The Economy of Ethnic C

In the wake of World War II the Sudetenland became the scene of ethnic cleansing, witnessing not only the expulsion of nearly 3 million German speakers, but also the influx of nearly 2 million resettlers. Yet mob violence and nationalist hatred were not the driving forces of ethnic cleansing; instead, greed, the search for power and property, and the general dislocation of post-war Central and Eastern Europe facilitated these expulsions and the transformation of the German-Czech borderlands. These overlapping migrations produced conflict among Czechs, hardship for Germans and facilitated the Communist Party's rise to power. Drawing on a wide range of materials from local and central archives, as well as expellee accounts, David Gerlach demonstrates how the lure of property and social mobility, as well as economic necessities, shaped the course and consequences of ethnic cleansing.

David W. Gerlach is Associate Professor at Saint Peter's University, New Jersey. He was awarded the R. John Rath Prize for Best Article in the 2007 Austrian History Yearbook and the 2006–2007 Best Dissertation by the Austrian Cultural Forum. His most recent publication is "Toward a Material Culture of Jewish Loss," in the journal *Jewish Culture and History*. He was awarded a Richard M. Hunt Fellowship for the Study of German Politics, Society, and Culture by the American Council on Germany in 2017. In addition to the study of forced migration, his current research explores restitution, reparation, and other compensation programs stemming from World War II.

The Economy of Ethnic Cleansing

The Transformation of the German-Czech Borderlands after World War II

David W. Gerlach

Saint Peter's University, New Jersey

CAMBRIDGE
UNIVERSITY PRESS

University Printing House, Cambridge CB2 8BS, United Kingdom

One Liberty Plaza, 20th Floor, New York, NY 10006, USA

477 Williamstown Road, Port Melbourne, VIC 3207, Australia

314-321, 3rd Floor, Plot 3, Splendor Forum, Jasola District Centre, New Delhi - 110025, India

79 Anson Road, #06-04/06, Singapore 079906

Cambridge University Press is part of the University of Cambridge.

It furthers the University's mission by disseminating knowledge in the pursuit of
education, learning and research at the highest international levels of excellence.

www.cambridge.org
Information on this title: www.cambridge.org/9781316647196
DOI: 10.1017/9781108164559

First published 2017
First paperback edition 2019

A catalogue record for this publication is available from the British Library

ISBN 978-1-107-19619-3 Hardback
ISBN 978-1-316-64719-6 Paperback

Contents

Figures

Maps

Acknowledgments

Books are also journeys. This one began at the University of Pittsburgh in a seminar on nationalism led by the late Dennison Rusinow. Its deeper roots lay in a semester spent abroad in Prague in 1992, when I first experienced a fascination with Central Europe at a most exhilarating time. My interest in the region and the topic returned as I began graduate school, which happened to coincide with the war in Kosovo and a conference on ethnic cleansing at nearby Duquesne University. Such are the vagaries of history. I thank Bob Donnorummo, not only for his ongoing support, but also for getting this trip started by giving me the opportunity to present my earliest findings at the Center for Russian and East European Studies under the very title of this book. The hard work of the dissertation came much later, and I had the good fortune of being guided by Irina Livezeanu. Her dedication to my project, keen editorial skills and ongoing enthusiasm helped ensure that the book reached its final destination. The rest of my dissertation committee – Bill Chase, Ilya Prizel, Werner Troesken and Christian Gerlach (no relation) – deserves much credit for their insight, critiques and support.

Nancy Wingfield served as an outside reader for the dissertation, and has been a constant companion ever since. I thank her for her advice and assistance over the past several years. Pieter Judson and Gregor Thum each read portions of the manuscript and offered valuable observations and suggestions, for which I am very grateful. Ben Frommer joined the trip near its completion and he, along with a still anonymous reader, provided much needed comments and queries for further fine-tuning and improvement. They made a world of difference. I would also like to thank Lew Bateman at Cambridge University Press for seeing the potential in this project, and Michael Watson for skillfully shepherding it to its conclusion. The shortcomings that still exist in this book remain mine alone.

I benefited from generous funding for the dissertation from Department of Education, the Department of Defense, and the American Council for Learned Societies. A follow-up research trip in

2010 was supported by a fellowship from the Conference Group for Central European History. Saint Peter's University, through the Professional Development of Faculty Committee, provided additional support. Chapter 4 is an expanded and revised version of an article I published in the 2007 *Austrian History Yearbook*. Certain portions of Chapters 2 and 5 derive from my article "Beyond Expulsion: The Emergence of 'Unwanted Elements' in the Czech Borderlands, 1945–1950," *East European Politics and Society* 24 no. 2 (May, 2010): 269–93. I visited many archives during my research and enjoyed meeting and working with many different archivists across the borderlands. They all deserve my heartfelt thanks for their help.

Colleagues whom I met along the way helped me to develop as a scholar and also became friends. They include: Adrian von Arburg, Max Bergholz, Theodora Dragostinova, Anna Hajková, Krista Hegberg, Tara Zahra, and Kimberley Zarecor. Michael DeGruccio read portions of the manuscript and always provided sound advice. Paul Almonte and Daniel Murphy have been close confidantes for the past decade. My other colleagues at Saint Peter's University, especially those in the History Department, also supported me in a variety of ways for which I am grateful. A special note of thanks to Yo Cuomo for her creative energy and time spent on the cover art.

My personal network sustained me as I traveled near and far. In many cases they have been along for the ride, in one way or another. They are: Justin Ceccerelli, Pat Chila, Larry Costello, Craig Finn, Dylan Gifford, Matt Magura, Tom Malec, Courtney McKnight, Anthony Meyer, Liza Meyer, Chris Mitchell, Tom Rockafeller, Steve Reuter, and John Varholak. Miroslav and Klaudia Babej-Kmec provided me lodging and sustenance on my extended stays in the Czech Republic. They have been more than friends and made this voyage so much easier and more enjoyable than it would have been without them.

Along the way I received material and moral support from an extended family that has really made this trek possible. This includes my brother, Jay, and his daughter, as well as my sister, Audrey, her husband John, and their children. The Chabra family has been exceptionally generous and encouraging and I count them as some of my greatest blessings. My parents were there every step of the way. My mom was consistently reassuring and sympathetic. My dad always provided sage counsel and whatever assistance I required. I thank my boys, Max, Elliot and Theo, who grew up with this book, for their many, varied and sometimes inopportune detours; they always remind me of what is truly important in life. My partner on this journey, Meera, has supported me throughout. Her companionship and love carried me through to my destination. I cannot thank her enough.

Abbreviations

a.j.	– archivní jednotek (archive unit number)
AM	– Archiv města (City Archive)
f.	– fond (fund)
FNO	– Fond národní obnovy (National Renewal Fund)
inv. č.	– inventární číslo (inventory number)
k.	– karton (carton)
kn.	– kniha (book)
KSČ	– Kommunistická strána Československu (Czechoslovak Communist Party)
LAA	– Lastenausgleich Archiv (Equalization of Burdens Archive)
MěNV	– Městský národní výbor (Municipal National Committee)
MNV	– Místní národní výbor (Local National Committee)
MOPSP	– Ministerstvo ochrany práce a sociální péče (Ministry for the Protection of Labor and Social Welfare)
MP	– Ministerstvo průmysl (Ministry of Industry)
MSK	– Místní správní komise (Local Administrative Commission)
MV	– Ministerstvo vnitra (Interior Ministry)
NA	– Národní archiv (National Archive of the Czech Republic)
NPF	– Národní pozemkový fond (National Land Fund)
OKD	– Ostrava-Karviná doly (Ostrava-Karviná Mines)
ONV	– Okresní národní výbor (District National Committee)
OSK	– Okresní správní komise (District Administrative Commission)
OÚ	– Osidlovací úřad (Settlement Office)
SHD	– Severočeský hnědouhelné doly (Northern Bohemian Brown Coal Mines)
sign.	– signatura (signature)
SOA	– státní oblastní archiv (state regional archive)
SOkA	– státní okresní archiv (state district archive)
ÚKVO	– Ústřední komise vnitřího osidlování (Central Commission for Interior Settlement)

ÚPV   – Úřad předsednictva vlády (Office of the Government
                Cabinet)
ÚVOD   – Ústřední vedení odboje domácího (Central Leadership of the
                Domestic Resistance)
VHA   – Vojenský historický archive (Military History Archive)
ZA   – zemský archiv (regional archive)
ZNV   – Zemský národní výbor (Provincial National Committee)

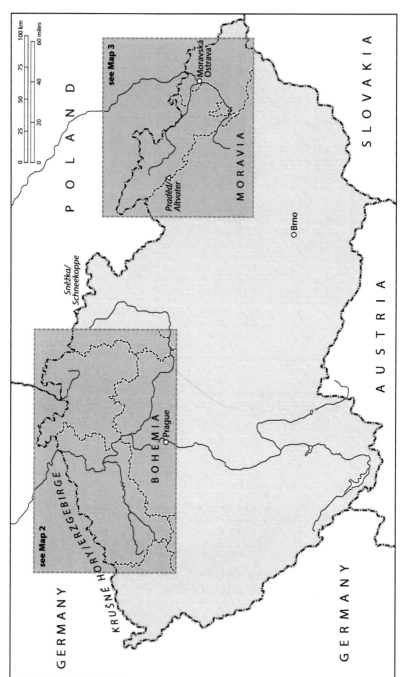

Map 1 Bohemia, Moravia and Silesia

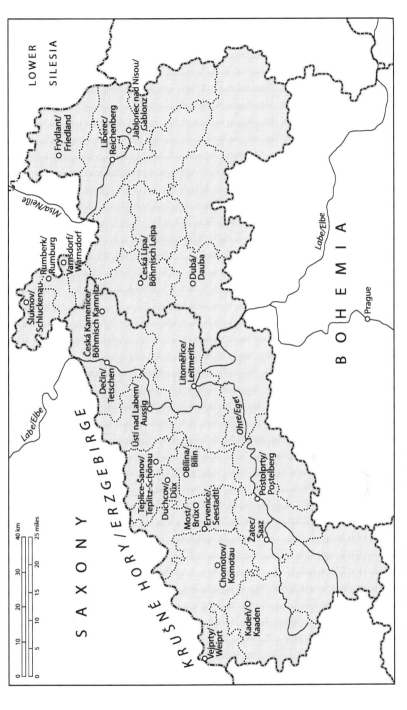

Map 2 North Bohemian borderlands

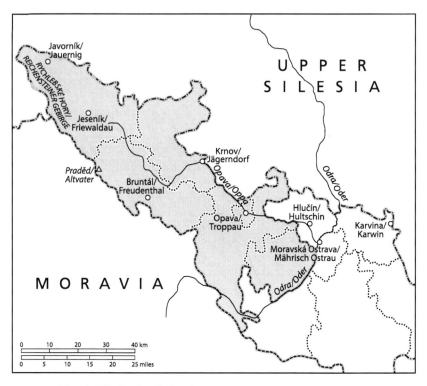

Map 3 Silesian borderlands

Introduction

> [O]n June 20, I had to leave the homeland with the first transport to Hernskretschen, together with my daughter and two grandchildren, where we reached the Reich German border. The transport was awful . . . At 5 am [we] gathered with all of our belongings that we were allowed in rucksacks. The rest of our possessions including valuables and other assets with great sorrow we had to leave behind, so that naked we had to leave our homeland.[1]

Thus began the difficult voyage for one Sudeten German in 1945, just as it had for millions of other people during World War II. If we changed the year to 1939 or 1943 we would find similar scenes occurring in numerous places across Central and Eastern Europe. These migrants trekked on foot or traveled by freight train from their ancestral homes to internal internment camps or across borders to unknown futures. Soldiers and civilians stripped them of virtually all of their possessions; a traumatic experience itself, as the above memory suggests. Some expellees faced forced labor and others were brutalized and killed. While the experience of being uprooted and people's ultimate fate varied widely, the moments of fear and uncertainty and the large-scale human displacement embodied the spirit of the times in Central and Eastern Europe between the late 1930s and early 1950s.

But not all wartime migrations were forced. Indeed, one key component of ethnic cleansing during this period was the parallel goal of using so-called reliable settlers to reshape cleansed territories. These migrants responded to the promise of a better future that came at the price of others' expulsion and despair. States distributed expellees' expropriated homes and farms to new settlers whom authorities deemed ethnically suitable and who provided a basis for rebuilding these areas. In some cases, the newcomers met and interacted with those being thrown out. In other cases, they arrived long after the original owners had been removed. Despite the widespread seizure of farms and homes, the resettlement of ethnically cleansed lands

---

[1] Erlebnisbericht. Lastenausgleich Archiv, Bayreuth, Germany (LAA). Ost-Dokumentation (Ost-Dok) 2, Böhmisch Leipa 244, 7.

rarely ran smoothly. Administrative conflicts, a lack of suitable settlers, labor shortages, property squabbles – just to name a few of the problems – beset many resettlement actions. As a result, settlement areas, many of which were in borderland regions, remained distinct and disconnected from the core part of their respective countries. For settlers, the opportunities for an improved existence often faded, as did leaders' grandiose visions of ethnically pure and economically progressive space.

This study examines the German–Czech borderlands where ethnic cleansing and a rapid reshuffling of populations occurred after the war.[2] The Munich Agreement of September 29, 1938, stipulated that Czechoslovakia hand over to Germany those border areas where a large number of ethnic Germans lived. As a result, in October the northern and western borderlands of Czechoslovakia were integrated into Germany as Reichsgau Sudetenland. After the war the interim National Front government of Czechoslovakia expelled roughly three million German speakers, most of them from these borderlands where their ancestors had lived for centuries. New settlers simultaneously moved into the borderlands in large numbers – more than one million by May 1947. The transformation of the borderlands began with ethnic cleansing and the immigration of new settlers. The two vectors of migration overlapped and influenced each other in key ways; indeed, they were part of a single process. It ended not with the complete removal of Germans, tens of thousands of whom remained behind, but rather when migration to, from and within the borderlands had slowed, when the economy stabilized and when a new political system took root. Only then did a new society emerge from the upheavals of the war.

The Sudetenland and Sudeten Germans

The Sudetenland was a unique mixture of industrial hamlets, mining towns, spa resorts and farmland amidst rolling hills, small mountains and forests. In fact, using "Sudetenland" as a geographical indicator is

---

[2] The borderlands (*pohraničí*) designate areas annexed by Germany following the Munich Agreement. This was largely synonymous with the term, "Sudetenland," which became a geographical designation in the 1920s and '30s based on political criteria that included the regions of Czechoslovakia along the borders of Austria and Germany where significant numbers of German speakers lived. I use the terms "borderlands" and "Sudetenland" more or less interchangeably and as geographic markers. For a list of the districts which officially comprised the borderlands, see 24.341/46 Vymezení pojmu pohraničí from Osidlovací úřad, June 6, 1946. *Předpisy z oboru působnosti OÚ a FNO: Zákony (dekrety), vládní nařízení, vyhlášky* (Prague, 1947) 2:488–89. For a discussion of the varying interpretations of the borderlands, see Matěj Spurný, "Nejsou jako my: Sociální marginalizace a integrace v období budování nového řádu na příkladu menšin v českém pohraničí, 1945–1960" (Dissertation, Charles University, Prague, 2010), 35–36.

somewhat misleading because it neither conforms to a single set of topo-graphical markers nor to a single region. The Sudetes mountain range, from which the German speakers of the Bohemian Crown Lands acquired their name, stretch along the northern border from Liberec/Reichenberg to Bruntál/Freudenthal.[3] The highest peak in the western part of the range, Sněžka/Schneekoppe (Snow top), stands at 5,259 feet and as the highest point in the border mountains did not present a real barrier to migration. The Praděd/Altvater (Grandfather) peak reaches 4,893 feet and signals the eastern terminus of the mountain range in what was Austrian Silesia. To the west, the Krušné Hory/Erzgebirge (Ore Mountains) provide a natural boundary between Bohemia and Saxony, though their highest peaks fail to reach those in the Sudetes. As their name suggests, the rich mineral deposits helped to fuel mining and industrial development on both sides of the mountains. The western edge of the borderlands juts into Germany, marked by hills and forests, and was famous for its spa towns of Karlový Váry/Carlsbad and Mariánské Lázně/Marienbad. Along the southern bor-der of Bohemia sits the Šumava/Böhmerwald (Bohemian Forest) with similarly modest mountain peaks, which, again, hindered but did not prevent the movement of German speakers across them. In South Moravia, where German speakers inhabited areas just across the Austrian border, the geography is comparably tame.

Each of these regions in the German-speaking borderlands had its own character, though defining it in this way still glosses over the many local variations. Western Bohemia, for instance, was famous for its spas, but it also had several thriving cottage industries such as musical-instrument production, glove making and porcelain goods. In South Moravia, viti-culture marked the land and economy. In this book, the focus lies pri-marily to the northern and northwestern parts of the borderlands for several reasons. One reason was simply practical – I would not have been able to delve deeply enough into all of the regions where German speakers resided given the scope of the research involved. While the Silesian and north Bohemian regions differed in some particular ways, they shared more similarities than with areas in the south and west. Both had key mining concerns and many textile firms, which gives some

---

[3] During the Habsburg era the Bohemian Crown Lands included Bohemia, Moravia and Austrian Silesia. Today, the latter province is often called Czech Silesia and these lands comprise the current Czech Republic. In Czech, *české zemi* could be translated either as "the Czech lands" or "the Bohemian lands," and can be considered as referring to all three provinces. The historical trend has been to move away from using "the Czech lands," however, as it suggests a nationalist classification of territory that was historically multi-ethnic. In order to avoid confusion, Bohemia is used only in reference to that specific province, while "the Bohemian lands" refers to the three provinces as they existed since the eighteenth century.

consistency to the industrial and labor transformations discussed in this book. They also were both subsumed into Germany as part of Reichsgau Sudetenland, which meant that their wartime experience was to some degree similar. After the war the Soviet armies occupied these regions, while the US army controlled the western borderlands, pointing to another parallel. While I kept comparative questions in mind, and highlight the key postwar differences when appropriate, the regional variations were far less noteworthy than were local differences from town to town.

The northern borderlands were heavily involved in textile production, with factories often nestled into the hilly landscape, their smokestacks competing for dominance with church spires and town halls. One business often dominated a town's economy, but also supported the rise of local competitors and the specialization in a particular product. Liberec represented the region's central city, though it was not significantly larger than its neighbors. It was also the largest textile producer and sometimes referred to as "Bohemian Manchester" or "Vienna of the North." As Liberec grew its population spread into the surrounding countryside and, aside from some intervening peaks, nearly connects with nearby Jablonec nad Nisou/Gablonz an der Neiße. Jablonec became a center for glass production of jewelery, beads and buttons, which spread to nearby villages, and was known throughout Europe. The city of Ústí nad Labem/Aussig sits on the Elbe River, which winds its way northward all the way to Hamburg. This made Aussig a transport hub, though its distinguishing industry was chemical production. To the west of Ústí begins the brown coal basin that runs all the way to Chomutov/Komotau and shaped the region into an important mining and industrial center. To the south lay mostly agricultural lands, with the noteworthy town of Žatec/Saaz, which remains world-renowned for the hops that are grown in its vicinity. Thanks in large part to the rise of these profitable industries, the local economies could support a thriving service sector as well. Traces of the prosperous past can still be seen in the streets and restored squares in many of these towns today.

In the Silesian borderlands a similarly variegated picture appears, with some attractive spas interspersed with quarries, small factories and an important mining center to the south. In Frývaldov/Friewaldau (today Jeseník) where the mountains reach substantial heights and local waters provided for a small but popular spa resort, a tourist industry emerged that included hiking and skiing. High-quality rock deposits also supported a granite industry. In Bruntál and Krnov/Jägerndorf, textile firms dominated the local economies and specialized in linen and wollen fabrics, respectively. Further to the south, Opava/Troppau became the administrative center of Czech Sileisa after Word War I and was surrounded by farmland. Ostrava, a city that straddles the Oder River and sits in both Moravia and Silesia, served as a magnet for industrial workers. The majority of the city is technically in Moravia, and thus it is often referred to as Moravian Ostrava (Moravská Ostrava/Mährisch Ostrau). In nearby Karviná, hard coal deposits established a thriving mining industry and provided the necessary coking coal to support the metalworks in Ostrava.

What defined the Sudetenland were the German-speaking inhabitants who ringed the state borders between Czechoslovakia and Germany/Austria after 1918. The ethno-linguistic composition of these borderland regions held a geographic dimension in the sense that the further north one traveled the more German speakers predominated. While using the 1930 census figures to outline ethnic composition is hazardous, they do provide the basis for showing the overall trends. Very few Czech speakers lived in the two northern promontories that cut into Germany. In Šluknov/Schluckenau and Frýdlant/Friedland the portion of Czech speakers was 3 and 5 percent, respectively. In Jablonec nad Nisou roughly 18 percent of the population was Czech speaking.[4] This figure is representative for many bigger towns and small cities in Northern Bohemia for this time. The Silesian cities, by contrast, were more heavily dominated by German speakers. As one moved south, the picture became more mixed. Opava and Ostrava were very much mixed regions, with Czech speakers actually in the majority. A bit to the east of there, Polish speakers were a sizable minority and natives in the area of Hlučín/Hultschin did not fit neatly into any national category. It should also be noted that German speakers comprised a large number of inhabitants in certain interior "language islands," particularly in the Moravian capital of Brno/Brünn and in Jihlava/Iglau. These Germans, as well as those in Prague and elsewhere, were eventually subsumed under the broad title of Sudeten Germans.

German leaders' attempts to form four autonomous regions from the former Bohemian Crown Lands that would be attached to the Republic of German Austria demonstrate the regional nature of German identity after World War I. Only after the failed attempts to break away from the new Czechoslovak state, which involved armed conflict in some places, did the notion of a broader Sudeten German identity begin to take shape.[5] What

---

[4] *Sčítání lidu v republice Československé ze dne 1. prosince 1930*. Díl I, Růst, koncentrace a hustota obyvatelstva, pohlaví, věkove rozvrstvení, rodinný stav, státní příslušnost, narodnost, náboženské vyznání (Prague, 1934), xvii–xxiii.

[5] For more on the interwar history of Sudeten Germans and the question of their identity, see Michael Campbell, "The Making of the 'March-Fallen': March 4, 1919 and the Subversive Potential of Occupation," *Central European History* 39, no. 1 (2006): 1–29; Karl F. Bahm, "The Inconveniences of Nationality: German Bohemians, the Disintegration of the Habsburg Monarchy and the Attempt to Create a 'Sudeten

that meant in practice is more difficult to tell. As many recent studies have shown, particularly in the Bohemian lands, ascribing national belonging was a slippery task at best. Some people switched between national groups, while others did not feel affinity for any particular nationality.[6] While individuals may have had little concern about their own national affiliation, political leaders and state officials often did. These "national activists" helped to promote the salience of nation in politics, whereby they framed various political debates in national terms.[7] Such appeals worked less well in the 1920s when the Czechoslovak Republic had earned some legitimacy and when most German parties agreed to work within its political framework. By the 1930s, however, with the effects of the Great Depression hurting many borderland towns and the success of the Nazis in neighboring Germany, politics became increasingly nationalized. The *Sudetendeutsche Partei* (SdP), led by Konrad Henlein, continued to gain support among German speakers in the borderlands. Henlein, who had been a leader of the nationalist gymnastics movement (*Turnverband*), was just one of many Sudeten Germans who actively worked to propagate a movement that sought the recognition of German rights and autonomy in interwar Czechoslovakia.[8] Yet only in the worsening economic conditions did their work bear fruit. In the 1935 elections, for instance, the SdP garnered more than 60 percent of the German vote.[9] While the SdP sought the support of the Nazis in order to further its domestic political agenda, Hitler seized the opportunity to expand his power. As a direct result of the Munich Agreement, in October 1938 Germany annexed predominantly German-speaking areas of Bohemia, Moravia and Silesia that had been part of interwar Czechoslovakia. By all accounts, most Sudeten Germans initially welcomed the arrival of Nazi troops across the border. They sought the

German' Identity," *Nationalities Papers*, 27, no.3 (1999): 375–405; Jan Křen, "Changes in Identity: Germans in Bohemia and Moravia in the Nineteenth and Twentieth Centuries," in Mikuláš Teich, ed., *Bohemia in History* (Cambridge, 1998); Herman Kopecek, "*Zusammenarbeit* and *Spoluprace*: Sudeten German-Czech Cooperation in Interwar Czechoslovakia," *Nationalities Papers* 24, no. 1 (1996): 63–78.

[6] Jeremy King, *Budweisers into Czechs and Germans: A Local History of Bohemian Politics* (Princeton, 2002); Tara Zahra, *Kidnapped Souls: National Indifference and the Battle for Children in the Bohemian Lands, 1900–1948* (Ithaca, 2008).

[7] On national activists, see Pieter Judson, *Guardians of the Nation: Activists on the Language Frontiers of Imperial Austria* (Cambridge, 2007). On the nationalizing politics, see Rogers Brubaker, Nationalism Reframed: *Nationhood and the National Question in the New Europe* (Cambridge, 1996).

[8] See, for example, the recent study on Heinz Rutha: Mark Cornwall, *The Devil's Wall: The Nationalist Youth Mission of Heinz Rutha* (Cambridge, 2012).

[9] Ronald Smelser, *The Sudeten Problem 1933–1938: Volkstumspolitik and the Formation of Nazi Foreign Policy* (Middletown, 1975), 160.

benefits of an apparently booming Reich German economy.[10] The Nazis then engaged in a massive propaganda effort to promote the takeover that culminated in a kind of referendum vote on December 4, 1938. In addition to a concerted press campaign, parades and radio broadcasts urged Germans to thank the Führer for bringing the Sudetenland into the Reich. More than 98 percent of them did so.

Aside from gaining certain short-term economic benefits, however, Sudeten Germans relinquished their long-term future to the Reich. As Volker Zimmermann remarks: "The Reichsgau Sudetenland represented a further step on the way to the 'Führer state'."[11] This meant that political power and local interests became subordinate to the central government in Berlin, despite the efforts of Sudeten German leaders to retain some autonomy. The Nazi regime installed a new system of local administration with combined powers of self-governance and state administrator. This system meshed with Nazi efforts to streamline the Reich's administration.[12] Likewise, the Sudetenland economy became subordinated to the Reich's needs. German economic planners and regulators placed Sudetenland industries under their control. While initially the hope among many Sudeten German industrialists was that attachment to the Reich would lead to better market opportunities, Reich Germans appeared to reap more benefits than their Sudeten German counterparts. Tara Zahra describes a scene in 1940 where Sudeten German women brawled with Reich German women because the latter had easy office jobs while the former were forced to work in factories.[13] The Sudeten German visions of greater prosperity under Nazi leadership faded as Reich Germans immigrated for jobs and cheap goods, and wartime needs demanded greater sacrifice.

After the Nazis occupied the Sudetenland many inhabitants – Czechs, Jews, German Social Democrats and Communists – fled to the interior parts of the country. Hundreds of others were arrested in the first weeks and months following the Anschluss. Jews had been increasingly isolated in the summer of 1938 through the spread of anti-Semitic propaganda by the SdP, a boycott of Jewish businesses and sporadic episodes of

---

[10] Jürgen Tämpke, *Czech-German Relations and the Politics of Central Europe: From Bohemia to the EU* (New York, 2003), 58; for a similar explanation, see Volker Zimmermann, *Die Sudetendeutschen im NS-Staat: Politik und Stimmung der Bevölkerung im Reichsgau Sudetenland* (1938–1945) (Essen, 1999), 71–74, 116.

[11] Zimmermann, 142; 108–15.

[12] Václav Kural, Zdeněk Radvanovský et al., *"Sudety" pod hákovým křížem* (Ústí nad Labem, 2002), 92–95. For more on the administrative changes, see Ralf Gebel, *'Heim ins Reich!' Konrad Henlein under Reichsgau Sudetenland* (Munich, 1999), 145–235.

[13] Zahra, 180.

robbery.[14] Nazis and SdP leaders next prevented Jews from practicing their professions and confiscated their property. These processes culminated in *Kristallnacht* in November 1938, when pogroms swept through the borderlands and synagogues were burned to the ground.[15] Many of the Sudetenland Jews had already left the region prior to the Nazis' arrival. Between 15,000–17,000 out of roughly 27,000–30,000 Sudetenland Jews fled to the interior parts of the country and, in particular, to Prague by November 1938.[16] Many others continued to flow into the interior after the annexation. From there they emigrated abroad, if they could.

Czechs and German antifascists also left the Sudetenland. This migration has been labeled an expulsion in its own right by some Czechs who experienced it.[17] It was certainly influenced by the takeover of the Sudetenland and the reorganization of its political and economic space. However, many of the roughly 160,000 people who left did so by choice, rather than being forced to move by armed military units.[18] Some had lost their jobs, either as part of the change in state administration or because Germans demanded their positions. Others, though, certainly fled from fear of persecution. In one case, some local "Henleiners" threw a Czech settler out of his home and "beat him in the hallway and drove him out into the street terror, where he was thrown to his countrymen. The most fanatic was a neighbor from a nearby home, who threatened my brother with an axe. Of course, the purpose wasn't to kill him, but to put Czechs 'on notice' that they would be turned out of Ledvice."[19] Still others did not wish to live in a different country, especially under Nazi leadership, and departed of their own accord. German citizenship transferred to German speakers in the Sudetenland, but Czechs and others were left without rights.

In March 1939, the Nazis finished dismantling Czechoslovakia. The Protectorate of Bohemia and Moravia was created under the pretext of continuing Czech–German conflicts. Slovakia seceded and achieved its first taste of independence under Nazi tutelage. From a Czech nationalist perspective, Czechs became the subjects of their age-old enemy. Czech universities were closed, and Czech professionals and intelligentsia were

---

[14] Jörg Osterloh, *Nationalsozialistische Judenverfolgung im Reichsgau Sudetenland, 1938–1945* (Munich: Oldenbourg, 2006), 152–54; Livia Rothkirchen, *The Jews of Bohemia and Moravia* (Jerusalem, 2005), 60; Kural and Radvanovský, 52–54; Zimmermann, 73–94.

[15] Rothkirchen, 79–80. Kural and Radvanovský, 81–82.   [16] Rothkirchen, 78.

[17] Karel Zelený, ed., *Vyhnání Čechů z pohraničí 1938: Vzpomínky* (Prague, 1996).

[18] Kural and Radvanovský, 50–65. Included in this figure are several thousand Jews and German antifascists. See also Zimmermann, 98–100; Vladimir Srb, *Populační, ekonomický a národnostní vývoj pohraničích okresů ČSR od roku 1930 do roku 2010* (Prague, 1989), 4.

[19] Zelený, 84.

forced to work for the Nazi war economy. Other efforts at Germanization followed. Some plans involved resettling *Volksdeutsche* (i.e. German speakers living outside of the German Reich) to the Protectorate; others centered on Germanizing the vast majority of Czechs and leaving the remainder to be deported or exterminated.[20] Occupational authorities imprisoned and killed some of the population, but did not target the Czechs as a whole. Jews and Roma, by contrast, did not fare as well. Less than 15 percent of their prewar communities in the Bohemian lands survived the Holocaust.[21]

Vojtech Mastny notes that because of the initial smooth transition of power, people's daily lives did not change much in the Protectorate. He argues that Czech attitudes toward Germans "though certainly not friendly, at least encouraged accommodation to the new conditions."[22] Other historians also corroborate the general picture of Czechs' acceptance of the situation, though they differ on the extent and type of resistance.[23] Chad Bryant, on the other hand, argues that Czechs did what they could to resist Nazi plans for Germanization by "acting nationally." Rather than seeing resistance only through the paradigm of gun in hand, he suggests that many Czechs adopted nationalist attitudes and a variety of practices, such as meeting in clubs and reading pro-Czech materials, to protest German control.[24] What most scholars have found is that traditional labels of resistance and collaboration do not neatly fit the complex swirl of political, economic and cultural policies when measured against individuals' reactions to them during the war. Indeed, it may have been "the norm in occupied Czechoslovakia to collaborate and resist at the same time."[25] Such nuanced views were largely absent by the end of the war, however, which facilitated the move toward ethnic cleansing.

[20] Chad Bryant, *Prague in Black: Nazi Rule and Czech Nationalism* (Harvard, 2007), 114–28; Götz Aly, *Final Solution: Nazi Population Policy and the Murder of the European Jews*, trans. Belinda Cooper and Allison Brown (London, 1999), 118; Vojtech Mastny, *The Czechs under Nazi Rule: The Failure of National Resistance, 1939–1942* (New York, Columbia, 1977), 127.

[21] Helena Krejčová gives 18,970 Jewish survivors in 1945 from a prewar population of over 120,000: see Helena Krejčová, "Židovská očekávání a zklamání po roce 1945," in *Češi a Němci: ztracené dějiny?* (Prague, 1995), 245–47; Tomáš Staněk lists more than 22,000 Jews in 1946: Tomáš Staněk, "Němečtí židé v Československu v letech 1945–1948," *Dějiny a současnost* 5 (1991): 42. Of roughly 6,500 Roma in the Bohemian lands only 600 survived: see Nina Pavelčíková, "Romské obyvatelstvo ČSR v letech 1945–1954," in *Sborník studií k národnostní politice Československa (1945–1954)*, ed. Helena Nosková (Prague, 2001), 41; Bryant, 3.

[22] Mastny, 57.

[23] Tämpke, 58–72; Radomir Luža, *Transfer of the Sudeten Germans: A Study of Czech-German Relations, 1933–1962* (New York, 1964), 187–222.

[24] Bryant.   [25] Zahra, 233.

The Economy of Ethnic Cleansing

This book explores ethnic cleansing by examining the economic motives, debates, policies and relationships that emerged after the war. It argues that economic factors played a decisive role in shaping the way that ethnic cleansing unfolded, the experience of Germans and the fate of the post-war borderlands. This is not an argument based on economic determinism; that is, economic factors did not drive every outcome. For instance, the killing of Germans rarely had a direct economic motive and often involved a host of other factors. The causes for the expulsion policy were connected to the war, international politics and the postwar Czechoslovak government's need for legitimacy. Nonetheless, economic enticements and logic shaped local events and individual encounters. One way this happened was through the rapid migration of settlers, primarily Czechs from the interior parts of the country, to the borderlands in search of enrichment. A series of Presidential Decrees, popularly known as the Beneš Decrees after President Edvard Beneš, expropriated German property and stripped Germans of their citizenship. "National administrators" were then established as property trustees for seized homes, farms and businesses, and many new settlers sought to acquire these positions with the hope of eventually taking ownership. Others, known derisively as gold-diggers (*zlatokopové*), moved through the borderlands for plunder or staged a temporary existence as a national administrator to live from the spoils of German property with no intention of permanently residing there. The hundreds of thousands of settlers who arrived in the border-lands in 1945 and 1946 became effective agents of ethnic cleansing by stripping Germans of their homes and livelihoods.

At every stage of the expulsion process, economic considerations permeated its planning, organization and implementation. Early plans revolved around keeping German labor available for critical industries and farming. The earliest orders for expulsions specified that those who were able-bodied and had particular skills should remain, while less useful people should go. This reasoning continued to guide decisions about the so-called organized transfer of Germans in 1946. In some cases, Czechoslovak authorities considered work as a form of punishment and put Germans in mines and on farms to do heavy manual labor with little in the way of food or compensation. At its worst, this meant hard labor in the mines accompanied by beatings and prison-like accommodations. At its best, it meant manual farm labor with small rations and makeshift shelter. Economic demands also prompted the retention of tens of thousands of experienced German workers. As early as May 1945, some Czechs began protecting German workers from the expulsion in order to save local

businesses. As the expulsions began to sap labor from borderland industries and mines, these practices developed into concrete policies to retain
experienced German workers. Czech authorities and national administrators offered these Germans better wages and living conditions in the
hopes of increasing their productivity. Had some Czech managers and
officials had their way, they would have kept even more. Yet, because the
retention of German workers ran counter to the goal of solving the
German question once and for all, other Czech officials forced many
skilled German workers from the country. Czech settlers failed to make
up the difference, primarily because they sought more easily won gains.
The resulting deficit of workers, in turn, attracted Slovaks, Roma and
others to the borderlands for work and dashed leaders' plans for an
exclusively Czech society there. Labor demands operated as a key organizational principle for the expulsions, influenced the individual treatment of Germans and shaped the future of local economies.

The reorganization of the borderlands' industrial capacity stemmed
from the confiscation of German property and labor shortages, thus
wedding ethnic cleansing to structural changes in the Czechoslovak economy. As part of postwar Czechoslovakia's "national and democratic
revolution," socialist political parties within the National Front government sought to remake the economic foundations of the country through
a broad nationalization program. The state nationalized large-scale
industrial enterprises and gave factory councils a role in the management
of production. In the borderlands, where many German-owned small and
medium-sized firms operated, the extent and meaning of nationalization
dramatically expanded. Until early 1947 hundreds of factories, work-
shops and spas remained in ownerless limbo between the private and
nationalized sectors. This situation fostered political debate and worker
demands for the nationalization of these firms. Ultimately, a case of
restitution involving a formerly Jewish-owned factory and striking workers turned the tide in favor of nationalization. Although greater concentration began prior to 1948 through the allocation of confiscated firms to
the nationalized sector, Communist policies during the First Five-Year
Plan (1949–53) accelerated this process. Communist authorities often
closed, dismantled and relocated confiscated German factories despite
the protests of borderland officials and workers. These policies dovetailed
with Communist leaders' greater attention to heavy industry and the
demands of the early Cold War. Ethnic cleansing offered material incentives not only to individuals seeking property like homes and furniture,
but also to government leaders and administrators who sought to expand
their power and to implement far-reaching socio-economic changes.

Communist goals fused with the consequences of ethnic cleansing to remodel the borderland economy.

The focus of this study is less about why ethnic cleansing happened in postwar Czechoslovakia and more about how it occurred and its consequences for the people and places involved. The specific story of the expulsion policy and the international negotiations and decision making that led to its acceptance and implementation – the "why" – has been sufficiently covered elsewhere.[26] The manner of Sudeten German expulsions, on the other hand, has been only partially examined, and its broader consequences and links to the early Cold War rarely analyzed. In part, the focus on violence and lack of attention to competing dynamics can be explained by how the study of ethnic cleansing evolved. The wars and violence in the former Yugoslavia in the 1990s generated scholarly interest in the topic of ethnic cleansing and its previous manifestations in the history of Europe. Much had already been written about individual cases of the post–World War II expulsions, but these works tended to be narrowly focused, victim-centered narratives. While these studies offered many details about the victims' experiences and the general outline of events, they were usually heavily biased and in many cases exaggerated the levels of violence and death.[27] Nonetheless, these works played an important role in the historiography of the expulsions by establishing violence as the key dynamic, which historians continue to highlight in order to explain ethnic cleansing.

In the case of the postwar German expulsions, an explicit political program that aimed at creating and propagating a picture of German wartime and postwar suffering emerged and intended, among other things, to keep alive the possibility of regaining lost territory and property. Part of this program involved the collection and publication of testimonies from German expellees, which the Federal Republic of Germany supported through a separate ministry dedicated to expellees, refugees and war victims.[28] As Eva Hahnová and Hans Henning Hahn argue:

[26] Detlef Brandes, *Der Weg zur Vertreibung, 1938–1945: Pläne und Entscheidungen zum "Transfer"der Deutschen aus der Tschechislowakei und aus Polen* (Munich, 2001); Václav Kural, *Místo společenství – konflikt! Češi a Němci ve Velkoněmecké říši a cesta k odsunu, 1938–1945* (Prague, 1994).

[27] See, for example, Gerhard Ziemer, *Deutscher Exodus: Vertreibung und Eingliederung von 15 Millionen Ostdeutschen* (Stuttgart, 1973), 94–103; Emil Franzel *Die Vertreibung Sudetenland, 1945–1946* (Munich, 1979).

[28] Theodor Schieder, ed., *Dokumentation der Vertreibung der Deutschen aus Ost-Mitteleuropa,* vol. 4/2, *Die Vertreibung der deutschen Bevölkerung aus der Tschechoslowakei* (Bonn, 1957); Theodor Schieder, ed., *Documents on the Expulsion of the Germans from Eastern-Central-Europe,* vol. 4: *The Expulsion of the Germans from Czechoslovakia,* trans. G.H. de Sausmarez (Bonn, 1960). For background on the project see Matthais Beer, "Im Spannungsfeld von Politik und Zeitgeschichte: Das Grossforschungsprojekt

"Individual memories were transformed into mere symbols and useful arguments for the benefit of demands articulated by West German politicians toward eastern neighbors of Germany."[29] This project also provided a way for other Germans to accept the mantle of victimhood that expellees and remaining POWs in the USSR offered them. The image of the *Volksdeutsche* as victims held particular resonance in Germany because Nazi propaganda had already portrayed them as victims in 1939 during the prelude to war.[30] The horrid tales of expellees, in this sense, seemed to support ex post facto the prewar claims of the Nazis about the unjust treatment of the *Volksdeutsche*. Robert Moeller points out that even more problematic has been the way in which these testimonies and the editors' accompanying narratives suggest the comparability of the German expellees' experience with that of the Jews during the Holocaust.[31] Some testimonies explicitly equate their camp experience with that of Jewish suffering during the Holocaust. In one account, for instance, a Sudeten German reflecting on the crowded conditions of the internment camp in Krnov (Jägerndorf) remarked: "It could not possibly have been worse in a concentration camp."[32] The editor of one volume, Theodor Schieder, writes "As reports confirm again and again, the Czechs often deliberately copied the practice and methods of the concentration camps of the National Socialist regime."[33] The so-called Scriptorium that edits online testimonies of Sudeten German expellees goes so far as to compare the Czech internment camps to Majdanek and Bergen-Belsen.[34] Connecting the expulsion of Germans to the extermination of the Jews in this way not only downplays the extent of Jewish

'Dokumentation der Vertreibung der Deutschen aus Ost-Mitteleuropa,'" *Vierteljahrshefte für Zeitgeschichte* 49 (1998): 345–89. For the best treatment in English see Robert Moeller, *War Stories: In Search for a Useable Past in the Federal Republic of Germany* (Berkeley, 2001), chapter 3. On Schieder, see Aly, *Final Solution*, 6–7; and Fred Kautz, *The German Historians: Hitler's Willing Executioners and Daniel Goldhagen* (Montreal, 2003), 92–3.

[29] Eva Hahnová and Hans Henning Hahn, *Sudetoněmecká vzpomínání a zapomínání* (Prague, 2002), 130.

[30] Doris Bergen, "Instrumentalization of *Volksdeutschen* in German Propaganda in 1939: Replacing/Erasing Poles, Jews, and Other Victims," *American Historical Review* 31, no. 3 (2008): 447–70. This image extended back to the Weimar period as well. See James E. Casteel, "The Russian Germans in the Interwar German National Imaginary," *Central European History* 40, no. 3 (2007): 429–66.

[31] Moeller, 78.   [32] Schieder, *Documents on the Expulsion of the Germans*, 4: 455.

[33] Ibid., 447, n.7.

[34] The Scriptorium is the online continuation of a Sudeten German interest group that first published its own set of documents as Wilhelm Turnwald, ed., *Documents on the Expulsion of the Sudeten Germans*. Trans. Gerta Johannsen (Munich, 1951). See the comment in Report 129, N.N., May 23, 1946, Bodenbach. Scriptorium, accessed on August 23, 2016, www.wintersonnenwende.com/scriptorium/english/archives/whitebook/desg39.html.

suffering during the war, it also misrepresents the nature and scale of Sudeten German suffering in the postwar borderlands. It is this misleading portrait of the expulsions that have helped to shape both popular and scholarly accounts of these events to date.

Recent scholarly surveys of ethnic cleansing have done much to broaden the focus beyond the victims by clarifying the scope and definition of ethnic cleansing and by offering new methodologies for its analysis. The majority of these scholars agree that ethnic cleansing is a modern phenomenon that has its roots in the concept of the nation-state. Norman Naimark's seminal study highlights the continuity of cases throughout twentieth-century Europe. He argues that the modern state's "impetus to homogenize" along with the rise of "racist nationalism" set the stage for ethnic cleansing.[35] Other scholars share this position, though their books highlight other factors or choose different starting points for the rise of ethnic cleansing.[36] Several edited volumes on the topic have also appeared in recent years, some with focused attention on the postwar expulsion of Germans.[37] Philipp Ther's study has broadened the scholarly framework for ethnic cleansing by clarifying previous inconsistencies and by positing some new methods for its study.[38] For instance, Ther challenges several longstanding notions regarding the extent of popular violence, and he offers a more nuanced view of expellee experiences. Raymond Douglas's recent examination of the postwar Polish and Czechoslovak expulsions of Germans does an exceptional job of synthesizing much of the recent literature and echoes Ther's approach.[39] In this way, his study serves as a useful counterweight to the influence of Alfred de Zayas's work, which mirrors the focus of earlier German accounts.[40]

---

[35] Norman Naimark, *Fires of Hatred: Ethnic Cleansing in Twentieth Century Europe* (Cambridge, 2001).

[36] Andrei Bell-Fialkoff, *Ethnic Cleansing* (New York, 1996); Michael Mann, *The Dark Side of Democracy: Explaining Ethnic Cleansing* (Cambridge, 2004); Benjamin Lieberman, *Terrible Fate: Ethnic Cleansing and the Making of Modern Europe* (Chicago, 2006); Michael Schwartz, *Ethnische "Säuberungen" in der Moderne: Globale Wechselwirkungen Nationalistischer und Rassistischer Gewaltpolitik im 19. und 20. Jahrhundert* (Munich, 2013).

[37] Philipp Ther and Ana Siljak, eds., *Redrawing Nations: Ethnic Cleansing in East-Central Europe, 1944–1948* (Lanham, 2001); Steven B. Várdy and T. Hunt Tooley, eds., *Ethnic Cleansing in 20th Century Europe* (Boulder, 2003); Alfred J. Rieber, ed., *Forced Migration in Central and Eastern Europe, 1939–1950* (London, 2002).

[38] The study was first published in German in 2011; the English version appeared in 2014. Philipp Ther, *Die Dunkle Seite der Nationalstaaten: "Ethnische Säuberungen" im Modernen Europa*, (Göttingen, 2011); Philipp Ther, *The Dark Side of Nation-States: Ethnic Cleansing in Modern Europe*, trans. *Charlotte Kreutzmüller* (New York, 2014).

[39] R.M. Douglas, *Orderly and Humane: The Expulsion of Germans after the Second World War* (New Haven, 2012).

[40] Alfred de Zayas, *Nemesis at Potsdam: The Expulsion of the Germans from the East*, 2nd edn. (Lincoln, 1989). See also de Zayas, *A Terrible Revenge: The Ethnic Cleansing of the East*

The postwar German expulsions from Poland have generated some important new approaches to ethnic cleansing as well.[41] Most noteworthy in this regard is Gregor Thum's study of Breslau/Wrocław, which explores one city's transformation following ethnic cleansing. He traces the physical and cultural makeover of the city as well as the psychological evolution of resettlers as they tried to make the city Polish.[42]

The topic of the Sudeten German expulsions was largely absent from academic research and debate in Czechoslovakia until the late 1960s. At that time, Czech historians and dissidents started discussing the moral implications and legal aspects of the expulsions.[43] Only in the late 1980s were historians able to begin exploring the history of the expulsions on the basis of archival materials. Tomáš Staněk's 1991 groundbreaking study, *Odsun němců z Československa* ("The Transfer of Germans from Czechoslovakia"), still represents the most comprehensive account of the expulsions.[44] Since then he has continued to publish works that highlight some of their darkest episodes.[45] Staněk and Adrian von Arburg have also clarified the military's role in the expulsion process, and they have published some important document collections concerning the history of expulsions and resettlement.[46] Recent studies by

European Germans 1944–1950, 2nd edn. (New York, 2006). The German version of *Nemesis at Potsdam* is in its 14th edition.

[41] One of the key works is Philipp Ther, *Deutsche und polnische Vertriebene: Gesellschaft und Vertriebenenpolitik in der SBZ/DDR und in Polen 1945–1956* (Göttingen, 1998). In English see T. David Curp, *A Clean Sweep? The Politics of Ethnic Cleansing in Western Poland, 1945–1960* (Rochester, 2006); Andrew Demshuk, *The Lost German East: Forced Migration and the Politics of Memory, 1945–1970* (Cambridge, 2014); Hugo Service, *Germans to Poles: Communism, Nationalism and Ethnic Cleansing after the Second World War* (Cambridge, 2015).

[42] Gregor Thum, *Uprooted: How Breslau Became Worcław During the Century of Expulsions*, trans. Tom Lampert and Allison Brown (Princeton, 2011).

[43] *Češi, němci, odsun" Discuse nezávislých historiků* (Prague, 1990). For an analysis see, Bradley F. Abrams, "Morality, Wisdom and Revision: The Czech Opposition of the 1970s and the Expulsion of the Sudeten Germans," *East European Politics and Societies* 9, no. 2 (1997): 234–55. The Czech émigré historian Radomír Luža's work might also be included in this context. Radomir Luža, *Transfer of the Sudeten Germans: A Study of Czech-German Relations, 1933–1962* (New York, 1964).

[44] Tomáš Staněk, *Odsun Němců z Československu, 1945–1948* (Prague, 1991). His work confirmed many of the findings in the earlier publication, S. Biman and R. Cílek. *Poslední mrtví, první živí: České pohraničí květen až srpen 1945* (Ústí nad Labem, 1989). See also Jaroslav Kučera, *Odsun nebo vyhnání?* (Prague, 1992); Zdeněk Radvanovský, *Konec Česko.Německého soužití v ústecké oblastíi.* (Ústí nad Labem, 1997).

[45] Tomáš Staněk, *Poválečné "excessy" v českých zemích v roce 1945 a jejich vyšetřováni* (Prague, 2005); Tomáš Staněk, *Perzekuce 1945* (Prague, 1996); Tomás Staněk, *Tábory v českých zemích, 1945–1948* (Opava, 1996).

[46] Adrian von Arburg and Tomáš Staněk, eds., *Vysídleni Němců a proměny českého pohraničí, 1945–1951: Dokumenty z českých archivů*, 6 vols. (Středokluky, 2011). Tomáš Staněk and Adrian von Arburg "Organizované divoké odsuny? Úloha z ústředních státních orgánů při prováděni 'evakuace' německého obyvatelstva (květín až září 1945)," 1 část.

American scholars have also investigated certain aspects of the expulsions. Benjamin Frommer explores how the expulsion of Germans was entangled with Czechoslovakia's postwar attempts to reckon with collaborators. He argues that the punishment of low-level German functionaries and the expulsion, rather than prosecution, of German collaborators weakened the authority of the courts and the very nature of retribution. Chad Bryant's study of the Nazi Protectorate of Bohemia and Moravia examines the continuities between Nazi occupation and the postwar expulsions. Eagle Glassheim, on the other hand, emphasizes the connections between the expulsions, resettlement and ensuing environmental devastation in the borderlands.[47] Other recent studies have highlighted the complex interethnic dynamics of resettlement.[48] My study of the expulsions and resettlement draws on these important findings.

Despite the extensive scholarship to date, however, scant attention has been given to how economic factors have shaped ethnic cleansing, particularly at the local and individual levels. This is perhaps unsurprising given scholars' penchant for studying violence and its essential role in ethnic cleansing. While some recent studies have begun to move away from this focus, it continues to dominate this time period and topic. Timothy Snyder's publication, *Bloodlands*, reinforces this trend, even though Snyder recognizes the key role that economic plans and factors played in the horrors of the World War II era.[49] While Hitler and Stalin shaped the context of violence and elaborate resettlement schemes in Central and Eastern Europe, national leaders and local actors performed the work of ethnic cleansing. The scholarship on ethnic cleansing has highlighted the role of state leaders as well as their victims. What it has

---

"Předpoklady a vývoj do konce května 1945," *Soudobé dějiny* 12, no. 3–4 (2005), 465–533; 2 část. "Československá armáda vytváří 'hotové skutečnosti', vláda je před cizinou legitimizuje," *Soudobé dějiny* 13, no. 1–2 (2006), 13–49; 3 část. "Snaha vlády a civilních úřadů o řízení 'divokého odsunu'," *Soudobé dějiny* 13, no. 3–4 (2006) 321–76. See also, Adrian von Arburg, "Tak či onak." *Soudobé Dějiny* 10, no. 3 (2003): 253–92.

[47] Benjamin Frommer, *National Cleansing: Retribution Against Nazi Collaborators in Postwar Czechoslovakia* (Cambridge, 2005). See also his article on mixed marriage: "Expulsion or Integration: Unmixing Interethnic Marriage in Postwar Czechoslovakia," *East European Politics and Societies* 14, no.2 (2000): 381–410. Bryant; Eagle Glassheim, "Ethnic Cleansing, Communism and Environmental Devastation in Czechoslovakia's Borderlands, 1945–1989," *Journal of Modern History* 78 (2006): 65–92; Eagle Glassheim, "Most the Town That Moved: Coal, Communists and the 'Gypsy Question' in Post-War Czechoslovakia," *Environment and History* 13 (2007): 463–69.

[48] František Čapka, Lubomír Slezák and Jaroslav Vaculík, *Nové osidlení pohraničí po druhé světové válce* (Brno, 2005); Andreas Wiedemann, *"Komm mit uns das Grenzland aufbauen!": Ansiedlung und neue Strukturen in den ehemaligen Sudetengebieten 1945–1952* (Essen, 2007); Matěj Spurný, *Nejsou jako my: Česká společnost a menšiny v pohraničí (1945–1960)* (Prague, 2011).

[49] Timothy Snyder, *Bloodlands: Europe between Stalin and Hitler* (New York, 2010).

done less well is to explain the role of individual perpetrators and how settlers fueled expulsion dynamics. This study brings settlers out of the shadows and underscores how local authorities' economic concerns shaped central government policies and Sudeten Germans' lives.

In order to examine what was happening on the ground, I approach the study of ethnic cleansing regionally through various local examples. No one person or place takes center stage, but instead the narrative moves through different locales in an effort to draw broader conclusions about the borderlands, Czechoslovakia and Central and Eastern Europe. In particular, I focus on the records of national committees, which comprised the basis of the local postwar administration and coordinated expulsions, controlled the distribution of confiscated property and helped to restructure the local economy. Because national committees functioned as one of the primary intermediaries between individuals and the central government, their records offer a broad picture of people's actions and attitudes in the borderlands. These organs also crucially affected the state's operations because they provided local information for decision makers in Prague and enforced central government policies. This dual role means that their records offer an excellent vantage to understand both policy-making and its implementation. In most cases, national committees put community interests before the wishes of Prague policy makers. This dynamic came to play a key role in the expulsion and resettlement actions. In addition to local records, my sources include military records as well as the debates and decisions of several ministries and central government offices, most crucially the Interior Ministry and the Settlement Office. Finally, my research integrates the testimonies of Sudeten Germans themselves as they reflected on the experience of expulsion and its meaning after their journey to Germany. Despite the problematic nature of these accounts, as discussed above, they do provide one window into Sudeten Germans' experiences following the war.

By examining this range of sources, the importance of Czech–German divisions recedes. Instead, diverse groups of actors, whose outlooks and behavior do not fit neatly within national or political parameters, transformed the borderlands into competing interests for property and power. In this sense, this book suggests a move away from nationality politics as the frame of reference for postwar Czechoslovak history, even during a period of national cleansing or "revolution." Czechs were far from united; they included "old settlers," Czech speakers who lived in the borderlands even before the war and had close relationships with Germans, and "new settlers," those who came for the first time to the borderlands following the war. The latter were further divided as some new settlers came from interior parts of the country, while others returned from abroad. One key group were Czech immigrants from Volhynia, many of whom were soldiers, who returned as part of the conquering army and as victors seeking justice. Sudeten Germans too were divided by class, occupation, geography and other factors, such as the timing of their expulsion. Although being labeled "German" designated one for expulsion, it did not determine what German speakers faced in the postwar borderlands or during their expulsion. Close examination of individual attitudes, actions and experiences reveals a vibrant portrait of borderland life, in which national identities comprised only one part of the spectrum. In short, ethnic cleansing was not simply about ethnicity.

Looking beyond the boundaries of Czechoslovakia provides another key perspective on the expulsions. The World War II period spawned new waves of population movements across Central and Eastern Europe. The Soviet and Nazi states each implemented vast population movements during the war which prompted the postwar migrations. Scholars of the Soviet Union and Nazi Germany now employ the term ethnic cleansing to capture shifting policies toward national minorities in the USSR in the 1930s and to describe the evolution of Nazi policies toward Jews prior to 1941.[50] The expulsion of Germans was common policy in several Eastern European countries. Though individual experiences differed greatly, each case was conditioned by the war and shared several key features. Ethnic cleansing involved resettlement actions as leaders drove people from their homes and offered them to selected groups. Thus, the dynamics involved in moving populations often had consequences that reshaped more than the ethnic diversity of a given area. Property transfers, regime change, new cultures and economies were some of the main transformations accompanying ethnic cleansing. These changes were not simply by products either; they affected how ethnic cleansing was carried out and experienced. Briefly outlining the history of ethnic cleansing in Central and Eastern Europe underscores how the Sudeten German expulsions and the resettlement of the borderlands fit into this larger context of World War II forced migrations.

Ethnic Cleansing in Central and Eastern Europe

In the 1990s the breakup of the Soviet Union, Yugoslavia and Czechoslovakia and the reunification of Germany revamped the political,

---

[50] On the Soviet Union, see Terry Martin, *The Affirmative Action Empire: Nations and Nationalism in the Soviet Union, 1923–1939* (Ithaca, 2001), 320–43; Kate Brown, *A Biography of No Place: From Ethnic Borderland to Soviet Heartland* (Cambridge, 2004). On Nazi Germany, see Christopher Browning, *Nazi Policy, Jewish Workers, German Killers* (Cambridge, 2000), chapter 1. See also Christopher Browning, *Origins of the Final Solution: The Evolution of Nazi Jewish Policy, September 1939-March 1942* (Lincoln, 2004), especially chapter 3. Also important in this context is Timothy Snyder, *The Reconstruction of Nations: Poland, Ukraine, Lithuania and Belarus* (New Haven, 2003).

social and economic composition of Central and Eastern Europe. The Communist system, though leaving a lasting imprint on these societies, now appears tenuous and temporary in the long-term history of this region. Yet the dispersion of millions of people through state-engineered population movements after the war proved to be one of Europe's most significant and lasting changes. Particularly in the region of Central, Eastern and Southeastern Europe, corresponding to the lands of the former multinational empires – Russian, Ottoman, Habsburg and even German before 1918 – ethnic cleansing became a key feature of the region's twentieth-century history.

Ethnic cleansing has been primarily defined as the forced removal of an ethnic group from a particular area. Naimark argues that the goal of ethnic cleansing is "to get rid of the 'alien' nationality, ethnic or religious group, and to seize the control of the territory they had formerly inhabited."[51] This is a good starting point as it suggests a broader way of conceiving ethnic cleansing beyond simply ethnicity. It also highlights the transfer of land, which is a crucial aspect of ethnic cleansing. Naimark and Ther both point to additional factors that define ethnic cleansing, including the role of the modern bureaucratic state and its leaders' desire for national homogeneity. The rise of nationalism along with increasing state power and its use of statistical methods and population policies, Ther argues, established the preconditions for ethnic cleansing in the modern world.[52] There are several factors which have caused ethnic cleansing in twentieth century Europe and several aspects characterize individual cases to different degrees, all of which makes a simplistic definition difficult to acheive. While definitions vary and the concept has often been abused for political ends, I argue that ethnic cleansing acts as a transformative force driven by migration and property transfers as much as by violence and nation-state goals. It begins with forced removals of people and the confiscation of their homes and continues as new people move in and settle the land. It ends when those migrations subside and new inhabitants control the territory and establish new communities there. Varying levels of violence, suffering, greed, government agency and individual actions shape the character of each case of ethnic cleansing. Still, the movement of people and the confiscation of property remain at the core. Only through these mechanisms can the goal to create or to refashion nation-states be realized.

Ethnic cleansing did not commence in 1939 Europe. During the Russo-Turkish War of 1877–78 and the Balkan Wars of 1912–13, for

---

[51] Naimark, 3.   [52] Ther, *Dark Side of Nation-States*, 4–8.

instance, as military fronts shifted people fled or were forced to move as soldiers and locals attacked minorities.[53] In the Russian and Ottoman Empires particular ethnic groups were driven from their homes prior to World War I. During the war the persecution and forced migration of minorities continued. For example, in the western borders of the Russian Empire, where a panoply of ethnic groups lived, compulsory deportations began with war's outbreak in 1914. That December the Russian military began to relocate all "enemy" inhabitants from western Polish provinces. They also deported some 200,000 German speakers to the Russian interior for similar reasons. Although security concerns were part of the impetus, the policy of expulsion expanded to target those who posed little threat to the Russian state. For instance, the government removed more than 600,000 Jews from Russian Poland and the Pale of Settlement by the end of 1915.[54] Frequent pogroms gave Jews another reason to flee. As Eric Lohr argues, there were certain similarities between these policies and modern ethnic cleansing, "which almost invariably includes security concerns about ethnic groups with kin outside the boundaries of the state, an ideological component, and emancipatory nationalist rhetoric of removing one group to promote another."[55]

Forced migrations did not cease at the end of World War I. In 1919, Bulgaria and Greece signed a Convention for the Emigration of Minorities, which promoted voluntary migrations of their respective minorities. These migrations, some of them actually forced, were underway as waves of Greek refugees also moved into Western Thrace as a result of Greek and Turkish fighting. This influx of Ottoman Greeks and the cession of Western Thrace to Greece prevented the continued resettlement of Bulgarian Greeks there.[56] The Lausanne Conference of 1922–23, which ended the fighting between Greece and Turkey, included a "compulsory exchange" of populations. While many Greeks had already been expelled or fled from Turkey, the Lausanne Convention authorized the removal of 1.2 million Orthodox Greeks from Turkey and roughly 350,000 Muslims from Greece. Greece's postwar population

[53] Lieberman, 15–79; Michael Marrus, *The Unwanted: European Refugees in the Twentieth Century* (Oxford, 1985), 23–48; Theodora Dragostinova, *Between Two Motherlands: Nationality and Emigration among the Greeks of Bulgaria, 1900–1949* (Ithaca, 2011), 77–103.

[54] Alexander V. Prusin, *The Lands Between: Conflict in the European Borderlands, 1870–1992* (Oxford, 2010), 54–59; Eric Lohr, *Nationalizing the Russian Empire: The Campaign against Enemy Aliens during World War I* (Cambridge, 2003), 124, 138; Joshua Sanborn, "Unsettling the Empire: Violent Migration and Social Disaster in Russia during World War I," *The Journal of Modern History* 77, no. 2 (June, 2005): 290–324; Marrus, 27–71; Eugene M. Kulischer, *Europe on the Move: War and Population Changes, 1917–47* (New York, 1948), 31.

[55] Lohr, 154.   [56] Dragostinova, 125–42; Marrus, 106–8.

increased by 25 percent as a result, and the refugees suffered tremendous hardship.[57] Muslim minorities from Balkan states not involved in official transfers also moved or were forced to migrate to Turkey, often replacing the Greeks.[58] Political leaders and some scholars considered the Turkish–Greek and Greek–Bulgarian "population exchanges" after World War I as successful examples of how to diffuse minority conflicts. Indeed, they cited them as evidence to support the call for population transfers following World War II.[59]

Despite the deportations in World War I and the "ethnic unmixing" engendered by the peace accords that followed, the population movements of the World War I years differed in key ways from those of the World War II era. First and foremost, the failure of World War I border and minority settlements and the "success" of the Lausanne Convention served as important precedents. In addition, during the World War II era the scale of migration, death and dislocation increased dramatically, particularly in Central and Eastern Europe. Robert Magosci calculates that from 1939 to 1948, 46,000,000 people were uprooted in East Central Europe.[60] Krystyna Kersten has noted that a quarter of Poland's population moved at least once between 1939 and 1950.[61] In Czechoslovakia, thanks primarily to the postwar expulsion and resettlement, more than a third of the prewar population migrated. While not all of these people were forcibly targeted and removed from a given territory because of their ethnicity, ethnic cleansing played the primary role in the vast population movements of this period.

The Soviet and Nazi regimes increased the scope and reshaped the character of population movements during the World War II era. Beginning in the 1930s, the Soviet Union conducted similar actions against its borderland populations as Imperial Russia had twenty years earlier.[62] Ethnic groups increasingly became targets of deportation

---

[57] Marrus, 97–106; Bruce Clark, *Twice a Stranger: The Mass Expulsions that Forged Modern Greece and Modern Turkey* (Cambridge, 2006); Onur Yildirim, *Diplomacy and Displacement: Reconsidering the Turco-Greek Exchange of Populations, 1922–1934* (New York, 2006).

[58] Klaus Bade, *Migration in European History*, trans. Allison Brown (Malden, Mass., 2003), 199.

[59] Ahonen, Pertti, Gustavo Corni, and Jerzy Kochanowski. *People on the Move: Forced Population Movements in Europe in the Second World War and Its Aftermath* (Berg, 2008), 10; Naimark, 110; Joseph B. Schechtman, *Postwar Population Transfers in Europe, 1945–1955* (Philadelphia, 1962), 458.

[60] Robert Magosci, *Historical Atlas of East Central Europe* (Seattle, 1993), 164. See also Schechtman, *Postwar Population Transfers*, 363.

[61] Krystyna Kersten, *The Establishment of Communist Rule in Poland, 1943–1948*, trans. John Micgiel and Michael Bernhard (Berkeley, 1991), 165.

[62] Peter Holquist, "To Count, to Extract and to Exterminate: Population Statistics and Population Politics in Late Imperial and Soviet Russia," in *A State of Nations: Empire and*

policies beginning first in the Far East and soon thereafter in the western borderlands. In the mid-1930s the Soviet secret police rounded up Poles and Germans and sent them to Kazakhstan.[63] This policy continued in 1939 as Soviet authority expanded into Poland and Bessarabia, through the Nazi–Soviet Non-Aggression Pact, and ensured that borders would be redrawn and populations moved. Indeed, the Soviet Union deported somewhere around 330,000 Polish citizens after it took control of eastern Poland prior to the Nazi invasion in 1941.[64] During this period the USSR also sent German speakers to Nazi territory through a series of negotiated agreements. From Volhynia alone nearly 65,000 *Volksdeutsche* were relocated between December 1939 and February 1940 as part of this larger resettlement action.[65] Baltic Germans and other German speakers became the subject of resettlement actions as well. After the 1941 invasion, the USSR deported nearly 750,000 Soviet German speakers to parts of Central Asia. Hundreds of thousands of other ethnic Germans followed, many of them after the war.[66] As the Red Army moved westward at the end of the war, the Soviet government again engaged in massive population dislocations. The Soviet Union's approach to ethnic minorities both reflected and accelerated the shift toward ethnic homogenization through forced migration.[67]

Nazi goals to expand the Third Reich eastwards hinged on population restructuring, property transfers and productivity needs. Adam Tooze argues that economic demands were in lock step with Nazis' racist ideology and drove their wartime goals.[68] Hitler's desires for *Lebensraum* in the East shaped their strategies, with disastrous consequences for local populations and Soviet POWs. The German army and *Einsatzgruppen*

Nation-Making in the Age of Lenin and Stalin, eds. Ronald Grigor Suny and Terry Martin (Oxford, 2001), 111–44; Snyder, *Bloodlands*, 89–118.

[63] Brown; Martin, *The Affirmative Action Empire*, 320–43.

[64] Jan Gross, *Revolution from Abroad: The Soviet Conquest of Poland's Western Ukraine and Western Belorussia* (Princeton, 1988); Pavel Polian, *Against Their Will: The History and Geography of Forced Migrations in the USSR*, trans. Anna Yastrzhembska (Budapest, 2004), 115–20; Prusin, 125–48. Gross's figures of the numbers expelled from the region have been revised and are presented here; see Mark Kramer, "Introduction," in *Redrawing Nations*, 3; Ther, "A Century of Forced Migration," in *Redrawing Nations*, 51; Snyder, *Bloodlands*, 151.

[65] Joseph B. Schechtman, *European Population Transfers, 1939–1945* (New York, 1971), 150; Timothy Snyder, "The Life and Death of Western Volhynian Jewry, 1921–1945," in *The Shoah in Ukraine: History, Testimony, Memorialization*, eds. Ray Brandon and Wendy Lower (Bloomington, 2009), 86.

[66] Polian, 126–39; Naimark, 88–89; J. Otto Pohl, *Ethnic Cleansing in the USSR, 1937–1949* (Westport, 1999), 30–46.

[67] Brown, 230; Snyder, *Bloodlands*.

[68] Adam Tooze, *The Wages of Destruction: The Making and Breaking of the Nazi Economy* (New York, 2006).

removed Jews from areas in the east, first through expulsion and, after 1941, through murder. German officials also relocated German-speaking communities throughout Eastern Europe to occupied Poland as outposts of German settlement. As these policies were put into motion after 1939, creating space for German settlers also meant clearing the territory of Poles, who owned the farmsteads on which many ethnic Germans from the east were to be resettled. Nazi expropriation policies proved that the transfer of property could be harnessed to the needs of the state and could serve as a method of repression. Yet, replacing Poles and Jews with Germans proved unworkable. German occupation officials, for instance, attempted to halt the flow of Jewish and Polish refugees to their districts, slowing the resettlement process and leaving German settlers stranded in temporary resettlement camps.[69] By the end of 1941 Polish and Jewish fates drastically diverged. Poles who were dispossessed of their farms to make room for German-speaking farmers were often sent to the Reich as forced laborers.[70] This forced migration, in turn, helped to alleviate growing labor shortages in the Reich and demonstrates well the way that migration and economic needs often overlapped. Jews, on the other hand, were systematically rounded up and killed. While the Holocaust involved many complex factors, the failed efforts at restructuring populations in favor of German settlers played a decisive role in directing Nazi policies toward Jews.

The plans to refashion the social landscape of Eastern Europe and to create a Greater German Reich crumbled with Nazi Germany's defeat. Following the war German speakers, some of whom had already been resettled once, were cleansed from communities across Central and Eastern Europe. Redrawing the Polish–German borders involved the expulsion of more than 3,000,000 Germans from territories in what had been prewar Germany's east. This followed the flight and expulsion of more than 5,000,000 Germans from areas of East Prussia, Silesia, West Prussia, Danzig and eastern portions of Pomerania and Brandenburg. German speakers were also expelled from Hungary, Yugoslavia and Romania, most being sent to Germany, though others were deported to the Soviet Union. In all, some 12,000,000 German speakers were forced

---

[69] Aly, *Final Solution*; Christopher Browning, *Nazi Policy, Jewish Workers, German Killers* (Cambridge, 2000); Browning, *Origins*; Robert Koehl, *RKFDV German Resettlement and Population Policy, 1939–1945: A History of the Reich Commission for the Strengthening of Germandom* (Cambridge, 1957); and Anna C. Bramwell, "The Re-settlement of Ethnic Germans, 1939–41," in *Refugees in the Age of Total War*, ed. Anna C. Bramwell (London, 1988), 112–32.

[70] Götz Aly and Susan Heim, *Architects of Annihilation: Auschwitz and the Logic of Destruction*, trans. A.G. Blunden (Princeton, 2002), 73–8–8; Aly, *Final Solution*, 43.

to leave their homes by 1948. Although Nazi planners had earlier envisioned their migration into the Third Reich as a form of promotion, their flight and "transfer" to postwar Germany turned into a form of punishment. In the broader history of forced migration during World War II, the German expulsions belong to its final chapter.

Nazi policies and actions alone were not responsible for population upheavals and ethnic cleansing during the war. In Poland, as in Yugoslavia and elsewhere, conflicts emerged within the context of the broader war that pitted locals against one another in the name of ethnic purity. For instance, ethnic cleansing helped to define the nation-state projects of both Ukrainian and Polish nationalists during World War II. Ukrainian leaders believed that by removing Poles, they had a better chance of establishing an independent state.[71] For all postwar Polish leaders, making Poland ethnically homogeneous became a central goal. In addition to expelling Germans they began major efforts to de-Germanize and to Polonize the western regions taken from Germany. Polish officials renamed streets, resurfaced tombstones and relocated monuments.[72] Poles migrated to these regions from territories in the east that the Soviet Union had annexed as well as from central Poland. The Polish government continued to implement repressive ethnic policies into 1947 when it carried out *Akcja Wisla* (Operation Vistula), which forcibly dispersed Lemkos and remaining Ukrainians throughout Poland.[73]

World War II unleashed these mass expulsions and resettlement projects that dramatically reshaped postwar states and societies across Central and Eastern Europe. As Jan Gross has argued, the revolutionary changes often associated with the establishment of Communist regimes in the region really began with the war and were made possible because of it.[74] According to Gross, two key aspects of this "revolution" were the migratory flows of millions of people and economic changes in property relations and work. Expulsion policies proved popular in Poland and Czechoslovakia and provided a pool of readily available property to support demand for goods and social mobility that had been restricted by the

---

[71] Snyder, *Reconstruction of Nations*; Alexander V. Prusin, "Ethnic Cleansing in Western Ukraine: The OUN-UPA Assault against Polish Settlements in Volhynia and Eastern Galicia, 1943–1944," in *Ethnic Cleansing in 20th Century Europe*, 517–35; Prusin, *The Lands Between*, 125–48.

[72] Thum, *Uprooted*, chapters 8 and 9.

[73] Snyder, *The Reconstruction of Nations*, chapters 8 and 9; Naimark, 122–36; Curp, 34–54. See also the chapters on Poland in *Ethnic Cleansing in 20th Century Europe* and *Redrawing Nations*.

[74] Jan Gross, "War as Revolution," in *The Politics of Retribution in Europe: World War II and Its Aftermath*, eds. Istvan Deak, Jan Gross and Tony Judt (Princeton, 2000), 17–40, here 24–25. Bradley Abrams makes a similar argument in "The Second World War and the East European Revolution," *East European Politics and Societies* 16, no. 3 (2002): 623–64.

war. Land reform policies and the nationalization of industry began with the expropriation of so-called enemies. Labor control also became a focus of postwar regimes, and in Czechoslovakia was closely tied to the expulsions and resettlement of the borderlands. Situating the expulsion of Sudeten Germans as part of the World War II population movements across Central and Eastern Europe demonstrates that it was not merely a matter between Czechs and Germans, but closely coupled to the war, other cases of ethnic cleansing and the emerging Cold War.

The Communist Party of Czechoslovakia (KSČ) served as a conduit of these changes rather than as their catalyst. While historians generally credit Communists with great success related to the expulsion and resettlement agendas, the picture was actually more mixed. Communists received political patronage through the management of confiscated property and they were able to utilize confiscated German factories to further expand the nationalized industrial sector in 1947. However, the KSČ did not dictate all of the changes in the borderlands. In Czechoslovakia the Communists did not yet possess total control after the war and the other parties in the National Front government mostly supported the use of expropriated property for socialist goals. Moreover, people moved to the borderlands and seized property without any oversight by the central government or with the direct help of any political party. Finally, as this study makes clear, the Communist Party of Czechoslovakia was itself anything but a unified force in the late 1940s. Communists living in the borderlands often worked against the policies initiated by their leaders in Prague. Party membership was also in constant flux in the postwar borderlands. This began to change in the early 1950s as the Communist Party's leadership reorganized the administration of the country, but even then, local policies did not necessarily flow from the center.

As part of the final chapter of ethnic cleansing in Central and Eastern Europe, the expulsion of Germans from the Sudetenland represented a turning point for the country and the region. It was the end of engineered population restructuring and it wound back the clock on centuries of migration in a matter of months. It demonstrated that a nominally democratic transitional government could carry out ethnic cleansing, thanks to the war and shifting international politics in 1945. It had not only become feasible, but also, in many people's minds, desirable. The expulsions were not only a form of collective punishment, they were also viewed as a preventive measure against future conflict. This was sadly ironic given that the expulsions fostered Cold War divisions and brought Czechoslovakia closer to the Soviet orbit, while Sudeten German organizations in the Federal Republic pushed hard for redress. It also represents one of the most costly cases of ethnic cleansing. To calculate even an approximate figure of Sudeten Germans' losses would be next to impossible; suffice it to say that of the roughly 3,000,000 expellees most lost nearly everything. Their loss, however, was others' gain, and in this sense profitable for state and society. Yet, the benefits were mostly short term as Cold War priorities turned the Sudetenland from a series of unique productive towns into a Soviet-style behemoth with all of the associated social, economic and environmental degradation. It is still digging itself out of that history.

The book is organized thematically and Chapters 1 through 5 each run chronologically from the immediate postwar to the late 1940s. Chapter 6 covers the period after the Communist takeover and into the early 1950s. The book begins by examining the experience, organization and operation of the expulsions and postwar life through both German and Czech eyes. It challenges the notion of "wild expulsions" in which Czechs unleashed their fury against Germans, and instead argues that the violence was sporadic, but specific, allowing most Germans to escape unscathed. The second chapter outlines the establishment of local government and the relations among settlers. It demonstrates how competing visions of the borderlands emerged as different groups of people, not simply Czechs and Germans, began to refashion the region. Chapters 3 through 5 investigate more deeply the key intersections of ethnic cleansing and economic change: property confiscation, labor relations and industrial overhaul. These economic issues played a central role in shaping the policies and the experiences of expulsion and resettlement. Chapter 6 explores the borderlands' final transition into a Sovietized polity and economy during the early Cold War and the Sudeten Germans' position within it. The KSČ attempted to lure the remaining Germans in Czechoslovakia to work for the construction of a socialist society by offering them cultural and material incentives that were unimaginable a few years earlier. Rather than providing the foundation for a successful socialist society, however, the economy of ethnic cleansing wasted the wealth and work of German inhabitants and left the borderlands divided and impoverished.

1   In The Wake of War: Expulsions, Violence and Borderland Life

> The years 1945 and 1946 will remain forever written in the history of our nation as a great turning point in its development. In the maelstrom of historic events, many of the constructive efforts that our nation is self-lessly and heroically developing in these years – stimulated by our national and democratic revolution – will gradually fade. But the reality that after this revolution our republic once and for all time truly became a national state of Czechs and Slovaks, without minorities, will remain the unforgettable fruit of our revolution.[1]
>
> Miroslav Kreysa, Chairman of the Settlement Office

From War to "The Wild Transfer"

While seventy years might not be long enough to call Miroslav Kreysa's statement prophetic, of all the changes emanating from the war years in the Bohemian lands the removal of the Sudeten Germans has seemingly been the most enduring. Communist rule ended, as did the accompanying Cold War. Even the Czechoslovak state is gone, replaced with two separate national states thanks, in part, to the postwar cleansing of minorities. Kreysa, as a Communist Party leader, was trying to claim responsibility and praise for the expulsions, and, as the leader of the borderlands' resettlement program, he had an audience of settlers with a vested interest in getting rid of Germans. His attitude toward the expulsions and the party's efforts to gain political capital from them was common across the political leadership of postwar Czechoslovakia. Slovak leaders, it should be noted, were simultaneously attempting to expel Hungarians. In fact, these were popular programs in many parts of Central and Eastern Europe after the war. The Nazis' annihilation of the Jews and their attempts to redraw the ethnic landscape set off a series of similar policies throughout the region. In addition, the brutality of the war, particularly in the east, meant that Soviet reprisals were devastating as well. Together,

[1] Miroslav Kreysa, "Osidlovací politika lidově demokratického státu," *Osidlování* May 5, 1946.

these factors helped facilitate the expulsion of Germans after the war. In this sense, the ethnic cleansing that swept through borderland regions of Czechoslovakia was part of a much broader revolutionary pattern than Kreysa was willing to admit.

The war did not wreak the kind of death and destruction in Czechoslovakia that it did further east. The Nazi destruction of the town of Lidice and the murdering of its male inhabitants in June 1942 represented the most noteworthy act of aggression in the country during the war. This was in retaliation for the assassination of Reinhard Heydrich, the Nazi leader of the Protectorate. There were, to be sure, other acts of terror and arrests. Czech resentment toward Germanization policies and other restrictions grew throughout the war. This sentiment was most evident among the underground resistance itself, known as the Central Leadership of the Domestic Resistance (*Ústřední vedení odboje domácího*, ÚVOD). They had lost the most, and had the most to lose, and thus voiced a particularly sharp desire for revenge. In 1944, for instance, one report from ÚVOD noted that "Anti-German feeling has changed into hatred … The overwhelming opinion, as among political leaders, is that Germans must be removed and the Republic will become a nation-state without Germans."[2] The resistance movement certainly emphasized widespread feelings of hatred among the general populace, which served to support its calls for a total expulsion of the German population. For other Czechs, gauging the level of animosity is more difficult. It would seem appropriate to argue that, as with judging people's levels of collaboration and resistance during the occupation, we assume that a range of emotions and attitudes characterized the Czech populace after the war.

This has not been the favored interpretation of most historians, however. The majority of scholars continue to argue that Czechs, as a whole, felt a deep-seated hatred toward Germans as the war came to an end.[3] The term "wild transfer" (*divoký odsun*) has been used to characterize the

---

[2] Doc.137. Report from August 17, 1944. Jitka Vondorová, ed., *Češi a sudetoněmecká otázka, 1939–1945* (Prague, 1994), 281.

[3] Tomáš Staněk, *Perzekuce 1945* (Prague, 1996), 49. Tomáš Staněk, *Odsun Němců z Československu, 1945–1948* (Prague, 1991), 56–60; Norman Naimark, *Fires of Hatred: Ethnic Cleansing in Twentieth Century Europe* (Cambridge, 2001), 114–22; Benjamin Frommer, *National Cleansing: Retribution Against Nazi Collaborators in Postwar Czechoslovakia* (Cambridge, 2005), 38–45; Chad Bryant, *Prague in Black: Nazi Rule and Czech Nationalism* (Harvard, 2007), 219–25; Jürgen Tämpke, *Czech-German Relations and the Politics of Central Europe: From Bohemia to the EU* (New York, 2003), 65–70; Eagle Glassheim, "National Mythologies and Ethnic Cleansing: The Expulsion of Czechoslovak Germans in 1945," *Central European History* 33, no.4 (2000): 463–86; Eagle Glassheim, "Mechanics of Ethnic Cleansing: The Expulsion of Germans from Czechoslovakia, 1945–1947," in *Redrawing Nations: Ethnic Cleansing in East-Central Europe, 1944–1948*, eds. Philipp Ther and Ana Siljak (Lanham, 2001), 205–8.

early postwar months when Czechs carried out expulsions, and connotes the notion of widespread violence. This image emerged with the expellees' postwar accounts of the expulsions and continues to influence historical scholarship. Chad Bryant, for instance, argues: "Hating the Germans became the only clear, unambiguous aspect of Czech national identity that survived the war." Drawing from Roger Peterson's work, he continues, "emotions . . . readied Czechs to beat, kill, and humiliate their neighbors."[4] No doubt this was the case for a certain part of the population, and Czech leaders called for violent reprisals against Germans. Some responded, and violence ensued. Yet, this picture is at once both vague and conclusive. For instance, one recent study noted that "the first wave of expulsions from the Sudetenland took place in a maelstrom of fury, vengeance, nationalism and popular rage."[5] Another account states: "As the German armies retreated, Czechs went on a violent rampage against the German population in a number of localities. This violence was brutal, indiscriminate, and aimed to humiliate."[6] Such an image suggests that all Czechs were willing participants in terrorizing Germans because they hated them.

The notion of the "wild transfer" misrepresents the character of the expulsions and the violence against Germans for several reasons. First, a commission of Czech and German historians places the number of deaths resulting from the expulsions at 30,000. Of these, they argue that the number killed directly at the hands of Czechs was less than 7,000.[7] While not all scholars agree with these findings, they suggest that widespread popular violence does not accurately characterize Czech actions against Germans. Of course, killings were not the only form of violence, and physical assaults were widespread. Still, violence was usually located in specific contexts, such as internment camps, and during moments of expulsion, when compulsion was used to get people to move and to instill fear in others. In this sense, the violence was not "wild" at all, but rather served specific ends. In addition, the two main examples that scholars use to support this idea of wild and hate-driven expulsions turn out to be some of the more exceptional cases of violence in postwar Czechoslovakia. The first one occurred in Brno at the end of May 1945 and the other one

---

[4] Bryant, *Prague in Black*, 220–21. See also Roger Peterson, *Understanding Ethnic Violence: Fear, Hatred, and Resentment in Twentieth-Century Eastern Europe* (Cambridge, 2002).

[5] Anne Applebaum, *Iron Curtain, 1944–1956: The Crushing of Eastern Europe* (New York, 2012), 120.

[6] Beth Wilner, "Czechoslovakia, 1848–1998," in Peterson, *Understanding Ethnic Violence*, 200.

[7] *Konfliktní společenství, katastrofa, uvolnění: Náčrt výkladu německo-českých dějin od 19. století* (Prague, 1996). The other estimated deaths occurred as a result of crowded camp conditions, disease and malnourishment.

happened in Ústí nad Labem at the end of July. Each case was very different, but neither one of them was a good representation of what happened during the ethnic cleansing of the borderlands.

The following account of the 1945 summer expulsions attempts to place the violence in its local context and to examine more closely the actors and conditions involved. By doing so, the picture of wholesale mob violence recedes while more specific perpetrators, mostly associated with the Czech military and partisan units, move to the fore. Recent research has clarified that the Czechoslovak military conducted the majority of expulsions, which the central government had ordered it to implement.[8] The first Czechs to enter the borderlands were military units and paramilitary groups that treated the area as a land to be conquered. They regarded everyone as suspect, including the Czech speakers living there. After they solidified their presence in the region they began to organize and carry out expulsions. What emerges, then, is not a picture of widespread nationally motivated mob violence, but a military campaign to force Germans from the country with groups of young men, and occasionally women, who engaged in particularly brutal or sadistic acts of violence when given the opportunity.

By late March 1945, the Red Army had entered the Bohemian lands in Silesia and began the drive against German forces in Moravia. In May, additional Soviet forces moved south from Saxony and began to drive toward Prague, which they liberated on May 9. As they occupied the borderlands they instituted a reign of terror on local German populations. While they arrived as ostensible liberators for Czechs, they came as conquerors to the borderlands and treated Sudeten Germans no differently than Germans in the Old Reich.[9] Soviet soldiers raped, pillaged and tormented local German communities as they moved through the borderlands. German testimonies are filled with such reports: "The first Russians came riding in, followed by stronger units and the night from 8 to 9 May was the beginning of the ensuing time of terror. Robbing and plundering were of the daily order, the violation of women and girls were the horrific side effects."[10] Another German described the arrival of

---

[8] Tomáš Staněk and Adrian von Arburg "Organizované divoké odsuny? Úlohá z ústředních státních orgánů pří provádění 'evakuace' německého obyvatelstva (květín až září 1945)," 1 část. "Předpoklady a vývoj do konce května 1945," Soudobé dějiny 12, no. 3–4 (2005), 465–533; 2 část. "Československá armáda vytváří 'hotové skutečností', vláda je před cizinou legitimizuje," Soudobé dějiny 13, no. 1–2 (2006), 13–49; 3 část. "Snaha vlády a civilních úřadů o řízení 'divokého odsunu'," Soudobé dějiny 13, no. 3–4 (2006) 321–76.

[9] Norman Naimark, The Russians in Germany: A History of the Soviet Occupation Zone, 1945–1949 (Cambridge, 1995).

[10] Erlebnisbericht, Josef Eckert, March 19, 1951. Lastenausgleich Archiv, Bayreuth, Germany (LAA). Ost-Dokumentation (Ost-Dok) 2, Brüx 246, 2.

Russians in this way: "Not only shots were heard, but the screams of women and girls of all ages raped by the Russians."[11] The editor of the Sudeten German testimonies suggests that Czechs frequently aided and abetted Russian soldiers who sought to rape Germans.[12]

Red Army soldiers not only terrorized Germans, but also became a thorn in the side of Czech authorities. Reports of soldiers taking livestock, food, clothing and other necessities abounded. One borderland town reported that they had been working on several cases where Red Army soldiers stole things "not only in apartments evacuated by Germans but also in various storage facilities and the like."[13] Soviet soldiers sometimes even helped Germans at the expense of Czechs. Several reports indicate that Soviet soldiers aided Germans' flight, often including the shipment of their belongings. Sometimes the soldiers even returned for the Germans' property after they had already reached Germany. For instance, on July 10, 1945, Czech officials reported that Soviet soldiers crossed the Czech–Saxon border with two trucks and transported the family of the photographer Max Nowak back to Germany with all of their belongings, including furniture.[14] Soviet forces continued to harass officials and undermined the restoration of order in the borderlands until their withdrawal in December 1945. As noteworthy, however, was the fact that regardless of how poorly Soviet soldiers treated Germans, the German testimonies, almost without exception, state that when the Czechs arrived the situation became much worse. That is because whatever the transgressions of the Russians, the Czechs came to expel the Germans from their homes.

The situation in the borderlands differed greatly from that of interior towns and cities where Germans lived. Here, Germans were often more at the mercy of Czechs, who greatly outnumbered them. In Prague, for instance, Czechs forced Germans to do menial work and terrorized them in various ways. In Brno, local Czechs took matters into their own hands to expel Germans from the city. What became known as "The Brno Death March" claimed the lives of hundreds, many in its aftermath.[15]

[11] Erlebnisbericht, Erwin Brendel, n.d. LAA, Ost-Dok 2, Freiwaldau 252, 24.
[12] Theodor Schieder, ed., Documents on the Expulsion of the Germans from Eastern-Central-Europe, vol. 4: The Expulsion of the Germans from Czechoslovakia, trans. G.H. de Sausmarez (Bonn, 1960), 29.
[13] Report from police commissioner, October 9, 1945. Státní Okresní Archiv (SOkA) Jablonec nad Nisou (Jablonec n. N) fond (f.) ONV Jablonec n. N., karton (k.) 18 inventární čislo (inv. č.), 39.
[14] Information report to Minister of National Defense. Archiv Města (AM) Ústí nad Labem (Ústí n. L.), f. ONV Ústí n. L., k. 111 inv. č. 749.
[15] Staněk and von Arburg, "Organizované divoké odsuny?" 1 čast; Hans Hertl et al., Němci ven! Brněnský pochod smrti 1945, trans. Jana Šlajchrtová (Prague, 2001); Vojtěch Žampach, "The Expulsion of the Germans from Brno and the Immediate

The reasons for the expulsion from Brno involved a combination of popular anger, desire for German property, especially housing, and the radicalized political atmosphere in the country. President Beneš had delivered an invective against Germans in the city two weeks before the expulsion.[16] Tomáš Staněk argues that "[p]ressure for the expulsions combined with the incomparable conditions in the city, which led to increasing radical demands and exacerbated national passions."[17] The lack of housing was part of these difficult conditions and likely hastened calls for expulsion.[18] Property demands and local resentments, combined with leaders' calls to expel Germans, pressured local officials to authorize the action. On May 30, armed factory workers and various security units forced more than 20,000 Germans to march south from the city toward Austria. Along the way, security officials added as many as 10,000 other Sudeten Germans to the moving columns of humanity from nearby towns and villages. Those in charge, however, had not secured permission from officials in Austria to accept these Germans or made provisions for them once they were refused entry. While difficult to assess, in addition to dozens of Germans who appear to have perished en route, hundreds more died in the makeshift camps in Pohořelice and once across the border in Austria.[19]

Popular pressure and the wider involvement of Czechs in this expulsion appear more pertinent in this case than in any other during that summer. That local factory workers played a large role in gathering and expelling Germans, for example, was exceptional compared to the general course of the expulsions. Another reason that popular demands for revenge surfaced to the degree that they did in Brno is due to the fact that Germans were a minority in the city. Popular anger had a much better chance of surfacing there than in the borderlands, where Sudeten Germans comprised the majority of inhabitants well into 1946. Other historians note an important distinction between events in the borderlands and those in the interior. One pair of Czech historians considers the borderlands and the former Protectorate as "two separate worlds" at this time.[20] The domestic resistance's actions against Nazi units in Prague in early May, along with the severe treatment of Germans in the city, leads Staněk to argue that

---

Consequences, 30 May to 7 July 1945," *The Prague Yearbook of Contemporary History* (Prague, 1999), 85–156; Staněk, *Perzekuce*, 87–90; Glassheim, "National Mythologies," 481–86.

[16] Glassheim, "National Mythologies," 481–82.   [17] Staněk, *Perzekuce*, 87.

[18] Glassheim, "National Mythologies," 482, 485; Staněk and Arburg, "Organizované divoké odsuny? Úloha z ústředních státních orgánů," 524.

[19] Staněk, *Perzekuce*, 89–90; Staněk and Arburg, "Organizované divoké odsuny? Úlohá z ústředních státních orgánů," 525–33.

[20] S. Biman, and R. Cílek. *Poslední mrtví, první živí: České pohraničí květen až srpen 1945* (Ústí nad Labem, 1989), 14.

Prague "had an undoubtedly exceptional position in comparison with the situation of Germans" elsewhere in May 1945.[21] Inland cities and towns were more likely to be dangerous places for Germans than the borderlands immediately after the war.

Popular uprisings like the one in Brno were in fact extremely rare in the borderlands, and it took time before expulsions there got underway. Standing military orders were issued in mid-May to "deport all Germans from the historic borders."[22] Despite these instructions, however, few expulsions occurred. In some places disagreements among Czechs slowed progress toward getting rid of the Germans. In Liberec, for example, a series of different security organs came through the town and complicated the expulsions by looting and terrorizing both Czechs and Germans.[23] In late May, a frustrated military commander in the borderlands characterized the situation as follows:

No cleansing (čistka) or expulsion to the Reich is being carried out. Germans everywhere remain in their places, and they even continue with their former pride, working publicly and threatening Czech people ... Relevant sector commanders, when they are notified about the weakness towards Germans, blame it on national committees in the borderlands, which hinder the activities of units in the borderlands and directly prohibit severe policy towards Germans, with the claim, that only they are the responsible authority in this region.[24]

In May 1945, national committees and military organs had not yet established clear lines of authority. They would continue to battle over control of German inhabitants throughout the summer. Despite the commander's view that national committees were preventing ethnic cleansing, national committees were often willing to expel Germans, but did not have the means to engineer many large operations or force them across the border.[25] At the same time, national committees proved reluctant to allow military forces to control expulsions from their towns because they wanted to be in charge. As the expulsions continued, military authorities stepped up their pressure and stepped over national committees' authority to conduct expulsions.

Orders to deport Germans in the middle of May meant little given the few preparations for such expulsions. Many of the military's early instructions

[21] Staněk, *Perzekuce*, 66–73.
[22] Dodatek to č.45/45 from Velitelství gen. Alex, May 15, 1945. Vojenský historický archiv (VHA) Prague, f. Velitelství první oblasti (VO1), k. 1 inv. č. 6; Biman and Cílek, *Poslední mrtví, první živí*, 31; Staněk, *Perzekuce*, 23.
[23] Staněk, *Perzekuce*, 90–93.
[24] Situanční hlášení oper. skupiny [sic] za den May 26, 1945, Velitelství 3 Čs. divise. VHA, f. VO1, k.1 inv. č. 6.
[25] See, for example, Report from Fryváldov, June 6, 1945. NA, f. Ministerstvo vnitra – Nosek (MV-N), k. 227 inv. č. 146.

did not directly call for a general expulsion, but spoke of securing the borders and beginning operations against remaining Nazi formations and suspected German guerrilla groups, known as "Werewolves." In addition to members of the reconstituted Czechoslovak Army, special armed detachments of partisans and others moved into the borderlands. Their assignment included securing the transportation network around the Most coal basin.[26] Once accomplished, these basic security measures allowed military officials to turn to the process of ethnic cleansing. On June 7, 1945, the commander of the Northern Bohemia region issued some of the first concrete instructions regarding the expulsion procedures. The "transfer," as he called it, would be carried out by Czechoslovak units in agreement with national committees, and after reaching the border Red Army units would assume control. Transfers would start in the interior parts of the country, from areas where Germans comprised less than 60 percent of the inhabitants.[27] These and other plans prepared the way for military authorities to take greater control of the expulsions, which the government authorized on June 15, 1945.[28]

The military's first expulsions were often directed against Nazi Party members and citizens of Nazi Germany who had moved to the Sudetenland or the Protectorate after the Munich Agreement. More extensive expulsions only began to take shape in June. Near the town of Děčín, 1,328 German inhabitants were expelled as a "test case" (zkušební případ) on June 4, 1945.[29] Reports from other places show how expulsions quickly assumed routine forms. One report noted, for example: "In Teplice-Šanov Germans are being moved out systematically home by home and they are transported by trucks to Cinvald, where they undergo a thorough search by the border guards. After the search they are sent on foot across the border."[30] These actions, which took place just prior to

[26] Postup při obsazení Sudet, Generál Novák, May 20, 1945. VHA, f. VO1, k. 1 inv. č. 6; Situační hlášení, Vel. 3 Čs. divise, May 27, 1945, ibid.; Biman and Cílek, Poslední mrtví, první živí, 25–51.

[27] 0536/taj.1.odd.1945, VO1, June 7, 1945. VHA, f. VO1, k. 49 inv.č. 267; see also Staněk and von Arburg "Organizované divoké odsuny?" 2. část: "Československá armáda vytváří,"13–49.

[28] Meeting of the government, June 15, 1945. Karel Jech and Karel Kaplan, eds., Dekrety prezidenta republiky 1940–1945: Dokumenty 2 vols. (Brno, 1995), 1: 372–73. For other plans see: Instructions from Ministry of National Defense, June 12, 1945. VHA, f. VO1, k. 2 inv.č. 21; Biman and Cílek, Poslední mrtví, první živí, 31; Staněk, Odsun Němců, 64–65. This helps explain why the Provincial National Committee in Prague ordered national committees to stop further expulsions on their own as of June 14, 1945. See Glassheim, "National Mythologies," 478.

[29] Situace 9 June 1945 v prostoru Děčín-Podmokly-Teplice-Šanov, from VO1, June 13, 1945, VÚA, f. VO1, k. 48 inv. č. 263; Report from VO1, July 25, 1945. VHA, f. Vojenská kancelář presidenta republiky (VKPR), č.j. 1070.

[30] Situace 9 June 1945 v prostoru Děčín-Podmokly-Teplice-Šanov, from VO1, June 13, 1945, VHA, f. VO1, k. 48 inv.č. 263.

June 15, presaged the move toward a general cleansing of Sudeten Germans. On June 19, the Headquarters of the First Army Corps issued a general "transfer" order to military units operating in the borderlands. First, non-productive Germans, business owners and others, such as teachers, lawyers and office personnel, were to be concentrated according to local conditions and made available for transfer. Important workers and farmers were to be kept until the Czechs could replace them.[31]

Even though the military leadership worked to better organize the expulsion process, this should not mask the violence that ethnic cleansing entailed. Local commanders could shape the nature of expulsions in particularly brutal ways. In Chomutov, for example, on June 9 the local Czech military authorities forced all the men in the city, some 5,000–6,000 of them, to assemble at the local sports stadium. Somewhere around 10–20 members of the SS were identified, tortured and killed. Following this, Staff Captain Karel Prašil ordered the forced march of the men to the Saxony border, some 20 kilometers away. Along the way, the Germans were beaten with whips and several were shot. One Czech participant counted 27 killed, many of whom were shot in the back. A German source listed many more dead. When they reached the border the Soviet commander refused to allow the transport to cross. Prašil, it appears, attempted to carry out this expulsion without prior preparation or approval. After a few days at the border they marched the Germans to an internment camp in nearby Most to work at the synthetic fuel plant there.[32]

Partisan units that roamed throughout the borderlands in May and June also added to the arbitrary nature of violence and ethnic cleansing for some Germans. Many partisan groups, often referred to as Revolutionary Guards, came to the borderlands from Prague, where they had already been engaged in fighting against Germans. Some units formed only as the war ended, and with the express purpose to go to the borderlands to pacify the region. Rather than restoring order, however, these groups often created chaos. Czech officials, both local and central, continually complained

---

[31] Čj.75 Taj.1.odděl.1945, Odsun německého za hranice, from Velitelství I. sboru (VS1), June 19, 1945. VHA, f. VO1, k. 48 inv. č. 263; Entry for June 19, 1945. VHA, f. Kronika velitelství 13 divise, k. 1, kronika.

[32] For details surrounding the Chomutov March, see Report no. 55. Theodor Schieder, ed., *Dokumentation der Vertreibung der Deutschen aus Ost-Mitteleuropa*, vol. 4/2, *Die Vertreibung der deutschen Bevölkerung aus der Tschechoslowakei* (Bonn, 1957), 292–94; Report no. 90. Schieder, ed., *The Expulsion of the Germans from Czechoslovakia*, 4: 469–72; Record of the Ministry of Interior on events in Chomutov in June 1945 and of the brutal offenses at the internment camp there. November 28, 1947; Doc. 91, Arburg and Staněk, eds., *Vysídlení Němců*, II.3: 267.

about the actions of partisan groups. An officer from the Third Division reported: "Aside from military units operating in this sector several detachments of partisans ... behave undisciplined, do not heed orders from the regional headquarters, plunder, and simply do as they please."[33] Germans mostly bore the brunt of partisan independence. "On Sunday, 13 May 1945 Czech Partisans came into our apartment, rummaged through boxes and closets, and held my husband and I under the threat of pistols aimed at the back of our necks. They did this with sadistic joy and lust and were seemingly prepared for a long extension of their visit," wrote one Sudeten German.[34] While most partisans were out for material gain, the space between war and ethnic cleansing provided opportunities to those who wished to threaten and attack Germans. Already in June the military began making efforts to contain and control partisan units and, aside from a few hold outs, by July 1945 most partisan units had been disbanded and the men and women who comprised them assumed other responsibilities, often as camp guards or as members of local police forces. Despite their actions and the different ways that they shaped early postwar borderland life, partisans had little power to carry out expulsions across the border and played a mostly auxiliary role to the regular army.

The military's involvement and the clearer delineation of responsibility helped to accelerate expulsions in mid-June; they became increasingly intense in July. For instance, the Twelfth Division, operating in Northern Bohemia, oversaw the expulsion of 70,727 Sudeten Germans before July, but in that month alone they forced more than twice that number of Germans across the border.[35] The troop's presence along the German and Polish frontier determined the options for Czechoslovakia's military seeking to expel Germans. For example, on June 8, 1945, Polish forces closed the border between Czechoslovakia and newly demarcated Polish territory. They prevented Sudeten Germans from being driven into territory the Poles had just occupied because they too were forcibly moving Germans westward.[36] Their forces cut off a direct northward route from borderland districts in eastern Bohemia and northern Moravia and Silesia. American forces likewise did what they could to prohibit expulsions from western Bohemia, much of which they occupied until the end of the year. In 1945, the majority of expellees were sent to

---

[33] Výpis ze situačního hlášení vel. divisí. May 27, 1945. VHA, f. VO1, k. 1 inv. č. 6.

[34] Erlebnisbericht Margarete Kaulfersch, June 16, 1950. LAA, Ost-Dok 2, Gablonz 255, 11.

[35] Postup vysídlování obyvatelstva německé národnosti, 12 divise, from First Divisional Headquarters, August 9, 1945. VHA, f. VO1, k. 49 inv. č. 271.

[36] Report on the difficulties of the evacuations of Germans from late July 1945. VHA, f. VO1, k. 49 inv. č. 267; Biman and Cílek, *Poslední mrtví, první živí*, 95.

Saxony with the consent of Soviet Army officials, though at times local Soviet commanders needed a bit of coaxing.[37] The army and irregular units forced tens of thousands of Sudeten Germans living in the south, in addition to inhabitants from Brno, across the Austrian border.[38] However, expulsion across the border was not the only means of ethnic cleansing. Hundreds of thousands of other Sudeten Germans were driven from their homes and sent to holding camps or to work in the interior parts of the country. Thus, while military units forced only some of the Germans abroad in 1945, they nonetheless threw out many others from their homes. A national committee report from one small town in the Česká Lípa (Böhmisch Leipa) district provided a typical breakdown of the summer expulsions' effects on borderland Germans. It noted that seventy-five local Germans had been sent to the interior parts of the country, seventy-three had been taken away by soldiers, and more than one hundred others remained working in the town.[39] In this sense, the individual paths to expulsion varied widely.

Certain army units specialized in ethnic cleansing. The 28th Infantry Regiment was one such unit; easily distinguished by their unique uniforms, its members became known as "Svoboda's men."[40] This regiment moved among various divisions and carried out numerous cleansing operations, at times without the knowledge of superior officers. Just as the general expulsions began in mid-June, it carried out the first extensive operations in and around Česká Lípa.[41] In one instance, local authorities complained that the regiment expelled protected German glass specialists and carried off truckloads of pilfered German property. Although investigations into the incident were conducted, the regiment's work had already been done and it moved on to other towns. When the 28th Infantry Regiment's second battalion arrived to carry out a planned expulsion of German speakers from Děčín on July 12, 1945, its leaders concluded that preparations had not been made and that the District Administrative Commission (Okresní správní komise, OSK) wished to postpone the action by several days. After being told that, despite the lack of preparation, "the evacuation" could take place as scheduled the

---

[37] See, for example, Report from Štáb-2.oddělení VO1, July 7, 1945. VHA, k. 48 inv. č. 264; Report from Štáb-1.oddělení VO1, July 16, 1945. Ibid., k. 49 inv. č. 67.

[38] Staněk gives the figure of 200,000. See Odsun němců, 73.

[39] Report from MNV Medonosy, August 8, 1945. SOkA Česká Lípa, f. ONV Duba, k. 43, inv. č. 98.

[40] Jan Havel, Vladimír Kaiser, Otfrid Pustejovsky, Stalo se Ústí nad Labem 31 července 1945 (Ústí nad Labem, 2005), 15.

[41] Entries in June, Chronicle of Division 13. VHA, f. Kronika velitelství 13 divise, k.1, kronika; Report from Velitelství 13 pěší divise, June 20, 1945. VHA, f. VO1, k. 48 inv. č. 264.

following day, district officials produced just over 1,000 German speakers for transfer. Displeased with the low figure, one of the regiment's commanders and two officers demanded another expulsion, which they carried out the next day, despite the protests of district and local officials. Police units under the OSK's authority attempted to thwart the expulsion by occupying the train station, but to no avail. While the dispute was later explained as a misunderstanding, local officials remained stung by the incident.[42] Despite such difficulties between the 28th Infantry Regiment units and national committees, military authorities continued to dispatch it for cleansing operations. A similar conflict occurred in Varnsdorf just a few weeks later. Officials reporting on the incident noted that the soldiers did not cooperate with local officials, pillaged, disregarded the exemptions for antifascists and industrial specialists, and even mistreated Czechs.[43] According to incomplete records, this regiment alone expelled more than 90,000 Germans by the end of July.[44]

Throughout June and July 1945, the plans and policies regarding the expulsions were revised and refined. By late June, military officials had established twelve routes for expelling Germans into Saxony.[45] Further instructions directed national committees and military authorities to ensure that Germans were properly provisioned with clothing and food for at least three days and that exile columns did not exceed 1,000 people. Military officials feared that if they were not so prepared, Red Army officers might not accept further transports.[46] Similar fears about losing the opportunity to transfer the Germans emerged as the Big Three deliberated the question of population transfers from Czechoslovakia, Poland and elsewhere at the Potsdam Conference. In late July the Minister of Defense requested that military officials make plans to increase the number of expulsions. At a meeting of military officials on July 28, 1945, the record noted that the Allied powers did not take the transfer seriously enough and were overly concerned about the humane treatment of Sudeten Germans on both sides of the border. While military officials at the meeting suggested that the Czechoslovak government would respect these wishes, the report also stated

[42] Compare reports from Místní národní výbor Děčín, July 15, 1945. SOkA Děčín, f. MNV Děčín, k. 1 inv. č. 39 and Velitelství 13 divise, July 23, 1945. VHA, f. VO1, k. 49 inv. č. 269. See also reports from local authorities, July 15, 1945. Doc 300B. Arburg and Staněk, ed., *Vysídlení Němců*, II.1: accompanying CD-ROM.
[43] Report of František Lis, July 1945. Doc 342; Report of Captain Václav Strejček, July 25 1945. Doc 327F. Arburg and Staněk, eds., *Vysídlení Němců*, II.1:727 and accompanying CD-ROM.
[44] Report from Velitelství 13 divise, July 23, 1945. VHA, f. VO1, k. 49 inv. č. 269. See also various figures for expulsions in ibid., inv. č. 271.
[45] Čj. 97/taj.1.odděl.1945, Velitelství I. sboru, June 26, 1945. Ibid., k. 48 inv. č. 263.
[46] Evakuace Němců-pokyny, Velitelství 13 divise, July 12, 1945. VHA. f. 13 Divise, k. 13 inv. č. 3.

that the government "does not wish to waste time and wants to place before the Allied leaders a *fait accompli*. Therefore, the expulsion (*vyhoštování*) must be carried out as fast as possible."[47] Just as the Allied powers prepared to sanction the expulsion of Germans from the country, Czechoslovak authorities sought to seize the moment and expedite the process, already under way. While military forces were not responsible for all of the expulsions, their operations permitted a more massive and rapid process desired by central officials. Incomplete military records indicate that by the end of July 1945 at least 450,000 Germans had been expelled into Saxony.[48]

Germans who were expelled during the summer of 1945 felt dread, suffering and loss. Because few expulsions had occurred in the first month after the war, the suddenness of expulsions in mid-June took most Germans by surprise:

We had to leave our homes as early as 17 June 1945, having been informed by the Czechs at 2 a.m. of the previous night. Some 60 percent of the population had been given this terrible news. We were allowed to take 30 kilograms of luggage, but no cash or jewelry. The people were seized by a paralyzing fear, as nobody had the slightest idea what would be their destination.[49]

The first expellees were given very little time to pack and had to leave almost everything behind. "In my understandable panic, I packed a suit and some underwear and other little things together in a suitcase and a rucksack, and bread in a briefcase and loaded them on a small hand wagon, which I took with me to the instructed meeting place."[50] Sudeten Germans were later stripped of these wagons and other possessions as they continued via train, truck or on foot during their journey to Germany. The expulsions were painful for those who experienced them in the summer of 1945. For some Germans that pain was direct, physical and sometimes deadly.

Postelberg and Aussig: The Dynamics of Local Violence

The expulsions during the summer of 1945 involved significant violence and brutality. Hundreds, if not thousands of incidents involving

---

[47] Interior memo about the decisions, July 29, 1945, and Minutes from the meeting at the main headquarters, July 28, 1945. VHA, f. VO1, k. 49 inv. č. 267; Staněk, *Perzekuce*, 131.

[48] Unofficial report: Postup vysídlení něm. obyvatelstva 1.oblasti, Velitelství 1. oblast, July 31, 1945. VHA, f. VO1, k. 49 inv. č. 271. These figures do not include those expelled into Austria. In a government meeting on July 24, 1945, the Minister of National Defense reported that half a million Sudeten Germans had been expelled. He noted "that a more radical transfer will be possible after the harvest and when the necessary Czechs assume positions in factories." Jech and Kaplan, *Dekrety*, 2: 865.

[49] Report no. 80. Schieder, ed., *The Expulsion of the Germans from Czechoslovakia*, 4: 463.

[50] Report no. 81. Schieder, ed., *Dokumentation der Vertreibung*, 4/2:391.

everything from gun shots to a push in the back drove Germans from their homes. Yet the notion of the "wild transfer" – of unbridled popular violence against Germans – fails to adequately characterize the violence of the expulsions, the experience of Germans, or the actions of ordinary Czechs. A closer examination of two cases of violence against Germans in Postoloprty (Postelberg) and Ústí nad Labem (Aussig) reveals a different picture. Both of these cases of borderland violence are noteworthy. Postoloprty was, numerically speaking, the site of the greatest massacre of Germans during the expulsions, yet has not received much analysis from historians. Ústí nad Labem, by contrast, serves as one of the standard measures of violence against Sudeten Germans, in part, because it has been portrayed as a spontaneous and popular attack. Czechs most certainly beat, raped and killed Germans during the ethnic cleansing of the borderlands. Yet, there is little evidence to suggest that they did so because they were Czech.

The situation in Postoloprty in May 1945 was similar to other regions of the borderlands. Following the German capitulation, the only real authority in the town was the so-called Revolutionary Guard, comprised of some local volunteers, led by an old settler named Bohuslav Marek. Germans moved around more or less freely, unencumbered by strict curfews or regulations.[51] All that changed when military units began to arrive at the end of May. The first group of soldiers was a security detachment of the army's Military Intelligence (*Obranné zpravodajství*, OBZ), under the leadership of Lieutenant Jan Čubka. Captain Vojtěch Černý controlled a second unit connected to the headquarters of the army's First Division, which was to prepare the way for the relocation of the regional army command there. A third unit was led by First Lieutenant Jan Zicha, who ran intelligence operations. Together with Marek, these three military officers created conditions and supported their men in the slaughter of roughly 800 people.[52]

---

[51] Protocol of Karel Kácel, August 8, 1947. Arburg and Staněk, ed., *Vysídlení Němců*, II.3: 267.

[52] Exactly who was responsible and how many were killed, and even what exact days the events took place, remain elusive. In 1947, following several anonymous letters to officials in Prague, a special committee of parliament was sent to investigate the claims of mass graves around Postoloprty. With the help of the Regional police office in Most, this committee interviewed several participants, including Marek, Zicha, Čubka, and Černý. Their testimonies are provided in Arburg and Staněk, eds., *Vysídlení Němců*, II.3: 246–60. Although no one took responsibility for ordering the killings and no one was ultimately held accountable for them, the government ordered the exhumation of the bodies: 763 in all were found. Tomáš Staněk argues that it is likely that the number could be even higher. For his account of these events, see Tomáš Staněk, *Poválečné "excessy" v českých zemích v roce 1945 a jejich vyšetřování* (Prague, 2005), 114–29, here 127.

The military units began arriving around May 26 and their leaders met with national committee members to plan the roundup of Germans. On the next day these units, together with some support from local police, assembled all of the inhabitants. Marek had been enlisted by the OBZ to help sort out Czechs from Germans and those Germans who had been punished by the Nazis. The remaining men were sent to the barracks while the women, children and elderly were sent to a former Nazi internment camp at the so-called "pheasant run." Another group of Germans, many of them Nazi leaders from the SA and SS or government leaders, were taken to the prison, where some local Germans were already being held. The shootings began that night. According to one survivor, at midnight the prisoners were separated and at 1 a.m. twelve soldiers returned from the first execution. At that point they dragged two young women into the neighboring room and raped them. The survivor, who escaped from the shooting squad at the last moment, describes what followed:

At 4 a.m. in the morning the last fifteen condemned, including myself and three women, were brought to the place of execution. As it was 4:30 when we arrived it was quite light out and we were able to see the murdered victims lying in the grave. The soldiers created a ring around us and drove us with curses and rifle butts – at the sight of the dead we were naturally horrified and staggered back – into the grave.[53]

Although there is no way to verify his account, if accurate, he likely escaped from the pheasant run grave, where thirty-four bodies were later discovered, including three women.[54]

A few days later, on June 3, just up the road in Žatec the soldiers and police gathered the men from the town in the market square and forced them to march the fifteen kilometers back to Postoloprty. The scene was chaotic: "Some 5,000 were assembled there. Many of them were knocked about by the soldiers there and then; any who were particularly noticeable or who, as a result of clumsiness or weakness, did not stay properly in line or who provoked the Czechs by wearing German national costume, were severely maltreated. A straggler was shot down."[55] The women and children were left behind. Ten days later they too were rounded up and placed

---

[53] Erlebnisbericht Egon Putz, August 30, 1948. LAA, Ost-Dok 2, Saaz 282, 4.

[54] Other accounts of the timing of this execution and the numbers involved corroborate this story. See Porevoluční události v Postolorptech, Oblastní úřadovna státní bezpečnosti, Most. August 13, 1947. Archiv bezpečnostních složek, Kanice (ABS-Ka), f. Sekretariát ministra vnitra (A2/1), k. 57 inv. č. 1765; Testimony of Bohuslav Marek, July 30, 1947. Arburg and Staněk, eds., *Vysídlení Němců*, II.3: 247.

[55] Report 85, Saaz-Postelberg. Scriptorium, accessed on August 23, 2016, www.winterson nenwende.com/scriptorium/english/archives/whitebook/desg29.html; Report of E.M., November 1945. Schieder, ed., *Documents on the Expulsion of Germans*, 4: 440.

in a camp in Žatec. They had to hand over all of their valuables and possessions, including the keys to their homes. Life in the camps was horrible. For three days there was no food; when it did come it consisted of watery soup, a bit of bread, and some black coffee. Many of the women and men were sent to work on local farms, mines or factories. Families were separated and faced constant harassment and humiliation from Czech guards.[56] Germans singled out Marek, in particular, for his brutality and held him responsible for many of the worst offenses. According to one German, the guards regularly threatened to execute inmates for their own amusement. When former military members complained about this torment "they were shot in front of our eyes by Marek personally."[57] Yet, as much as Marek acted in cruel and even sadistic ways, it was the arrival of the Czechoslovak military that escalated the killings.

The three leaders of the military units stationed in Postoloprty came from diverse backgrounds, but had all participated as soldiers on the eastern front. The oldest of the three, forty-one-year-old Jan Zicha, was a former school teacher at several different minority Czech schools in the German borderland regions during the interwar years. As such, he could be considered a nationalist zealot. Indeed, when he arrived in Žatec, he asked the chairman of the Local Administrative Commission if he wanted to make Žatec "Czech," before proceeding to remove the German men from the town.[58] Captain Černý was a twenty-eight-year-old who had begun fighting with partisans in Poland already in 1939. Jan Čubka, the youngest of the three at twenty-six, was a Slovak.[59] All of them eventually joined the Czechoslovak Army under Red Army command in the Soviet Union and fought for the liberation of Czechoslovakia. Which one of these officers was primarily responsible for the killings at Postoloprty remains a mystery. Only Černý admitted giving Marek the order to shoot five youths who been accused of attempting to escape from one of the camps. Their deaths were particularly horrifying for the Germans who witnessed them.[60] Otherwise, none of the officers took responsibility for

[56] Erlebnisbericht of Wilhelmine Jäckl, LAA, Ost-Dok 2, Saaz 282, 51–55; Report 60, E.D., July 27, 1947, Saaz. Schieder, ed., *Dokumentation der Vertreibung*, 4/2: 314–5.
[57] Report of Hans Enders, November 15, 1946. Schieder, *Documents on the Expulsion of Germans*, 4: 433.
[58] Testimony of Antonín Roška, July 30, 1947. Arburg and Staněk, ed., *Vysídlení Němců*, II.3: 244. For the background on Zicha see his testimony in ibid., 250–51. On interwar teachers see, Zahra, 135.
[59] For the background on these soldiers, see Arburg and Staněk, eds., *Vysídlení Němců*, II.3: 239 n. 6 and 12.
[60] Testimony of Vojtěch Černy, July 31, 1947. Ibid., 254. See the related German testimonies for accounts of the killings.

the killings or even admitted to knowing the extent of what had taken place. By the time of the investigation in 1947, Zicha had become the chairman of the District National Committee in Žatec and was a member of the Communist Party. As such, the investigation held serious political ramifications. Moreover, as one report noted, many of those who gave testimony participated in these events and feared possible repercussions, and therefore did not offer information about everything that they knew.[61] Because of these factors, assigning individual responsibility for the killings remains impossible from the existing evidence.

The details that do exist, however, provide great insight into the nature of violence in this case and its extent in the postwar borderlands. The Czechoslovak military controlled the situation and played the most active role in the shootings. While Marek and the local police had been involved in some particular acts of brutality prior to the military's arrival, the entire dynamic changed once the soldiers arrived. Marek claims that after he delivered the women and children to the camp Zicha ordered him to deliver 100 shovels and hoes to the shooting sites at the school and the prison barracks. When he arrived the next day, he found what he estimated to be 500 bodies dumped into an anti-tank ditch. He said that Zicha ordered him to use Germans from the camp to fill in the ditch.[62] While Marek might be judged as an unreliable source, given his involvement in these events, other sources generally corroborate his testimony. After the first night of executions in Postoloprty, the shootings continued some days after the arrival of the men from Žatec. In one summary report from 1947, the timeline for the executions suggests that they began on May 26 and ended on May 30. However, some witnesses recalled digging mass graves for the purpose of burying the victims after this date. Soldiers placed Arnošt Šedivý, an old settler from a mixed marriage, in the Postoloprty prison during the round up on May 27–28. He spoke of how, some five days later, he and sixty to seventy other men were taken under guard to dig three graves six meters long, four meters wide and three meters deep. One Saaz German, who was brought to Postoloprty on June 3, recalled: "During the following nights we heard occasional shooting all through the night coming from the guards at the stable doors."[63] The scattered graves that dotted the landscape around the town point to a

[61] Porevoluční události v Postoloprtech, Oblastní úřadovna státní bezpečnosti, Most. August 13, 1947. ABS-Ka, f. Sekretariát ministra vnitra (A2/1), k. 57 inv. č. 1765.
[62] Testimony of Bohuslav Marek, July 30, 1947. Arburg and Staněk, eds., *Vysídlení Němců* II.3: 247.
[63] Report of Hans Enders, November 15, 1946. Schieder, *Documents on the Expulsion of Germans*, 4: 433. See also, Report 85, Saaz-Postelberg, Scriptorium, accessed on July 28, 2013, www.wintersonnenwende.com/scriptorium/english/archives/whitebook/des g29.html

series of shooting incidents rather than a single isolated event. Nine graves in all were located during the exhumation of bodies in 1947, though even more may remain undiscovered. There were three mass graves of more than one hundred bodies each in Postoloprty following the terror. It appears that at least in these mass graves, the killings occurred in a few short episodes, requiring at least a small contingent of armed men to carry them out.

Only the military had the means and authority to carry out these mass executions. In most cases where national committees had been established by local residents, which meant a mix of old settlers, a few new settlers, and even Germans, the arrival of the Czechoslovak military shifted the balance of power in its favor. In this particular case, the soldiers' orders to clear the region of Germans had a practical component because the First Division headquarters was to be relocated there. In addition, generals encouraged the soldiers to act mercilessly. General Španiel reportedly told his men that the fewer Germans that crossed the border the better, because they would become their enemies, and he reminded them that the only good German, was a dead German.[64] While none of the officers present in Postoloprty admitted to giving orders to kill, Černý and Čubka both suggested that their men may have taken matters into their own hands. Černý noted that most of his thirty-five-man contingent was comprised of Sub-Carpathian Ukrainians who "came from the front and very often they had to determine independently, they were able to decide themselves, to shoot captured Germans without receiving an order from me."[65] Čubka likewise spoke of how his soldiers, mostly Sub-Carpathian Ukrainians (i.e. Ukrainian speakers, possibly Ruthenians, living in the easternmost parts of Czechoslovakia) and Volhynian Czechs, did not require specific orders to carry out actions against Germans: "Therefore it isn't out of the question, that without my knowledge several German SS men were shot somewhere."[66]

Despite the disingenuous suggestion that they knew nothing of the shootings, Čubka's and Černý's statements about their men point to an important connection with the war. Many of the soldiers involved in the shooting were not Czechs from interwar Czechoslovakia, and had a very different wartime experience. Large contingents of Czech-speaking soldiers from Volhynia, which is now in Ukraine, had helped to form the First Czechoslovak Army Corps in 1941 under Red Army command, and

---

[64] Testimony of Jan Čubka, July 31, 1947. Arburg and Staněk, ed., *Vysídlení Němců*, II.3: 253. See also the testimony of General Španiel, August 13, 1947. Ibid., 266.

[65] Testimony of Vojtěch Černy, July 31, 1947. Arburg and Staněk, ed., *Vysídlení Němců*, II.3: 255.

[66] Testimony of Jan Čubka, July 31, 1947. Ibid., 254.

continued to fill its ranks during the war. These Czech speakers were descendants of Czechs who had emigrated primarily as agriculturalists to Volhynia during the late nineteenth century. The territory had been under Russian administration from 1795 until World War I. In the 1897 Russian census, 27,000 Czechs were among the inhabitants of Volhynia.[67] Following the restoration of Poland after World War I, one part of this émigré community lived in Poland until 1939, while the other lived in Ukraine, where it experienced Soviet collectivization and other repressive policies. Nonetheless, they remained in distinct districts around Rovno and Luck. The incidence of intermarriage remained rather low and they maintained the cultural traditions of the past.[68] Following the Nazi–Soviet agreement to divide Poland in 1939, both groups faced Soviet rule. This experience proved decisive for many Volhynian Czechs who decided to leave after the war.

The more immediate factor for Czech speakers enlisting in the First Czechoslovak Army Corps, also known as the Svoboda Army, named after General Ludvik Svoboda, was the war. While the closed nature of Volhynian Czech communities may have protected them from Nazi brutality for a time, or also perhaps because other targets – Bolsheviks, Jews, Poles, Ukrainians, Germans – were plentiful in comparison, by 1943 the situation became more difficult. The Nazi war effort hung in the balance while the Holocaust increased in intensity. On July 13, 1943, the Nazis surrounded the village of Český Malín and killed all of the inhabitants, the vast majority of whom were Czechs, and then destroyed the village. The alleged reason for the attack was that these people had been supporting the Ukrainian Insurgent Army (UPA).[69] The UPA had begun an effort to cleanse the region of Poles and other minorities. As the front swung through Volhynia, and the larger war on Soviet soil drew to a close in 1943 and early 1944, the Polish Home Army responded in kind.[70] The Nazi claim to justify the death and destruction at Český Malín was sadly ironic as Czechs themselves had become targets of the UPA in its efforts to cleanse the region of Poles. As one member of the UPA recalled,

[67] Jaroslav Vaculík, *České menšiné ve Evropě a ve světě* (Prague, 2009), 219. For the most comprehensive history of the Volhynian Czechs, see Jaroslav Vaculík, *Dějiny Volyňskych Čechů*, vols. 1–3 (Prague, 1997–2003).
[68] Jana Nosková, *Reemigrace a usídlování volyňských Čechů v interpretacích aktérů a odborné literatury* (Brno, 2007). This book contains several interviews with Czechs from Volhynia made in the early 2000s.
[69] Zápis o vyvraždění obyvatelstva, spálení a vyloupení obce Český Malín hitlerovskými zločinci, April 3, 1944, accessed on August 23, 2016, www.valka.cz/newdesign/v900/clanek_11445.html.
[70] Timothy Snyder, *The Reconstruction of Nations: Poland, Ukraine, Lithuania and Belarus* (New Haven, 2003), 174.

the guidelines for actions in Volhynia in 1943 was to "Kill all Poles, Czechs, and Jews on the spot."[71] The secondary war that emerged between Ukrainian and Polish forces was particularly brutal as it targeted civilians who were already facing occupied administrations. The unrest provided by the war within the war that was the Ukrainian–Polish conflict over Volhynia and Galicia proved central to Volhynian Czechs' decision to enlist in the Czechoslovak Army with the hope of emigrating after the war.

Nearly 12,000 Volhynian Czechs volunteered to fight in the Svoboda Army. They formed the core of the postwar Czechoslovak Army and were instrumental in the cleansing of the borderlands. In addition to experiencing Nazi occupation and the horrors that ethnic cleansing unleashed in the Polish–Ukrainian borderlands, they also fought in several intense engagements as the Red Army swept westward, most notably at the Battle of Dukla Pass in September 1944. Many of the soldiers at Postoloprty and Žatec had lived through these traumas and had lost loved ones during the war. General Kapálek later reported in his testimony that the Postoloprty unit was comprised in the greater part by Volhynian Czechs who had lost relatives in the USSR at the hands of the Germans, and thus it was not surprising that they had treated the Germans roughly.[72] In General Španiel's testimony to the investigating commission, he too mentioned that the majority of the soldiers were from Volhynia and had on their minds the desire to avenge the Volhynian Lidice – Český Malín.[73] While it might seem like these were just convenient explanations to help exonerate the individuals responsible for the killings at Postoloprty, these soldiers were different from Czechs who remained in the country during the war. Some, at least, wished to make the Germans pay for what the Nazis had done during the war.

Understanding who the victims were is as important as understanding who the shooters were. In this case, it appears that, in the first place, those targeted for execution were members of the SS, the NSDAP or other functionaries of the Nazi administration. The first people executed in Postoloprty were those who had already been imprisoned by local authorities for their wartime activities. For the military authorities who arrived in late May, their status as guilty Germans was easily accepted, if not proven. For the rest of the Germans rounded up in Postoloprty and Žatec,

[71] Ibid., 169, n. 46.
[72] Testimony of Karel Kapálek, August 9, 1947. Arburg and Staněk, eds., *Vysídlení Němců*, II.3: 247; Tomáš Staněk, *Perzekuce, 1945* (Prague, 1996), 113; Staněk, *Poválečné "excessy,"* 128–29.
[73] Testimony of General Španiel, August 13, 1947. Arburg and Staněk, eds., *Vysídlení Němců*, II.3: 265.

they underwent a screening process to determine if they belonged to one of these groups. Marek's testimony gives the greatest detail on the screening process. He noted that it took them about a week to classify the Germans that had been brought from Žatec. They performed a body search in order to locate any physical markings to indicate whether a German was a member of the SS or not. In the end, according to him, there were roughly 500 Germans who were left in this category. Marek continued:

As I then found out, 100 people from this group were sent to Levonický pheasant run, where they dug four pits, and where that evening all of the roughly 500 men were shot ... In this number of 500 were also functionaries of the NSDAP party and its affiliates, some who voluntarily reported to the call, and some who were named by already apprehended functionaries of the party.[74]

Other witnesses note that many of the Germans who were killed and could be identified were party members or "fanatical" Germans. Of course, this process of classification could hardly be called just, and, as Tomáš Staněk notes, there were undoubtedly some caught up in this process who had done nothing wrong.[75] Nevertheless, it appears that some effort was made to target those who had participated most willingly with the Nazi regime. In other words, this episode was not a random outburst of violence at the hands of Czech mobs, but a military style execution of Germans suspected of actively supporting the Nazi regime.

The attacks in Ústí nad Labem (Ústí) appear at first glance to resemble more closely a popular response to a perceived act of German sabotage. On the afternoon of July 31, 1945 a munitions storage facility in Krasné Březno, a village just outside Ústí, exploded into flames.[76] What caused the explosion remains a matter of debate among historians. Some argue that Czech authorities set off the explosion intentionally in order to put pressure on Allied officials meeting in Potsdam at the time to approve a large-scale expulsion of Germans. Others suggest that it was probably an accident. Czech officials declared that it was an act of German sabotage. Whatever the cause, the blast killed thirty-three people and injured

---

[74] Testimony of Bohuslav Marek, July 30, 1947. Ibid., 248.
[75] Staněk, *Poválečné "excessy,"* 119.
[76] For other detailed accounts of the events see Zdeněk Radvanovský, "Události 31. července 1945 v Ústí nad Labem," in *Studie o sudetoněmecké otázce*, ed. Vacláv Kural (Prague, 1996), 120–31; Tomáš Staněk, "Co se stalo v Ústí nad Labem 31. července 1945?" *Dějiny a současnost* 2 (1990): 48–51; Staněk, *Perzekuce*, 131–37; Havel, Kaiser, Pustejovsky; Otfrid Pustejovsky, *Die Konferenz von Potsdam und das Massaker von Aussig am 31. Juli 1945: Untersuchung und Dokumentation* (Munich, 2001); Vladimir Kaiser, "Výbuch muničního skladiště v Krásném Březně a masakr německého obyvatelstva 31. července 1945," accessed on August 23, 2016, www.usti-nad-labem.cz/dejiny/1945-95/ul-8-9.htm.

dozens more. The explosion was clearly visible from Ústí, and in the immediate aftermath various military personnel and others attacked local Germans in parts of the city center. These people confronted Sudeten Germans in the town square, in front of the train station and on a bridge crossing the Elbe River. Many scholars have characterized the event, known as "The Massacre in Ústí" (*Aussiger Massaker* in German), as exemplary of the treatment of the Germans during the "wild transfer." Like the situation in Postoloprty, however, a closer examination of the violence suggests that more was involved than a Czech mob-response to the explosion.

The violence in Ústí spread quickly and was exceptionally brutal, even though the number of victims was relatively low. German sources present the most vivid accounts of the violence. One person reported that on Mozartstrasse, "Czechs with sticks and clubs began hitting German passersby."[77] Another German recalled: "I saw how the Germans were hunted down, how often three to four Czechs were clubbing down women, in front of the door lay a corpse."[78] The focal point for many of them was the murders and violence on the bridge that spanned the Elbe River. German workers returning from their morning shifts at the Schicht factory had to cross the bridge to return to Ústí. There they were trapped with others and faced the fury of Czechs. "On the Aussig end we were received by hundreds of Czechs, armed with clubs and iron bars. I received several serious head injuries, whilst my companion, a sixty-seven-year-old fore-man, had his skull smashed in." Another testimony states: "I ran to the bridge that crosses the Elbe River, and here I saw hundreds of workers who were coming from the Schicht manufacturing plant, being thrown into the Elbe."[79] One particularly vivid memory shared by witnesses was that of a mother and her baby carriage being tossed from the bridge.[80]

Several explanations for what triggered the violence have emerged. Czech authorities were quick to suggest that the explosion was an act of sabotage, which led local Czech forces to take their revenge on Germans. Minister of Interior Václav Nosek, reporting to the government in the

---

[77] Erlebnisbericht, unknown author. LAA, Ost-Dok 2, Aussig 240, 139.   [78] Ibid., 83.

[79] Report 2, Therese Mager, August 11, 1946, Aussig and Report 4, Max Becher, 14 December 1946 Aussig. Scriptorium, accessed on August 23, 2016, www.wintersonnen wende.com/scriptorium/english/archives/whitebook/desg04.html#002.

[80] Erlebnisbericht, unknown author. LAA, Ost-Dok 2, Aussig 240, 139; Erlebnisbericht, Georg Otto, n.d. LAA, Ost-Dok 2, Aussig 240, 131; Report 53 from a member of the OSK Ústí nad Labem, reprinted in *Londonské listy*, July 15, 1948; Schieder, *Documents on the Expulsion of Germans*, 4: 431–32; Report 1, A.U. 8 February 1951, Aussig and Report 2, Therese Mager, August 11, 1946, Aussig, accessed on August 23, 2016, www.winter sonnenwende.com/scriptorium/english/archives/whitebook/desg04.html; Report 43, Jiří T., 1990 and Report 44a, J.K., 1991. Vladimír Kaiser, ed., *Intolerance: Češi, Němci a Židé na ústecku 1938–1948* (Ústí nad Labem, 1998), 89, 91.

aftermath, said: "The situation in Northern Bohemia is unsettled. Almost daily members of the Hitler Youth and also older people, who are armed, and in various places operate Werewolf organizations hunt our security organs. They carry out systematic acts of sabotage."[81] Government officials continued to promote this interpretation even when competing accounts had emerged. This argument also jibed with the continuous reports of German Werewolf groups and purported sabotage. Borderland security reports blamed such groups for vandalism, destruction of property, forest fires and attacks on Czechs. While efforts had in fact been made to establish such units, they existed more on paper than in reality.[82] Some German sabotage did occur in the transition from war to peace, but this was mostly done by individuals acting alone. The notion that Czechs were under constant threat from German attacks was simply false.

Other explanations for the violence point to specific actors. For instance, one Czech old settler, who was in front of the train station when the explosion occurred, later testified that a "fifty-year-old bald-headed heavy set man in civilian clothing immediately called out: 'The Germans are guilty!' and pummeled several Germans wearing white armbands on their sides and heads with sticks and fists." After going to the bridge, but finding it impassable, the old settler returned to the train station, where the bald-headed man was still in a rage: "he had completely bloodstained hands, which he wrapped with rags. About a dozen Germans lay around on the ground not moving, three or four Czechs in civilian clothes joined with the raging bald guy and wildly kicked those laying on the ground."[83] Others claimed that the melee on the bridge began after a Reich German called out: "Germany lives! Cheers for Germany!" following the explosion. This act incited Czechs to attack him and throw him into the river.[84] Some historians suggest that the Czechoslovak government planned the entire operation in order to convince the Allies that Germans could not remain in the country. They argue that the Ministry of Interior and Military Intelligence planned and carried out the explosion and coordinated attacks on local Germans in the aftermath. No specific piece of evidence suggests that this was the case, though the simultaneity of the Allied meetings concerning "population

---

[81] Minutes of the 43rd meeting of the National Front Government, 3 August 1945. Arburg and Staněk, eds., *Vysídlení Němců*, II.3: 206.
[82] For official reports on Werewolf organizations see: NA, f. Úřad předsednictva vlády-tajné (ÚPV-T), k. 306 inv. č. 1636 sign. 127/13.
[83] Report 43, Jiří T., 1990. Kaiser, ed., *Intolerance*, 89.
[84] Report of the Regional Information Center for the Minister of Information, early August 1945. Arburg and Staněk, eds., *Vysídlení Němců* II.3: 212. See also Report of the Chief of Staff for the First Military Region, August 3, 1945. Ibid., 204; Staněk, *Poválečné "excessy,"* 152.

transfers" makes sense as a motive for government officials to demonstrate that Germans simply had to go. Some reports, for instance, claim that several hundred suspect individuals arrived on the noon train from Prague, just prior to the explosion. These individuals, like the bald-headed man above, appear as provocateurs in some testimonies.[85]

The extent of civilian involvement in the attacks remains difficult to decipher, though it is clear that some inhabitants took part. Czechs who joined in the attacks were identified as strangers – not surprising given the influx of some 60,000 new settlers to the district by July. The immigration of new settlers had created housing shortages, which also contributed to tensions in the city. In the aftermath, the chairman of the Local National Committee blamed the violence on "the fluctuation of inhabitants, who came from the interior to the borderlands in order to enrich themselves."[86] Indeed, some Czechs, particularly old settlers, went out of their way to protect Germans or to aid those who had been attacked. There is little consensus about how the general Czech populace acted during the killing spree. There was clearly a range of attitudes and behaviors that led some to take part, while others helped Germans, and still others remained bystanders. Such an interpretation, however, still undermines the image of the "wild transfer" and the notion that the explosion provided an opportunity for bloodthirsty Czechs to unleash their fury against Germans.

A closer examination of the various witness testimonies, both Czech and German, demonstrate that various security units in the area played a key role in the killings. These included members of the 28th Infantry Regiment, Red Army soldiers, other Czechoslovak Army units and police forces from the area.[87] In the days leading up to the explosion, new units had moved into the city and heightened tensions. Two days prior there had been a gathering to celebrate the creation of a new unit in the Ústí nad

[85] See Report 1, A.U. February 8, 1951, Aussig. Scriptorium, accessed on August 23, 2016, www.wintersonnenwende.com/scriptorium/english/archives/whitebook/des g04.html; Radvanovský, "Události," 122. For historians who pursue the claim that the explosion and attacks were deliberate, see Havel, Kaiser, and Pustejovsky; Pustejovsky, *Die Konferenz*.

[86] Report of the Regional Information Center for the Minister of Information, early August 1945. Arburg and Staněk, eds., *Vysídlení Němců* II.3: 214. On the influx of settlers see, Zdeněk Radvanovský, "The Social and Economic Effects of Resettling Czechs into Northwestern Bohemia, 1945–1947," in *Redrawing Nations: Ethnic Cleansing in East-Central Europe, 1944–1948*, eds. Philipp Ther and Ana Siljak (Lanham, 2001), 246. On the housing shortage, see Plans to move Germans to relieve housing problems, September 1, 1945. AM Ústí n. L., f. ONV Ústí n. L., k. 5 inv. č. 407.

[87] Report on events in Ústí n. L., August 1, 1945. VHA, f. VO1, k.49 inv. č. 269; Radvanovský, "Události," 122; Pustejovsky, *Konferenz von Potsdam*, 234–41; Arburg and Staněk, eds., *Vysídlení Němců* II.3: 198, n.4.

Labem police forces. Another police detachment from Prague attended, and the Interior Minister delivered a speech demanding "the cleansing of the country from the Fascist threat."[88] One eyewitness reported that the day before the explosion he came upon members of the Svoboda Army who had just arrived in the city, which likely refers to members of the 28th Infantry Regiment, who were stationed there the day before. They "were attacking the Germans wearing the white armbands, driving them from the sidewalks and even knocking them down."[89] Following the explosion these units quickly moved into the city center and established positions there. They were joined by other military and police personnel, including Red Army soldiers, as a range of witnesses and reports relate. In the aftermath of the killings, local authorities sent a letter to the Ministry of Defense about the "illegal actions of Russian soldiers" and requested that local soldiers receive instructions from their commanders about the need to respect national committee officials.[90] A defense official reported that the local army garrison had several new recruits, who were blamed for getting out of hand.[91] German testimonies also point to a military presence. "These Czechs were mostly wearing black uniforms with red armbands (SNB men)." Another German noted: "Soldiers of the Svoboda-army and individual Russians took part in it."[92]

Local officials primarily blamed Czechoslovak soldiers for the incident. In a meeting with the Minister of Interior and Minister of Defense, who traveled to Ústí in order to investigate the events in the immediate aftermath, they aired a number of grievances against the military units. One official stated that "some of the troops increased the chaos and whipped up the civilian inhabitants to a bloody outrage ... Several soldiers were armed with rubber truncheons and clubs, with which they beat German inhabitants without difference." Echoing these sentiments about the soldiers' behavior, the Vice Chairman of the District Administrative Commission asked: "who gave the order for the soldiers to conduct

[88] "V očistě našeho národního života budeme tvrdě pokračovat," *Rudé pravo* July 31, 1945.
[89] Report 1, A.U., February 8, 1951, Aussig. Scriptorium, accessed on August 23, 2016. www.wintersonnenwende.com/scriptorium/english/archives/whitebook/desg04.html.
    On the movement of the unit, see Zvláštní operační rozkaz 130, July 26, 1945. VHA, f. VO1, k. 49 inv. č. 268; Havel, Kaiser, and Pustejovsky, *Stalo se*, 15–18; Report from Ministry of Defense 1947. NA, f. Ministerstvo vnitra – tajná (MV-T), k. 12 inv. č. 199 s. T-B 13; Staněk, *Perzekuce*, 135.
[90] Minutes from the meeting of the OSK Ústí nad Labem, August 2, 1945. AM Ústí n. L., f. ONV Ústí n. L., k. 5 inv. č. 407.
[91] Report from Ministry of Defense 1947. NA, f. MV-T, k. 12 inv. č. 199 s. T-B 13; Staněk, *Perzekuce*, 135.
[92] Report 1, A.U., February 8, 1951, Aussig and Report 2, Therese Mager, August 11, 1946, Aussig. Scriptorium, accessed on August 23, 2016, www.wintersonnenwende.com/scriptorium/english/archives/whitebook/desg04.html.

their duty with whips, leather straps, and rubber truncheons?" Such observations suggest that the military personnel were ready for a fight, whether it was ordered or not. The security chief of the Commission, a Communist, reportedly commented: "The focus of the incident was on the bridge of President Beneš, where the 28th Infantry Regiment performed guard duty. The soldiers' indiscipline was a further impulse to the violence. If the military watch had intervened in time, it would not have come to that. Intervention in the incidents was impossible because of the troops' position."[93] The 28th Infantry Regiment's leading role in the violence is unsurprising given its role in the ethnic cleansing of the borderlands up to this point. In addition, not only did both German and Czech testimonies point to "Svoboda soldiers" as the ringleaders, they were also the most organized force in the city, aside from the police, who were not as widely accused of assaults.

The number of victims has remained a source of debate. The Sudeten German testimonies frequently offer figures of those who were killed that day, with estimates ranging from 400 to 1,000.[94] The foundation for these claims remains unstated and appears to be based on little more than their impressions. Given the horrors of witnessing such events, such figures are understandable, if also untenable. German historians have likewise arrived at a variety of figures for the massacre that day, reaching as high as 2,700.[95] This figure has appeared in recent English language publications as well.[96] Czech historians, however, place the figure somewhere closer to 100, noting in a much more balanced way that this figure is disputed, and they attempt to provide some concrete evidence to support their cases.[97] Given the confusion and conflicting claims, there may be no way to arrive at a figure that would be acceptable to both Czechs and Germans.

The dynamics of local violence in Postoloprty and Ústí involved a complex range of motives and causes. It is difficult to gauge the soldiers' mindsets, but revenge for wartime actions and atrocities likely played a part for some. Following the Ústí massacres, Nosek noted that the soldiers had participated in some particularly fierce fighting and lost many of their best people. The army "experienced indescribable hardship. All of

---

[93] Report of the Regional Information Center for the Minister of Information, early August 1945. Arburg and Staněk, ed., *Vysídlení Němců* II.3: 213–14.

[94] Report 1, A.U. February 8, 1951, Aussig and Report 3, Herbert Schernstein, December 9, 1945, Aussig. Scriptorium, accessed on August 23, 2016, www.winter sonnenwende.com/scriptorium/english/archives/whitebook/desg04.html.

[95] Schieder, *Documents on the Expulsion of Germans*, 4: 431 n.3.

[96] See, for example, Naimark, *Fires of Hatred*, 116; Alfred de Zayas, *A Terrible Revenge: The Ethnic Cleansing of the East European Germans 1944–1950* (New York, 1994), 91.

[97] Staněk, *Perzekuce*, 136; Radvanovský, "Události 31. července 1945," 126.

this led the soldiers of this army to the principle, that the best German is a dead German."[98] While these explanations might seem to be completely self-serving and unconvincing they point to a reality often overlooked when analyzing the Sudeten German expulsions. For the soldiers involved in these cases, this was very much still a wartime action. Because many of the soldiers were from Volhynia and had suffered through some of the worst parts of the war, their actions must be seen in this context. Their desire to wreak revenge on Sudeten Germans was not rooted in a shared but volatile past stretching back hundreds of years; rather, the violence fit into the wartime context and their plans for the future. As one Volhynian Czech later stated: "We Czechs wanted to go voluntarily to stamp out the Germans, to annihilate the Germans, so that we could return to the Czech lands."[99] Indeed, the desire to cleanse the region of Germans in order to create space for themselves may also have played into the killings. Like a foreign army, the Czechoslovak military entered and took over the borderland regions. This was not, in other words, a matter of neighbors turning on neighbors and subjecting them to the worst kinds of brutality. This kind of violence emerged elsewhere in eastern and southeastern Europe during the war and requires a different kind of explanation.[100] Here the situation resembled much more an occupation of foreign lands, and the displacement of local populations, in this case through ethnic cleansing. This insight into these cases of mass violence does not dismiss the pain, suffering and loss of those Germans and their families. What it does demonstrate is that Czechs did not rise up as a nation to attack and kill Germans.

Everyday Expulsions

The more commonplace experiences of postwar borderland Germans did not involve the direct threat of violence; instead, they faced a range of regulations which Czech authorities used to control and punish them. Sudeten Germans were forced to wear special armbands with a capital "N" for German (*Němec*, in Czech). Their rations were lower than those offered to Czechs. Property was confiscated and other restrictions, such as against the use of public transportation, reduced shopping hours and

---

[98] Report of the Regional Information Center for the Minister of Information, early August 1945. Arburg and Staněk, eds., *Vysídlení Němců* II.3: 215.
[99] Nosková, *Reemigrace a usídlování*, 77.
[100] See, for example, Jan Gross, *Neighbors: The Destruction of the Jewish Community in Jedwabne Poland* (Princeton, 2001); Max Bergholz, "Sudden Nationhood: The Microdynamics of Intercommunal Relations in Bosnia-Hercegovina after World War II," *American Historical Review* 118, no.3 (June 2013): 679–707.

curfews, also often applied. Many Sudeten Germans also had to work. At the immediate end of the war, they were forced to clean up towns and repair roads. While these policies were hard for many Germans, they reflected the war experience and represented victor's justice – one which Nazi Germany had applied to the Bohemian lands and much of Eastern Europe only a few years before. At the same time, most German speakers remained in their homes for the first weeks following the war. Some were able to stay until the general expulsions of 1946. Much depended on their profession and where they lived. More remote areas sometimes remained isolated from the wave of expulsions that occurred throughout the summer of 1945. Czech settlers inundated more desirable cities, on the other hand, and often forced Germans into pitiful quarters. Ethnic cleansing was rarely a single day's experience. For many Sudeten Germans the experience lasted several months and involved varying degrees of suffering and loss.

Some Sudeten Germans were unfortunate enough to wind up in internment camps, where they faced some of the worst conditions. Rather than being centrally directed, the camp system emerged under local authority. The central government had, in fact, discouraged putting Germans into camps. In its June 15, 1945, decision to give the army authority to carry out the expulsions, it stipulated that "German inhabitants will not be driven without difference into concentration camps, but rather in terms of technical possibilities they will be put into work groups and kept at work."[101] Many camps were first referred to as "concentration camps" and only later did officials change the names to collection centers, internment camps or labor camps. In some cases, they had been POW camps used by the Nazis for forced labor and simply changed hands after the war.[102] While officials had incarcerated those suspected of serious offenses in makeshift camps, they quickly became barracks for Germans who were forced from their permanent homes. In the region of Frývaldov, for instance, one German noted that in the weeks following the arrival of Russian soldiers, "Czechs had flooded the entire area and therefore internment camps were created for Germans in Ober-Thomasdorf and Adelsdorf."[103] Indeed, it was the pressure to find housing for new settlers that forced local officials to create camps in several places. Still, fewer than a thousand Germans lived in most camps, many of which were attached to local factories and housed only a small number of workers.

[101] Intimovany výnos, Ministerstvo vnitra (MV) 2118/45. NA, f. Ministerstvo ochrany práce a sociální péče, 1945–1951 (MOPSP), k. 556 inv. č. 1131 s. 2246.
[102] Petr Joza, Rabštejnské údolí (Děčín, 2002).
[103] Report 40, W.M., February 14, 1947, Troppau. Schieder, ed., Dokumentation der Vertreibung, 4/2: 229.

Other camps became prisons holding suspects of serious wartime crimes, including some Czechs. Overall, more than 300 camps existed in the Bohemian lands by the end of August 1945, housing some 100,000 people.[104]

The various internment, concentration, labor and collection camps were undoubtedly the most dangerous places for Sudeten Germans in 1945, and their prominence in the published testimonies can be justified to a certain degree on these grounds. Tomáš Staněk notes how the treatment of Germans hinged on the background and personalities of individual camp personnel. He states that "[m]onstrous beatings, torture, killing as a result of cruelty and shootings, suicide, humiliation and various intrusions became part of the daily order."[105] Sudeten German testimonies are filled with graphic and gruesome details of shootings, rapes, beatings, starvation, unsanitary living conditions, cramped quarters and so on. The testimonies often paint a similar picture regardless of where the camp was situated, who was relating the incident or in which source it appears. One German described the scene in Concentration Camp number twenty-eight near Most in Northern Bohemia: "The beatings were carried out with fists, whips and rubber truncheons; they went on day and night. There was never a quiet night, but always blows, screams and the crack of whips and shots."[106] A woman who spent time in a distant camp in Silesia reported: "Continuous shooting went on in the camp day and night, whips were cracking, so that the inmates were naturally in a continuous state of worry."[107]

Although the camps were often the most horrific sites of violence for Germans during the expulsions, they were not the common experience for the majority of Sudeten Germans. By November 1945, the number of interned Germans was approximately 152,000, which was roughly 6–7 percent of the total number of German inhabitants at that time.[108] A recent German publication estimates that 350,000 German speakers – just over 10 percent of the total number of Sudeten Germans – spent some time in a camp prior to their expulsion.[109] The numbers from local archives support this general assessment. So, while German testimonies

[104] Tomás Staněk, *Tábory v českých zemích, 1945–1948* (Opava, 1996), 52.
[105] Ibid., 77. For more on the general violence in the camps, see ibid., 76–87; Schieder, *Documents on the Expulsion of Germans*, 4: 87–88.
[106] Report 17, Carl Grimm, 3 December 1950, Brüx. Scriptorium, accessed on August 23, 2016, www.wintersonnenwende.com/scriptorium/english/archives/whitebook/desg08.html.
[107] Report 37 Hubert Schütz, January 4, 1947, Jägerndorf. Schieder, *Documents on the Expulsion of Germans*, 4: 412.
[108] Staněk, *Tábory*, 105.
[109] K. Erik Franzen, *Die Vertriebenen: Hitlers letzte Opfer* (Munich, 2002), 203.

Figure 1.1 Awaiting expulsion. Courtesy of the Central Military Archives in Prague

are dominated by horrible images from the internment camps, it should be kept in mind that relatively few Germans suffered in this way.

German experiences in the postwar borderlands fit into a broad range that extended from violent encounters to friendly and even amorous relations with Czechs. Even within the Sudeten German testimonies one can find evidence of daily life that did not involve violence. In addition, reports from the Czech archives provide accounts of Czechs and Germans doing more than just getting along. In one report, for instance, a frustrated Czech military policeman recounted his attempts to break up a dance party at a pub in Běhánky in early 1946. The official noted that local Czechs refused to cooperate and prevented the officials from carrying out a thorough search, but that they were able to register thirty-two Germans as they left the place. When the authorities departed, however, many of those same Germans reportedly returned to the party.[110] Such instances point to a very different kind of story than that presented in the expellee testimonies. Yet even there, the stories provide glimpses into a life not filled by violence and fear, but with the mundane or normal minutiae of everyday getting by. The history of the Sudeten German expulsions was one punctuated by moments of jarring dislocation, but generally fit into the context of postwar shortages and privations that many people across the wrecked European landscape endured.

For many Germans the first weeks and months after the armistice passed without major incident. One Sudeten German's testimony opens with a relatively innocuous introduction:

Together with my wife and two sons, I lived in a three-room flat in Bodenbach. Until 5 September 1945 we were spared any persecution – aside from comparatively minor harassment. I had already lost my job earlier, since the firm with which I had been employed for many years had been dissolved. I had found temporary employment as construction assistant, as had my younger son.[111]

While he goes on to describe some brutal mistreatment at the hands of Czechoslovak soldiers, what is telling here is the absence of any noteworthy events from May to September. Many of the testimonies, in fact, do not even begin their stories until late June or July when the expulsions picked up in volume and intensity. In communities off the main road or in larger towns where people could avoid direct confrontation with military units, many Germans went about their daily life in ways that deviated only slightly from the wartime past. Though at some point a reckoning with the forces of ethnic cleansing occurred, it was not necessarily immediate or violent in the summer months.

For most German speakers life after the war was characterized by an immediate and significant drop in their social and economic status.

[110] Report from March 18, 1946. SOkA Teplice-Šanov, f. ONV Teplice-Šanov k. 238 inv. č. 269 063.
[111] Report 129, N.N., May 23, 1946. Scriptorium, accessed on August 23, 2016, www.wintersonnenwende.com/scriptorium/english/archives/whitebook/desg39.html.

Farmers often had to work their own land, but no longer for themselves and often without pay. Many white collar employees lost their positions as well. Germans' valuable property was confiscated, particularly cars, radios and musical instruments. In many places they were forced to move into cramped quarters, either in their own homes, in cellars or attics, or into other nearby buildings, as Czech settlers began arriving in larger and larger numbers. Otherwise, they remained put. Security reports from the district of Opava-venkov in July and August 1945 captured the varied conditions well. The official from the town of Komárov reported that because of insufficient housing Germans were housed together. In nearby Vávrovice, on the other hand, no concentration of Germans had occurred. In Štablovice, they placed Germans with local farmers who were happy to have the extra help during the harvest.[112] In one case, a German farmer in northern Moravia recorded a diary that mirrors the creeping process of ethnic cleansing in the borderlands: "8 June 1945. The first farm was settled." On June 10, 1945, Germans had to relinquish all valuable items like radios, bicycles, cameras, etc. to the town's authorities. On the 20th they had to begin wearing a large "N" on their left breast. In July a host of forced labor measures involved work in camps or locally as domestic help. In August during church services German songs, sermons and prayers were forbidden for four weeks. Beginning in early October, Germans had to pay rent for their housing, and housing was becoming scarcer as settlers continued to flow into the town.[113] These are each moments of ethnic cleansing, as the government and settlers began identifying Germans, restricting their freedom and slowly displacing them, all without violence. Instead, the force of local fiat, heavy immigration and losers' compliance dictated Germans' movement.

The day-to-day contact between settlers and native inhabitants during ethnic cleansing was often hostile, particularly when the new settlers met or lived with the old homeowners. In one case, a German reported that one family sharing living quarters was not allowed to use the front door, and instead had to come and go through a window. They were not allowed to use the common toilet, and their mail was often opened. The Czech children, she noted, behaved "in the most inconsiderate way."[114] When Germans' testimonies involved situations of cohabitation, they often portray the new settler of the property as incompetent, poor and

[112] Monthly security reports. SOkA Opava, f. ONV Opava-venkov, k. 16 inv. č. 117.
[113] Report 43, Marianne Benisch, March 18, 1947. Schieder, *Dokumentation der Vertreibung*, 4/2: 240–45.
[114] Erlebnisbericht, f. Lichtblau. January 19, 1947. LAA Bayreuth. f. Ost-Dok 2, Freiwaldau 252, 127.

mean, sometimes abusive. This was not always the case, though. In some testimonies, Sudeten Germans differentiate between individuals who acted cruelly and those settlers and local officials who behaved decently. For instance, one German noted that the Czech settler who came to live in his house allowed him to take his linens and clothes with him when he was relocated in town: "He treated me very friendly, even fed me, and promised me then that he would look after my things and the property."[115] Such sentiments are few and far between in the German testimonies, though this is unsurprising given their goals and methodology. Even so, such indicators suggest that starting an analysis of the expulsions from the perspective of national hatreds overlooks such personal interactions, which demonstrate that what often mattered most was how individuals treated one another.

Germans were not always passive victims, either. As one Czech family was moving into a home, the Germans who lived there demanded their things, yelling: "That is still our house, we earned it." The Czech man replied that he considered it repayment for his unpaid labor in Germany over the past three years. Still, the Germans yelled from the street, calling the Czechs "swine" and telling them to get out.[116] In a few places there were attempts to organize some armed resistance, though these rarely involved more than a small group of people and did not amount to serious attacks. Rather than being collective, most German resistance involved some sort of individual act, either through displaying the Nazi flag or drawing a swastika on a tree. Some Germans expressed their anger against the expulsions and even the Czechoslovak state. One woman reportedly warned new Czech settlers that the Germans would return and throw them out.[117] It would not have been unusual, in this sense, for a German to say, or for a Czech to believe that he said, "Long live Germany!" in the aftermath of the explosion outside Ústí nad Labem. Germans challenged the Czechoslovak state in a number of other ways as well. In towns located in the immediate vicinity of the frontier, for instance, Germans traveled across the border, despite security officials' attempts to shut down this traffic. Czech officials saw such movements as serious security breaches, but the reality was much more mundane. The scarcities of life in postwar Germany promoted expellee efforts to bring goods across the border, before, during and after their expulsion. The sanctity of states' borders

[115] Erlebnisbericht, unknown. n.d. LAA Bayreuth. f. Ost-Dok 2, Friedland, 254, 33.
[116] Erlebnisbericht, Maria Hafranke. May 3, 1948. LAA Bayreuth. f. Ost-Dok 2, Jägerndorf 260, 107–9.
[117] Monthly Security Report ONV Frývaldov, November 15, 1945. SOkA Jeseník. f. ONV Jeseník, k. 2 inv. č. 63.

meant little to Germans who had been, from their perspective, illegitimately tossed from their homes.

Despite the frequent claims of German sabotage or Werewolf activities in the press and by central authorities, Germans were not generally considered a threat to public order or the restructuring of the borderlands. In the vast majority of reports from the borderlands, security officials stated that the Germans behaved passively (*klidně*). At times their "mood" varied from positive, based on rumors that the western powers would put a halt to the expulsions, to negative, based on the arrival of settlers or local expulsions. While these reports cannot be taken as necessarily representative of all Germans, they suggest that German actions and attitudes varied. Much of that dynamic appears in the following chapters, but one example here reinforces the point. A report from a Czech official simply noted that three German guys were fined 200 crowns each or faced 30 days in jail for forgetting to wear their armbands with the "N."[118] Whether or not this was an act of protest is difficult to tell; wearing the armbands tended to dissipate as common practice across the borderlands at different times. Nevertheless, that these guys were out for a beer at the time of the incident suggest a normalcy unassociated with fear or repression. Thus, while violence reigned in certain places and times, other Germans continued to live and work amid ethnic cleansing.

The Czechoslovak government waited for the official Allied approval of the expulsions before it formally stripped the Sudeten Germans' of their citizenship. Decree 33, which President Beneš signed on August 2, 1945, declared: "Czechoslovak state citizens of German or Magyar nationality, who according to the regulations of the occupying powers acquired German or Magyar citizenship, lost Czechoslovak citizenship rights on the date of the acquisition of such citizenship."[119] This applied to all Germans who lived in the borderlands after the Munich Agreement, although the use of nationality presented some obstacles to officials who had to determine this in individual cases. Nevertheless, the implications were clear: all Germans were considered guilty. Decree 33 did allow those Germans and Magyars who "remained true to the republic" or "suffered under Nazi or fascist terror" to apply to keep their Czechoslovak citizenship.[120] The criteria were subjective and the cases were divisive. Czech officials granted few such exceptions and there was no option of appealing once someone had already been expelled. While debates about

---

[118] Report, September 1945. SOkA Teplice-Šanov. f. Teplice-Šanov ONV, k. 238 inv. č. 94.

[119] Decree 33, Part 1 sec. 1, August 2, 1945. Jech and Kaplan, *Dekrety*, 1:345.

[120] Decree 33, Part 2 sec. 1. Ibid.

the legality of the decree continue to this day, and the nationality questions raised by the decree demonstrate the protean nature of national
categories, for Germans the decree sanctioned their permanent removal.
The rumors that expulsions might end were sorely misguided. Even after
the Potsdam Agreement was signed in August expulsions continued,
though their intensity slowed during the fall. Soviet military officials did
not halt the forced migration of Sudeten Germans into Saxony until the
end of the year.[121] Trying to determine the exact number of expellees for
1945 is nearly impossible considering the number of Germans already on
the move at war's end, the lack of precise data for war losses and the biases
informing the figures that do exist. German speakers moved throughout
the country in different directions, for different reasons and at different
times. Some Sudeten Germans fled the imposing front and then returned,
while others kept moving to Germany. Some expelled Germans were
Reich Germans who had relocated to the Sudetengau or the Protectorate
during the war. Other German speakers had also moved to Czechoslovakia
from the east in advance of the military front. In addition, some Sudeten
Germans left voluntarily, perhaps thinking that this was the best option.
Despite the migratory chaos, a general range of the forced exodus can be
drawn. Estimates of the number expelled during the summer range from
650,000 to 800,000.[122] From September 1945 to the end of the year
expulsions slowed dramatically; roughly 150,000 Germans were expelled
or left during this period. The Allied-sanctioned transfer began in January
1946 and lasted until the end of 1946, during which nearly 2.2 million
more German speakers were expelled.[123] Voluntary departures continued
as well. This left some 200,000–300,000 Sudeten Germans in the country.
Some of these Germans later made their way to Germany under both
official and unofficial auspices, others remained where they were, and

---

[121] The Soviet commander gave the order to halt the acceptance of expellees on December
21, 1945. He stated that, by that time, 773,840 Germans from Czechoslovakia had
crossed the border. T.V. Volokitina et al., eds., *Vostochnaia Evropa: V Dokumentakh
Rossiiskikh Arxikhov*, vol. 1 (Moscow, 1997), 388–89, n. 8. For reports on continued
expulsions during these months, see Situation reports from September 1945. SOkA
Chomutov, f. ONV Chomutov, k. 1 inv. č. 175; U.S. Department of State. Historical
Office, *Foreign Relations of the United States [FRUS], 1945*, vol. 2 (Washington, DC,
1960), 1274–75, 1280, 1315.

[122] Vladimir Srb, *Populační, ekonomický a národnostní vývoj pohraničích okresů ČSR od roku
1930 do roku 2010* (Prague, 1989), 8; Schieder, *Documents on the Expulsion of Germans*, 4:
105. These figures match the tenor of the findings of Staněk and Arburg as well. See
"Organizované divoký odsun? Úlohá z ústředních státních orgánů pří provádění 'evakuace' německého obyvatelstva (květín až září 1945)." 3 část. "Snaha vlády a civilních
úřadů o řízení 'divokého odsunu'," *Soudobé dějiny* 13, no. 3–4 (2006): 370–74.

[123] Souhrnná zpráva pro československou vládu o dosavadím průběhu odsunu Němců
z Československé republiky, November 29, 1945. NA, f. Úřad předsednictva vlády –
běžná spísovna (ÚPV-B), k. 720, inv. č. 2908 s. 753/4.

still others were dispersed to interior parts of the country. For most Sudeten Germans, then, expulsion came with international approval and systematic routine.

The "official transfer," a label used to distinguish the Allied-sanctioned expulsions after the Potsdam Agreement from the earlier "wild transfer," was still ethnic cleansing. Local national committees organized collection points where Germans gathered prior to being sent to a district collection center. Czechoslovak officials allowed them 30 kg of belongings, later increased to 50 kg because of American officials' demands. Germans could bring up to 1,000 Reichsmarks per person and were supposed to have at least 200 RM, but no other currency or valuables. They were also supposed to have seven days' worth of food.[124] They were then loaded into trains, sometimes in passenger cars, but in most cases in freight wagons. The Czechoslovak military managed the movement of expellees to the state border where Allied officials checked the passengers and then the trains continued to specific destination points where they were left under Allied control. There were also variations between Soviet and American regulations. In many ways, the operation reflected the system established in 1945, though it happened with greater regularity and less violence. Still, problems emerged. For instance, local officials had trouble securing enough money to send with the Germans. An even greater problem was the failure to send the Germans as a family unit. Often certain members of the family had been sent to other towns for work prior to their expulsion, but because the regulations insisted that Germans leave as a family, and from their original place of residence, national committees scrambled to have those Germans released from work and returned in time for transfer. One collection center leader issued a list of thirteen shortcomings to the Bruntál District Administrative Commission about the transfer process in June 1946. Some of the complaints were administrative; others noted that Germans did not have the proper provisions, but that they nonetheless carried too many personal things in their suitcases. He also complained that one of the guards who brought Germans to the camp was drunk.[125] Ministry of Interior officials charged with overseeing the official transfer feared that such problems could derail the transfer's success. In July 1946, Antonín Kučera, the

---

[124] B-300/1990. Směrnice k provádění soustavného odsunu (transferu) Němců z území Československé republiky. Ministerstvo vnitra, December 31, 1945. SOkA Bruntál, f. ONV Bruntál k.14 inv. č. 81; Č.j. 32.657/46-IV/5 Ministerstov financi, February 6, 1946. Ibid.; B300/1129 Odsun Němců. (Instrukce) Informace ohledně vybavováni odsunovaných Němců markovými platidly. Ministerstvo vnitra, February 15, 1946. Ibid.

[125] Letter to OSK Bruntál, June 20, 1946. Ibid.

government representative charged with organizing the transfer, appealed to lower level officials' "historical responsibility" in order to overcome such problems and to ensure the smooth operation of the remaining expulsions.[126] The obstacles were indeed overcome, such that Václav Nosek in his summary report about the official transfer declared that comparing the number of Germans in 1930 to that of November 1946 "should be an unadulterated source of joy about the completed cleansing of Germans from the Czech lands."[127]

For Sudeten Germans, the experience of the Allied-sponsored "transfer" in 1946 was mixed with loss and uncertainty, and anticipation and relief. The hardship of losing everything and having to live in cramped conditions with limited food and having to work in poor circumstances meant that many Germans looked forward to getting out of the country. At the border crossings, many transports broke into song – some nostalgic, like "Riesengebirglers Heimatlied," others more patriotic, like "Deutschland, Deutschland über alles." The discarding of the despised white armbands was another expression of the Germans' relief at their departure. As one German wistfully recalled: "At the border past Eger beautiful little birch trees stood along the train tracks and from one of them fluttered German armbands and many people did not want to leave the armbands on the branch of the tree, but to hold onto their memory." Others tossed them with pleasure.[128] For most people, the 1946 transports were filled with miseries and discomfort, but did not entail the abruptness and harsh cruelty of the early expulsions. For the expelled Germans their difficulties often continued beyond the border, while for Germans who remained behind Czechoslovak officials were already beginning to dismantle the discriminatory regulations against them.

When examined from the level of individual relations, the ethnic cleansing of Sudeten Germans appears less like nationally driven rage and more like a limited military campaign, contingent upon local factors and forces. The conditions certainly permitted some sadistic individuals to brutalize Germans, and the military nature of the borderlands' takeover and the camp system that emerged in its wake fostered rape and other forms of violence. Still, the scenes in places such as Ústí nad Labem and Postoloprty were more exceptional than usual. In addition, the focus

---

[126] B 300/5365 Odsun Němců. Odstranění všech závad brzdících jeho provádění a dokočení. Ministerstvo vnitra, July 3, 1946. Ibid.

[127] Souhrnná zpráva pro československou vládu o dosavadím průběhu odsunu Němců z Československé republiky, November 29, 1945. NA, f. ÚPV-B, k. 720, inv. č. 2908 s. 753/4.

[128] Erlebnisbericht, f. Kirwein. May 31, 1950. LAA Bayreuth. f. Ost-Dok 2, Außig 240, 57. For more on the songs and armbands see Erlebnisbericht, Erika Zippe, n.d. Ibid., 222; Schieder, *Documents on the Expulsion of the Germans*, 4: 489–509.

on violence often obscures other dynamics that shaped the process of ethnic cleansing in key ways. Not only did relations between Czechs and Germans matter, so too did the development of local politics and relations among Czechs themselves. As Czechs flooded the borderlands in search of power, wealth and prosperity, they affected the way that Germans were treated and the nature of the expulsions as well. It is to that story that we now turn.

2 Divisions Within the Nation: Resettlement, Local Power and Settler Conflicts

Česká Kamenice: Local Power Conflicts

As wartime hostilities ended in May 1945, a handful of Czechs formed a "revolutionary national committee" in Česká Kamenice (*Böhmisch Kamnitz*) in order to establish administrative control as Nazi authorities fled. This committee renamed itself the Local National Committee (*Místní národní výbor*; MNV) on May 28 to mark President Edvard Beneš's birthday and to meet the state's new official nomenclature for local administrative organs.[1] Candidate lists for the national committee were distributed at a public gathering of the few hundred Czechs that lived in the town, including military personnel stationed there, and those gathered unanimously approved the list with a round of applause.[2] Karel Caidler, a thirty-six-year-old reserve lieutenant who had recently arrived after participating in the so-called Prague Uprising, became the chairperson. Caidler was born and raised in Teplice-Šanov, another borderland town, but like thousands of other so-called old settlers (*starousedlíci*) he departed for the rump Czechoslovak interior after the Nazis annexed the region following the Munich Agreement.[3] The term "old settlers" marked a distinction in the postwar borderlands between Czechs who had lived there before the war, and the so-called new settlers (*novousedlíci*), who arrived for the first time following the war. This distinction proved to be one of many among postwar inhabitants of the borderlands. Even old settlers were a divided group; some had decided to remain in the borderlands during the war, while others had moved or were forced to move to the interior. Those old settlers who decided to stay often had personal reasons

---

[1] I use national committees as the general term to cover local and district national committees, and local and district revolutionary committees, and local and district administrative commissions. There were some key differences among these different local government organs, which will be outlined in more detail in this chapter.

[2] Protocols of Karel Caidler, March 15, 1947 and Hynek Kašpar, May 6, 1946. Národní archiv, Prague (NA), f. Ministerstvo vnitra – nová registratura (MV-NR), karton (k.) 1943 inventární číslo (inv. č.) 1602 signatura (sign.) B2111.

[3] Václav Kural and Zdeněk Radvanovský, eds., *"Sudety" pod hákovým křížem* (Ústí nad Labem, 2002), 45–69.

for doing so. Caidler's sister, for instance, married a German-speaking glass manufacturer from Česká Kamenice and joined the thousands of other ethnically mixed-marriage couples in the country.

This chapter shifts the focus of ethnic cleansing to consider the influence of incoming settlers and the administrative power structures that shaped settlement policies in the borderlands. While the events in Česká Kamenice were not typical in terms of the extent of the conflicts that arose there, they reveal the character of the political vacuum that emerged at war's end and how that void was filled. They also point to the internal conflicts among Czech speakers that became an important feature of postwar borderland life. Despite the claims of national unity that came with ethnic cleansing, using Czechs as a category of analysis makes little sense when trying to understand the transformations that occurred there.[4] First, there were many divisions among Czechs speakers. Second, the expulsion of Germans encouraged the migration of non-Czechs to the borderlands too. A host of different people, from various countries, with diverse backgrounds and customs moved to the borderlands, including some against their will. In addition to contradicting the notion of national unity, the diversity of people who came to reside there challenged the visions of settlement planners who sought to erase the distinctions between the borderlands and the interior and to create an ethnically pure space. Settlement officials also struggled against the ambitions and decisions of national committees, which emerged as competing loci of power. Rather than any single agenda or single authority controlling resettlement, migration pressures and intragovernmental tensions were key factors that shaped the reconfiguration of the borderlands.

Many of the Czech members of the first Local National Committee in Česká Kamenice had German relatives or marriage partners. Such relationships made many of the newly created national committees suspect in the eyes of Czechs who resided in the Protectorate during the war. Early reports from Czechoslovak military commanders in the borderlands demonstrated the high degree of mistrust they felt toward many local Czechs and borderland national committees. Not only old settlers, but Sudeten Germans, even some who had joined the Nazis, were able to position themselves on national committees.[5] Fears emerged that such

---

[4] For a critique of using nations as categories of analysis, see Rogers Brubaker, *Nationalism Reframed: Nationhood and the National Question in the New Europe* (Cambridge, 1996).

[5] In one unusual case, a Sudeten German became the chairman of the national committee in Krnov and his brother, reportedly a former SS member, declared that he had received authority from the Ministry of Interior to take control of the district security forces. It took the assistance of a partisan unit from nearby Olomouc to remove the two brothers from power. However, after the partisans moved them to Olomouc the brothers apparently returned briefly to Krnov. From there they were escorted by the NKVD to Ostrava and

national committees would protect local Germans from expulsions. In a general military report about borderland conditions in June 1945, the entry for Česká Kamenice ominously read: "The national committee is bound by its familial relations to the civilian population, it works very slowly; preparation of a list of about 1,000 Germans, who should be expatriated (vysidlování), took this national committee three weeks [to compile]."[6] Such reports were not uncommon, and demonstrated the impatience of military officials with deliberations that considered allowing any Germans to remain.

However, the disputes between military officials and national committees had little to do with finding enough Germans to expel. In June 1945, expulsions had only just begun; German inhabitants lived everywhere in the borderlands. Instead, military organs and borderland national committees challenged each other's authority, which went beyond old settlers' attempts to protect Germans with whom they had personal connections. The conflict between old settlers and security units often involved control of local government and access to confiscated property. The first new settlers arriving in 1945 likewise sought immediate access to Sudeten German property. In Česká Kamenice, as elsewhere, the MNV immediately began drawing up lists of Germans to expel, confiscating their property, and attending to other day-to-day matters of local administration. Caidler, like many national committee members elsewhere, took a practical approach to the problems facing the town. For example, he distributed confiscated German clothing, shoes and linens equally to all Czechs in the area, but ensured that valuables such as jewelry, furs and Persian rugs were safe-guarded or sent to Prague. His actions, while in line with official regulations issued by the Provincial National Committee in Prague, met the approbation of new settlers and others in search of Sudeten German property. As Caidler later recalled: "Considering that I openly declared my efforts to protect national property and enacted a whole series of provisions, which had protected it from theft, I was very unpopular among a definite part of the inhabitants."[7] Military personnel in the town looked upon such equanimity with even greater displeasure.

then disappeared. Situation reports, Národní sbor bezpečnosti (SNB), June 14, July 8 and 11, 1945; Státní okresní archiv (SOkA) Bruntál, f. Okresní národní výbor (ONV) Krnov I, dodatek, k. 11 inv. č. 92; Minutes from the Okresní správy komise (OSK), Krnov, June 16 1945. Ibid. k. 7 inv. č. 63; Report on Krnov affair, Velitelství VI sborů odd. Obrané zpravodajství (OBZ), Olomouc, June 14, 1945. Vojenský historický archiv, Prague (VHA), f. Vojenská kancelář presidenta republiky (VKPR), č. j. 1014.
[6] Report on the difficulties of the evacuations of Germans, June–July 1945. VHA, f. Velitelství oblast 1 (VO1), k. 49 inv. č. 267.
[7] Protocol of Karel Caidler, March 15, 1947. NA, f. MV-NR, k. 1943 inv. č. 1602 sign. B2111.

As was the case across the borderlands, a variety of military forces surfaced in Česká Kamenice. The army had established one garrison there and other military detachments came through to help carry out expulsions. In addition, a Defense Intelligence unit under the leadership of Vilem Dovara established operations there. A small partisan group of thirty-five to fifty members under Adolf Charous also arrived in the town.[8] The relations between the Local National Committee and these security organs quickly deteriorated, but disputes about the progress of expulsions were not at the heart of the conflict. Despite the reports of the MNV's foot-dragging, Caidler helped "evacuate" or sent to the district collection center nearly two-thirds of the town's Germans during his short tenure as the chairperson.[9] It was Caidler's unwillingness to permit wide-scale looting that became the major point of contention between himself and Dovara. Dovara and his unit engaged in massive expropriation. They were particularly fond of collecting motor vehicles. They even broke into the national committee's garage and seized a Mercedes and another car despite the protests of Caidler's pregnant wife. The turning point, however, came following a search by Dovara's men of the local German doctor's house, during which countless valuables, including a Persian rug valued at more than 100,000 Kčs, were confiscated. The doctor had been slated for an upcoming expulsion, but because of the shortage of qualified medical personnel, he was temporarily allowed to remain. Caidler reported the incident to the local police, thus threatening to bring down Dovara's pillaging operation.[10]

However, Dovara found an ally in Charous, the partisan leader, and gained the upper hand. Together they had Caidler and several other members of the national committee arrested for connections to alleged German Werewolf groups. Such accusations sufficed to have Caidler taken into custody and keep him in the basement of the former district court, where he underwent torturous beatings and witnessed the merciless behavior of Charous' and Dovara's personnel against Czechs and Germans alike. With the blessing of one member of the District Administrative Commission (OSK) in nearby Děčín, Charous became the town's commissar and declared to a public audience, with whip in hand: "Gentlemen, this is our new people's democracy and I will govern

[8] For more on the following events in Česká Kamenice, see Michal Mareš, "Opět propagujeme vlčí svobodu," *Dnešek* March 6, 1947; Petr Joza, *Rabštejnské údolí* (Děčín, 2002), 174–90.
[9] Protokols of Karel Caidler, March 15, 1947 and Jaroslav Synek, May 10, 1946. NA, f. MV-NR, k. 1943 inv. č. 1602 sign. B2111. There were 6,800 inhabitants in Česká Kamenice at the end of the war; see *Česká Kamenice* (Česká Lípa, 2002), 340.
[10] Protocol of Karel Caidler, March 15, 1947. NA, f. MV-NR, k. 1943 inv. č. 1602 sign. B2111.

here by this."[11] Aside from the reign of terror in the town, Charous and Dovara also garnered support by handing out confiscated German businesses to their followers and by encouraging looting. As one former policeman in the town reported, the pillaging got so out of control that the police did not have time to investigate the actions of Germans.[12]

The turbulent conditions in Česká Kamenice in the immediate postwar period is just one example demonstrating how the chaos in the borderlands stemmed from the struggle among Czechs over property and administrative control in conjunction with the expulsion of Germans. As new lines of authority emerged and the National Front government reorganized the state's administration, opportunities abounded for people like Dovara and Charous to assume powerful positions in the borderlands. The expulsions provided excellent cover for their actions. Military personnel roamed freely and were not subject to clear hierarchies of authority. The suspicions against Germans and old settlers justified harsh measures of repression without solid evidence of guilt or wrongdoing. On one level, the story of Česká Kamenice demonstrated peoples' motivation for personal gain. On another level, it showed the difficulty of creating democratic conditions amid ethnic cleansing. For a partisan leader to become a local commissar made more sense under such circumstances than the emergence of democratic local rule.

Local power remained fluid for the first months after the war and depended upon the kinds of people who moved to the borderlands. They not only shaped the long-term changes, they also played a pivotal role in the lives of Germans and Czechs already living there. In some places people like Charous emerged, which is unsurprising given the context of ethnic cleansing. Nonetheless, the picture was mixed. In other towns national committees developed without such drama and they sought to build new communities and economies as they saw fit. Such goals, however, often ran counter to the plans of central officials and the realities on the ground. As the plans and processes of settlement progressed, the borderlands grew more diverse and borderland communities became riddled with conflicts despite central leaders' goal of creating a homogenous nation-state.

---

[11] Various protocols. NA, f. MV-NR, k. 1943 inv. č. 1602 sign. B2111; Joza, 180. Caidler remained in jail for several weeks in Česká Kamenice before being transferred to a prison in Děčín. He was finally released sometime in October 1945.

[12] Protocol of former SNB officer in Česká Kamenice, September 7, 1945. NA, f. MV-NR, k. 1943 inv. č. 1602 sign. B2111. In his testimony the officer also reported that he replaced his predecessor because he suffered from bad nerves caused by conditions in the town.

National Committees and the Establishment of Local Power

The idea of using national committees as the basis for postwar administration of Czechoslovakia emerged during President Beneš's visit to Moscow in December 1943. During the war, so-called "revolutionary national committees" had emerged in larger borderland towns, often within factories, but the Gestapo successfully infiltrated and disbanded them. The Communist underground had been instrumental in their organization and leaders in Moscow had generally supported them.[13] In their meetings with Beneš, Czechoslovak Communists proposed national committees as the basis for the postwar reorganization of state power. Beneš likewise sought to reform the prewar state administration and considered national committees as possible postwar institutions of democratic governance.[14] National committees were not entirely new to the Czech political scene. During the 1848 Revolutions, political leaders established a National Committee in Prague, which pursued the unification of Bohemia, Moravia and Silesia.[15] During World War I, a National Committee was created in Prague to provide support to Czechs, and it formed the basis for an interim government after the fighting ended.[16] The post–World War II versions, by contrast, became permanent institutions and had far-reaching powers to control everything from security to schools.

An organized system of national committees developed slowly through a series of problems, scandals and readjustments in the borderlands. Decree 18, issued on December 4, 1944, formally established national committees as the organs of public administration in postwar Czechoslovakia. It presented only rough guidelines about the form and

[13] Jinřich Pecka, "Revoluční národní výbory jako prostor pro místní elity," in *Politické elity v Československu 1918–1938* (Prague, 1994), 233–37; František Cvrk, "Vznik a vývoj národních výborů v letech 1945–1946 a přihlédnutím k vývoji na Děčínsku," in *6. vědecká archivní konference Revoluční národní vybory, osídlování pohraničí a význam národních vyborů při zajišťování národně-demokratického procesu v ČSR v letech 1944–1948* (Ústí nad Labem, 1990), 31–32; Karel Bertelman, *Vývoj národních vyborů do ústavy 9. května* (Prague, 1964), 23; Zdeněk Radvanovský, "Národní výbory ústecké průmyslové oblasti a jejich podíl na osídlování pohraničí v letech poválečného revolučního procesu," in *6. vědecká archivní konference*, 7; Paul Zinner, *Communist Strategy and Tactics in Czechoslovakia, 1918–1948* (New York, 1963), 74.
[14] Eduard Beneš, *The Memoirs of Dr. Eduard Beneš: From Munich to New War and New Victory*, trans. Godfrey Lias (London, 1954), 270–71; Zinner, 81.
[15] Stanley Pech, *The Czech Revolution of 1848* (Chapel Hill, 1969), 119–22.
[16] Radvanovský, "Národní výbory ústecké průmyslové oblasti," 3–5; Anthony Paleček, "Formative Years of the First Republic of Czechoslovakia. The Statesmanship of Antonín Švehla," in *Czechoslovakia Past and Present*, ed. Miroslav Rechcigl (The Hague, 1968), 1: 30–34.

purpose of national committees, and those guidelines reflected the wartime context and certain leaders' assumption that they would remain merely temporary bodies. The decree called on people to create national committees in order to fight the Nazis and to provide the basis for transitional local government following the war.[17] However, administrative commissions or individual commissars, as in the case of Česká Kamenice, usually replaced these revolutionary national committees by the end of May 1945. The Ministry of Interior established administrative commissions to provide provisional authority in places where Czechs comprised less than a majority of the inhabitants – that is, in the borderlands. In smaller towns and communities, individual "administrative commissars" were installed to govern until a significant Czech population arrived.[18] The Interior Ministry controlled the appointments to district-level administrative commissions, which in turn appointed local administrative commissioners or commissars.[19] In theory, this meant that district officials possessed tremendous authority to manage the appointment of local commissars and administrative commission members. In practice, the development of local power depended on who was present in the borderlands and how they chose to handle their new authority. In addition, the administrative commissions that appeared in most borderland towns were supposed to adhere to the principle of parity among the National Front political parties. This was particularly problematic when one or more parties did not have any representation in a particular town. In general, the Communist Party benefited from this situation as its members, many of them brand new, came to dominate national committees in the borderlands.

Regardless of whether a commissar, administrative commission or national committee governed a given locality, they all carried out similar functions. In the borderlands where conditions remained in flux after the war, national committees helped to plan and execute the expulsion of Sudeten Germans. This role involved balancing the competing agendas of getting rid of Germans, but ensuring the continued functioning of the economy and making enough space for new settlers. In Teplice-Šanov, for instance, during one meeting the District Administrative Commission reorganized the housing office, discussed how factory committees were requesting to exempt German workers from the transfer, and decided on vacation policy for district workers (which was set at one week). National

[17] Decree 18, December 4, 1944. Karel Jech and Karel Kaplan, eds., *Dekrety prezidenta republiky 1940–1945: Dokumenty* 2 vols. (Brno, 1995), 1: 123–125.
[18] Decree 18, Article 4. Jech and Kaplan, *Dekrety*, 1: 123.
[19] Směrnice Ministerstvo vnitra pro Národní výbory mistní a okresní, May 19, 1945. *Úřední list* č.7, May 23, 1945.

committees were also responsible for arresting those guilty of collaboration and important Nazi functionaries. At the same meeting in Teplice-Šanov they investigated the background of forty-one local Czechs. In addition, like the national committee in Česká Kamenice, national committees played a significant role in collecting, protecting and distributing confiscated Sudeten German property. The Teplice-Šanov OSK reported that various secret police units had been taking confiscated goods from local warehouses and making off with them, and it discussed ways to halt this practice.[20] In addition to dealing with settlement and expulsion matters, national committees were responsible for a host of other functions. They looked after public health, developed cultural and recreational institutions, established new schools and oversaw public works projects. Although their finances were linked to the central government, they had some control over their own budgets.[21]

The agenda facing national committees and administrative commissions in the borderlands was quite large and, in general, they were ill-equipped to handle it. Administrative commissions in nearly all borderland towns faced a shortage of personnel. According to official regulations, district-level administrative commissions ranged from six to twelve members, while local administrative commissions had three to six members, depending on the size of the population. National committees, on the other hand, had much larger memberships. District national committees consisted of twenty to thirty-six members, and local national committees had between nine and sixty members, again depending on population size.[22] Individual commissars generally existed only in smaller communities where almost no Czech inhabitants lived. While the Interior Ministry officials who composed such rules were concerned that few "reliable inhabitants" existed to staff borderland national committees, by limiting the number of people appointed to administrative commissions they hindered them from completing their duties and concentrated power in the hands of a few. The result of this policy, as the example of Česká Kamenice illustrates, sometimes facilitated corruption and the abuse of power.

National committees replaced administrative commissions and individual commissars as the number of Czechs in the borderlands grew in late

---

[20] Minutes from the meeting of the OSK Teplice-Šanov, July 19, 1945. SOkA Teplice-Šanov. f. Teplice-Šanov ONV, k. 8 inv. č. 239.

[21] For the official regulations concerning national committees functions, see Směrnice Ministerstvo vnitra pro Národní výbory místní a okresní, May 19, 1945. Úřední list č.7, May 23, 1945.

[22] Ibid.; Bertelman, 207–8; J. Fusek Organisace a činnost okresních národních výborů (Prague: 1946), 47; Cvrk, 33–34.

1945 and early 1946. There were forty-five district administrative commissions in July 1945, which accounted for nearly all of the borderland districts.[23] During preparations for the Provisional National Assembly elections in September and October 1945, towns with enough Czechs elected national committees and eliminated administrative commissions. Similarly, in connection with the May 1946 elections to the Constituent National Assembly, further changes were made and nearly all of the administrative commissions disappeared. By 1947, 3,805 local national committees existed, with more than 50,000 members in the borderlands.[24] District national committees had a similar structure to local national committees, except that the former had a Presidium, which included the chairperson and three deputies. The Presidium supervised MNVs and maintained contact with central officials, such as the government ministries and the provincial national committees.[25] In this sense, ONVs were critical intermediate bodies, linking the central government to local officials. Three provincial national committees (ZNV), based in Prague, Brno and Ostrava, controlled district- and local-level national committees in Bohemia, Moravia and Silesia, respectively. Prior to the creation of other government organs with greater control over the expulsion and settlement, the ZNVs also served as policy makers for borderland national committees.

National committees' composition in the immediate postwar period reflected the unpredictable circumstances brought by the war, expulsion and resettlement. Many Czech partisans or Revolutionary Guard members remained in positions of authority, especially in local police forces or as commanders for camps holding Germans, but also as national committee members.[26] At times, this was a natural progression for those partisans who had been politically active prior to the war, went underground during it and resumed a leading position following liberation. For example, the vice chairman of the Jablonec nad Nisou MNV had been active in Czech nationalist circles before the war.[27] For others, national

---

[23] Bertelman, 209. Slezák reports that there were 34 districts fully settled in the Bohemian borderlands and 12 in Moravia and Silesia. In addition, there were 50 partly settled districts. Lubomír Slezák, *Zemědělské osídlování pohraničí českých zemí po druhé světové válce* (Brno, 1978), 44–46, 112.

[24] Ervín Polák, *Čísla mluví o voličích a o národních výborech* (Prague, 1947), Table IIa, 90.

[25] Fusek, 67–70.

[26] Miroslav Kocich, *Boj KSČ za prosazení národních výborů jako lidových orgánů státní moci a správy* (Ostrava, 1981); Cvrk, 32.

[27] On the day before the Local Administrative Commission in Jablonec became a Local National Committee, it awarded the vice chairman a large sum of money for having given books to the "minority library" in the town prior to the war. Minutes from the meeting of the Mistní správní komise (MSK), April 11, 1946. SOkA Jablonec nad Nisou (Jablonec n. N), f. Městský národní výbor (MěNV) Jablonec n. N., kniha (kn.) 1 inv. č. 1.

committee membership offered the option to maintain positions of authority, which they gained through the expulsions. Adolf Charous began his postwar career in the notoriously brutal camp for Germans in Kolín.[28] By the end of June 1945, he found himself on the edge of authority when partisan units were being disbanded and sought a more legitimate and permanent position. Other military and security personnel involved in expulsions attempted the switch to politics as well. The chairman of the District National Committee in Bruntál had been the head of district security just after the war. Captain Ctibor Novák, a former partisan, was slated to be the security chief at the ONV in Frývaldov. His checkered past and German wife, however, likely prevented him from consideration for the post by early 1946.[29]

The wide-ranging authority given to administrative commissions, commissars and national committees often led to abuses of power. National committee members' transgressions most commonly involved using their positions to benefit, either personally or politically, from confiscated German property. For instance, in one farming community, members of the Local Administrative Commission placed themselves as national administrators on confiscated farms and did not include in their inventories some of the livestock, which they then sold on the black market.[30] Incoming settlers often complained of local officials' petty abuses of power. That national committee members used confiscated automobiles and scarce fuel for personal trips irked settlers who had trouble even finding a place to live.[31] Other abuses were more serious. One police investigation in the outlying reaches of northern Silesia led to the arrest of several people, including two brothers, for, among other things, the rape of a fourteen-year-old German girl and the attempted rape of another. The first offender was a twenty-three-year-old commissar of two small towns near the Polish border, where few settlers ventured. Another one of the arrested individuals, a member of a Local Administrative Commission, had been extorting sex from another Sudeten German

---

[28] *Dnešek*, May 15, 1947.

[29] Security report, ONV Frývaldov, November 15, 1945. SOkA Jeseník, f. ONV Jeseník, k. 2 inv. č. 63. Novák had spent some time as a camp commander in the Frývaldov district after the war. See Jana Hradilová, *Nucené společenství: Internace německého obyvatelstva v adolfovickém táboře 1945(1946)* Diplomová práce (Olomouc, 2002); Jan Němeček, *Mašínové: Zpráva o dvou generacích* (Prague, 1998), 193–212.

[30] Punishment proceedings in the Settlement Committee, ONV Chomutov. February 1946. SOkA Chomutov, f. ONV Chomutov, k. 1446 inv. č. 1646. For more general reports about such abuses of power, see NA, f. MV-NR, k. 1943 inv. č. 1602 sign. B2111.

[31] "Okénko z frývaldovská," *Hraničář Protifašistický list okresu Frývaldova*, August 25, 1945; Monthly security report, OSK Frývaldov, September 25, 1945. SOkA Jeseník, f. ONV Jeseník, k. 2 inv. č. 63.

woman by threatening to prevent her appeal for citizenship.[32] Such commissars had tremendous power to take advantage of Sudeten Germans' fears. Because of the many transgressions associated with national committees, people came to see them as corrupt and bureaucratic.

Many commissars and administrative commission members accused of wrongdoing belonged to the Communist Party. This should not be surprising, given that Communists comprised nearly 40 percent of Local National Committee members and a near majority of the leadership positions in 1945.[33] They also seemed the least inhibited from aggressive behavior, and perhaps with good reason. As Tomáš Staněk has noted, "In a series of cases, these people's unlimited power was legalized or at least tolerated by higher authorities. They intervened against them only after a long interval or the perpetration of especially serious criminal acts. At the same time, the legitimacy of the Communist Party or the intercession of its functionaries gave many reliable cover."[34] Indeed, once the incidents in Česká Kamenice were brought to light in 1946 and early 1947, Dovara and Charous, both Communist Party members, received only minimal punishments. Following the Communist seizure of power in early 1948, Dovara became an undercover agent for the State Security Police.[35] In other instances, however, the Communists paid a price for such "adventurers." In the Frývaldov district, the disclosure of a series of disreputable Communists, including another whip-toting commissar like Charous, discredited the KSČ and forced it to carry out an internal purge.[36]

Despite the disgraceful acts of several of its functionaries, the Communist Party's influence within national committees has been portrayed as a critical ingredient in its postwar seizure of power. The Communist Party proved more than capable in placing their people on administrative commissions, especially just after the war. Soviet army intelligence and even NKVD officers had connections with the Defense Intelligence units of the Czechoslovak military and sometimes helped

[32] Weekly criminal report, OSK Krnov-kriminální úřad, January 26, 1946. SOkA Bruntál, f. ONV Krnov I, k. 2 inv. č. 60.

[33] Bertelman, 172; Karel Kaplan, *Nekrvavá revoluce* (Prague, 1993), 50 n. 13.

[34] Staněk, *Perzekuce*, 63.

[35] Ibid., 62; Joza, 188–89. Caidler spent several weeks in the Děčín district jail and then was released when neither Dovara nor Charous agreed to testify against him. He immediately pressed charges against them, but the investigation lagged. In early 1947 he gave his story to Michal Mareš who, upon further investigation, published it. See Mareš, "Opět propagujeme."

[36] Monthly security report, OSK Frývaldov, November 15, 1945. SOkA Jeseník, f. ONV Jeseník, k. 2 inv. č. 63.

ensure that Communists moved into positions of authority.[37] The Interior Ministry, which oversaw the appointment of commissars and administrative commissioners, also worked to create a strong Communist influence in these organs. However, the process was not as straightforward as Bradley Abrams has suggested occurred in other countries of Eastern Europe, where the Red Army installed "whatever local Communists were at hand."[38] Instead, it seems that Czechs received spots on national committees as they became Communists, especially just after the war. For instance, in Česká Kamenice, the local KSČ organizer first offered Karel Caidler a chance to take the chairperson position of the local Communist Party organization, which Caidler refused because he wished to remain above party politics.[39] The Communists' flexibility in membership decisions not only opened the party's door to adventurers, but suggests that many of its local leaders were not hard core ideologues. The significance of Communist prevalence on borderland national committees must be judged accordingly.

In addition, the extent of Communist influence must also be approached with caution. First, national committees were constantly evolving. In addition to the structural changes – from revolutionary national committees, to popularly supported national committees, to administrative commissions, to properly elected national committees – internal membership frequently varied. From July 1945 to the end of the year, more than 20 percent of District Administrative Commission members were recalled or resigned.[40] Local national committees also had high turnover rates. One reason for this resulted from non-Communist parties demanding their right to seats on national committees based on the parity agreement, though these changes were not as significant or rapid as these parties had hoped. The dismissal of those caught for corruption or other offenses also brought substitutions. Despite the abuses committed by some national committee members, responsible leaders did emerge during the summer and fall of 1945. Among other things, they worked to remove young commissars, who, like Charous, ruled as local dictators.[41] Although KSČ members were most often linked to scandals and misuse of official power, this image did not define the party or detract from its popularity. Following the May 1946 elections, in which the Communist

---

[37] Staněk, *Perzekuce*, 61–62.
[38] Bradley Abrams, "The Second World War and the *East European Revolution*," *East European Politics and Societies* 16, no.3 (2002): 627.
[39] Protocol of Hynek Kašpar, May 6, 1946. NA, MV-NR, k. 1943 inv. č. 1602 sign. B2111.
[40] Bertelman, 109.
[41] See, for example, Minutes from the ONV Opava-venkov, July 3 and September 7, 1945. SOkA Opava, f. ONV Opava-venkov, k. 1, inv. č. 111.

Party secured a high percentage of the vote in borderland districts, Communist control of national committees in the borderlands actually increased well beyond that of 1945. In this sense, their control of borderland national committees was not simply a source of their popularity, but a reflection of it.

National committees, whether Communist-dominated or not, faced common hurdles in the borderlands, brought by expulsion and resettlement. These massive migrations destabilized local economic, cultural and social life in numerous ways. To mention just one example here, the housing agenda of national committees grew to tremendous proportions as they removed Germans from their homes and often had to deal with multiple requests for a single apartment and incoming settlers' constant movement from house to house. For instance, in Děčín people took over apartments as they pleased and local housing officials, often new to their jobs, could not keep pace with the changing conditions. Already in late May 1945, the revolutionary Local National Committee instructed people to register with the national committee before occupying a home. On July 2, 1945, the housing department in Děčín requested permission from the national committee council to allot fifty apartments a day in order to keep pace with the growing number of settlers.[42] Yet the sheer volume of arriving settlers overwhelmed housing officials. The committee had an insufficient number of employees and they did not keep track of the requests for apartments or retain evidence about the homes they had allotted. The result, as a later report noted, was that settlers continued to take over apartments as they wished and "in many cases enriched themselves at the state's expense."[43] The constant movement of people through borderland towns frequently strained national committees to breaking point.

National committees faced the initial onslaught of settlers on their own and devised solutions to problems as they emerged. First and foremost, national committees sought to restore order, even if only to consolidate certain gains – either political, economic or both.[44] Through their initial control of the settlement agenda, national committees and administrative commissions both experienced and developed the administrative

---

[42] Minutes of the revolutionary MěNV Děčín, May 25, and July 2, 1945. SOkA Děčín, f. MěNV Děčín, k. 1 inv. č. 39.

[43] Zpráva o výsledku revise činnosti bytového úřadu, Podmokly, January 1947. SOkA Děčín, f. MěNV Děčín, k. 254, inv. č. 775.

[44] Frommer agrees. He writes: "National committees, for all their faults, had a vested interest in establishing order within their jurisdictions and concentrating power in their own hands, not those of vigilantes and paramilitaries." Benjamin Frommer, *National Cleansing: Retribution Against Nazi Collaborators in Postwar Czechoslovakia* (Cambridge, 2005), 57.

autonomy promised to national committees as the people's representatives. National committees quickly became a powerful political force of their own, drawn together in many ways by the numerous obstacles and conflicts that they faced. They proposed different ways to better organize resettlement. For example, in July 1945, a group of borderland national committees petitioned to pair interior national committees with borderland ones in order to coordinate the flow of hitherto unplanned migrations.[45] As we shall see in the following chapters, their actions, though often hampered by internal conflicts, were guided more by their sense of knowing what was best for their communities rather than any dedication to the Communist cause, or even the national one. This sense of autonomy grew out of necessity in 1945 and became problematic only as central authorities later sought to claim control of the borderlands.

Resettlement Realities and Borderland Visions

New settlers played a central role in ethnic cleansing by dispossessing Sudeten Germans of their homes, land and businesses. In 1945, the migration of Czechs to the borderlands matched the pace and extent of the expulsions. Although data concerning the migration of people to and around the borderlands during the summer of 1945 are not completely reliable, a general picture of settlers' arrival can be reconstructed. According to Vladimír Srb, 1.2 million Czechs lived in the borderlands by the middle of August 1945, of which between 400,000 and 500,000 were already there at the beginning of May.[46] Some of these Czechs had arrived during the war to work in the borderlands, but most were old settlers who had lived there prior to the war. Old settlers were a further divided group; some of them had remained in the borderlands during the war, while others had left for the country's interior when the Nazis annexed the Sudetenland in October 1939. These latter old settlers – so-called returnees (*navrátlíci*) – were among the first to make it to the

---

[45] Letters from national committees in northeastern Bohemia, July 12, 1945. NA, f. MV-NR, k. 7443 inv. č. 4148 sign. B300. This policy was used particularly in agricultural settlement plans.

[46] Vladimír Srb, *Materiály k problematice novoosídleneckého pohraničí* (Prague, 1984), 76–77; *Soupisy obyvatelstva v Československu v letech 1946–1947* (Prague, 1951), 528. This table gives 729,126 as the number of inhabitants in borderland communities on May 1, 1945, including Germans still present in May 1947. The number of Germans, according to Srb elsewhere, was 180,000: see Vladimír Srb, *Populační, ekonomický a národnostní vývoj*, 7. The Settlement Office gave the figure of 350,000 Czechs living in the borderlands at the beginning of May 1945. These figures do not include 100,000 workers, which Settlement officials argued returned to the interior of the country following the war. See, for example, "Rok úsilovné práce," *Osídlování*, 25 September 1946; Report on settlement, Osídlovací úřad (OÚ), January 28, 1946. NA, f. Osídlovací komise při ÚV KSČ (f. 23), a. j. 359.

borderlands in May 1945. Together with a huge influx of newcomers, they comprised the 500,000–650,000 Czechs who arrived between May and August 1945.[47] Miroslav Kreysa, the chairperson of the Settlement Office, spoke about a settlement rate of more than 200,000 per month during the summer of 1945. As he noted, "the original borderland settlement by Czechs occurred entirely spontaneously and without central direction."[48]

The first settlers moved to the most desirable locations in search of the best opportunities. These places were mostly towns with nice homes and a range of potentially profitable businesses, based on their prewar reputations. They were also easily accessible. Czechs quickly moved from their homes in the interior, found a former German home or business in a popular town, and had the Local National Committee appoint them as the national administrator. One newspaper article drew attention to this phenomenon, arguing that too many settlers were heading to places like Karlový Váry and Liberec – two of the more picturesque borderland towns.[49] In Liberec, for instance, the OSK had stopped accepting applications for the national administrator positions of former Sudeten German businesses by June 8, 1945.[50] Many people hoped to become an independent proprietor and perhaps future owner of a farm, a small shop or a pub. Settlers moved in and began working immediately, sometimes investing their own money for necessary repairs or supplies. Other settlers occupied national administrator positions in more than one place, hoping to improve their chances of permanently obtaining choice property.

The rate of settlement began to slow in the fall of 1945, but still hundreds of thousands of Czechs and others arrived. Between September and the year's end, nearly 500,000 additional settlers moved into these areas, bringing the total borderland population to over 3,500,000 people, more than had lived there at the beginning of the war.[51] The year 1946 brought relief from the crowded conditions in many borderland towns, and large concentrations of Germans in outlying areas began to diminish. The Allied-sponsored expulsion of Sudeten Germans accomplished much in this regard, but so too did a slowdown in the arrival of settlers. During 1946 the monthly increase in settlers'

---

[47] Srb, *Materialy*, 76–77.   [48] Miroslav Kreysa, *České pohraničí* (Prague, 1947), 8.
[49] "V pohraničí nejsou jen K. Vary," *Svobodné slovo*, July 7, 1945.
[50] *Stráž severu*, June 8, 1945.
[51] Population figures vary. See Srb, *Materialy*, 76–77 for continued settlement figures. Also see population data in NA, f.23, a.j. 315. And report on settlement čj. 3421/46 Osidlovaci úřad, Prague, February 1946. Ibid., a.j. 359. For a broader analysis of population development in the borderlands, see Srb, *Populační, ekonomický a národnostní vývoj*.

arrival, measured by the distribution of their ration cards, never neared 100,000, which it had far exceeded for nearly every month in 1945. For instance, August 1946, one of the biggest months for expulsions, witnessed only a small increase in the number of settlers. In fact, some of the first settlers had already begun returning to the interior, which partially offset the complications that their rapid and large-scale arrival brought in the summer of 1945. There were mixed reactions to this. For instance, a reporter for *Sentinel of the North* (*Stráž severu*) was worried about the ability to successfully "Czechify" the borderlands if settlers returned to the interior "at the first sign of frost."[52] Others welcomed the departures. The National Socialist Party (a longtime moderate socialist Czech political party, not to be confused with the Nazis) used its paper *Free Word* (*Svobodné slovo*) to argue that the departures were a sign that "the inhabitants of the borderlands themselves are beginning to defend against the theft of their regions by unwanted elements and to finally prosecute the post-revolutionary gold-diggers, who have already disappeared from the borderlands and now are likely hidden in the interior." It noted that in June 1946 Czechs continued to return to the interior, but in decreasing numbers.[53] The expulsion of tens of thousands of Germans every week combined with the steady arrival and departure of Czechs, Slovaks and others meant that the previous year's fluctuating conditions persisted.

The variable rates of incoming settlers and the early departures created serious difficulties for central officials charged with overseeing resettlement of the borderlands. Centralized control over settlement policies developed on two separate tracks. On July 17, 1945, Presidential Decree 27 formally established the Central Committee for Interior Settlement (ÚKVO) and two Settlement Offices (OÚ), one in Prague and one in Bratislava, to separately administer resettlement in both parts of the country. The ÚKVO – comprised of various ministerial representatives – helped to ensure that settlement policies were coordinated with other government offices and agencies.[54] In addition to the Settlement Office, the Ministry of Agriculture controlled confiscated German farmland. It established a separate department within the ministry to focus exclusively on the distribution of these farms to new settlers. This department worked closely with special local farming commissions that were formally attached to national committees, but had exclusive authority on matters related to land and livestock. Because the distribution of

---

[52] "Jak žije a pracuje naše pohraničí: Lidé se stěhují z pohraničí," *Stráž severu*, January 3, 1946.

[53] "Nesnáze v osidlování pohraničí," *Svobodné slovo*, June 20, 1946.

[54] For the official designation of these offices duties, see Decree 27, July 17, 1945. Jech and Kaplan, 1: 318–19.

confiscated farms fell under the land reform provisions following the war, agricultural officials had an easier time allocating farmland than OÚ officials had finalizing procedures and policies regarding other confiscated property.

The Settlement Office in Prague, which finally began its work in September 1945, planned and promoted borderland settlement. Miroslav Kreysa, the OÚ's chairman, once referred to its role as "our settlement's Čedok," which was the name for the country's largest travel bureau.[55] Indeed, the Settlement Office began promoting the borderlands in a number of ways to encourage migration to the borderlands. The OÚ established its own newspaper, Settlement (Osidlování), for this purpose and published several pamphlets to advertise the available resettlement opportunities. The newspaper often featured stories about particular borderland towns and factories in order to highlight successes and to encourage further migration. In addition, the Settlement Office supported a large exhibition in Prague to stress the "Czechness" of the borderlands.[56] Settlement officials sought an organized approach to repopulating the borderlands with Czech inhabitants, who could contribute to the rebuilding of the postwar economy.

The Settlement Office's main efforts focused on planning and policymaking. It spent enormous time on and made detailed plans for the reorganization of the borderlands. What settlement officials termed "settlement politics" (osidlovací politika) meant a set of plans to encourage resettlement to the borderlands. Settlement politics depended on favorable policies using property and wages in efforts to stimulate particular immigration to the former Sudetenland. As Kreysa stated, settlement politics rested on the idea "that we must not force anyone to go to the borderlands; that settlement politics must be carried out so that the necessary categories of workers, and in general that all necessary people move to the borderlands of their own free will."[57] This was a rational approach, rather than one motivated by ideology, and utilized the advantages in hand. Sudeten German property represented a cheap means to attract settlers. Indeed, the OÚ established several regulations to offer cheap housing and other advantages in order to attract much needed workers there.[58] Settlement politics also offered a seemingly viable way

---

[55] Minutes from the meeting of the Settlement Commission of the Communist Party's Central Committee, July 17, 1945. NA, f. 23, a.j. 14.

[56] Eagle Glassheim, "Ethnic Cleansing, Communism and Environmental Devastation in Czechoslovakia's Borderlands, 1945–1989," *Journal of Modern History* 78 (2006): 74.

[57] Miroslav Kreysa, *Budujeme pohraničí* (Prague, 1946), 13; Kreysa, *České pohraničí*, 24–27; See also The Programmatic Declaration delivered at the third meeting of ÚKVO, September 18, 1945. NA, f. MV-NR, k. 12145, sign.1651/2.

[58] See text and references to key policies in Kreysa, *Budujeme pohraničí*, 11–13.

to mold the borderlands into a particular vision of what postwar Czech society should resemble.

One goal of the resettlement planners involved the erasure of distinctions between the borderlands and the interior parts of the country. On a practical level this meant raising the availability of food and other provisions in the borderlands to countrywide levels, which the government's program for the Two-Year Plan (1947–1948) formally stipulated.[59] Reconnecting the borderlands with the rest of the country likewise raised more general notions about unifying the nation-state. The Programmatic Declaration of the Settlement Office, for instance, proclaimed that settlement should support the efforts "to attach the borderlands to the entire structure of our republic as a state of Czechs and Slovaks." It further noted that this meant cultivating its economic potential for the benefit of the entire republic.[60] Indeed, economic restructuring brought by the expulsion and resettlement was a welcomed event for many political leaders. This was particularly the case for Communists, who sought to promote social change through the resettlement process.[61] For example, Kreysa, who was a Communist Party leader, placed resettlement in the general framework of postwar economic restructuring. He declared:

the directed and planned settlement can and must increase the well-being of the economic sectors of our state, to the marked improvement of productivity and a higher living standard of our people; that the confiscation of enemy property and its new division will partly help us solve the most pressing postwar social problems and partly establish an entirely new social structure for our nation, much healthier, than before now.[62]

Communists and other leaders considered resettlement not as an isolated policy, but as part of a larger rebuilding process for the country as a whole.

The visions of the resettlement program also connected with broader notions of security, territory and culture. The first concern reflected the broader sense of ethnic cleansing, in which resettlement served to protect the country against the possible return of Germans. One settlement official underscored settlers' importance in this regard: "these new settlers are used to create a stable barrier and secure defense against any kind

---

[59] Kreysa, *Budujeme pohraničí*, 12.
[60] The Programmatic Declaration delivered at the third meeting of ÚKVO, 18 September 1945. NA, f. MV-NR, k. 12145, sign. 1651/2; Arburg, "Tak či oňak," 266; Radvanovský, "Resettling Czechs," 243.
[61] Matěj Spurný, "Nejsou jako my: Sociální marginalizace a integrace v období budování nového řádu na příkladu menšin v českém pohraničí, 1945–1960" (Dissertation, Charles University, Prague, 2010), 49–50; Glassheim, "Ethnic Cleansing," 78.
[62] Miroslav Kreysa, "Osidlovací politika lidově demokratického státu," *Osidlování*, May 17, 1946.

of German danger." He argued that "[t]heir fate must also be our fate, because only if we have a secure border against the Germans, will we be able to feel secure."[63] President Beneš argued that the settlement question needs much care not only for economic reasons, but also "to ensure that the Germans will never be able to return."[64] This was not simply rhetoric. Even after the Allied-sponsored expulsions began in 1946, rumors of an impending American/Soviet conflict had Sudeten Germans claiming that they would soon return to take over their homes.[65] Even though far from true, settling the borderlands with "reliable" Czechs became an important deterrent in the minds of Prague officials to any possible revision of the Potsdam decision to expel Germans. Other leaders stretched settlement's meaning even further. "Czechification" (počeštění) of the borderlands meant, in part, ensuring that Czechs occupied the physical space in the borderlands, in order to align ethnic and state borders. It particularly surfaced in discussions concerning the confiscation and allocation of Sudeten German farmland. Jiří Koťátko, the Communist head of agricultural settlement, repeatedly emphasized the need for "the complete Czechification of our borderland countryside."[66] During a debate about what to do with the farmland of German antifascists, Klement Gottwald, then Deputy Prime Minister, argued that "they could otherwise be compensated and that the state's endeavor must be that land is in the hands of Czech and Slovak farmers."[67] The goal of making the borderlands Czech likewise entailed removing physical signs that the Sudeten Germans had ever been there, and drew on the national symbols familiar to Czechs in order to create a homogeneous Czech culture. Through holidays, public spaces and cultural events commemorating the nation, a postwar Czech identity – increasingly infused with Communist overtones – was promoted throughout the borderlands.[68]

The grand visions associated with the borderlands and resettlement, however, conflicted with the realities on the ground in late 1945 and early

---

[63] A. Vodička, "A už se nikdy nevracejte ...," Osidlování, November 10, 1946.
[64] Edvard Beneš, Edvard Beneš: Odsun němců z Československa, ed. Karel Novotný (Prague, 1996), 192.
[65] Similar rumors circulated in Poland. See Krystyna Kersten, "Forced Migration and the Transformation of Polish Society in the Postwar Period," in Redrawing Nations: Ethnic Cleansing in East-Central Europe, 1944–1948, eds. Philipp Ther and Ana Siljak (Lanham, 2001), 81.
[66] Jiří Koťátko, Zemědělská osidlovací politika v pohraničí (Prague, 1946), 9; Koťátko, Konfiskace, rozdělování a osidlování půdy, 8.
[67] Minutes from the 30th government meeting, June 21, 1945. Jech and Kaplan, Dekrety, 1:338.
[68] Nancy M. Wingfield, "The Politics of Memory: Constructing National Identity in the Czech Lands, 1945–1948," East European Politics and Societies 14, no.2 (2000): 246–67; Glassheim, "Ethnic Cleansing," 71–83.

1946. Settlement patterns were uneven and tended to thin out toward the frontier. In less attractive places, often geographically isolated, under-developed or situated directly on the state border, the lack of settlers left Sudeten Germans in their homes and at their jobs. For instance, a late July 1945 business report from the towns of Černá Voda, Supíkovice, and Zighartice, which sit in the mountainous region of Silesia near present-day Poland, showed that the vast majority of local firms had yet to be taken over by national administrators.[69] In the district of Rumburk, located in a northern Bohemian promontory, German farmers remained on 80 percent of the farms, and Germans comprised 90 percent of the industrial workers in mid-October 1945.[70] Prospective settlers remained wary of such towns' futures. Because these places were already off the beaten track, the continued presence of Sudeten Germans became an impediment to further resettlement. In some towns, local officials requested expulsions for German homes not because new settlers had demanded them, but because they had not.[71]

In addition, the belief that resettlement could be directed from Prague overlooked the fact that the bulk of settlers had already moved to the borderlands by the time the Settlement Office began its work in earnest. Settlement plans and policies called for a population of 2.5 million Czech and Slovak inhabitants to reside in the borderlands by 1949.[72] Yet, nearly 1,000,000 people had already relocated to the borderlands by the end of 1945, which, in addition to the 400,000 to 500,000 Czechs already living there at the end of the war, meant that well over half of settlement officials' intended 2,500,000 Slavic settlers were already there. Because the initial rush of settlers focused on acquiring desirable property, most of the businesses and farms were already occupied by this time.[73] This was part of the reason why the OÚ focused on bringing industrial and agri-cultural workers to the borderlands. In early 1946 the Settlement Office began discussing methods to encourage such migration, such as offering a stipend for workers who moved there and raising wage levels in border-land industries, among other things.[74] Settlement officials were also

[69] See reports from these towns in July 1945. SOkA Jeseník, f. ONV Jeseník, k. 134 inv. č. 117.
[70] See *Inventář ONV Rumburk*, 2. SOkA Děčín, f. ONV Rumburk.
[71] Situation report, Liptan, September 9, 1945. SOkA Bruntál, f. ONV Krnov I, dodatek, k. 11, inv. č. 92. Monthly report, SNB Heřmanice, August 30, 1945. SOkA Opava, f. ONV Opava-venkov, k. 16 inv. č. 117.
[72] Kreysa, *České pohraničí*, 23–24; Kreysa, *Budujeme pohraničí*, 8–9.
[73] Report of the General Secretary of the Central Commission for Interior Settlement on the 5th plenary meeting, November 29, 1945. NA, f. MV-NR, k. 12145 sign. 1651/2.
[74] Report on the Implementation of Settlement, č.j. 3421/46, likely March 1946. NA, f. 23, a.j. 359.

committed to the idea of bringing Czech and Slovak emigrants back to the country, whom they termed "re-emigrants," and, following the logic of settlement politics, the OÚ sought to use confiscated property as an enticement. However, the efforts to sequester property and to remove settlers in order to make room for them became another source of conflict in the borderlands. The extensive and disorganized resettlement in 1945 created specific realities that undermined settlement officials' visions and plans. Ethnic cleansing had not made the borderlands a blank slate, but rather a land of competing interests for property and power.

Old Settlers and New Settlers: Past, Present and Future

The postwar conflicts concerning the borderlands were not only about the future, though. Past experience shaped the way that settlers wrestled with questions of collaboration and resistance, guilt and innocence. The Nazi annexation of the Sudetenland had overturned the social order there and halted the Czech nationalists' efforts to expand the Czech presence in the borderlands. While thousands of old settler Czechs had left the Sudetenland during the war, other Czechs had arrived to work in Nazi-run industries, so the ethnic balance at the war's end had changed only slightly. Even so, settlement officials expected that many of the Czech workers in the borderlands would return to the interior and that replacing both these workers and expelled Germans would require a concerted effort. Still, Czechs flocked to the borderlands without the need for centralized plans and, worse yet, from the planners' perspective, many Czechs supported Germans and wanted them to remain. In part, this support stemmed from concerns about the future of local economies that depended on skilled German labor.[75] In other cases, personal relations between Czechs and Germans hampered efforts to expel every last German. Over 90,000 mixed-marriage couples existed in 1945, and as Czechs increasingly moved to the borderlands more interethnic relationships emerged.[76] In the 1939 Nazi census of Czechoslovak districts attached to the Reich, some 15,000 Germans listed Czech as their mother tongue and another 13,000 were recorded as bilingual.[77] These figures indicate that even under Nazi rule thousands of people did not necessarily conform to well-defined national categories. These ambiguities, as well as personal relationships among Czech and German speakers, quickly

---

[75] See Chapter 4.

[76] Benjamin Frommer, "Expulsion or Integration: Unmixing Interethnic Marriage in Postwar Czechoslovakia," *East European Politics and Societies* 14, no.2 (2000): 382.

[77] Jaroslav Kučera, *Odsunové ztráty sudetoněmeckého obyvatelstva: Problémy jejich přesného vyčislení* (Prague, 1992), 10.

became contentious in the postwar borderlands as officials moved to determine nationality once and for all.

At the war's end, old settlers often took the lead in establishing so-called revolutionary national committees in the borderlands, just as they had in Česká Kamenice. In many cases, Germans were also early members. This made sense given that they predominately inhabited the region. Old settlers and Sudeten Germans worked together to re-establish control over their towns as Nazi officials fled and German authority melted away. Many old settlers did not see a problem with this. In an early dispatch from the town of Jablonec nad Nisou, the leader of the national committee, an old settler, wrote to Prague officials for clarification about the position of Germans in mixed marriages, Czechs who had declared themselves German during the war and what he called "democratic Germans." He wrote:

Personally I was of the opinion that we keep democratic Germans in the republic. I stayed in touch with them, they did guard duty with us, etc. in 1938 and now. It seems to me like a fraud from my side, if I am unable to do something for them (The day before yesterday an employee of the [national] committee was killed, he lives six years with a German who doesn't know Czech, are we to let her be thrown out? Isn't that harsh?)[78]

Such sentiments reflected old settlers' past experiences with Germans and conditioned them to be sympathetic and to consider each German as an individual to be judged on their actions and beliefs. Old settlers understood that not all Germans were Nazis and that even membership in certain Nazi organizations did not mean unyielding loyalty to the regime. They viewed matters of nationality and guilt for Nazi occupation through a complex lens shaped by prewar and wartime experiences. Precisely for this reason, Czechs from the interior saw old settlers as suspect.

Not all old settlers were sympathetic toward Germans. Many of the earliest Czechs to arrive from the interior were returnees, who had left or whom Nazis had forced from the borderlands after 1938.[79] They demanded that their property and positions be restored, or simply took matters into their own hands. Because their fate had been determined by the Nazi takeover, they had less reason to treat Germans well. Some old settlers had been active in Czech nationalist organizations, such as the Czech National Union, and considered themselves to be part of the

---

[78] Doc. 19. Pamětní spis Svazu Národních jednot a matic. May 12, 1945. Adrian von Arburg and Tomáš Staněk, eds., *Vysídlení Němců a proměny českého pohraničí, 1945– 1951: Dokumenty z českých archivů*, vol. II *part 1 Duben-srpen/září 1945: „Divoký odsun "a počátky osídlování* (Středokluky, 2011), 255–57.

[79] Zdeněk Radvanovský, "The Social and Economic Effects of Resettling Czechs into Northwestern Bohemia, 1945–1947," in *Redrawing Nations: Ethnic Cleansing in East-Central Europe, 1944–1948*, eds. Philipp Ther and Ana Siljak (Lanham, 2001), 241.

vanguard of Czechness in a sea of Germandom. They claimed the mantle of the loyal frontiersman (hraničář), who struggled directly against Germans during the prewar years, thus proving their national pedigree. As early as May 12, 1945, the League of National Associations and Culture petitioned the government to "unconditionally and immediately evict all Germans and Magyars" and to undo all of the changes that had accompanied the Nazi takeover of the Sudetenland. They also sought to ensure that old settlers be placed in charge of local offices because they knew local conditions best.[80] That old settlers' attitudes toward Germans varied should not be surprising given the complexity of the borderland population and its history. Some old settlers were impassioned nationalists who saw Germans as their long-term enemy; others lived with and loved Germans.

New settlers who moved to the borderlands for the first time after the war were also a divided group. One fault line opened over the access to confiscated property. In particular, settlers who reached the borderlands by autumn 1945, whom I call "first comers" or "early settlers," held a distinct advantage in acquiring and retaining former German-owned property. Those who arrived later had fewer auspicious choices, despite settlement officials' continued promises of cheap attractive property. Determining who should receive the final allocation of this property became a contested process that the government did not easily resolve, and is taken up in the following chapter. The class background of new settlers, although difficult to substantiate because so many settlers changed professions or became independent farmers through settlement itself, suggests a more variegated picture than the commonly held assumption that all new settlers were from the lowest strata of the population.[81] While factory owners and independent farmers were almost entirely absent from the settlement process, a variety of employment openings drew settlers from different backgrounds. Settlers with advanced technical degrees and/or experience came to help manage borderland industries. So too did skilled workers, for much the same reasons. In addition, an array of state officials took up posts vacated by Nazi and Sudeten German administrators.[82] Even professionals, such as doctors, lawyers, accountants and teachers, assumed positions in the borderlands, although they remained in high demand. One indication that not all settlers were from the lowest social strata was the observation by one reporter that one-third of the settlers had blocked savings accounts from before or during the war, which they could put toward purchasing confiscated homes.[83]

---

[80] Doc. 38, Arburg and Staněk, *Vysídlení Němců*, II/1:279.

[81] Karel Kaplan, *The Short March: The Communist Takeover in Czechoslovakia, 1945–1948* (London, 1987), 28; Karl Kaplan, *Právda o Československu* (Prague, 1990) 135.

[82] Wingfield, 254–55.

[83] "Dejte osídlencům, co jejich jest," *Stráž severu*, May 26, 1945.

Figure 2.1 New settlers. Courtesy of the State District Archive, Jeseník

Thus, while members of the industrial and agricultural working class, as well as those whom might be called service personnel – waiters, mechanics, tailors and others – made up the majority of those who moved to the borderlands, a broader range of social backgrounds marked new settlers than historians generally have suggested.

By other measures, the overall portrait of new settlers' backgrounds appeared more homogeneous. Settlers were generally young. By May 1947, those aged thirty-four years old and under comprised nearly 63 percent of the population.[84] As Bradley Abrams points out, this demographic trend bolstered Communist movements throughout Eastern Europe after the war. He argues that, considering the experience of the young generation during the Great Depression and war, "an urge for radical social change seems expected, not just excusable."[85] In this light,

---

[84] *Soupisy obyvatelstva v Československu v letech 1946–1947*, Table 29, 540. The corresponding figure for the interior was nearly 50 percent.
[85] Abrams, 658.

many young settlers may have set out to support the efforts to construct a model society in the borderlands and, thus, shared a similar mindset with each other and settlement officials. In addition, despite a variety of regional origins, agricultural settlers largely followed similar migratory paths to the borderlands, which meant that in some places new settlers already knew each other. Enhancing this trend, the Ministry of Agriculture sponsored the relocation of settler groups from specific interior districts to specific borderland districts in late 1945.[86] While this policy had largely organizational and economic motives, in some places it likely eased settlers' transition. It also likely contributed to the creation of factions in some towns as no one town was completely homogeneous in terms of settler origins, and those of similar background often stuck together.

While it would be wrong to place too much emphasis on the similarities of any one group, certain divisions proved more important than others. Old settlers and new settlers had very different attitudes toward each other. Early military reports provide a glimpse of the suspicions against old settlers who had remained in the Sudetenland during the war. One report from Liberec, formerly the center of the *Sudetendeutsche Partei*, noted: "In the area of Liberec there are no really true (*správných*) Czechs, because those who remained here during the German occupation (which is about 25 percent of the prewar state of the Czech population) out of property motives or other greedy reasons necessarily cooperated with Germans. The majority of the current Czech population here cannot be considered reliable."[87] Old settlers sometimes provided the fodder for such attacks. The first chairman of the national committee in Josefodol, for instance, issued 683 certificates of antifascist legitimacy to a town with a prewar population of roughly 4,000 people. He later ruined his reputation when he partied with several German women, none of them his wife, on New Year's Eve in 1945. Apparently he and a few other locals used a plush confiscated villa to stage their party, where, incidentally, the Minister of Interior Václav Nosek had stayed when he had visited the region with some other officials over Christmas. All of this and more led to an investigation which later revealed that he had declared himself a German in 1939 and had attempted to join the German army during the war, but as a "Czech" his application had been rejected.[88] Such

---

[86] Slezák, *Zemědělské osidlování*, 87–99; Zprávy o činnosti Osidlovací komise Ministerstva zemědělství, various. NA, f. Národní pozemkový fond (NPF), k.10–12 inv. č. 16.

[87] Situation report from Third Division Headquarters, May 27, 1945. VHA, f. VO1, k.1 inv. č. 6. See also Doc. 80, Arburg and Staněk, *Vysídlení Němců*, II.1: 330.

[88] Investigative Report, Criminal Division of the Provincial National Committee in Prague, Branch in Jablonec nad Nisou, June 2, 1947. Report from the police headquarters in Jablonec n. N., December 4, 1945. SOkA Jablonec n. N., f. ONV, k. 29 inv. č. 52; NA, f. MV-NR k. 1808 inv. č. 1602.

national "side switchers" or "amphibians," though small in number, worked to further tarnish the reputation of all old settlers who were considered as "unreliable."[89]

Old settlers often held similarly uncompromising feelings toward their Czech brethren from the interior of the country. They blamed new settlers for the chaos and rampant pillaging immediately following the war. One old settler newspaper claimed that many settlers who came during May were Nazi collaborators or simply sought to enrich themselves at the expense of the nation. It continued, "The size of these categories is quite large and from them comes much of the resistance which we encounter during the fulfillment of the historic work in the borderlands' construction."[90] These claims meshed with the emerging image of the borderlands as a corrupt and lawless place, and shifted the focus from old settlers' supposed protection of Germans to the reckless actions of newcomers or those seeking to hide their collaborationist past. At the same time, old settlers worked to repair the image of the borderlands. They founded or re-established organizations which promoted their interests and which gave them a voice in the political control of the borderlands. In one case a Regional Committee for the Borderlands of the Czechoslovak Republic was called to order in early 1946. One of the main reasons for its creation was that its members "objected to the incorrect opinion that the interior of the state had toward the borderlands."[91] They sought to address a wide assortment of shortcomings in the borderlands, from poor housing to the lack of teachers and newspapers, by relying on regional solutions led by national committees. In this sense, old settlers hoped to control local power and reshape the borderlands according to their own priorities.

The divergent perspectives among old and new settlers about the borderlands' past and future led to some of the sharpest conflicts between them. One debate involved mixed-marriage couples, which laid bare several key issues regarding citizenship and nationality. As Benjamin Frommer argues, deliberations about the fate of mixed marriages even

---

[89] For more on amphibians and side switchers, see Chad Bryant, "Either German or Czech: Fixing Nationality in Bohemia and Moravia, 1939–1946," *Slavic Review* 61, no. 4 (2002): 683–706; Frommer, *National Cleansing*, 199–204, 243–7; Jeremy King, *Budweisers into Czechs and Germans: A Local History of Bohemian Politics* (Princeton, 2002), 194–202. For more on the category of "unreliable" inhabitants in the borderlands, see David Gerlach, "Beyond Expulsion: The Emergence of Unreliable Elements in the Postwar Czech Borderlands, 1945–1950," *East European Politics and Societies* 24, no. 2 (2010): 269–293.

[90] Jan Harus, "*Hraničář*," *Hraničář-Ústřední orgán národní jednoty severočeské*, September 27, 1946.

[91] Zápis z ustavujícího sjezdu Regionálního sboru pro pohraničí Československé republiky, February 2, 1946. SOkA Chomutov, f. ONV Vejprty, k. 2 inv. č. 53.

threw the legitimacy of the expulsions into question as some people supported Czechs married to Germans, while others considered them complicit in collaboration and sought to get rid of them.[92] Decree 33, which rescinded citizenship from Germans, stated that married women and children of Czechoslovak citizens would be allowed to apply to retain citizenship. This meant that German women married to Czechs had a way in, while German men married to Czech women were left out. Indeed, many Czech-speaking women married to German men were expelled, along with their children, and those who remained in the country were under constant attack and suspicion. Yet the debate about expelling Czechs, even those in mixed marriages, raised doubts about the total nature of the expulsions in people's minds, particularly as the organized expulsions took shape. Old settlers supported those who had often been their neighbors. For example, in April 1946 a public meeting of "frontiersmen–old settlers" pressed the president's office to find a solution to the question of German men married to Czech women.[93] This kind of pressure forced central officials to finally lift many of the repressive provisions for Germans living in mixed marriages with Czech speakers. In May 1946, the government formally restored citizenship to male German spouses, including rights such as full wages and freedom of movement.[94] The official shift in government policy, however, did not alleviate the troubles that faced mixed-marriage couples in the borderlands. Many Czechs continued to be expelled along with their German spouses, and their property continued to be confiscated.

The status of German antifascists also caused great debate in the borderlands. The provisions of Decree 33 permitted Germans who had fought against the Nazi regime to retain their citizenship. While the process of establishing someone's antifascist credentials took some time to become officially sanctioned, national committees initially distributed certificates of antifascist legitimacy in large numbers in an attempt to protect some German speakers from expulsion. This effort should not be seen as simply self-serving. That old settlers or even Sudeten German Communists or Social Democrats had a broad view of what constituted antifascist behavior demonstrated their nuanced view of the Nazi occupation. The public response to the idea of allowing antifascists to remain was much more one-sided. Articles in the press demanded recounts of the

---

[92] Frommer, "Expulsion or Integration."
[93] Letter from Ústí nad Labem, April 7, 1946. NA, f. Úřad předsednictva vlády – Běžná spisovna (ÚPV-B), k. 1032 inv. č. 11752 sign. 1364.
[94] Směrnice o úlevách pro některé osoby německé národnosti, May 27, 1946. *Předpisy z oboru působnosti OÚ a FNO: Zákony (dekrety), vládní nařízení*, vyhlášky (Prague, 1947), 2: 305–12; Frommer, "Expulsion or Integration."

antifascist certificates, and argued that all Germans were the same and needed to go. The National Socialist Party members were particularly vociferous in their condemnation of antifascists. Their pressure, in part, led the Czech Communists to disavow their German comrades and to encourage them to leave the country.[95] While the government instituted a host of measures to support and protect antifascists, they became increasingly isolated and many decided it would be better to leave. Ultimately, the antifascist label was reserved for German Communist Party members and some Social Democrats. The conditions for their transfer to Germany included the retention of their property and special transports. Roughly 100,000 antifascists and their family members left Czechoslovakia, with slightly more of them going to the western occupation zones by the end of 1946.[96]

Even determining a person's nationality became an avenue for debate between new and old settlers after the war. In late 1946 a sharp dispute erupted in Jablonec about the nationality commission of the Local National Committee on just these issues. This commission was established to ascertain which individuals should receive certificates of national reliability. It did not have the final say on citizenship – that was a matter for the District National Committee to decide – but it carried out the initial background checks and made recommendations about who should be considered a Czech. Which members of the national committee would comprise the nationality commission thus became an important matter because they would determine the future of hundreds of people in the town based on their past decisions and actions. During a plenary meeting in August 1946 the security chief of the MNV, Vladimír Škarvada, criticized a recent proposal to include old settlers on the MNV's nationality commission, arguing that they too often sympathized with Germans. The current chairman of the commission, himself an old settler, had requested the inclusion of old settlers because he believed only they understood local conditions and witnessed these people's behavior before and during the war, and therefore had better insight into the question of who was truly Czech and should retain Czechoslovak citizenship. Indeed, the Interior Ministry had ruled that a person's behavior, and not necessarily their designated nationality, should determine citizenship.[97]

---

[95] Staněk, *Odsun němců*, 281–83.

[96] Ibid., 283–84. For a more thorough treatment of the situation facing antifascists in Czechoslovakia after 1947, see Adrian von Arburg, "Zwischen Vertreibung und Integration: Tschechische Deutschenpolitik, 1947–1953." (Dissertation, Charles University, Prague 2004), 390–412.

[97] Jan Kuklík, *Mýty a realita takzvaných Benešových dekretů* (Prague, 2002), 287. For a similar connection with the Nazi designation of Jews in Germany, see Raul Hilberg, *The Destruction of European Jews*, 3rd edn. (New Haven, 2003), 1: 72–74.

However, Škarvada emphasized the possible dangers of letting old settlers influence these decisions. He noted, for example, that the first chairman of the nationality commission had a German wife whose brother had been in the *Sturmabteilung* (SA). In addition, he complained that Germans who appealed for Czechoslovak citizenship and possessed local businesses hindered settlement by leaving the national administrators uncertain about their future. He even argued that the local schools were overfilled with children who could not understand Czech, threatening the education of true Czechs.[98]

Underlying the dispute over the nationality commission was a deeper division between old and new settlers. Škarvada complained that old settlers allowed unreliable people to assume leading positions in the town after the war and thereby compromised the town's well-being. He also noted that old settlers occupied a privileged position in the town's administrative and economic life. The current nationality commission chairman argued otherwise. He questioned Škarvada's portrayal of old settlers, stating: "We suffered here far more than Czechs from the interior." He drew attention to the example of working-class Czech women who came to the region for work during the interwar period and married Germans, when such relationships were unproblematic. Because their husbands often listed them as Germans during the 1930 census, he argued that they deserved a chance to retain Czech citizenship.[99] In a later meeting on the question, Škarvada resumed his attacks against old settlers, noting that while some had proven themselves to be worthy Czechs, they were the exceptions. He then reviewed forty-one cases in which the nationality commission had approved the citizenship requests of people who had connections to Nazi organizations or questionable pasts. Other members of the MNV challenged Škarvada's presentation; the nationality commission chairperson noted that many of the cases he cited had already been overturned. Others defended old settlers' cautious approach to the nationality question. One member, for instance, argued that old settlers had worked to defend Jablonec from unreliable Czechs who moved to the borderlands to escape their collaborationist past. Another member noted that even the Interior Ministry had changed its position on the nationality question and that things were stricter now than before.[100] Both sides in this standoff couched their arguments in terms of past actions and present dilemmas about solving the nationality question.

[98] Minutes from the plenum MNV Jablonec n. N., August 13, 1946. SOkA Jablonec. n. N., f. MěNV Jablonec n. N., kn. 17, inv. č. 17.
[99] Ibid.   [100] Minutes from the plenum MěNV Jablonec n. N., October 17, 1946. Ibid.

The future of the nationality question remained uncertain. Although Škarvada was successful in limiting the influence of old settlers on the nationality committee in the short term, this did little to resolve the nationality question in Jablonec once and for all. One key difficulty was the provision from Decree 33 that gave exceptions from the loss of citizenship for Czechs who applied for German nationality because they "were forced by pressure or other special circumstances."[101] The Jablonec nationality commission struggled to define what this meant. One situation they could not resolve, for example, involved a woman who likely declared herself German because she feared losing her job. The commission also debated another set of circumstances surrounding women in mixed marriages. The commission offered two examples. The first one – where pressure was present, they argued – was when a husband declared his wife a German in her presence. The other was a case when the woman, not in her husband's presence, declared herself German and thus, it was argued, she was not pressured into doing so. The intricacies of these cases and the minutiae upon which a person's status as a Czech or German hinged made a final resolution to the nationality question impossible in many borderland towns. Out of thirty-one cases decided at the June 23, 1947, meeting, the commission recommended fifteen people for receiving Czech status, refused seven applications, and left nine without recommendation for district officials to decide.[102] That a resolution to nationality questions remained contentious two years after the war had ended reflected the ongoing power struggles between new and old settlers as much as the elusive nature of nationality itself.

Emerging Diversity in the Borderlands

The disagreements and differences between old and new settlers over nationality were just as much about resolving the past as they were about determining the future of the borderlands. Yet, these conflicts were only one aspect of the growing complexity brought by expulsion and resettlement that officials and settlers had to face. By May 1947, the new settler population in the borderlands numbered more than 1.3 million, out of a total borderland population of just over 2.2 million.[103] The vast majority of these new settlers were Czechs, mostly from the interior. Some,

---

[101] See Decree 33, sec. 5. Jech and Kaplan, *Dekrety*, 2:346.

[102] Minutes from the nationality committee, Council of the MěNV, June 21 and 23, 1947. SOkA Jablonec. n. N., f. MěNV Jablonec n. N., kn. 4, inv. č.4.

[103] Srb, *Populační, ekonomický a národnostní vývoj*, 8–11. The figures do not include children under the age of 2. The number of children born between 1945 and 1947 was 118,536,

however, were Czechs who had spent the war abroad and had repatriated after the war ended to take advantage of the benefits that resettlement offered. Others were Czech speakers from foreign countries whose ancestors had emigrated, sometimes centuries earlier, and had now returned. While together these groups of Czechs gave officials some reason to celebrate the Czechification of the region, they masked the heterogeneity and the deep divisions that existed among them. Other settler groups included Slovaks, some from Slovakia and others from Romania, Hungary and Bulgaria, again re-emigrants. Slovak speakers were at least officially welcomed as "Slavic" settlers, who would, at the very least, promote the de-Germanization of the borderlands. Still others arrived in the borderlands, including Roma, Magyars and Jews. Given that Germans and old settlers also remained, by the late 1940s the borderlands were becoming a mix of peoples with different backgrounds and with different expectations for the future.[104]

The policy of attracting re-emigrants to the borderlands meshed with the goal of making the borderlands Czech and the real need to attract more settlers in order to support the local economies. Initially, officials hoped that roughly 700,000 Czechs and Slovaks would return from foreign countries, even from beyond Europe.[105] Negotiations with various groups of Czech speakers abroad began immediately after the war. The Czechoslovak government met with a delegation of Czechs from Vienna, which represented some 40,000 Czech speakers, in the hopes of bringing many of these compatriots home. Discussions and efforts to make connections with other groups of emigrant Czechs soon followed.[106] However, it proved impossible to manufacture migration to the borderlands, for a host of reasons. People did not want to leave their current home for the unstable political and economic conditions in postwar Czechoslovakia. While officials attempted to lure Czech emigrants with offers of property, interstate negotiations over property for would-be re-emigrants were long and left them uncertain that they would receive adequate compensation for things left behind. In short, the advantages

---

most of whom were from new settler families. The difference between the two figures comprised old settlers and remaining Germans.

[104] Spurný.

[105] Helena Nosková, "Osídlovací komise ÚV KSČ a reemigrace v letech 1945–1948," *Historické studie* (1998): 118.

[106] See for instance, Doc. 26. Arburg and Staněk, *Vysídlení Němců*, II/1: 262–63; Doc. 54. Arburg and Staněk, *Vysídlení Němců*, II/1, 298–99; Doc. 73. Arburg and Staněk, *Vysídlení Němců*, II/1: 322; Joseph B. Schechtman, *Postwar Population Transfers in Europe, 1945–1955* (Philadelphia, 1962), 123–24.

for most Czech speakers living abroad did not outweigh the costs and risks that repatriation involved. In the end, only about 200,000 re-emigrants returned to Czechoslovakia after the war, and only half of those went to the borderlands by May 1947.[107]

The majority of re-emigrants came from Germany and the Soviet Union – two places that faced the greatest social and economic dislocations after the war. Many of those coming from Germany differed only slightly from repatriates (those who had left Czechoslovakia after 1938) in that they had gone to work in Germany in the 1930s and had little hope of sustaining themselves there after the war. The Czechs coming from Volhynia in the Soviet Union had even fewer options, having lived through Soviet collectivization in the 1930s, the Nazi occupation and Holocaust, as well as Polish–Ukrainian battles over the region. By that time, postwar Soviet life appeared anything but promising. Moreover, because a majority of Volhynian Czechs had served in the military and were re-emigrants, they stood to profit greatly from the benefits offered by the Settlement Office. Postwar discussions about the repatriation of Volhynian Czechs who still remained in the Soviet Union, more than 30,000 of them, were prolonged and difficult. In December 1945, representatives for the Volhynian Czechs requested that the Czechoslovak government begin to press the issue more forcefully with the Soviet government. It noted that already in April 1945 the National Front government had pledged to negotiate for the resettlement of their families, but that nothing had yet happened.[108] Soviet foot-dragging and issues of property compensation led to protracted negotiations. Several Volhynian Czechs returned to the Soviet Union rather than endure the separation. Finally, in July 1946 Czechoslovakia and the Soviet Union signed a formal agreement to permit their departure. Still, because of the difficulties in planning and organizing this large-scale migration, the Czech speakers remaining in Volhynia had to wait until 1947 to reunite with family members already living in Czechoslovakia.[109]

By 1948 more than 38,000 Volhynian Czechs had resettled in Czechoslovakia, about 26,000 of them in the borderlands. They were concentrated in large numbers only in a few places, such as the hop-growing

---

[107] Nosková, "Osídlovací komise," 118; *Soupisy obyvatelstva v Československu v letech 1946–1947*, 528; Srb, *Populační, ekonomický a národnostní vývoj*, 8. For more on re-emigrants see Jaroslav Vaculík, *Reemigrace zahraničích Čechů a Slováků v letech, 1945–1950* (Brno: 2001); Andreas Wiedemann, *"Komm mit uns das Grenzland aufbauen!" Ansiedlung und neue Strukturen in den ehemaligen Sudetengebieten 1945–1952* (Essen, 2007), 255–76.

[108] Request Velitelství voj. skupina Žatec, December 4, 1945. VHA f. MNO 1945–1946 – Volynští Češi.

[109] Jaroslav Vaculík, *Dějiny Volyňských Čechů* (Prague, 2003), 3: 44–63.

regions of Žatec and Podbořany, where initially demobilized soldiers had sought to settle.[110] The difficulty of securing property in preferred areas was one reason that Volhynian Czechs were generally dispersed throughout the Bohemian lands. In addition, settlement officials and Communist Party functionaries did not want Volhynian Czechs to comprise compact settlements with significant numbers. For a number of reasons, settlement officials had trouble securing quality farms by 1947, particularly in individual regions. Communist Party leaders, for their part, were concerned that few Communist supporters could be found among the Volhynian Czechs in Žatec and that, at best, they held antipathetic views toward communism and the Soviet system they had left behind.[111] In addition, Volhynian Czechs made efforts to sustain their unique heritage. Volhynian Czechs formed their own union, published their own newspaper and were continually vocal in their demands for better settlement opportunities. Such actions did not win them favor among leaders who sought to build unity in the borderlands. Because of difficulties with finding farmland and many officials' reluctance to give in to their demands, Volhynian Czechs existed mainly as small minorities in many towns, cities and villages throughout the borderlands. For instance, out of the 1,431 agricultural families who had settled in the Chomutov region by early 1947, 187 were Volhynian Czechs. In the village of Stadice just outside Ústí nad Labem, 5 out of the roughly 70 homes in the village were occupied by Czechs from Volhynia, one of whom later moved away.[112] While Volhynian Czechs were not able to recreate the compact settlement patterns they had in the Soviet Union, they generally saw moving to Czechoslovakia as a preferable option to staying where they were.

Slovaks were another source of recruits that settlement officials hoped to tap in order to offset the shortfall of workers and residents in the borderlands. In the official proclamations surrounding ethnic cleansing, postwar leaders spoke of Czechoslovakia as a national state of Czechs and Slovaks. Although official rhetoric about resettlement mostly revolved around Czechification, space still existed for the more general notion of welcoming Slavic settlers. Miroslav Kreysa referred to the resettlement of re-emigrants as a reversal of "the exodus of Slavic blood" that had characterized earlier periods, and that the return of Czechs and Slovaks to their homeland (*vlast'*) demonstrated success of the national revolution

---

[110] Report on reemigration, Osídlovací komise ÚV KSČ, September 25, 1948. H. Nosková, *Návrat Čechů z Volyně: Naděje a skutečnost let 1945–1954* (Prague, 1999), 141–44; Srb, *Populační, ekonomický a národnostní vývoj*, 8.

[111] Nosková, "Osídlovací komise," 126–28; Vaculík, *Reemigrace*, 90.

[112] For Chomutov, see Situation report from Osidlovaci komise, June 2, 1947. SOkA Chomutov, f. ONV Chomutov, k. 1446 inv. č. 1646; For Stadice see, Lists of national administrators, undated. AM Ústí nad Labem, f. MNV Stadice, k. 12 inv. č. 35.

and the National Front's politics.[113] What served as unifying rhetoric, however, differed from the practical needs that made Slovaks attractive to settlement officials. As the remaining Germans departed in the summer and fall of 1946, Slovaks appeared as potential laborers to fill job openings created by the German expulsions and Czech movement into other professions. In general, Slovaks in the Bohemian lands worked in low paying jobs, such as seasonal agricultural labor or construction work. They moved to the borderlands primarily in 1946 and 1947 where they also found work as miners and textile workers.[114] Many were also re-emigrants from Romania, Bulgaria and Yugoslavia. Yet Slovak speakers remained a mobile workforce; many returned to Slovakia after working for a short time in order to make some money or because conditions did not appear conducive to long-term settlement.[115]

Among the influx of settlers to the Czech borderlands were also Slovak and Hungarian speakers who were caught up in the politics of retribution facing Magyars in Slovakia. Initially Slovak officials had planned on expelling the entire Magyar population from Slovakia – nearly 600,000 of them – but due to Allied and Hungarian officials' resistance to such plans the two governments worked out an exchange, so that for every Slovak living in Hungary who returned to Czechoslovakia a Magyar living in Slovakia would have to move to Hungary. As equitable as this exchange may have seemed, from the start it was clear that more than half of the Magyars would remain in Czechoslovakia because there were only approximately 200,000 Slovaks living there. Slovak leaders decided to forcibly deport Magyars from southern Slovakia to the Czech borderlands. The Central Commission for Interior Settlement began discussions to move Magyars in late 1945 as labor shortages in agriculture began to surface, particularly in the interior parts of Bohemia and Moravia. The Czechoslovak government forced more than 9,000 Magyars to the Bohemian lands under work decrees in late 1945, but these were temporary and many later departed.[116] A more concerted effort to remove Magyars followed the signing of the exchange agreement in early 1946.

---

[113] Kreysa, *České pohraničí*, 24; Spurný, 71.

[114] Ol'ga Šrajerová and Karel Sommer, "Migrace Slováků do českých zemí v letech 1945–1948," *Slezský sborník* 96, no.1 (1998): 20–35. They note that in the borderland census of May 1947, 115,783 inhabitants had moved from Slovakia. While the vast majority of these people were Slovaks, the census was not based on ethnicity, but on place of residence in May 1945.

[115] Wiedemann, 248–55.

[116] Minutes from the 5th and 7th meetings of the ÚKVO, November 29, 1945, March 8, 1946. NA, f. MV-NR, k. 12145, s.1651/2; Adrian von Arburg, "Tak či onak," Soudobé dějiny 10, no.3 (2003): 276–77; Kaplan, *Právda o Československu*, 118–19.

While Czechoslovak officials hoped that all of the nearly 200,000 reported Slovak speakers living in Hungary would return under the deal, only some 75,000 did so.[117] As it became clear in the summer of 1946 that Slovak re-emigration from Hungary would be less than expected, Slovak leaders feared that they might lose the ability to remove the Magyar minority, which was a promise of "their" national revolution. Government leaders returned to the possibility of moving Magyars from Slovakia in 1946, again on the basis of work decrees. Government officials hoped to gain 250,000 new permanent settlers through these campaigns, but they were only able to deport some 45,000 Magyars, and, again, most of them later departed.[118]

Government leaders devised another plan to relieve pressure in southern Slovakia – one which demonstrated the hollowness of concerns for national purity in the Czech borderlands. Officials planned to "reslovakize" purported Slovaks who had been Magyarized by sending them to the former Sudetenland, where Czechification was the goal. How reslovakization was supposed to effectively function there was never fully elucidated. Emptying Slovakia of Magyars and filling the Czech borderlands with able-bodied workers were the real priorities. In a proposal from October 1946 the Settlement Office clarified plans to bring Slovaks and Magyars to the borderlands. Officials planned to disperse Hungarian speakers on farms throughout the borderlands, so that they comprised no more than 10 percent of local populations. In addition, only Hungarian speakers who had committed to reslovakization would be eligible to receive farmland. The others would have to reside in the interior parts of the country and work as wage laborers.[119] It remains unclear how many Magyarized Slovaks accepted the opportunity to move to the Czech borderlands as a part of this deal, though the figure was likely small. Despite the fact that the vast majority of Hungarian speakers applied for reslovakization, most sought merely to protect themselves from loss of property and possible expulsion from Slovakia. In 1947 the Central Reslovakization Commission approved over 200,000 requests for

[117] Several thousand Magyars were also expelled from Slovakia immediately after the war. For the situation on the Hungarian minority in Slovakia, see Štephan Šutaj, *Maďarská menšina na Slovensku v rokach 1945–1948* (Bratislava, 1993); Janics Kálmán, *Czechoslovak Policy and the Hungarian Minority, 1945–1948* (Boulder, 1982); Kaplan, *Pravda o Československu*, 85–129; Helena Nosková, "Slováci z Maďarska v národnostní politice Československa v letech 1945–1954," in *K problémům menšin v Československu v letech 1945–1989: sborník studií k národnostní politice*, ed. Helena Nosková (Prague, 2005): 53–82.
[118] There were also some 2,400 who voluntarily resettled, see Kaplan, *Pravda o Československu*, 118–21; Arburg, "Tak či oňak," 278–81.
[119] Osídlení uvolněných českých krajů slovenským a maďarským obyvatelstvem, October 30, 1946. NA. f. MPSP k. 401 inv. č.841 sign. 2306.

those who had some Czech or Slovak ancestors or spoke these languages at home; a year later, another 144,000 were approved.[120] Rather than moving to the Czech borderlands, however, most remained in temporary limbo until political conditions changed and Communist governments in Hungary and Czechoslovakia resolved their differences.

Roma became perhaps the most targeted group in the borderlands. During the first postwar years migrant Roma moved mostly from Slovakia to the Czech borderlands, particularly to the northern and western parts. In 1947 a special registration carried out by the Ministry of Interior found that nearly 17,000 of more than 100,000 Roma inhabitants statewide resided in the Bohemian lands. This figure, however, likely underestimates the actual number of Roma present there.[121] Many of the Roma migrated to the borderlands for the same reasons that brought other settlers there. As soon as they began arriving at the borderlands, however, national committees sought to limit their ability to settle in borderland towns and some took initiatives to remove them.[122] In a security report for February 1946, one official from Jablonec reported on the arrival of "gypsies" from Slovakia. He noted that they bring food which they sell to Germans or barter with them, and suggested that these gangs (*tlupy*) were engaged in other illegal activities, such as robbery. The police had recently apprehended two such gangs and dealt with them in the following way: "For the time being after a search these gangs are taken to the train station in Rychnov and from their own money a ticket to Slovakia is purchased for them. They are then sent away on the earliest train." He urgently recommended that central officials issue some instructions on the matter "so that a new gypsy question is not created."[123]

In general, however, resolving "the gypsy question" remained a local matter and one which local officials sought to directly confront. In September 1946, the District National Committee in Jablonec ordered

---

[120] Kaplan, *Pravda o Československu*, 116–17.

[121] Nina Pavelčíková, "Romské obyvatelstvo ČSR v letech 1945–1954," in *Sborník studií k národnostní politice Československa (1945–1954)*, ed. Helena Nosková (Prague, 2001), 44–45; Tomáš Haišman, "Cikánské obyvatelstvo v českém pohraničí v prvních letech osidlování," in *Etnické procesy v novoosídleneckém pohraničí- dělnictvo v etnických procesech* (Prague, 1986), 1:117.

[122] See, for instance, Minutes from ONV Jablonec n. N., September 9, 1946, SOkA Jablonec. n. N., f. MěNV Jablonec n. N., kn. 3, inv. č. 3; Minutes from meeting of MSK Vejprty, November 26, 1946. SOkA Chomutov, f. MNV Vejprty, k. 2 inv. č 12–15; Minutes from MNV Ervěnice, March 11 and 26, 1947. SOkA Chomutov, f MěNV Ervěnice, k. 2 inv. č. 125; Minutes of the Local National Committee Česká Kamenice, April 20, 1946, SOkA Děčín, f. MNV Česká Kamenice, k. 1 inv. č. 40.

[123] Monthly report on political activities, Jablonec nad Nisou, March 1, 1946. SOkA Jablonec, f. ONV Jablonec, k. 29, inv. č. 52. See also Gerlach, "Beyond Expulsion," 280.

the creation of a labor camp for "gypsies and others shirking work."[124] Although the Ministry of Interior would later discuss similar plans, they did not lead to a formal statewide policy. Jablonec officials developed other plans that involved confining Roma to a few homes in the same area, "so that they would not be spread around the town."[125] Compared to the approach of some other districts, such treatment seemed mild. For example, in the district of Jeseník, the District National Committee simply noted in its January 2, 1947, meeting that, due to complaints against Roma, it forbade them from residing in the district and that those who were already there were to be expelled (*vyhoštění*).[126] Local officials' attitudes toward Roma remained intolerant and xenophobic during these years and they considered Roma as a visible blight on the borderlands.

Volhynian Czechs, Slovaks, Magyars and Roma, regardless of where they came from, were not easily integrated into the borderlands. Slovaks and Czech re-emigrants, who expected equal treatment and certain advantages owing to their Slavic status, were often disappointed by the situation there and departed. Despite the shortage of workers following the German expulsions, Slovaks were treated as second-class citizens. Employers often short-changed Slovak workers and these broken wage agreements encouraged more departures.[127] Slovaks and re-emigrants also faced discrimination that was usually reserved for Roma or Magyars. Indeed, in the postwar period one indication of the increasing diversity of the borderlands were the ways in which discrimination became indiscriminate; Czech settlers began to see all minorities as suspect. A report to security officials from July 1946 listed several difficulties facing re-emigrants and repatriates from Germany: they were imprisoned without hearings, put into internment camps, separated from their families and dispossessed of their property.[128] During the summer of 1946 as the town of Vejprty was experiencing a severe loss of workers because of German transfers, local officials took aim at immigrants from Slovakia. In August the Local Administrative Committee in Vejprty carried out health inspections of arriving Slovaks and Roma. It

---

[124] Letter to the Security referent at the ONV in Jablonec, October 3, 1946. SOkA Jablonec, f. ONV Jablonec, k. 18 inv. č. 39.

[125] Minutes from the meeting of the MěNV in Jablonec n. N., November 29, 1946 SOkA Jablonec n. N., f. MěNV Jablonec, kn. 3, inv. č. 3.

[126] Minutes from the meeting of the ONV Jeseník, January 2, 1947. SOkA Jeseník, f. ONV Jeseník, k. 135 inv. č. 119.

[127] Šrajerová and Sommer, 24, 29; Minutes from the meeting of government officials "The question of settling the borderlands," November 22, 1946. NA, f. 23 a.j. 349/1.

[128] Report on repatriation and reemigration, Sbor národní bezpečnosti, Zemské velitelství v Brné, July 2, 1946. SOkA Bruntál, f. ONV Krnov I k. 217. inv. č. 262.

also ordered that Slovaks without proof that they were delegated for work in Bohemia be sent back. This provision was later extended to Roma and Magyars as well. As Slovaks were being threatened with expulsion, local authorities accused one group of them of using furniture to heat their homes; they escaped arrest by leaving town.[129] An article in *Sentinel of the North*, published during the same period, expressed the frustrations that led to such rulings. The author was a Social Democratic leader and a member of the District National Committee in Liberec who supported the Czech vision of the borderlands. In addition to demanding the expulsion of all Germans at any price, he drew attention to a group of fifty "Magyar-speaking gypsies" from Slovakia who "in their short stay in the borderlands, has produced a fine file of SNB reports." He continued: "Are we replacing our hard-working people with Czech blood with descendants of the 'courageous' Arpad and their blood of related nomads?" He appealed for Czech souls who are able and have a taste for work to come to the borderlands, otherwise he feared the borderlands would remain filled with minorities.[130]

The various groups living in the borderlands by 1947 did little to support settlement leaders' vision of the borderlands as a Czechified region that stood in defense of the nation. In some ways settlement officials themselves worked against this goal by simply trying to find anyone "Czech" or "Slavic" enough to move in and take the place of Germans in the borderlands. Their rhetoric of Slav solidarity dissolved when faced with the practical needs of the borderlands. In many places a diverse mix of people had emerged, which in turn often elicited reproaches from local officials and early settlers. From another perspective, the diversity underscored the challenges facing resettlement officials. It has been estimated that together, re-emigrants, remaining Germans, Roma, Slovaks and other foreigners comprised roughly a third of the borderland population.[131] If we include old settlers into this equation, not to mention the different regions from which Czech settlers from the interior had moved, the diversity of origin and background in the postwar borderlands was greater than it ever had been. Despite the positive spin that settlement officials put on the overall numbers of settlers in the borderlands, the realities were not always what they seemed. The results were continued conflict, among settlers and between local and central

---

[129] Minutes from meeting of MSK Vejprty, August 14 and 28, September 18, November 6, 1946. SOkA Chomutov, f. MNV Vejprty, k. 2 inv. č 12–15.
[130] J. Veverka, "Ne svévole, ale pořadek," June 7, 1946, *Stráž severu.*
[131] František Čapka, Lubomír Slezák and Jaroslav Vaculík, *Nové osídlení pohraničí po druhé světové válce* (Brno, 2005), 188; Spurný, 125.

officials, and continued migration as many people left one borderland town in search of better prospects elsewhere, or departed from the borderlands altogether.

The mass migrations triggered by expulsion and resettlement in combination with the reorganization of state power following the war created instability and opportunity in the borderlands. Instability flowed from the huge influx of settlers and the conflicting agendas over local control. National committees were rife with divisions, not only because of party differences, but because of the different perspectives of old and new settlers, as well as the presence of many corrupt members. Further instability ensued from the composition of different settler groups, some of whom had been forced to move there. Czechs perceived them as outsiders who did not belong, and they targeted them for removal when possible. Such actions meshed with the tenor and practice of ethnic cleansing. Opportunities emerged for individuals to reap rewards in property and power, as the case of Česká Kamenice demonstrates. Resettlement also offered the opportunity for settlement officials to remake the borderlands. They sought a rational approach to this problem and believed they could control settlement through enticements and good planning. Their plans failed in a number of respects, however, as settlers had already flooded the borderlands, national committees staked out their own positions of power and increasing ethnic diversity undermined the goal of Czechification. As we shall see in the next chapters, these problems were exacerbated by conflicts over property and labor. While resettlement officials considered the borderlands a tabula rasa for their grandiose plans, postwar realities made such visions impossible to implement.

3   Persian Rugs and Well-Appointed Farms: The Politics of Expropriation

Confiscation Decrees

On February 14, 1946, authorities in Vejprty apprehended a national administrator sending a Persian rug from the Gammnitzer factory to his wife in Prague. When they searched his house, the police found other items from the firm already packed for shipping, including more rugs, some paintings, a table clock and a crystal punch bowl with cups. The man denied the accusation that he was attempting to steal national property. A German woman who worked at the factory knew better, however, and testified that the items indeed belonged to the confiscated factory's former owner and were thus state property. Other rugs and works of art from the factory, the police noted, were already missing. For the officials the worst aspect of the investigation was that they had to use Germans' testimonies to break the case; the officer noted that this was "very unfortunate for Czech honor." Indeed, it was a "humiliating act."[1] In another case, the police detained a man traveling by train from Ústí nad Labem to Prague with two rugs, which he claimed to have legitimately purchased. The police suspected that the man was illegally trafficking Persian rugs. When they searched his home they found eleven more rugs, which they believed he bought from Germans in Ústí and the surrounding area, even though Germans no longer had the right to sell their belongings.[2] Such cases, repeated countless times throughout the borderlands, were not only harmful to "Czech honor," but, more importantly, diminished the amount and quality of property left for new settlers and projected a negative image of the borderlands. These cases also reveal the multifaceted relationships that grew among Czechs and Germans in the postwar borderlands. Prior to their expulsion, Germans acted both as informants of Czechs' misdeeds and as suppliers of property. These stories remind us that governments and laws do not determine property relations, but that people do. In

[1] Case of Mr. B. Státní okresní archiv (SOkA) Chomutov, f. Místní národní výbor (MNV) Vejprty, karton (k.) 16 inventární číslo (inv. č.) 20.
[2] Archiv města (AM) Ústí n. L., f. Městský národní výbor (MěNV) Ústí n. L. Soupis majetku, k. 63 signatura (sign.) 350.

the same way, property relations are a reflection of human relations. Studying property transactions and transgressions in the postwar German–Czech borderlands demonstrates how people's interests in social mobility and personal gain fueled ethnic cleansing.

This chapter explores the varied ways in which property matters influenced the expulsions. Dispossessing Germans through legal means became one of the first and most widespread sanctions in the process of ethnic cleansing. Not only did these measures make Germans prostrate to local officials and marauding military units, it also gave the central government the ability to decide how such property should be distributed. Such decisions became a source of political debate and conflict, and highlight the degree to which central officials sought to gain power and influence through confiscated property. Of course, laws meant little to many Czechs after the war, who went to the borderlands in search of German wealth. These gold-diggers (*zlatokopové*) posed short-term problems for national committees that attempted to control the distribution of such property and simultaneously undermined the long-term potential of the resettlement program. Gold-diggers also established the image of the borderlands as a place of lawlessness and greed, which affected not only people's perceptions of the region, but also government policies for it. In this atmosphere of suspicion and mistrust, national administrators, who sought to start a new life in the borderlands based on confiscated property, remained without ownership rights and uncertain of their future. The government's attempts to remove unqualified or suspect national administrators through revisions only increased settlers' apprehensions and led to discord between local and central officials. Germans played an important role here too. They identified Czech gold-diggers and could be important informants about confiscated property. The means for appealing the confiscation decrees also opened avenues for Germans to challenge the very notion of the expulsions. Finally, this chapter explores how the Communist Party sought to utilize confiscated German property for its own political gains. While Communists were not the only party attempting to leverage confiscated property for their own ends, they were most effective at playing on settlers' fears, at securing national administrators' support and at using the national committee system to their benefit.

The confiscation of private property after World War II was hardly unique to Czechoslovakia. Plunder and expropriation were common features of warfare stretching back centuries. After World War I, the victors imposed a harsh settlement on the Central Powers that included the loss of territories and a large indemnity from Germany. The restructuring of property relations occurred across all of Central and Eastern

Europe. Most notably, in Soviet Russia the Bolsheviks altered property relations after the 1917 revolution by nationalizing factories and by allowing peasants to seize noble, state and church lands. The revolution in Russia, not to mention the Hungarian and German uprisings, underscored the threat of social unrest and fostered the political will to reorganize land ownership. Between the wars, many states in the region attempted to implement far-reaching land reform, though with only limited success. In Czechoslovakia a "Confiscation Act" was passed in 1919 that expropriated estates over 150 hectares, but still compensated owners.[3] One element of the interwar land reform policies was a latent effort to displace ethnic minority landholders in favor of those in the majority. In Poland, for instance, the government not only targeted German estate owners in the western provinces for land expropriation at a higher rate than Poles, it also only distributed land to Poles, particularly to veterans and political refugees from the Soviet Union.[4] Property policies in interwar Central and Eastern Europe served as a tool for nationalist politicians to align their goals with social and economic priorities.

Nazi rule in Central and Eastern Europe proved equally transformative regarding property and property rights. Nazis taxed and confiscated property to simultaneously isolate Jews and promote Germans. Aryanization, first understood as the forced sale of Jewish businesses to non-Jewish owners, was already "a creeping process" in different parts of Germany by 1933. German banks, businesses, and individuals hastened to acquire Jewish commercial property, even before official regulations permitted it. They used informal measures and direct pressure to gain access to Jewish businesses.[5] In Austria, following the March 1938 Anschluss with the Reich, so-called "wild commissars" seized Jewish businesses at will. These were not authorized government caretakers, as *Treuhänder* later became, but

---

[3] Ivan Berend, "Agriculture," in *Economic Structure and Performance between the Two Wars*, eds. M.C. Kaser and E.A. Radice, vol. 1 of *The Economic History of Eastern Europe, 1919–1975* (Oxford, 1985), 152–62; Joseph Rothschild, *East Central Europe between the Two World Wars* (Seattle, 1974), 12–13; Derek Aldcroft and Steven Morewood, *Economic Change in Eastern Europe since 1918* (Brookfield, 1995), 17–20.

[4] Richard Blanke, *Orphans of Versailles: The Germans in the Western Borderlands, 1918–1939* (Lexington, 1993), 112–15; Dieter Gosewinkel and Stefan Meyer, "Citizenship, Property Rights and Dispossession in Postwar Poland (1918 and 1945)," *European Review of History* 16, no. 4 (2009): 578–83.

[5] Frank Bajohr, '*Aryanisation*' *in Hamburg: The Economic Exclusion of Jews and the Confiscation of Their Property in Nazi Germany*, trans. George Wilkes (New York, 2002), 76; Hans Safrian, "Expediting Expropriation and Expulsion: The Impact of the 'Vienna Model' on Anti-Jewish Policies in Nazi Germany, 1938," *Holocaust and Genocide Studies* 14, no.3 (2000): 398; Raul Hilberg, *The Destruction of European Jews*, 3rd edn. (New Haven, 2003), 1: 97–98.

self-appointed managers out for personal gain.[6] Following *Kristallnacht* in November, the Nazi government further intensified and codified Aryanization in the Reich. By the end of 1938, the Nazis forced Jews to relinquish their property through administrative and legal means. Although top Nazi Party officials wanted to ensure that the process remained orderly and that qualified businessmen took over Jewish firms, a property rush, benefiting mainly lower-level party members, occurred.[7] Once the war began, the Nazis expanded and accelerated property expropriation. Denying Jews the right to existence in Germany and other occupied territories formed a core piece of Nazi ideology. By seizing their property, Nazi leaders made plans and policies for the Jews' expulsion and destruction easier to implement. At the same time, redistributing Jewish property provided one way for the Nazis to maintain the support of German citizens.[8] The Nazi program of confiscation fit both ideological and practical goals of the regime.

A similar blend of local actions and state intervention drove the process of property confiscation in the Czechoslovak borderlands and across Central and Eastern Europe after the war. First, Soviet armies pillaged and raped their way across much of the region. Looting and military occupation went hand in hand. Soviet soldiers took what they liked from the local inhabitants, but could only return home with movable property, which ranged from watches to wardrobes.[9] In postwar Poland, Red Army soldiers not only plundered Germans, they also harassed many Polish inhabitants.[10] Property confiscation often served as one of the first legal measures against Germans and other minorities prior to their expulsion. A Polish decree of March 2, 1945 subjected German property to seizure and became a prelude to widespread looting.[11] Local officials and actors often did not wait for central permission to commence expropriations, which quickly assumed the appearance of a gold rush. The *szabrownicy*, often Poles from districts bordering the so-called Recovered Territories, roamed throughout heavily German-populated

---

[6] Safrian, 395. The government also used commissars of Jewish property in the Sudetenland in 1938, see Harold James, *The Deutsche Bank and the Nazi Economic War against the Jews* (Cambridge, 2001), 164.

[7] Hilberg, 1: 122–27; Bajohr, 231–57.

[8] Götz Aly, *Hitler's Beneficiaries: Plunder, Racial War, and the The Nazi Welfare State*, trans. Jefferson Chase (New York, 2006).

[9] Norman Naimark, *Russians in Germany: A History of the Soviet Zone of Occupation, 1945–1949* (Cambridge, 1995), 167, 174.

[10] David Curp, *A Clean Sweep? The Politics of Ethnic Cleansing in Western Poland, 1945–1960* (Rochester, 2006), 51–52.

[11] Richard Blanke, "Polish-speaking Germans and Ethnic Cleansing of Germany East of the Oder-Neise," in *Ethnic Cleansing in Twentieth Century Europe*, eds. Steven Vardy and T. Hunt Tooley (Boulder, 2003), 287.

areas in search of enrichment.[12] Even after the Polish government established regulations governing property confiscation, local Polish officials
acted as they saw fit. Often this meant engaging in smuggling activities
themselves, which created "an atmosphere of officially sanctioned
lawlessness."[13] Similar processes occurred in Soviet-occupied Germany,
where local Soviet officials as well as German authorities sequestered the
property of accused Nazis.[14] As Jan Gross notes: "Such actions conspicu-
ously demonstrated that property rights were dependent on a state's good
will and could be eliminated with the stroke of a pen."[15]

The decrees and regulations which expropriated German property in
Czechoslovakia did not form a consistent and coherent whole, and the
leaders who wrote them sought maximum gains with little liability. The
property seized by the Czechoslovak state did not form part of the reparations that it received from Germany. At the Paris Conference on
Reparations in November and December 1945, Czechoslovak authorities
successfully excluded from their reparation receipts the property of
Germans who were not citizens of Germany "at the time of occupation
or annexation of this country by Germany."[16] This provision applied to
all Germans who had been citizens of Czechoslovakia until the Nazis
annexed the borderland areas in 1938. In a seemingly contradictory
fashion, the Czechoslovak government had used the fact that the Nazis
gave Reich citizenship to Sudeten Germans in November 1938 as a
means to deny them citizenship through Decree 33.[17] Furthermore, the
decrees that confiscated property did not take the Germans' prewar
citizenship status as the basis for their expropriation. Instead, the government confiscated property based on people's nationality, which it defined
in different ways. In the case of Decree 5, which established national
administrators as the state's caretakers of enemy property, and Decree 12,
which confiscated agricultural holdings, nationality was determined "by
their choice for German nationality in any census since 1929" or by virtue

[12] Curp, 42–43; Claudia Kraft, "Who is a Pole, and Who Is a German? The Province of Olsztyn
in 1945," in *Redrawing Nations: Ethnic Cleansing in East-Central Europe, 1944–1948*, eds.
Philipp Ther and Ana Siljak (Lanham, 2001), 114.
[13] Kraft, 114.   [14] Naimark, 171.
[15] Jan Gross, "War as Revolution," in *The Politics of Retribution in Europe: World War II and
Its Aftermath*, eds. Istvan Deak, Jan Gross, and Tony Judt (Princeton, 2000), 22.
[16] Yugoslav authorities also supported the measure. Jan Kuklík, *Mýty a realita takzvaných
Benešových dekretů* (Prague, 2002), 322. See Paris Agreement on Reparations, Part I,
Article 6, Section D, accessed on October 2, 2015, www.cvce.eu/content/publication/2
003/12/15/5c0dfcd9-2af2-431b-8cbf-e8e288aef30e/publishable_en.pdf.
[17] The Agreement on Citizenship that made borderlanders of German nationality into
Reich citizens came into effect on November 11, 1938. Other regulations followed. See
Karel Jech and Karel Kaplan, eds., *Dekrety prezidenta republiky 1940–1945: Dokumenty*. 2
vols. (Brno, 1995), 1:358–60.

of having joined any German group or organization."[18] Some ministers immediately realized the drawbacks of this principle. In May 1945, Interior Minister Václav Nosek noted that the previous census from December 1, 1930, did not request data about nationality, but was based on an individual's "mother tongue" (*mateřský jazyk*). Citing just one possible complication, he asked: "What will be the position of Austrian citizens?"[19]

The ad hoc manner in which the government constructed legal measures to expropriate Sudeten Germans reflected the nature of retributive justice. While Decree 33 legitimized the expulsions, the postwar confiscation decrees (i.e. Decrees 5, 12 and 108) explicitly penalized the Sudeten Germans for their prewar support of the *Sudetendeutsche Partei*. The confiscation decrees substantiated their guilt and demanded payment for their transgressions. For instance, the Justification Report attached to Decree 108, which confiscated German non-agricultural property in October 1945, stated: "[P]rimarily all Germans and Magyars, who identified with the program of Hitler and his willing accomplices in Hungary, accepted responsibility for all the crimes their regimes perpetrated and as a member of an enemy state became liable for damages they caused." The report noted that more than 90 percent of Sudeten German voters had supported the *Sudetendeutsche Partei* in the 1938 local elections, which, it claimed, aided the Nazi dismemberment of the country.[20] In one debate about confiscation, state leaders dismissed proposals to compensate Germans for their property by arguing that aside from those Sudeten Germans who had actively opposed the Nazis, the rest "carry collective responsibility for all the crimes committed by Germans against the Czech nation and republic, and therefore compensation does not belong to them."[21] Other explanations for expropriation and against compensation were more complex, but still rested on the idea of collective crime and punishment.[22]

While National Front leaders enjoyed claiming the right to German property in the name of the nation, the state ultimately controlled it. Seized German assets helped the state to implement economic restructuring

---

[18] Compare Decree 5, sec. 6 with Decree 12, sec.2; Jech and Kaplan, 1:216, 276.
[19] Excerpt from the minutes of the government meeting, May 25, 1945; Jech and Kaplan, 1:284.
[20] Důvodová zpráva k vládou schválenému znění dekretu o konfiskací nepřátelského majetku, October 13, 1945. Jech and Kaplan, 2:882.
[21] Proposed response to President Beneš' comments about confiscation Decree 12, June 13, 1945. Jech and Kaplan, 1:303.
[22] See for instance, Jan Procházka, *Konfiskace majětku nepřátel a zrádců v ČSR* (Prague, 1946); V. Řezníček, "Rozdělování konfiskovaného majetku, jeho předpoklady, přípravy a dosavadní průběh," *Osidlování*, December 12, 1946.

programs at little cost. Confiscated property paid for many of the resettlement program expenses, including loans to settler-farmers and a cash incentive offered to other settlers needed in critical borderland industries, such as mining.[23] Proceeds from the sale of confiscated property were used to help offset currency reform in 1953. Confiscated factories bolstered the nationalization of industry, as discussed in Chapter 5. Confiscated property also served as the basis for land reform, though government leaders did not always agree about the details. The Košice Program, which outlined the National Front government's agenda in April 1945, made land reform a cornerstone of its economic program. Article XI of that program contained the broad outlines of Decree 12. It demanded the confiscation of German and Hungarian lands without compensation and promised to sell such property to Czechs and Slovaks at low prices.[24] In June 1945, however, President Beneš raised objections to confiscating Sudeten German land without counting it toward the reparation payments. He had earlier promised Allied leaders that the property of transferred individuals would not be confiscated without compensation.[25] He was also worried about future claims that might arise if compensation was not made. Nevertheless, the rest of the government's leaders sought to take advantage of the opportunity to take what they could get from the Germans without having to account for it.

While National Front ministers unanimously agreed that the state should not compensate Germans for their property, the issue of how much settlers should pay for confiscated farmland created sharp debate. The Communists proposed that payments should be the equivalent of no more than two years' harvest. The Minister of Finance argued that such a payment grossly undervalued German farms and suggested that it be increased to three or more years. President Beneš and others supported this view, in part because they sought a bigger return from confiscated property to help offset losses from impending currency reform, which Nazi occupation had necessitated.[26] Communists overcame objections to their proposal through a mixture of

---

[23] The supplement was aimed primarily at state employees and industrial workers and amounted to only a small fraction of receipts from confiscated property. See Návrh vládního usnesení o jednorázovém platovém příspěku osídlovacím pro veřejně a některé jiné zaměstance v pohraničí, Osidlovácí úřad (OÚ), May 14, 1946. AM Ústí n. L., f. MěNV Ústí n. L., k. 2 inv.č. 24.

[24] *Program první Československé vlády Národní fronty* (Prague, 1955), 20–21.

[25] President Beneš' comments on the proposal for the decree on the confiscation of agricultural property (Decree 12), June 12, 1945. Jech and Kaplan, 1:295, 296 n.6; See also Jan Rychlík, "Pozemková reforma v českých zemích v letech 1945–1948." *Zemědělství na rozcestí, 1945–1948.* Sborník příspěvků z mezinárodní konference konané ve dnech 22–23 September 1998 (Uherské Hradiště, 1998), 9.

[26] Excerpt from the minutes from the 29th meeting of the government, June 13, 1945. Jech and Kaplan, 1:296–303.

nationalist and populist arguments. Party leader Klement Gottwald argued that "the confiscation of land should not lead to the enrichment of the state," but, rather, should be in the hands of the people.[27] The outspoken Communist Minister of Information, Václav Kopecký, attacked proposals to increase settlers' payments for farmland, arguing that it would appear that the government supported "the propertied strata." Julius Ďuriš, the Minister of Agriculture, made cheap land reform a matter of state survival. He argued that "such proposals and suggestions against the text of the decree from the highest echelons destroy national unity and particularly the unity of the state and both of its nations."[28] In the end, Communists successfully held the rest of the government to their terms for the sale of confiscated farmland. The broad agreement for the rapid redistribution of land and the fact that dispossessing Germans had cost the government little gave the Communists the necessary leverage to win this debate.

As central officials worked out the policies and laws in the summer and fall of 1945, Czechs scrambled to the borderlands and seized German property on their own, setting the stage for future disputes about who owned what. A sense that everyone was stealing former German property conditioned Czech settlers to behave in ways that gave little consideration to the government's policies. The question of how to best utilize seized assets became contentious and divisive among Czechs, both within the government and without. Settlers squabbled over the spoils, as did politicians, which hindered a definitive solution for transfer of ownership rights. Some Czechs turned to former Sudeten German owners for help in finding and managing seized property, even though they were labeled the enemy. Germans, in turn, buried their possessions or used personal relationships with Czechs in an effort to retain their belongings. As expulsions accelerated in 1945, so too did settlers', politicians' and Germans' attempts to control confiscated property.

Gold-diggers

"The gold-diggers (*Goldgräber*) poured into the German area like the ravens in the wild, nothing but shabbily dressed, uneducated characters. A picture of Stalin in a scraped up briefcase was all of the property these questionable people had."[29] Many expellees considered the first Czech

---

[27] Excerpt from the minutes from the 26th meeting of the government, June 4, 1945. Ibid., 1:289–90.
[28] Excerpt from the minutes from the 29th meeting of the government, June 13, 1945. Ibid., 1:296–303.
[29] Erlebnisbericht Arthur Becke, n.d. Lastenausgleich Archiv, Bayreuth, Germany (LAA), Ost-Dokumentation (Ost-Dok) 2, Supplement Freiwaldau-Gablonz 294b, 1.

arrivals in the borderlands as people simply in search of immediate spoils. Contemporary Czechs likewise equated gold-diggers with all settlers who moved to the borderlands in 1945. The widespread looting and misuse of confiscated German property was not simply a matter of image, either. Because property stood at the center of the resettlement program, protecting confiscated property became a necessary and important first step for rebuilding the borderlands. The postwar pilfering of Sudeten German property thus threatened to undermine the entire project. People who went to the borderlands with the sole intent of profiting from the expropriation of Sudeten Germans added to the instability and disorder brought by expulsions, and left little for later settlers who hoped to use German property to build a new existence there.

Gold-diggers can be defined in a number of ways. In contemporary terms, the definition evolved from those Czechs who rushed to the borderlands in the summer of 1945 in search of quick gain, to those who abused their positions as national administrators and lived well by embezzling the assets of confiscated businesses and farms. Strictly speaking, gold-diggers looted, but settlers who became national administrators of a Sudeten German farm, house or business in order to steal property, as in the Gammnitzer case mentioned earlier, or to siphon off the business's earnings were gold-diggers of a slightly higher order. Other settlers who sold goods on the black market were called gold-diggers, though Czechs in the interior who engaged in similar practices avoided this label. Despite the difficulty of drawing sharp distinctions between such practices, "gold-diggers" is used here to describe those who sought to remove or misuse confiscated property for their personal benefit. In this sense, Czechs from the interior as much as those who settled in the borderlands comprised the pool of possible gold-diggers.

Gold-diggers played a central role in shaping the postwar borderlands. First, they had a free-for-all attitude toward expropriated property that created an atmosphere in which people easily overlooked local and central government's regulations against the theft and false accounting of former German assets. Such actions and attitudes weakened settlement policies that revolved around offering confiscated property to lure would-be settlers. Farms, homes and businesses that had been stripped of furniture and equipment offered little to those settlers who came to start a new life with few possessions of their own. In addition, the borderlands came to be seen in the eyes of many Czechs as a land of gold-diggers.[30] Newspaper

---

[30] Gregor Thum suggests a similar image existed in cleansed areas of western Poland. Gregor Thum, "Cleansed Memory: The New Polish Wrocław (Breslau) and the Expulsion of the Germans," in *Ethnic Cleansing in Twentieth Century Europe*, 337–38;

reports, jokes and official commentary reinforced this image and painted a one-dimensional portrait of the borderlands focused solely on its short-comings. The sense that property was disappearing or being misused became prevalent among national committee members and settlement officials. This notion, in turn, supported invasive government policies, such as house and luggage searches and other restrictions, which further reinforced suspicions of corruption and illicit activity among Czechs and others in the borderlands.[31] In addition, the more that people believed that others engaged in the practice of "illegally" taking German property, the more they appeared willing to do so too. Although documenting the extent of gold-digging is difficult because of its surreptitious nature, during the summer and fall of 1945 a variety of sources demonstrate the ways that gold-diggers pilfered confiscated property and altered govern-ment plans and people's lives.

Military units pillaged first. Soviet soldiers in the northern parts of the country regularly raided local Sudeten Germans' property and took what they wanted or needed. "The Russians, after all, had been used to 'take' everything during the first days if they liked it. Especially watches. They took those wherever they found them, no matter whether the looter had already one or two. Jewelry of any description had also been taken. And first and foremost alcohol if it could be found anywhere."[32] As the Soviet army handed military operations over to Czechoslovak authorities during the summer, the Czechoslovak Army, partisans and Revolutionary Guards took up where the Soviets had left off. As one German put it: "Money and valuables appeared to be too little for the Czech partisans and he asked if we perhaps had not put out everything and threatened, that he would dump out our suitcase and rucksacks and drive us out of there without any linens or clothes."[33] The looting by military personnel continued into the fall and could take brutalizing turns. In one case, a search for hidden Persian rugs led to a German's imprisonment and torture:

The two NCOs then went at my back, loins, thighs and calves with leather belts, rubber truncheons and whips. I could hardly speak any more, but I kept trying to tell them that I could not possibly know what they wanted to know from me

Gregor Thum, *Uprooted: How Breslau Became Worcław During the Century of Expulsions*, trans. Tom Lampert and Allison Brown (Princeton, 2011), 118–26.

[31] Tomáš Staněk, *Odsun Němců z Československu, 1945–1948* (Prague, 1991) 72, 84; Lubomír Slezák, *Zemědělské osídlování pohraničí českých zemí po druhé, světové válce* (Brno, 1978), 45–47, 54–55.

[32] Report no. 12, Dr. August Lassmann, n.d.; Theodor Schieder, ed., *Documents on the Expulsion of the Germans from Eastern-Central Europe. The Expulsion of the German Population from Czechoslovakia*, vol. 4, trans. G.H. de Sausmarez (Bonn, 1960), 353.

[33] Erlebnisbericht Richard Klein, n.d., LAA, Ost-Dok 2, Aussig 240, 58.

because I had never seen and never owned the Persian rugs. Finally, after I was beaten half-unconscious again and my body was covered from top to bottom with welts suffused with blood (as my wife observed later), the two monsters left me alone.[34]

Local Czech officials constantly complained about military groups' banditry in the borderlands as well. In one investigation, the Local National Committee (MNV) in Polevsko complained that two companies of the 28th Infantry Regiment absconded with two motorcycles, four bikes, a couple of typewriters, dozens of provisions and other odds and ends from local Sudeten Germans after threatening to shoot them.[35]

Indeed, participation in military or paramilitary units in the borderlands provided an avenue for immediate enrichment. For instance, military authorities discovered a letter from a mother to a son in the army in which she pleaded: "Everyone already received full suitcases from the borderlands; only I have nothing still."[36] In another case, a camp guard found three watches in a Sudeten German's baby carriage during an entrance search at an internment camp. The guard, Anežka Rumplíková, returned the watches to their place and instructed another guard to bring the woman to her cell. A few minutes later Rumplíková came to the cell and removed the watches from their hiding place along with a ring and slid them into her own pocket, refusing to respond to the woman's pleas for compassion. Such incidents were common during the summer expulsions. Unique to this case was that officials caught Rumplíková and she had to answer to charges of theft. In her defense, she mentioned that she had joined the partisans at the end of the war to make the Germans pay for what they had done to her. Her defense for the theft of jewelry and other belongings was that "all the camp employees steal, so I was allowed to do this as well."[37] This comment led to a wider investigation, following which police officials charged the commander of the camp and another guard for embezzlement and fraud. Rumplíková finally tried to fool local authorities with a letter allegedly from the Defense Ministry, which requested that she be allowed to retain possession of these goods as payment for her services as a partisan. When this plot failed, she broke down and admitted that she had stolen the items, but she still believed that they truly belonged to her. The

[34] Report No. 129, N. N., May 23, 1946. Scriptorium, accessed on December 10, 2015, www.wintersonnenwende.com/scriptorium/english/archives/whitebook/desg39.html.
[35] Zápis o stěhovací akci, Národní výbor Polevsko, June 20, 1945. Vojenský historický archiv (VHA) Prague, f. Velitelství první oblasti (VO1), k. 49 inv. č. 2763–2801.
[36] Report from Hlávní velitelství Sbor národní bezpečnosti (SNB), Liberec, May 28, 1945. Narodni archive, Prague (NA), f. Ministerstvo vnitra – Nosek (MV-N), k. 227 inv. č. 146.
[37] Testimony of Anežka Rumplíková, October 31, 1945. Státní okresní archiv (SOkA) Bruntál, f. Okresní národní výbor (ONV) Krnov I, k. 1 inv. č. 60.

belief that "everyone was doing it" was a common refrain in property investigations. The leader of the 28th Infantry Regiment repeated this line during an investigation about theft accusations concerning his unit.[38] This notion emerged from widespread plundering and further supported it. It demonstrated people's sense of entitlement to German property based not on laws or popular justice, but as a developing social norm toward property.

The looting reached its peak during the summer of 1945 when the expulsions were in full swing. Much of the movable property was taken out of the borderlands. Sudeten Germans frequently referred to this dynamic in their testimonies. For instance, as one man reported: "Thousands came from inner Bohemia by train and on the road with empty bags and suitcases and a greater part of them soon returned with ample booty."[39] Popular accounts in the press corroborate the Germans' testimonies. Satirical journals frequently ridiculed gold-diggers, while borderland newspapers condemned their activities. Items that could be transported easily, such as rugs, radios, furniture and clothing, formed the bulk of outgoing goods. Many attempted to smuggle their goods by train. Prague was often the preferred destination, though many gold-diggers came from neighboring interior districts, as well.[40] Czechs found easy access to Sudeten German goods following local expulsions. For instance, on June 14, 1945 authorities rounded up resident Germans in the Krnov district and sent them to the school following a reported shooting incident. This offered an excellent opportunity for settlers to move from house to house and take what they wished, uninhibited by the presence of former owners and unhindered by local authorities who were busy collecting Germans.[41]

---

[38] Statement of František Voves, n.d., Doc. 328C. Adrian von Arburg and Tomáš Staněk, eds., *Vysídlení Němců a proměny českého pohraničí, 1945–1951: Dokumenty z českých archivů*, vol. II.3, *Akty hromadného násilí v roce 1945 a jejich vyšetřování* (Středokluky, 2011), accompanying CD-ROM.

[39] Erlebnisbericht Dr. Franz Bardachzi, Burghausen, August 31, 1948. LAA, Ost-Dok 2, Aussig 240, 8.

[40] See, for examples, KNS-214/114 z r.1946, Zemský národní výbor (ZNV) Prague, January 3, 1947. NA, f. Ministerstvo vnitra-Nová registratura (MV-NR), k. 2380, inv. č. 2030, s. B2620/1; Rabování v pohraničí spojené s odsunem Němců, MV, May 17, 1946. SOkA Opava, f. ONV Opava-venkov, k. 3 inv. č 113; Heda Margolius Kovály, Under a *Cruel Star: A Life in Prague*, trans. Franci and Helen Epstein (New York, 1989), 70; According to Zdeněk Radvanovský: "On May 18 and 19th Prague radio delivered an official report to the inhabitants, that family members of those who went to Ústí nad Labem and other cities go to the train station, because the guards would be returning and have heavy suitcases." See Zdeněk Radvanovský, "Nucené vysídlení a odsun Němců," in *Studie o sudetonemecké otazce*, eds. Vaclav Kural et al. (Prague, 1996), 137.

[41] See reports on Krnov expulsion. SOkA Bruntál, f. ONV Krnov I, k. 17 inv. č. 72, and f. ONV Krnov I, Dodatky, k. 11 inv. č. 92; Tomáš Staněk, *Perzekuce, 1945* (Prague, 1996), 126.

Official positions in local governments or police units offered another easy route to abscond with confiscated German property. Corruption ran rampant, especially during 1945. Individual commissars and local administrative commissions controlled many localities that were overwhelmingly German and had little effective oversight. For instance, the local commissar in Malkov and Zasada, Josef Kostka, had accumulated a cache of expropriated property in his nearby home. He had one radio, six lamps, a typewriter, one violin, four different cameras, a half a dozen sets of dinnerware, a cash register and a stove, in addition to 135 kilograms of seed and 43 kilos of grain.[42] In Rumburk an official investigation revealed a number of district administrative commissioners who had collected and sold confiscated valuables.[43] National committee members benefited not only through personal possession of such property, but also through its allocation to others. Such transactions helped national committee members to build personal and political support. For instance, Adolf Charous, the commissar in Česká Kamenice, went to great lengths to ensure that his people received desirable national administrator positions. After his misdeeds surfaced in March 1946, he lost his posts in the MNV and the KSČ, but through his remaining connections he received a national administrator position for a local business. Despite such obvious nepotism – or perhaps because of it – the local Communist Party achieved a rousing electoral victory two months later.[44]

Becoming a national administrator of a Sudeten German farm or business also offered an excellent opportunity to exploit confiscated property. These gold-diggers misreported inventories or earnings, sold goods on the black market or simply lived off the business with no intention of maintaining it, often keeping Germans working there as long as possible. In his monthly report concerning the more important cases of theft and gold-digging, one security official reported the following: "One national administrator of a restaurant had sold meat and wine without a license and for illegal prices; another sold a liter of cognac for 2,000 Kčs and six pieces of bread for 300 Kčs; a dental technician requested gasoline and a Persian rug from a Russian soldier for some dental work."[45] Other national administrators simply did not show up to work. District officials in Vejprty reported that one national administrator had three businesses in the district and did not fulfill any of his duties. Another national

---

[42] SOkA Chomutov, f. MNV Ervěnice, k. 47 inv. č. 170.
[43] Report on the Wagner case, NA, f. MV-NR, k. 1785 inv. č. 1579.
[44] *Česká Kamenice* (Česká Lípa, 2002), 339, 346; Minutes from the meeting of the MNV Česká Kamenice, April 9, 1946. SOkA Děčín, f. MNV Česká Kamenice, k. 1 inv. č. 40.
[45] Report from the police commissar in Jablonec n. N., October 9, 1945. SOkA Jablonec n. N., f. ONV Jablonec n. N., k. 18 inv. č. 39.

administrator of a clothing store, they noted, often did not open the store because she spent the majority of her time in Prague. This had been unproblematic until the original owner, who had run the shop for the woman in her absence, was expelled.[46] Such attitudes among some of the first Czech national administrators meant that Sudeten German property served only to enrich them during their stay and left little for others who followed in their wake. More importantly, these practices continued into 1946, extending the unrest and unease about the borderlands, and threatened the long-term success of the settlement program.

Although the majority of first settlers moved to the borderlands simply to start a new life, a negative image had already become associated with national administrators, settlers and the borderlands by 1945.[47] The borderlands became characterized as a land of gold-diggers. Humor played an important role in generating this image. The ever irreverent journal *Porcupine* (*Dikobraz*) published dozens of cartoons on the topic. For instance, in one cartoon a man with a rucksack, a suitcase and some paintings under his arm speaks with a well-dressed settler. In a play on words, the settler asks if there was a vacant (*prázdnej*) home in the town. The man replies, "Well, really I live in Prague, but I can tell you. The third home on the right. I just cleared it out (*vyprázdnil*)."[48] In another jab at the common looter the magazine projected the image of gold-digging to the entire region. Displaying a map of the country where the borderlands are whited out, one gentleman explains to another: "And there at the top, those white spots, there isn't anything there, our people pilfered them from us in their suitcases."[49]

More caustic commentaries also appeared. Michael Mareš, a reporter for Franitšek Peroutka's newspaper *Today* (*Dnešek*), focused much of his work on expulsion and resettlement misconduct. In a regular column entitled "Coming from the Periphery of the Republic," Mareš often reported about gold-digging. He painted the most cutting portrait of one national administrator who had taken over a German farm:

Newly designated master with an allocation of about 30 hectares of land. Wife is lazy as a louse and has no children. Mr. "Farmer" has long polished boots and tucked away behind one of them is a beautiful gold cane. Perhaps he also rides a horse? With an officer's impeccable shiny nickel spurs. An inheritance from the Gestapo or Wehrmacht? Green German hat on his head with a tuft of chamois fur. Perfect for a lazy stroll through the meadows. A dozen beef cattle, two pair of glistening well-kept horses, one looks with joy on such holdings. Naturally, this

[46] Report from the SNB in Přísečnice, November 29, 1945. SOkA Chomutov, f. ONV Vejprty, k. 1 inv. č. 52.
[47] Staněk, *Odsun Němců*, 84; Slezák, *Zemědělské osídlování*, 54–57.
[48] *Dikobraz*, October 10, 1945, 3.   [49] *Dikobraz*, September 5, 1945, 8.

man is against any kind of transfer of the Germans working on his property. Since Mr. Landowner does not even know how to mend his fence, the answer is clear to the question, "What will happen when the Germans leave?" He casually responds: "That is the point, is it some sort of problem? I arrived with an empty bag, I will leave with a full one, I had a festive two years, the trip to the borderlands was rewarding for me. So it was, so it will be."[50]

These portrayals of national administrators reinforced the idea that "everybody is doing it," and that the borderlands were filled with gold-diggers. Such images defied the hopes of settlement officials, who increased their calls for more experienced and reliable national adminis-trator candidates.

While gold-diggers often made out well, the properties they left behind suffered. In September 1945 a unit of the giant Stalinworks plant wrote to district officials asking that they issue an announcement to the public requesting the return of typewriters and calculators that had been taken during "the revolutionary days." They noted that the lack of these machines created a substantial loss for the firm.[51] Settlers coming to the borderlands later in 1945 and 1946 reported that almost no furniture remained in vacant apartments. Confiscated German possessions fre-quently moved within apartment buildings and later became the source of disputes between new neighbors. In early 1947, after the official "transfer" of Germans ended and Czechs began leaving the borderlands in greater numbers, the National Land Fund (*Národní pozemokvý fond*; NPF), which regulated confiscated farms, issued a circular warning against theft by departing national administrators. It noted that they not only failed to pay for the use of the land, but also tore out windows and floors and took equipment back to the interior.[52] The total loss that resulted from gold-digging can never be known. As the basis for border-land resettlement, gold-digging negatively affected the general economic recovery and the possibility for a seamless transition for new settlers. As a part of ethnic cleansing, gold-diggers made it clear that the Germans would leave the country with next to nothing.

Attempts to halt the influx of gold-diggers and the outflow of confis-cated property from the borderlands met with little success. It did not help matters that members of local administrative commissions and

[50] Michal Mareš, "Přicházím z periferie republiky, I." *Dnešek*, June 27, 1946. A later article noted that the green hat symbolized malicious excess, Josef Němeček, "Očistec a vykoupení štrálských Čechů," *Dnešek*, July 25, 1946.

[51] Letter from Čsl. tov. na motorová paliva, Horní Litvínov, September 21, 1945. SOkA Teplice-Šanov, f. ONV Teplice-Šanov, k. 1 inv. č. 1.

[52] NPF Circular č.22/47, March 5, 1947. NA, f. Národní pozemkový fond (NPF), k. 3. See also "Proti krádežím a ničení majetku v pohrančí postupuje NPF s nejvetší přísností," *Osidlování*, March 25, 1947.

security officials engaged in theft and corruption. Indeed, the very policies that they pursued in order to limit the loss of German property, such as house searches and storing confiscated property in warehouses, often led to further abuses of their authority. Yet many police officials, as well as national committees and even administrative commissions, tried hard to halt the process of gold-digging. An early announcement from the security department at the Provincial National Committee in Prague (ZNVP) called on all citizens to respect the nation's property and warned that anyone caught taking it would not avoid punishment.[53] In late June 1945, shortly following the expulsion and concentration of Sudeten Germans in Krnov, the District National Committee (ONV) established a three-member guard to check people's luggage at the train station. Police organs pushed for even stronger measures against gold-diggers.[54] The Ministry of Interior responded to such demands by calling on national committees to carry out searches at train stations and to limit the stay of outsiders at borderland hotels, despite the obvious difficulties this posed for incoming settlers.[55] In early July 1945, the Ministry of Interior warned more explicitly against the further theft of the republic's property. People were given three days to report possession of Sudeten German goods or they faced investigation.[56] The invasive tenor of such policies, however, did little to make new settlers feel welcome or to halt gold-digging. Officials in Vejprty posted a sign greeting passengers at the train station, which read "Gold-diggers go home."[57]

Continued reports and discoveries of property-related machinations, as well as harsh policies to deal with them, cast a shadow over the settlement program. One borderland reporter complained in early 1946 that gold-diggers hindered the consolidation of the borderlands and that they should be expelled.[58] A series of articles in *Settlement (Osidlování)*, the Settlement Office's periodical, reminded readers of the steep penalties

---

[53] Výhláška, ONV Semily, June 7, 1945. SOkA Jablonec n. N., f. ONV Jablonec n. N., k. 51 inv. č. 63.
[54] Zapisy z schůzí Okresní správní komise (OSK) Krnov, June 28, 1945. SOkA Bruntál, f. ONV Krnov I, k. 3 inv. č. 63.
[55] Výnos Z/II-2515/1945, MV, July 6, 1945, issued by ONV Opava-venkov as 138/pres from August 10, 1945. SOkA Opava, f. ONV Opava-venkov, k. 3 inv. č. 113. See also 4279-II/5–45, ZNV Brno, August 2, 1945. SOkA Opava, f. ONV Opava-venkov, k. 3 inv. č. 113.
[56] Oběžník č.j. 3250/45, ONV Jilemnice, July 3, 1945. VHA, f. Velitelství třetí oblasti (VO3), k. 23 inv. č. 7. See a similar proposal from the local police in Krnov, July 6, 1945. SOkA Bruntál, f. ONV Krnov I, k. 17 inv. č. 72.
[57] Minutes of the Místní správní komise (MSK) Vejprty, August 14, 1946. SOkA Chomutov, f. ONV Vejprty, k. 2 inv.č. 12–15.
[58] Rudolf Svoboda, "Očista životem, základem pořádku," *Hraničář: Protifašistický list okresu Frývaldova*, January 4, 1946.

they faced if they were caught embezzling national property.[59] In early 1947, the Communist Party in Jablonec proposed expelling from the borderlands all speculators and others who misused German property. While a statewide law that prosecuted speculators was already in place, the Communists in Jablonec justified the need for stronger measures against gold-diggers because, they argued, even if such people were forced out of one borderland town they would be able to continue their activities elsewhere. Their proposal sought to ban these people from the borderlands altogether.[60] While this policy can be understood, given the frustrations of officials attempting to bring stability to the borderlands, it also demonstrated how settlement policies could assume a repressive character in the context of ethnic cleansing.

While the number of Czechs punished for offenses against expropriated Sudeten German property remains unclear, the efforts to stop gold-digging practices were seemingly ineffective. A separate legal measure, Decree 38, punished property misdeeds during wartime as well as the postwar period and was not limited to the borderlands. In fact, during the decree's discussions in early June 1945, the Minister of Agriculture requested that a special provision be inserted to curtail the abuse of Sudeten German farmland already occurring in the borderlands.[61] Even without such a clause, in 1946 the Ministry of Interior reported that more than 3,000 arrests had occurred for offenses under the decree.[62] Decree 108 had its own provisions for punishment through fines and jail time for mishandling former German property. Although the exact number of convictions according to section 19 of Decree 108 is unknown, officials in Prague remained unhappy with the inconsequential punishments that national committees handed out for property transgressions. In August 1948, the Settlement Office issued a directive requesting that national committees give greater attention to issuing harsher penalties under section 19.[63] Gold-digging made it clear that people did not equate confiscating German property as part of a national goal. In addition, negative reports in the press and

[59] Dr. Václav Voborník, "Trestní ustanovení konfiskačního dekretu č. 108," *Osidlování*, June 10, 1946; Otakar Benda, "Pomáhejte k zajištění státního a národního majetku," *Osidlování*, July 10, 1946; Dr. Václav Voborník, "Chraňte národní majetek," *Osidlování*, August 25, 1946; Dr. Václav Voborník, "Pletichy podle dekretu č 108/45," *Osidlování*, September 10, 1946.
[60] Zapisy ze schůzí MSK Jablonec n.N., February 14, 1947. SOkA Jablonec n. N., f. MěNV Jablonec n. N., kn. 4, inv.č. 4.
[61] Comments of the Ministry of Agriculture on proposed decree. Jech and Kaplan, 1:343, n.1.
[62] Benjamin Frommer, *National Cleansing: Retribution Against Nazi Collaborators in Postwar Czechoslovakia* (Cambridge, 2005), 59; Radomir Luža, *Transfer of the Sudeten Germans: A Study of Czech-German Relations, 1933–1962* (New York, 1964), 269, n.9.
[63] Letter from OÚ, June 28, 1947. NA, f. MV-NR, k. 2380 inv.č. 2030 s. B-2620/1.

repressive government intervention made it difficult to sustain a positive image of the resettlement program and the borderlands more generally. Ethnic cleansing became an opportunity for individual gain and marked the borderlands as a land apart.

National Administrators: Social Mobility and the Expulsion of Germans

Property confiscation worked in tandem with military actions to remove Germans from their homes. It ensured that Sudeten Germans lost their means to remain in the country and served as a lasting punishment for being "German." Once stripped of their homes, Sudeten Germans began an uncertain journey that millions of other displaced and dispossessed Central and Eastern Europeans faced during the war. Although the Czechoslovak military forces controlled the expulsions, settlers also played a central role in this process. In the short term, Czechs who immediately moved into the borderlands and occupied German property increased pressure to expel Germans. In the long term, settlers were supposed to provide an effective barrier against the possible Sudeten Germans' return. In this sense, settlers both initiated and finalized the cleansing process. They not only seized the physical structures and land, but completely transformed the cultural, social and economic fabric of the borderlands.

Decree 5, issued on May 19, 1945, placed "national administrators" in charge of the permanent property of "state/nationally unreliable (*státní nespolehlivé*)" people. It defined as unreliable ethnic Germans and Magyars, regardless of state citizenship, as well as those who collaborated with the Nazis or fascists in Slovakia.[64] The Czechoslovak government established an extensive legal system to try those accused of collaboration. Popular people's courts, separate legal measures, and a National Court emerged in 1945–46 to adjudicate crimes specifically related to the war. In theory, this method of retribution did not differentiate between Czechs and Germans, though in practice Czech and German trials proceeded quite differently.[65] More importantly, Decree 5 and other decrees circumvented any possibility of ascertaining the level of individual guilt of Sudeten Germans and Magyars, and instead declared them all unreliable. Even before the Allies officially sanctioned the "transfer" of Germans, and before their Czechoslovak citizenship had been revoked, the Czechoslovak state began erecting a set of

---

[64] Decree 5, May 19, 1945. Jech and Kaplan, 1: 216.
[65] For more on the legal prosecution of such crimes, see Frommer.

legal measures that punished Sudeten Germans on the basis of their nationality.

Decree 5 fulfilled several purposes. In addition to its punitive aspect, the decree allowed Sudeten German businesses, factories and farmsteads to remain in operation until the government worked out a more permanent solution concerning the distribution of confiscated assets. The decree's temporary nature, however, did little to stabilize property relations. Instead, it offered central officials a method to ensure some control over the designation of national administrators at a time when problems of looting and mismanagement had already begun to surface. The decree on national administrators also encouraged Czechs to move to the borderlands. Becoming a national administrator did not guarantee future ownership of Sudeten Germans' permanent property, but many assumed that once they occupied a home or a farm they would have the right to remain. Therefore, while Decree 5 helped to evict Germans, it left open the question of ownership and failed to establish a definitive solution to the borderland's future.

On June 21, 1945, President Beneš signed into law Decree 12, which utilized the expropriated farms of Germans, Magyars and collaborators as the first stage of land reform. Unlike Decree 5, which covered all other confiscated property, the government pledged to quickly transfer ownership of seized farmland to qualified individuals. Part of the reason for the urgency involved immediate planting and harvest needs. For example, in July 1945 the Provincial National Committee in Prague had already promised settlers that they would receive ownership of German farms as long as they remained there and worked the fields.[66] Decree 28, from July 20, followed through on these promises and established concrete provisions for the distribution of agricultural holdings.[67] Agricultural officials sought to create borderland farms of 10–13 hectares, which they believed provided the optimum basis for small-scale production. In early 1946, the Ministry of Agriculture distributed ownership certificates to the national administrators of borderland farms, which, in theory, gave them some rights over their new holdings. Although these certificates did not finalize the transfer of property rights, they temporarily appeased settlers' expectations of becoming independent landholders. Unlike the question of ownership over other seized German assets, which remained unresolved beyond 1947, national administrators of agricultural property became quasi-owners in early 1946.

---

[66] Přidělení půdy, Okresní správní komise (OSK) Jablonec, July 25, 1945. Státní okresní archiv (SOkA) Jablonec n. N., f. Okresní národní výbor (ONV) Jablonec, k.50 inv.č.63.
[67] Decree 28, July 20, 1945. Jech and Kaplan, 1:331–35.

National committees, administrative commissions and commissars were in charge of installing people as national administrators. Local national committees handled small firms, farms and houses, and district national committees dealt with businesses that had between 20 and 300 employees, farms from 50 to 100 hectares, and houses and other property worth more than 5 million crowns. The three provincial national committees or a relevant ministry controlled larger firms and properties.[68] Those interested in obtaining a position as a national administrator of Sudeten German property had to apply to these officials and provide some basic background information to prove that they were suited to the post. Decree 5 outlined only general parameters in this regard. It stated that national administrator positions should be given to those people "with relevant training and practical knowledge, [who were] morally irreproachable and politically reliable."[69] Later guidelines supplemented these instructions and stressed the need to find experienced and reliable people. On June 18, 1945, the Ministry of Industry issued a comprehensive directive to help national committees regulate seized Sudeten German firms. It reminded them that "the choice of national administrators deserves the greatest care and diligence, because the orderly and uninterrupted operation of a firm depends on them. Just as this [choice] is in the national interest, so it is in the general and local economic interest and also in the interest of employees."[70] As problems concerning the control of national administrators later emerged, central officials blamed local officials for failing to place reliable people in these posts.

In reality, national committees initially had little control over who settled in their jurisdictions. New settlers flooded the region from areas adjacent to the borderlands or from the large urban centers in the country's interior. Radio announcements and government leaders promoted the quick settlement of the borderlands. In a radio address of May 11, 1945, Klement Gottwald encouraged small farmers and agricultural laborers to prepare for the confiscation of German land.[71] During June and July, Czechs inundated the borderlands in search of farms and businesses. The arrival of these settlers corresponded with the rising pace of the summer expulsions, which made it easier for them to find available property. In Ústí nad Labem, for example, only 129 national

---

[68] Decree 5, sec. 7. Jech and Kaplan, 1:217.   [69] Decree 5, sec. 16. Ibid., 1:219.
[70] Directive from Minister of Industry, č.j.II-129.782–1945. *Předpisy z oboru působnosti OÚ a FNO: Zákony (dekrety), vládní nařízení, vyhlášky* (Prague, 1946), 2:175.
[71] Tomáš Grulich, "Problematika počatku osídlování pohraničí a plany na osídlení," in *Etnické procesy v novoosidleneckém pohraniči- dělnictvo v etnických procesech* (Prague, 1986), 1:15–16.

administrators were established in May 1945, while from June 21 to the end of July 1945 nearly 1,500 national administrators were installed in local businesses.[72] Even in less desirable areas, the opportunity to run a pub or small shop drew immediate interest. In the northern Bohemian industrial town of Dubí, for instance, Czechs had seized roughly two-thirds of the German businesses by the end of July.[73] Similar practices emerged with farmland, where early settlers sought farms in the most attractive agricultural areas between Žatec and Česká Lípa in Bohemia and in the wine-growing areas of southern Moravia.[74] By moving spontaneously with general government support, Czechs quickly confiscated the best-quality farms and businesses available. This rapid migration left little room for local or central officials to plan or carry out an orderly transfer of German property. It also indicated that settlers were primarily interested in running a shop or farm, rather than working in factories – a trend that had serious implications for the future of borderland industries.[75]

A similar surge occurred in the occupation of German housing in 1945. Czechs rushed to the borderlands, putting a strain on available housing and forcing Germans out of their homes. National committees solved the housing demands in numerous ways. In some instances they forced Germans across the border to make room for incoming Czechs. When expulsions were impossible, national committees made other arrangements, such as establishing internment camps. More often they moved Sudeten Germans into shared quarters, which meant placing two or more families into small apartments or decrepit homes – a practice that became recognized policy during the summer.[76] For instance, in late August 1945, the Local Administrative Commission (MSK) in Podmokly needed to locate an additional 1,000 apartments for incoming settlers.

[72] Zdeněk Radvanovský, "Národní výbory ústecké průmyslové oblasti a jejich podíl na osídlování pohraničí v letech poválečného revolučního procesu," in 6. vědecká archivní conference Revoluční národní vybory, osídlování pohraničí a význam národních vyborů při zajišťování národně-democratického procesu v ČSR v letech 1944–1948 (Ústí nad Labem, 1990), 11–12.
[73] Cf. Zápisy plenum, Městský národní výbor (MěNV) Dubí, August 19, 1945. SOkA Teplice-Šanov, f. MěNV Dubí, k. 12 inv. č. 69; Reports on national administrators. Ibid., k. 4 inv. č. 67. Other reports also indicated that a majority of national administrators assumed their posts by the end of August 1945. See incomplete lists of national administrators by district. NA, f. MV-NR, k. 1770–1771 inv. č. 1576 s. B1470.
[74] Lubomír Slezák, Zemědělské osídlování pohraničí českých zemí po druhé světové válce (Brno, 1978), 59–60 Jiří Koťátko, Konfiskace, rozdělování a osidlování půdy (Prague, 1946), 7.
[75] See Chapter 4.
[76] See, for example, Oběžník 1680, Zemský národní výbor (ZNV) Prague, July 19, 1945. SOkA Teplice-Šanov, f. ONV Teplice-Šanov, k. 4 inv. č. 211 042.3. Also see various Sudeten German testimonies that describe this practice: LAA, Ost-Dok 2, Freiwaldau 252, 124; Tetschen 288, 3, 227; Friedland 254, 29–33; Aussig 240, 8.

It planned to use 200 uninhabited apartments, 700 apartments inhabited by Germans and 200 others that it hoped to find by consolidating settlers who had already taken up residence.[77] District officials in nearby Ústí nad Labem likewise called on local officials to make space for settlers by moving Germans. However, it instructed them not to relocate all the Germans to a single street, in order to prevent "a kind of ghetto" from being established.[78] They urged local officials to dedicate all of their resources to overcoming the "housing crisis" and to prevent a "calamity." In some places, Czechs and Germans were forced to live together, which often led to more strident demands. Metalworkers in Česká Ves, for instance, complained that they could no longer tolerate living with Germans in the same households. They reported that Germans did everything from spreading propaganda about an American invasion to spending too much time in the bathroom. They demanded that Sudeten Germans be expelled from twenty-eight homes or that strikes and bloodshed would result.[79]

The intensive immigration of settlers overwhelmed the limited resources of national committees. What oversight they did exercise often came after properties had been occupied. One difficulty was the lack of organization among housing departments in national committees, as this retrospective report from Podmokly indicates:

Applicants' lack of confidence in the housing office grew from the reality that evidence of submitted requests was not properly catalogued and during their processing were even lost. Many requests were refused and filed even though the requester was not informed, or requests were denied without any reason only with the remark "refused" so that it was not possible to give an explanation for the judgment on a specific case. This all gave the applicant the impression of prejudice, disorder and even protectionism. Therefore, it is not surprising that at the housing department there were several undesirable scenes.[80]

Administrative commissions in the summer of 1945 simply did not have the ability to keep up with demand. In August 1945 the housing department in Podmokly reported that they were issuing sixty-five to seventy housing decrees daily.[81] The process of securing an apartment or home

---

[77] Zpráva bytového referenta pro Podmokly, August 27, 1945. SOkA Děčín, f. MěNV Děčín, k. 1 inv. č. 40.

[78] OSK to MNV, September 1, 1945. AM Ústí n. L., f. ONV Ústí nad Labem, k. 407 inv. č. 5.

[79] Resolution of workers from the iron and steel factories in Česká Ves, October 9, 1945. ZA, f. ZNV Expozitura v Moravské Ostravě, k. 294 inv. č. 362.

[80] Zpráva o výsledku revize činnosti bytového úřadu, Děčín -Podmokly, January 1947. SOkA Děčín, f. MěNV Děčín, k. 254 inv. č. 775.

[81] Zpráva bytového referenta, August 27, 1945. SOkA Děčín, f. MěNV Děčín, k.1 inv. č. 40.

was as disorganized as it was mystifying. Settlers considered it another example of corruption, which led to ongoing feuds over German homes.

Another problem in distributing confiscated property was that many national administrators were unqualified for the positions that they assumed. Farms in particular suffered as few settlers were prepared or able to manage the demands of running a farm. Former miners often seized farms and factories. Waiters and cooks became national administrators of pubs and restaurants. While social mobility was a key facet of the resettlement program, it also had dire consequences for the borderland economy. Sudeten Germans commented bitterly on the changes that followed their displacement: "The Czech successors often arrived mostly in tatters with a briefcase or an empty suitcase, took over the farm, and played the master."[82] One German-speaking farmer noted how he was forced to work for seven months without pay for the new national administrator of his farm, a shoemaker by trade. Despite his efforts, he remarked "in just a short time our beautiful German fields were turning into wilderness."[83] Czech officials likewise catalogued the problems of unqualified people running German farms and businesses. One police report, for example, noted: "Several farmers/national administrators are in debt for the extravagant way of life and in many cases manage the property entrusted to them very negligently – even criminally."[84] Not all of the shortcomings can be attributed to gold-diggers, however. Many new settlers simply lacked the skills, resources, know-how and labor force to succeed.

New settlers continued the work of ethnic cleansing that the military had begun. By the pressure of their numbers, Czechs forced Germans to leave their homes, farms and businesses, and by remaining there guaranteed its permanence. Nearly 80,000 national administrators occupied German farmsteads by the end of 1945.[85] By the beginning of 1946, national committees and settlement officials had distributed 60,000–90,000 national administrator positions for expropriated businesses.[86]

---

[82] Report 98. Hedwig Ott, n.d. Theodor Schieder, ed., *Dokumentation der Vertreibung der Deutschen aus Ost-Mitteleuropa*, vol. 4/2: *Die Vertreibung der deutschen Bevölkerung aus der Tschechoslowakei* (Bonn, 1957), 456.
[83] Erlebnisbericht, LAA, Ost-Dok 2, Freiwaldau 252, 100.
[84] SNB Chomutov monthly report, July 22, 1946. SOkA Chomutov, f. ONV Chomutov k. 1 inv. č. 175.
[85] Problémy zemědělství v pohraničí, Ministry of Agriculture, December 1949. NA, f. Ministerstvo zemědělství – Sekretariat (MZ-S), k. 379 inv. č. 191. Jiří Koťátko gave 76,506 as the number of national administrators on farms by the end of 1945. Jiří Koťátko *Zemědělská osidlovací politika v pohraničí* (Prague, 1946), 38.
[86] Compare Report č.j.3421/46 from Osídlovací úřad (OÚ), February 1946. NA, f. Osídlovací komise při ÚV KSČ (f. 23), a.j. 359; Minutes from Osídlovací komise při Ústřední komise KSČ, December 15, 1945. Ibid., a.j. 15.

In addition, people who took over Germans' homes also became national administrators, though their numbers are more difficult to quantify. Individual apartments sometimes came under the management of a single national administrator, other times one individual managed an entire block of homes. One housing estimate put the number of apartments in the borderlands at 850,000.[87] On June 30, 1948, the Settlement Office reported that 231,222 family homes and 147,329 apartment buildings and other property had been confiscated.[88] Not all of these fell under the management of national administrators; some homes were uninhabitable and local offices and state officials seized other buildings. Nonetheless, by the end of 1945, it would be safe to argue that at least 400,000 settlers in the borderlands had become national administrators of the permanent property that formerly belonged to Sudeten Germans.

The same promise of social mobility that provided a significant influx of new settlers to displace the Sudeten Germans also fueled conflicts among Czechs. The most dramatic example of how property divided settlers was the policy of "priority rights" (*přednostní práva*). This policy offered better access and cheaper prices, among other things, to certain categories of Czechs. Priority rights served as reward as well as enticement. Re-emigrants, soldiers and those who had suffered from Nazi persecution (though not explicitly Jews) were eligible for priority status. Decree 12 first established the principle to grant partisans, soldiers and those who suffered from Nazi persecution, as well as their heirs, priority for German farmland. A host of decrees, laws and regulations then followed, extending privileged access to re-emigrants as well.[89] Different interest groups had lobbied for these provisions after the war. For instance, the League of National Associations and Culture requested such privileges for these groups when they met with officials at the Interior Ministry in early June 1945.[90] Officials at the Ministry of Defense likewise asked that soldiers receive special status for their service during the war. They proposed that soldiers should receive priority for confiscated property, in part because others who had not fought were reaping the benefits. One report stated: "It is impossible not to mention that the conditions created partly by non-soldiers' gain from German movable property and the incomparably improved conditions of other non-soldiers, who seized non-movable property, weigh heavily on the troops."

---

[87] Minutes from the meeting of the Advisory committee of the Settlement Office, April 20, 1946. NA, f. 23, a.j. 310.

[88] Letter from OÚ, June 30, 1948. NA, f. MV-NR, k. 2381 inv. č. 2030 s. 2620/1.

[89] Decree 12, sec. 7, para. 6. Jech and Kaplan, 1:278. See also, Decree 108, part 2, sec. 7, para.3. Jech and Kaplan, 2:853; Oběžník č.j. 49843, OÚ, 4 October 1946 and Směrnice č.j.26473/47, OÚ, February 10, 1947 for more specifics about priority qualifications. *Předpisy*, 2:431–35.

[90] Doc. 138. Arburg and Staněk, *Vysídlení Němců*, II/1, 421.

Giving soldiers preferential access to Sudeten German property, it continued, would help boost soldiers' morale.[91]

By the fall of 1945, the policy of setting aside property for returning emigrants and soldiers collided with the reality in the borderlands. For instance, one group of Czech emigrants in Vienna who specialized in cabinet making were considered a valuable pool of candidates for resettlement. However, the lack of suitable businesses presented a major obstacle to their return. One local national administrator seeking such workers blamed the fact that many confiscated businesses had already been occupied by unqualified people:

[T]he stumbling block is that our people from the interior, especially those without any sort of credit for the liberation of the country, immediately after the revolution flooded the shops and businesses and do not have any business license or experience. In this way our countrymen from Vienna do not find anything for themselves and return disappointed to Vienna, because everyone who had a business license in Vienna did not want to give it up and so they returned to German Vienna.[92]

On the face of it, that national administrators had been established for the majority of Sudeten German farms and homes by the end of the summer was not a problem for settlement officials. The rapid settlement of the land had been the government's priority from the start. However, mandating priority access to former German property for some, after hundreds of thousands of settlers had already staked their claim, provided fertile ground for conflicts between early settlers and those with priority rights. As each group attempted to get its hands on the better portions of Sudeten German property, political conflicts between them and between central and local officials deepened.

Volhynian Czechs clashed with new settlers who had already established control of national committees and possessed German property. In particular, the Volhynian Czechs wished to settle mainly in the world-renowned hop-growing region around Žatec. In June 1945, they sent a delegation to secure a number of former Sudeten German farms, but met resistance from members of the District Administrative Commission. As elsewhere, the best farms had already been occupied and first comers understood the threat that these re-emigrant soldiers posed to their newly won gains. Volhynian Czechs lobbied hard for confiscated property. They

---

[91] Letter from Velitelství 3 oblasti – hl. štab. 2. odd., June 26, 1945. VHA, f. VKPR, č.j. 1031.

[92] Letter from národní správce Dietze a Müller, Trnovany, October 4, 1945. SOkA Teplice-Šanov, f. ONV Teplice-Šanov, k. 1 inv. č. 1.

demanded the best property for themselves and their relatives and sometimes took matters into their own hands.[93] Though reported incidents of
violence were rare, the fear of so many demobilized soldiers in the area
who were not from the Czech interior and who had been promised easy
access to property reached to the highest levels of the government. As
each group sought to protect their right to seized property, divisions
between Volhynian Czechs and settlers in Žatec began to harden.[94]

The tensions that developed between re-emigrants and early settlers in
the borderlands also reflected the different attitudes of local and central
officials toward settlement. The idea of giving priority rights to re-emigrants, soldiers and victims of Nazi persecution initially found wide support in Prague. The Volhynian Czechs had some powerful backers, among
them the Minister of National Defense, who often wrote letters supporting
Volhynian Czechs' property claims. A special committee at the Ministry of
Agriculture was created to settle soldiers, including many Volhynian
Czechs, on expropriated German farmland.[95] First settlers, on the other
hand, turned to local authorities for help in securing their positions. Local
governments pursued a variety of strategies to prevent Volhynian Czechs
from settling in their districts. First, national committees simply refused to
meet their demands. Once it became apparent that some Volhynian
Czechs would be settled in their district, local officials in Žatec helped to
minimize their presence and influence by suggesting that they receive a
maximum quota of 30 percent of the farms in the district.[96] This figure
guaranteed that the majority of national administrators would not be
displaced. Other local governments attempted to protect current national
administrators by pointing to their diligence and service in the borderlands.
The ONV in Teplice-Šanov, for instance, argued that "countless national
administrators, who did not come to the borderlands solely for profit,
relatively quickly brought the entrusted property into order and with the
utmost effort succeeded in securing the harvest in proper time for planting.
It would be ungrateful if we throw them out now, simply because a foreign
soldier likes the farm."[97] Finally, borderland governments sought to use

---

[93] Letter from Office of the Cabinet of the Government, December 20, 1945. NA, f. MV-
NR, k. 7443 inv. č. 4148 s. B300.
[94] Report on trip to the borderlands Velitelství první oblasti, July 4–5, 1945. VHA, f. VO1,
k. 48, inv. č. 264. Report from Headquarters of the First Corps, late July 1945. Ibid., k. 49
inv. č. 271.
[95] Letter from Ministry of Agriculture, October 9, 1945. H. Nosková, *Návrat Čechů z
Volyně: Naděje a skutečnost let 1945–1954* (Prague, 1999), 100.
[96] Resoluce z Čeští zemědělci a národní správci zemědělských usedlosti, Žatec, September
6, 1945. NA, f. MV-NR, k. 7443 inv. č. 4148 s. B300.
[97] Opinion on settlement of foreign soldiers, November 15, 1945. SOkA Teplice-Šanov, f.
ONV Teplice-Šanov, kn.1 inv. č. 1.

the problem of settling priority applicants to reassert their own authority. One local government complained that Volhynian Czechs carried out their selection of farms with settlement officials, but not with the input of local authorities. They argued that this disrupted the work of already present national administrators, hurt the economy and weakened the power of independent people's organs.[98] For a variety of reasons, then, local officials supported the early settlers. They shared a common interest of protecting property from those whom they considered outsiders, already in 1945. Local officials also wanted to protect and project their own power in relation to central officials' efforts to control the borderlands. Early settlers' efforts at social mobility not only included the need to get rid of Germans, but also to protect these gains from the encroachment of later settlers, who had the support of the central government.

Resistance and Desperation

Although Sudeten Germans served mainly as sources of property and had little control over the ultimate fate of their belongings, they still had an important role to play in the politics of property after 1945. Unlike new settlers, Germans often knew the background and location of individual pieces of property. They assisted settlers in their transition as new owners by providing inventories and much-needed labor on farms and in businesses. Alternatively, some Germans chose to hamper this process by hiding their most valuable belongings and by appealing to the legal provisions against confiscation. Because of their knowledge of local property, German speakers also served as witnesses to the misdeeds of Czechs. While Sudeten German testimony mattered little in the case of violence against Germans, in the case of property transgressions their statements often proved essential to apprehending gold-diggers. A German woman who spoke Czech sealed the fate of Anna Rumplíková. In her testimony against Rumplíková, she stated that "I am in agreement with the fact that, as a German my property reverts to the state treasury; however, it is considerably worse for me, if our things would go to the possession of a person, who treated us so badly in the camp."[99] Sudeten Germans did possess the ability to influence the confiscation measures stacked against them. In the politics of expropriation, Germans not only played the role of victim; they also shaped the experiences of new settlers and challenged the idea of collective punishment that underpinned the confiscation decrees.

---

[98] Request of MěNV Pohořelice, November 7, 1945. H. Nosková, 101–2.
[99] Testimony of Anežka Pompová, October 30, 1945. SOkA Bruntál, f. ONV Krnov I, k. 1 inv. č. 60.

Hiding property was one way that Germans attempted to salvage some of their belongings. Often, Germans buried valuables in the yard or concealed them in their homes prior to the arrival of Soviet armies. One German explained how they stored several personal possessions in the corner of a factory cellar and bricked them in.[100] These efforts were often directed against the looting of Soviet soldiers rather than the Czechs, whom many Germans assumed would not treat them or their property in the same way as Red Army soldiers. Once it became clear, though, that the Czechs planned to completely expropriate their property, German speakers attempted to salvage what they could. In one case Czech authorities found 20 packages of 1000 crown banknotes – more than 2 million crowns in total – hidden in the hollow stand of a small table in the entranceway of a former German's apartment.[101] By attempting to hide their property, Germans sought to temporarily prevent others from getting their hands on it and hoped to retrieve it at a later date. Some Germans even crossed the border in order to retrieve goods they had stored somewhere prior to their expulsion, though it is unlikely that much property left the country in this manner.

Sudeten Germans also tried, with little success, to smuggle a few valuables or other items out of the country during their expulsion. Although regulations even during the summer 1945 expulsions permitted Germans to take a certain amount of luggage and other provisions, Czech military personnel and others often stripped them of even these meager possessions:

The crates and the luggage were weighed by the SNB [Sbor národní bezpečnosti (local police)] people and civilians and they rummaged through them. I willingly gave up the gold watch and an heirloom of my father. Meanwhile socks, quilt covers, linens, cigarettes flew out of the crate; the alarm clock, the iron, my slide rule, and the thermometer were 'discovered' with jubilee and set off to the side. With greater difficulty I succeeded in getting back the only winter coat of my wife. The children had an ordinary blanket strapped onto the backpack, this too was taken away.[102]

In response to such practices, some Germans packed only older, less desirable linens and clothes, which would be less tempting to would-be

---

[100] Report 12, Dr. August Lassmann, n.d. Schieder, ed., *Documents on the Expulsion of the Germans* 4:354. See also Erlebnisbericht Wilhelmine Jäckl, n.d., LAA, Ost-Dok 2, Saaz 282, 51.
[101] OSK Vejprty to ZNV Prague, May 13, 1946. SOkA Chomutov, f. ONV Vejprty, k. 1 inv. č. 52. For more reports about Germans hiding their property, see MV odbor pro celostátní politické zpravodajství report 12, April 16, 1946. ZA Opava, f. ZNVMO, k. 140 inv. č. 273; Erlebnisbericht Wilhelmine Jäckl, n.d. LAA, Ost-Dok 2, Saaz 282, 51.
[102] Erlebnisbericht, Alfred Porsche, April 30, 1953. LAA, Ost-Dok 2, Gablonz 255, 39.

plunderers. As the 1946 expulsions were carried out, searches became a bit more lax and German baggage was packed in advance and put on separate train carriages. This made it possible for some people to conceal at least a few small valuables. In 1946, the Interior Ministry issued a warning to national committees not to provide too much advance notice to Germans about their impending expulsion because of fears that the extra notice would allow them to hide things in their luggage or otherwise destroy their property.[103] Some attempted, when possible, to have the rights to their property transferred to a relative who had some other national status, especially Austrian, and who was therefore not liable to confiscation measures. In other cases Germans shipped packages abroad in an effort to avoid having to hand their property over to authorities.[104] Despite the thoroughgoing nature of expropriation and the efforts of officials and settlers, some Germans found ways to keep a few of their possessions during the expulsions.

When they could not bring their things with them, Germans sometimes resorted to destroying them. There were cases where Germans set fire to buildings or their fields and carried out other acts of sabotage prior to their departure. Such cases were frequently played up in the press and supported Czech officials' claims that all Germans were dangerous and should be expelled. Although Czech reports that Germans were setting fires in the borderlands should be viewed with some skepticism – especially because by 1947 officials reported that almost all fires in the borderlands were accidental – in some cases Germans did seek to destroy their property before relinquishing it to Czechs. Soon after Germany's capitulation these fires might have been used to destroy incriminating materials or as acts of pure destruction. Later, during 1946, sabotage was more clearly directed against the expulsion policy.[105] Such acts of desperation or defiance reflected the frustrations and anger of Germans at their fate. While many Germans assumed that there would be some price to pay for the war and occupation, few believed that they deserved to be completely dispossessed and

---

[103] MV Zs-3621–7/2–46, February 6, 1946. SOkA Opava. f. ONV Opava-venkov, k. 12 inv. č. 115.

[104] See the following for examples: ZNV Brno 37.231/11–13-1946, October 1, 1946. SOkA Bruntál, f. ONV Krnov I, k. 217 inv. č. 262; ZNV Brno 20.564 II/5–1946, April 30, 1946. SOkA Opava, f. UNV Opava, k. 163 inv.č. 265; Letter from ZNV Prague, June 5, 1946. NA, f. MV-NR, k. 1786 inv. č. 1581 sign. B1700.

[105] For various reports about fires in the borderlands, see Testimony of J.D., September 5, 1946. SOkA Bruntál, f. ONV Krnov I, k. 1 inv. č. 60; MV Z/XI-8986–23/4–46 from April 14, 1946. SOkA Opava, f. ONV Opava-venkov k. 12 inv. č. 115; *Stráž severu*, January 30, 1946; MV odbor pro celostátní politické zpravodajství reports, April–June 1946. ZA Opava, f. ZNVMO, k. 140 inv. č. 273.

expelled. Fighting back by controlling the fate of their belongings became a powerful weapon of the weak.

Evidence of German–Czech cooperation and negotiation involving officially confiscated property was widespread in the borderlands, suggesting a somewhat different paradigm for local relations than one based on hatred and revenge. Contacts between neighbors and relatives – that is, with old settlers – proved most frequent. Sudeten Germans who left things with people they knew could feel that they at least controlled who received their property. For example, one German tried unsuccessfully to give most of his valuables to his Czech brother-in-law. He had buried the goods in his backyard and was caught by chance as he unearthed them. Though the families did not even appear to be close, the idea of leaving his things to his sister's family obviously appealed more than abandoning them to unknown settlers or looters.[106] They may also have hoped to retrieve them at a later date. In other instances, Czechs did what they could to help Sudeten Germans. The police discovered one couple who protected several possessions for their Sudeten German neighbors. The Czech couple replied to the charges simply by saying that they had lived together in the same house for seventeen years and when the family asked them to store some valuables, they agreed.[107] In one exceptional case, a courier delivered Germans' belongings across the border to already expelled Germans. She took a 10 percent payment for the delivered goods, and over the course of about a year she transported items to more than sixteen people.[108] That such cases usually involved old settler assistance was yet another reason why new settlers suspected them of treachery.

Even new settlers, though, needed to deal with Sudeten Germans in order to locate, use and profit from confiscated property. While the military, police and local officials carried out house searches and used the threat of violence to force Sudeten Germans into relinquishing their property, others employed more refined methods. A lively exchange in confiscated valuables and money developed between Czechs and Germans. One popular case involved more than a dozen people in a black marketeering ring in the jewelry- and glass-making district of Jablonec. An underground trade in glass jewelry beads, which are still

---

[106] Investigation report, OSK Krnov, August 24, 1945. SOkA Bruntál, f. ONV Krnov, k. 17 inv. č. 72.
[107] AM, Ústí n. L., f. ONV Ústí n. L., k. 485 inv. č. 1413.
[108] Punishment proceedings, ONV Jablonec, May 19, 1948. SOkA Jablonec n. N., f. MěNV Jablonec n. N., k. 149 inv. č. 1482.

popular today in Jablonec, developed beginning in late 1945.[109] Prior to their expulsions, Sudeten Germans sold their semi-precious stones to others, both Czechs and Sudeten Germans who remained behind. In exchange, they often took money or provisions that met their immediate needs. These gold-diggers worked with Sudeten Germans in order to make a profit and were portrayed as worse offenders than ordinary plunderers. The regional paper, *Sentinel of the North*, saved its sharpest rebuke for the national administrators who sold the semi-precious stones on the black market and made a substantial profit.[110] The press and officials portrayed trading with Germans as a worse crime than simple theft or fraud because it seemed to benefit Germans at the expense of fellow Czechs.

Once the official expulsions under Allied control began in 1946 and Sudeten Germans knew that they would lose their property, they too had good reason to negotiate with Czechs. In Frývaldov, one official reported that Germans were selling valuable things still in their possession to Czechs for very low prices. At the same time, Germans were purchasing goods they were permitted to take with them or spent their money in local cafés. The consequences of this temporary trade are not difficult to imagine. After the Germans departed, cafés and other businesses lost customers and some went out of business.[111] National committees could do little to actively dissuade such activity and instead relied on informers to punish property crimes ex post facto. For instance, the District National Committee in Ústí nad Labem warned local national committees in September 1946 to watch out for Germans attempting to sell their possessions at low prices prior to their transfer. It advised the national committees "to quickly intervene, when many Czechs are allowed to be lured by a profitable purchase, such that they forget their national responsibility."[112] Few Czechs, however, considered such transactions in national terms. This helps explain, in part, why Czechs were willing to work with Germans, despite official efforts to prevent such relations. Even settlement officials had tacitly encouraged this sort of behavior by making confiscated property the cornerstone of attracting settlers to the borderlands. The sense that "everybody was doing it"

---

[109] For reports on this case, see SOkA Jablonec n. N., f. ONV Jablonec n. N., k. 29 inv. č. 52; SOkA Jablonec n.N., f. MěNV Jablonec n. N., k. 149 inv. č. 1482; *Stráž severu* 9, 13, February 16, 1947.

[110] *Stráž severu*, February 16, 1947.

[111] Security reports, OSK Frývaldov, April 14, July 15, and December 12, 1946. SOkA Jeseník, f. ONV Jeseník, k. 2 inv. č. 63.

[112] Rozprodávání nepřátelského majetku odsunovanými Němci, ONV Ústí n.L, October 23, 1946. AM Ústí n. L., f. ONV Ústí n.L., k. 9 inv. č. 49.

likewise persuaded some Czechs to cross national boundaries in pursuit of cheap wares.

Another method that Sudeten Germans employed to retain their property involved making appeals against the confiscation decrees. Each decree had its own mechanism for exceptions and appeals. Decree 108, which covered almost all personal possessions, for instance, permitted appeals for those who "remained true to the Czechoslovak republic, never harmed the Czech and Slovak nations, and actively participated in the struggle for its liberation or suffered under Nazi or fascist terror."[113] District national committees had to determine on a case-by-case basis whether individual Sudeten Germans met such criteria. This was no easy task. For instance, in the case of one Sudeten German, Herta Pražáková, conflicting stories dragged out her case for more than a year. Originally married to a German textile owner, she was expelled from Vejprty in early 1946 and then married a Czech, who had followed her to the American occupation zone in Germany. In late 1947, after returning to Vejprty with her new husband, she requested that her apartment furnishings be restored to her. The ONV in Vejprty denied her request, citing evidence presented by the SNB that she had been a well-known Nazi supporter. In her appeal to the Provincial National Committee in Prague, she argued that she had spent time in a concentration camp for supporting French POWs and had been given antifascist status for her actions. In response, the SNB replied that she had no proof of ever being in a concentration camp and her antifascist status had been given to her immediately after the war, when such certificates were widely available. They noted that these certificates had been revoked and the person responsible for issuing them had been given life imprisonment. Nevertheless, Pražáková and her new husband continued to appeal the case, although seemingly to no avail.[114]

Thousands of Sudeten Germans appealed the confiscation proceedings against them. National committees disregarded most requests because the Germans in question had often been transferred before they reviewed their cases. Even the cases that national committees did consider faced poor odds because applicants had to prove their "active participation" in the struggle against fascism.[115] Those Germans who had their requests

---

[113] Decree 108, part I, sec.1, par. 1, number (num.) 2. Jech and Kaplan, 2:848.

[114] See case of Herta Pražková. SOkA Chomutov, f. ONV Vejprty, k. 21 inv. č. 106. In September 1948 the ZNV in Prague was still requesting more information about the case, which was the last correspondence with district authorities.

[115] The concept of "active participation" as the sole means of exemption related to Decree 12, which confiscated German agricultural property. Decree 108, which confiscated other property, and Decree 33, which revoked Germans' citizenship, did not require "active participation" for exemption. Compare Decree 12, sec.1, par.2, Jech and

denied reacted with indignation. For example, a seventy-one-year-old Sudeten German argued that there was no possibility for him to fight with weapon in hand against the Nazis. Yet, he stated: "I hope that what is understood by active struggle is also a struggle of reason and intellectual acts, in which case I am convinced that I meet the stated conditions."[116] However, the appeals against confiscation did little to halt the thorough-going nature of expropriation and illustrate its connection to the expulsions. In some ways, the appeals further hardened Czechs' attitudes toward Germans. Large numbers of appeals appeared to undercut the premise of collective guilt upon which such policies were established, and therefore directly challenged the transfer and settlement agenda. In Frývaldov, for instance, 1,600 appeals against property provisions and loss of citizenship had been made by August 1945. By the time the official transfer concluded in late 1946, the number of appeals had reached more than 6,000. In addition, several appeals were written in Czech, which suggested to officials that at least some Czechs supported the continued presence of Germans.[117]

At a minimum, the appeal process had offered a chance for some Sudeten Germans to challenge the idea of collective punishment and demonstrate that they had not been Nazi supporters. In the end, it mattered little. In Frývaldov, 5,645 appeals for state citizenship had been rendered void simply by expelling those Sudeten Germans from the country.[118] Many Germans argued that they had participated in the struggle for liberation by listening to foreign radio or by helping POWs. Others could claim to have suffered under the Nazi regime because they went to jail or lost their jobs. To those people who had not had any stake in Nazi victory, the idea of losing everything they owned seemed unreasonably harsh and worthy of appeal. However, the vague qualifications for exemption, which may have offered hope to some Sudeten Germans, also allowed national committees to deny the vast majority of their requests. National committees, in fact, had little reason to support such requests. Expropriated property provided the basis for drawing settlers to the borderlands; thus, had national committees accepted the logic of the

---

Kaplan, 1:276, with Decree 108, part 1 sec.1 par.2, ibid., 2:848 and Decree 33, section 2, par.1, ibid., 2:345.

[116] Appeal of K.R., Vitkov. SOkA Opava, f. ONV Opava-venkov, k. 557 inv. č. 606.

[117] Compare Monthly Security Report, OSK Jeseník, August 14, 1945 and First Biannual Report, April 22, 1947. SOkA Jeseník, f. ONV Jeseník, k. 2 inv. č. 63.One security official remarked just as the official transfer began to pick up speed: "In the first instance, Czechs themselves are responsible for the growing courage of the Germans, partly those who in countless instances support them . . . and partly by not completely holding to the regulations for Germans." Monthly Security Report from OSK Jeseník, May 1946. Ibid.

[118] Report of the Security Chairman, ONV Frývaldov, April 22, 1947. SOkA Jeseník, f. ONV Jeseník, k. 2 inv. č. 63a.

Sudeten Germans' appeals, the entire process of ethnic cleansing would have been challenged.

Revise

Although many reports concerning the work of national administrators presented a bleak picture of laziness and greed, there were other reasons for national administrators' poor performance. The uncertainty involved in the process of expropriation and expulsion, for example, did not provide incentive to work hard. During the summer of 1945 there was no certainty that the Germans would leave; in other cases, Germans sometimes returned and attempted to reclaim their property. By 1946 the possibility that someone with priority rights would appear and take-over a farm further clouded the question of final ownership. Other national administrators simply struggled. At first they relied on German labor, and later were offered operational loans from the National Land Fund to keep them financially viable. Still, many could not succeed. National administrators' shortcomings and dubious behavior caused concern and debate about how to correct the situation. What emerged was a process the Czech government called "*revise*," which referred to general investigations, or revisions, of national administrators' performance, background and behavior. Already on June 6, 1945, before the flood of settlers and the expulsion of Germans had even reached their peaks, the Ministry of Finance offered to assist national committees in reviewing the work of national administrators.[119] *Revise* presented the opportunity to address the problem of gold-diggers and other unqualified national administrators once and for all. Yet, revision commissions were dominated by locals, which meant that settlers were often policing themselves. While *revise* were not necessarily corrupt, the majority of early settlers – often also a majority of national administrators and national committee members – shared a similar stake and experience, and therefore sought to minimize their potential destabilizing effects. Others, however, such as priority applicants, hoped that these investigations would bring them greater access to expropriated property. *Revise* thus became another battleground for the control of confiscated Sudeten German assets.

The *revise* of national administrators managing Sudeten German farms progressed rapidly, due in part to the separate administration of expropriated agricultural land. In the fall of 1945, the ZNV in Prague

---

[119] Letter from the Finance Ministry, June 6, 1945. NA, f. MV-NR, k. 1769 inv. č. 1576 sign. B1470.

established local commissions to conduct agricultural inspections consisting of three members from the local peasant commission, including one qualified applicant for a national administrator position, plus a member of the local police appointed by district officials.[120] Officials from the Ministry of Agriculture oversaw their progress and supported the commissions' work. The revision commissions confirmed whether national administrators had sent in the necessary forms and kept up with accounting. They checked current inventories against those from the day national administrator had taken possession of the farm. In addition, they evaluated whether the trustee met the three qualities for all national administrators: moral integrity, state/national reliability and economic capability.[121] In the end, agricultural investigation commissions recalled less than 15 percent of the national administrators in Bohemia; later results from Moravia and Silesia were roughly parallel.[122] Such an outcome appeared to contradict both the expectations of central authorities and the reports of pervasive gold-digging. For instance, the agricultural official at the Provincial National Committee in Moravská Ostrava had estimated that in Frývaldov, two-thirds of the national administrators managed poorly, and in nearby Bruntál it was over a third.[123]

Several reasons explain why the inspections failed to remove large numbers of national administrators. Most commissions had little time to closely investigate what national administrators had been doing. In the district of Dubá, a poor agricultural region near the interior, officials gave commissions only a week to make their decisions about national administrators.[124] The district of Chomutov began reviewing national administrators in the first week of October, and by the 13th it had finished its audits in fifty-two communities.[125] In both of these districts, more than 1,000 settlers managed confiscated farms. Agricultural *revise* were simply too perfunctory to have uncovered even significant transgressions. In addition, the composition of revision commissions favored the locals.

---

[120] Oběžník 2, Settlement Commission of the Ministry of Agriculture, Jablonec, October 8, 1945. NA, f. NPF k. 11 inv. č. 16; Přezkoušení všech národních správců, ONV Jablonec, November 13, 1945. SOkA Jablonec n.N., f. ONV Jablonec, k. 50 inv. č. 63; Jiří Koťátko, *Konfiskace, rozdělování a osidlování půdy* (Prague, 1946), 10.

[121] Přezkoušení všech národních správců zemědělského majetku č.j.9.256/45, OSK Dubá, October 3, 1945. SOkA Česká Lípa, f. ONV Dubá, k. 63 inv. č. 187.

[122] The average, according to a November 26, 1945 report, was 12 percent. NA, f. 23, a. j. 15.

[123] Settlement report for the week of 19 October 1945, ZNV Moravská Ostrava. ZA Opava, f.ZNV Expositura v Moravské Ostravě, k. 906 inv. č. 932.

[124] č.j.9.256/45, OSK Dubá, October 3, 1945. SOkA Česká Lípa, f. ONV Dubá, k. 63 inv. č. 187.

[125] See situation reports from Osidlováci komise, Chomutov, October 9 and 13, 1945. SOkA Chomutov, f. ONV Chomutov, k. 1446 inv. č. 1646.

In Česká Lípa and Liberec, agricultural officials performed so-called super-revisions to check the results of the first revision, which one of the districts reported had not been done "objectively enough."[126] Other revision commissions had been using their authority to eject national administrators from better holdings and place themselves or someone they knew in charge of the land. The Provincial National Committee in Brno chastised the behavior of certain revision commissioners who "in the first place look after themselves, their relatives or friends, etc."[127] While it is unclear whether the outside applicant on these commissions benefited in this way, the lack of general oversight certainly provided fertile ground for such practices.

In addition, the agriculture revision commissions sought to protect early settlers' gains from the possibility of being replaced by someone with priority rights. In Žatec, relations between Volhynian Czechs and native Czechs continued to deteriorate as the second wave of Czechs from Volhynia began arriving in the borderlands in early 1947. Central settlement officials at the Ministry of Agriculture, along with military officers representing Volhynian Czechs, requested that agricultural commissions in the borderlands carry out another *revise* of national administrators in order to reclassify them according to three levels. According to the plan, the second- and third-level national administrators would have been recalled to make space for Volhynian Czechs. In practice, all the agricultural commissions listed their national administrators at the first level.[128] Such actions proved that local officials tried to prevent the extension of priority access to Volhynian Czechs at the expense of early settlers.

Approving more than 85 percent of local national administrators also offered national committees a way to challenge higher authorities' assumptions about national committees and the popular image of the borderlands more generally. Officials could now claim that the number of gold-diggers was lower than many had believed and that those who remained had been removed through the *revise*.[129] As much as the inspections were about national administrators, they also reflected the work of national committees and administrative commissions. While many

---

[126] Zprávy o činnosti Osidlovací komise Ministerstva zemědělství, Česká Lípa, November 4 and 23, 1945. NA, f. NPF, k. 10 inv. č. 16; Zprávy o činnosti Osidlovací komise Ministerstva zemědělství, Liberec, October 31, 1945. Ibid., k. 12 inv. č. 16.

[127] Instructions 1410/VIII/28/46, ZNV Brno, January 16, 1946. Ibid. See also Zprávy o činnosti Osidlovací komise Ministerstva zemědělství, Litoměřice, October 23 and November 8, 1945. Ibid.

[128] Report of liaison officer attached to Minister of Agriculture to Ministry of National Defense, February 19, 1946. H. Nosková, 107.

[129] Zpráva o činnosti Osidlovací komise Ministerstva zemědělství, Litoměřice, November 8, 1945. NA, f. NPF k. 12 inv. č. 16; Koťátko, *Konfiskace, rozdělování a osidlování*, 9.

members of these bodies had already changed once by the end of 1945, they still seemed reluctant to, in effect, blame themselves for their decisions about who they had allowed to become national administrators. As one member of a district farmer's commission noted, removing less than 10 percent of national administrators proved that settlement had been carried out well.[130] In addition, national committees did not want to give central authorities further reason to meddle in their affairs. The ongoing stream of settlers in search of desirable property continued to apply pressure on national committees into early 1946. Had they condemned a large percentage of those looking after confiscated farms, it would have brought further chaos and central intervention to their districts. Agricultural officials recognized this danger and did not press *revise* to their fullest extent.

The revisions of national administrators in expropriated businesses followed a similar course, but were complicated by the overlapping authority to regulate such property. Settlement officials initially sought to carry out revisions in such a way that met the expectations of both priority applicants and early settlers and eliminated the interim use of national administrators. In November 1945, the General Secretary of the Central Commission for Interior Settlement outlined such an approach for the investigation of confiscated businesses. He argued: "For its political prominence it will be necessary to solve this problem very carefully and precisely, by throwing out morally unqualified national administrators and handing over this freed up permanent property to priority applicants." He went on to stress the importance of quickly giving legal assurance to national administrators through the final allocation of confiscated German property. He then concluded: "By the transfer of German inhabitants the borderlands' economic life will be protected to a certain extent and only the legal certainty through the acquisition of property will enable its quick renewal."[131] Initially, settlement officials did not see the contradiction in promoting certain groups of settlers by giving them priority status while at the same time pushing for the rapid transfer of ownership rights to already present national administrators. However, even among central officials the question of who should be in charge of the revision process led to disputes. While the Ministry of Finance wished to use its tax auditors to carry out the work, other officials wanted to use their personnel to administer the inspections of firms that fell under their provenance. For instance, the Ministry of Domestic Trade

---

[130] Minutes from the District Farmers' Commission, Opava-věnkov, January 25, 1945. SOkA Opava, f. ONV Opava-věnkov, k. 552 inv. č. 590.

[131] Report of the General Secretary of the ÚKVO, November 29, 1945. NA, f. MV-NR, k.12145 s.1651/2.

argued against using the tax auditors because they did not have the confidence of tradespersons and were not trained to evaluate companies' management.[132] The Finance Ministry later argued that "there is simply no reason that a feeling of 'distrust' would be created for a responsible national administrator" toward the ministry's inspectors. "For the loyal citizen," it continued, "a feeling of duty exists before an organ, whose purpose is to defend the selfless interest of the state and – in a democratic state – also his own interest."[133] Such arguments failed to convince the Ministries of Domestic Trade and Industry, which refused to give up oversight of inspections to a third ministry. Central authorities, like settlers and national committees, often became embroiled in disputes over the control of former German property.

The Settlement Office ultimately organized the overall process of inspecting and auditing former Sudeten German businesses. Revisions began in early 1946 and were scheduled to last a month. National administrators had to produce a mountain of documents concerning their background and business activities to date.[134] Revision commissions were comprised of one current national administrator, a national committee member, an official from the relevant economic group and, when possible, one unsatisfied applicant. They sent their findings to a district revision council, comprised of several different officials that made the final decisions regarding the recall of national administrators. A further complication in the inspection of small businesses was the Settlement Office's efforts to scale back the total number of businesses in the borderlands to correspond to the fewer inhabitants expected after the expulsions. They devised target figures for every type of business based on population figures. So, for instance, for every 12,000 inhabitants there would be one auto repair shop, for every 7,000 inhabitants a bookstore, for every 500 people a grocery store, and so on. This meant that in addition to recalling unqualified or corrupt national administrators to make space for those with priority status, district revision councils were also supposed to shut down a certain number of businesses.[135]

It remains unclear exactly how many national administrators were recalled through these first revisions. One settlement official claimed that, of the 60,000 national administrators investigated by the end of

[132] Meetings about revision services for national administrators, June 25 and 28, 1945. NA, f. MV-NR, k. 1769 inv. č. 1576 sign. B1470.
[133] Revise národních správ, Minister of Finance, December 4, 1945. Ibid.
[134] Revision of national administrators, Okresní revisní sbor při OSK, Chomutov, February 19, 1946. SOkA Chomutov, f. MNV Ervěnice, k. 45 inv. č. 168.
[135] Dodátek k instrukci pro sestavení a činnost okresních revisních sborů, OÚ, March 8, 1946. SOkA Opava, f. Ústřední národní výbor Opava, k. 163 inv. č. 264; Meeting from the Oversight board of the Settlement Office, April 20, 1946. NA, f. 23, a.j.310.

April 1946, 15,000 were recalled and 5,000 other confiscated businesses were closed.[136] However, these figures were only provisional, and it appears that the commissions recalled far fewer than 10,000 national administrators. A September 1946 report showed that revision commissions removed only 10 percent of national administrators in businesses, of which 51,000 existed in the Bohemian lands.[137] As in the case of agricultural revisions, the rapid pace of business inspections and the high degree of local control prevented a large turnover in the number of national administrators. As one critical parliamentarian commented: "the revision of national administrators in many places was really carried out by neighbors and with closed eyes."[138] Despite the lack of widespread recalls, settlement officials believed that there would be enough businesses to satisfy the needs of incoming settlers with priority rights, and national committees had been instructed to reserve these businesses for them. However, national committees did not always heed these instructions and continued to install national administrators without priority status.[139] Such actions led to further recalls, hampered the consolidation of local economies in the borderlands and increased tensions among settlers concerning the final distribution of confiscated German businesses.

By the fall of 1945, as expulsions slowed and incoming settlers numbered well over 500,000, several borderland towns experienced housing shortages and pressure on local officials to resolve the situation increased. Germans felt the brunt of these shortages, but settlers also demanded that local officials examine whether those who occupied confiscated houses and apartments really deserved them. In general, settlers wanted to know that single individuals or couples did not live in large multi-bedroom apartments or homes while working families had to make do in smaller abodes. Their calls for investigation reflected the negative image of a borderlands infested with gold-diggers, where officials looked out only for themselves and their mates. It likewise reflected the early rush to the borderlands after the war when local officials had only limited oversight of confiscated property. Many settlers had already come and gone and others had moved around within apartment buildings. While officials and settlers

[136] Meeting from the Oversight board of the Settlement Office, April 25, 1946. NA, f. 23, a. j. 310.
[137] Informace o živnostech a rodinných domcích pod národní správou, OÚ, September 16, 1946. NA, f. 100/34, a.j. 1042. I would like to thank Adrian von Arburg for sharing a copy of this document.
[138] "Osidlovací politika a přednostní práva účastníků odboje," Svobodné slovo September 8, 1946.
[139] See for instance, 23889/46 ONV Teplice-Šanov, September 24, 1946. SOkA Teplice-Šanov, f. MěNV Dubí, k. 3 inv. č. 66; VII/1-230.569/46 Ministersvto vnitrního obchodu, December 23, 1946. SOkA Chomutov, f. MNV Vejprty, k. 31 inv. č. 25.

wanted a more orderly approach to the distribution of expropriated housing, unraveling the summer settlement crunch required systematic revisions and the political will to challenge the position of first comers.

The reality, however, was that national committees did not have the
means to carry out these *revise* and, even if they could, there simply was
not enough suitable space for everyone. In Děčín-Podmokly, for instance,
as of November 7, 1945, there were 50,000 inhabitants in the city compared with 44,000 before the war.[140] Moreover, settlers' expectations
that they would be able to live in comparative luxury meant that their
desires could not be met. As the housing shortages escalated in many
borderland cities, central officials attempted to resolve the problem. In
November 1945, the Ministry for the Protection of Labor and Social
Welfare issued an emergency housing directive that applied to the borderlands and any interior town with over 3,000 people.[141] This directive
established principles to ensure that single individuals and those just
passing through did not end up in possession of large apartments at the
expense of families and those with full-time employment seeking to
permanently settle.

The *revise* carried out by local officials in connection with this directive
unsurprisingly failed to change the situation. In Podmokly local officials
had already conducted a housing revision in the fall of 1945. In early
1946, a second revision, which the housing office attempted after the
Ministry's emergency directive, was never completed. Only as conditions
on the housing market worsened during the summer of 1946 did officials
take more drastic measures. In July 1946, the ONV issued new regulations to alleviate "the housing crisis" which was "reaching a climax."
These regulations included forcing unemployed persons to move outside
the city and placing individuals into so-called *garconkas*, or studio apartments. It justified these and other restrictive measures in the interest of
the statewide economy and the extraordinary pressure on the housing
market.[142] These provisions exceeded those approved in a new law concerning housing welfare. The law's provisions for the borderlands gave
national committees the right to intervene and to make housing available
for settlers, but not with such blanket provisions as those in Podmokly.[143]
The third revision in Podmokly, which occurred in the fall of 1946,
following the promulgation of the new law, found only ten uninhabited

---

[140] Minutes from meeting of MSK on November 7, 1945. SOkA Děčín, f. MěNV Děčín, k.
1 inv. č. 40.
[141] See directive for local national committees from Ministerstvo ochraný práce a socialní
peče, November 28, 1945. SOkA Děčín, f. MNV Česká Kamenice, k. 76 inv. č. 128.
[142] Vyhláška č.29.902/46, ONV Děčín, July 26, 1946. Ibid.
[143] See Law 163/46, July 18, 1946. *Sbírka zákonů a nařízení Československu*, 1946.

apartments. The housing official noted the extreme difficulties of carrying out such *revise* in the borderlands, "where several places are only temporary stations."[144] This was especially true during the summer of 1946 when expulsions reached their highest rate and created new housing opportunities for settlers. Authorities in Podmokly could not overcome the administrative complexities involved in the transfer of the town's entire residential property and the whims of settlers who continued to seek the best possible accommodations.

Revise raised questions about the borderlands' future as well as its immediate past and assured, if nothing else, conflict among settlers. National administrators, a majority of whom were first comers, considered revisions not only a threat to their newly established livelihood in the borderlands, but also a rejection of the promise that settlement offered attractive benefits such as better housing and employment opportunities. Requests for houses reflected a sense of entitlement in exchange for past or present hardships. For instance, one miner, in his request for an apartment in Ervěnice, noted that he had been a miner for twenty-six years, had not missed a shift since liberation and that his brother had been tortured to death at the camp in Terezín. Therefore, he reasoned, "according to current circumstances I have a right to a proper apartment with enough daily sunlight."[145] Another report from September 1945 stated that the "majority of national administrators consider these homes as if they own them, invest money into the buildings without the approval of the MNV, make changes, etc." It noted that such national administrators assumed they would have priority for the final allocation of confiscated property.[146]

Given these assumptions, it should come as no surprise that first comers reacted sharply against *revise*, which they feared would remove them as national administrators in order to make space for soldiers, reemigrants and others with priority rights. In one example, a delegation of 1,620 national administrators in Litoměřice wrote: "Working people are widely convinced that priority rights do not exist, and if they will be enforced, they will create the impression of injustice and protectionism and will be regarded as a brake on the progressive efforts of the working people of the Czech borderlands."[147] First settlers' protests underscored their service during the early stages of the expulsion and settlement when

---

[144] Zpráva o výsledku revize činnosti bytového úřadu, Podmokly, January 1947. SOkA Děčín, f. MěNV Děčín, k. 254 inv. č. 775.

[145] See request of V.T., SOkA Chomutov, f. MNV Ervěnice, k. 50 inv. č. 173.

[146] OSK in Ústí n. L. to MNVs, September 18, 1945. NA, f. MV-NR, k. 1769 inv. č. 1576 s. B1470.

[147] Resoluce národnich spravců, Litomerice, September 2, 1945. Nosková, 92.

Figure 3.1 Assessing the value of confiscated housewares. Alexandr
Hampl, CTK

they heeded government calls and helped protect the borderlands. For
instance, one national administrator argued: "I listened to the calls that it
is necessary for Czechs to occupy this land, and immediately I decided . . .
not to wait like other people, who decided to see what would happen with
the remark 'we will wait [to see] that the Germans are not driven back to
you.'"[148] Despite the interim nature of national administrators as legal
entities, settlers who were national administrators felt they had earned the
right to own the confiscated property that they managed.

---

[148] Letter from national administrator, May 26, 1948. SOkA Jeseník, f. ONV Jeseník, k. 71
inv. č. 109.

Settlers with priority rights likewise felt entitled to expropriated property and compelled the government to recognize their privileges. They appealed not only to the sense of justice for past service to the nation, but also to the future needs of the borderlands. In one resolution, a group of organizations representing those with priority rights argued that it was in the state's interest to settle "particularly those who proved their allegiance to the state and who guarantee that never again is a regime created that resists democracy and socialism in our land."[149] They also implied that, unlike many in the borderlands, they were "reliable people" who could help bring stability to the economy. By early 1946 officials in Prague and the borderlands wanted to make national administrators a thing of the past. However, the delicate question of how to finally allocate former German shops, companies and dwellings made it vulnerable to partisan politics. More than 200,000 national administrators had still not been given guarantees about their legal claim to property they occupied, and thousands of soldiers, returning emigrants and others with priority rights to confiscated property demanded their due. Revisions had failed to placate either group. Thus, it fell to politicians to work out who deserved to become owners of the remaining confiscated German property.

"The north must be red"

Throughout 1946 and 1947, the political parties of the National Front government engaged in heated debates regarding the final allotment of small businesses and homes. In late 1945 the Communist Party (KSČ) leadership declared: "The north must be red," and borderland party members largely delivered on this request.[150] Non-Communist parties felt that Communists benefited the most from the way in which the ownership of confiscated farms had been resolved. During the May 1946 elections the KSČ received over 50 percent of the votes in most borderland districts, much higher than its returns in other parts of the country. It successfully pushed forward the allocation agenda for expropriated farmland, and promised cheap prices as well. While the other parties of the National Front did not oppose this policy, they could not capitalize on the political advantages that it offered. Instead, when the KSČ advanced a similar position on confiscated homes and small

---

[149] Request from Svaz osvobozených politických vězňů a pozůstalých po obětech nacismu, Svaz Národní Revoluce, Sdružení zahraničních vojáků druhého odboje při Československé obci legionářské, May 22, 1946. NA, f. Úřad předsednictva vlády – Běžná spisovna (ÚPV-B), k. 999 inv. č. 4671 sign. 1341/10.

[150] Minutes of the Communist Party's Settlement Committee of the Central Committee, September 15, 1945. NA, f. 23, a.j. 15.

businesses, the other parties blocked it. They could not allow the KSČ to be the only party claiming to represent early settlers' interests in the distribution of confiscated property; the political cost was simply too steep.

By the end of 1945, roughly 80,000 national administrators occupied former Sudeten German farms in the borderlands.[151] Following revisions, some of these were replaced by other, usually priority, applicants. Still, borderland agriculture faced significant shortcomings. At a meeting of regional representatives for the Ministry of Agriculture in early 1946, one district leader reported that the *revise* did little to resolve the problems with national administrators. He noted that many of them were on national committees and had little interest in handing over money to the National Land Fund. Under the current conditions, he argued, not one district could be considered ready for the transfer of ownership. Nevertheless, the Communist chairman of the NPF, Josef Smrkovský, insisted that ownership decrees be distributed as quickly as possible in order to eliminate the temporary position of national administrators. He argued: "When a farmer works on someone else's land, of course he does not work as he would for himself. He is unable to make plans [or] projects and cannot create a program. If he receives ownership of the land, he will know that now it is his, and will have greater interest in working."[152]

Communist leaders in charge of the settlement program had not always supported such a stance. For example, Jiří Koťátko, a Communist at the Ministry of Agriculture, whose department oversaw agricultural settlement planning, had previously condemned the unorganized process of settling the borderlands. In late August 1945, he argued that national administrators would have to step aside to make room for those with priority rights and for those who had remained in the interior to finish that year's harvesting.[153] Soon after, however, Communist policy shifted to supporting early settlers' claims to confiscated farms over those of other priority applicants. In September 1945, at a meeting of the Communist Party's Settlement Committee, one member explained the reason for this shift: "Politically the party gains very much through this [policy], because according to information we received, in a majority of cases they are members or supporters of the party."[154] Communist policy did not

---

[151] Koťátko, *Konfiskace, rozdělování a osidlování*, 7.

[152] Minutes from the meeting of the chiefs of the NPF branches, February 22, 1946. NA, f. NPF, k. 6 inv. č. 12.

[153] Všeodborový archiv ČMKOS, Prague, f. Ústřední rada odborů – Národohospodářská komise, k. 22 inv. č. 62. I would like to thank Adrian von Arburg for this document.

[154] Minutes from the meeting of the Settlement Committee of the Central Committee of the KSČ, September 26, 1945. NA, f.23, a.j. 15.

initially involve building support in the borderlands by doling out confiscated property. Indeed, the party did not have the organizational cohesion to implement such an agenda in 1945, and the rush of settlers precluded it. Instead, party leaders later realized the potential risk of losing supporters already installed as national administrators and sought to protect them. This realization likely contributed to the low number of national administrators who were recalled through the revision process. The same speaker noted prophetically that roughly 80 percent of agricultural settlers would be verified and would keep their positions during the upcoming revisions.

In early 1946, the Ministry of Agriculture, under the Communist leadership of Julius Ďuriš, decided to issue formal ownership decrees to national administrators. Timed to precede the first postwar elections in May 1946, these decrees became a political tool rather than an administrative one. The decrees did not legally transfer ownership, because that would have required rewriting the land registers and other time-consuming measures. Nonetheless, in late March, the ministry issued orders to remove all obstacles slowing the distribution of ownership decrees. The orders permitted ownership decrees not only for those national administrators who had passed the revision process, but even to those who had not carried out proper accounting procedures. These accounts involved the sale and purchase of confiscated livestock as well as harvest deliveries from 1945. The ministry warned officials to overcome all obstacles because distributing the decrees "held national importance which, according to the promise of the government, must be quickly fulfilled."[155] Even before the election returns proved the benefits of the Communist initiative to quickly turn national administrators into owners of confiscated farms, the other parties witnessed the KSČ's ability to tailor the property distribution process to its propaganda purposes. One Social Democrat remarked, for instance, that during the celebrations at which the decrees for farmsteads were distributed, only one party's [KSČ] representatives and highest officials were present.[156] Indeed, the Communists did everything they could to receive praise for quickly and cheaply distributing confiscated agricultural property. The party newspaper, for instance, ran several articles in early 1946 that highlighted their efforts to hand out ownership decrees.[157] Even the ownership decree itself reflected Communist control of confiscated land distribution; it included a line honoring the Red Army for its help in the country's liberation.

---

[155] 48.745/46-IX/2, MZ, March 27, 1946. SOkA Česká Lípa, f. ONV Dubá, k. 63 inv. č. 187.

[156] Pavel Sajal, *Za 300 miliard hodnot vrací se do rukou českého národa* (Prague, 1946), 12.

[157] See, for example, *Rudé právo*, February 19 and 24 and March 5, 1946.

While the actual extent to which the Communist Party benefited through the distribution of ownership decrees for former German farms remains unclear, the other parties feared allowing the Communist-controlled Settlement Office to oversee the same process for national administrators of homes and businesses. As the ownership decrees were being distributed to national administrators of farms, the KSČ and the Settlement Office proposed to circumvent the legal provisions in Decree 108 that gave allocation commissions, comprised of local officials, the authority to distribute other property to individual applicants. Instead, Communists wanted to hand over property to national administrators who had been certified through the revisions. The timing of this proposal coincided with the upcoming elections and was accompanied by a publicity campaign to pressure the government to accept it. For instance, the Communist Party issued a policy paper for circulation to lower officials to convey its proposal at public meetings of national administrators, in which it raised the specter that many of them would be replaced by those with priority rights through the current allocation provisions. The KSČ urged national administrators to sign a resolution supporting its position, which many did.[158]

The promise to quickly resolve the uncertainty surrounding national administrators offered potentially significant rewards in terms of political patronage. Therefore, the other Czech parties of the National Front rallied against the Communist proposal. Pavel Sajal, a Social Democratic member of the Provisional National Assembly's Settlement Committee, referred to the ownership decrees in agriculture in order to condemn the latest Communist proposal. He warned: "It is clear that such decrees only serve to create the impression of legal assurance for those awaiting allocation, [who are] ignorant of laws, which in reality they do not receive. It would be the same with the decision about the assignment of businesses, homes and other property according to general plans."[159] On May 25, 1946, the day before the elections, an article entitled "Once More to the Allocation of Businesses," in the Social Democratic borderland newspaper *Sentinel of the North*, referred to the Communist proposal to allocate businesses in similar terms. It stated: "Illegal allocation would not help in the first place to convince national administrators, for it would be possible to cancel their ownership at any time, even if they had as many as ten paper

---

[158] Referát pro veřejné schůze národních správců v pohraničí, 15 April 1946. NA, f. 100/24, a.j. 1042. I would like to thank Adrian von Arburg for sharing this document; See resolutions and demands that followed. NA, f. MV-NR, k. 480 inv. č. 1028 sign. A2826; NA, f.23, a.j.314; *Hraničář Protifašistický list okresu Frývaldova*, May 3, 1946.
[159] Sajal, *Za 300 miliard hodnot*, 12.

decrees for it."[160] The article argued that Communists should stick to the law and allow national committees and settlers to control the allocation process. Due to pressure from the other National Front parties the Communist plan stalled.

Throughout 1946 various proposals continued to emerge regarding the transfer of homes and businesses to final ownership. In the end, the parties reached a compromise whereby the Settlement Office gained the final say in which businesses remained in operation, but had to take into account the input of local authorities. Law 31, issued on February 14, 1947, was supposed to speed up the allocation provisions by removing the local ten-member allocation commissions that were originally designated to choose which national administrators would become owners. Instead, under the provisions of Law 31, the Settlement Office gained the power to dismiss national administrators, close down businesses and oversee the entire allocation process. National administrators who had taken possession of property prior to May 1, 1946, were given the right to apply for ownership of the property they had managed over priority applicants.[161] Of course, all of the parties wanted to take credit for resolving the tension between priority applicants and current national administrators. Communists argued that had the other parties been willing to go along with their original proposal, settlers would already be living under their own roof.[162] Social Democrats responded that they too had presented a proposal in May 1946, which protected the interests of national administrators already in place. Their representative noted: "Consequently it was not our Communist colleagues, who were the first to recognize the merits of certified national administrators; on the contrary, it was Social Democrats, who prepared a proposed law for their defense and benefit."[163] Though the law had been passed, additional disputes, delays and *revise* continued to hamper the final transfer of confiscated property. After the Communists took power in early 1948, another revision of national administrators occurred and renewed questions about who would gain the right to own seized permanent property.

The politics surrounding the ownership of non-agricultural property stalled in part because of party politics and the efforts of non-Communist parties to sap the support garnered by the KSČ in the first elections. The

---

[160] J. Veverka, "Ještě přidělování živností," *Stráž severu*, May 25, 1946.

[161] See Karel Petrželka, *Příděl konfiskovaných drobných živností a rodinných domků* (Prague, 1947). For background to this legislation see NA, f. MV-NR, k. 478–482, inv. č. 1028 s. A2826.

[162] From a special section for the borderlands in *Rudé právo*, February 14, 1947. NA, f. 23, a.j. 345.

[163] J. Veverka, "Další krok k úspěšní konsolidaci pohraničí." *Stráž severu*, February 16, 1947.

Communist Party's success, however, did not rest on a master plan that took advantage of confiscated property for political gain. Instead, the Communist Party sided with those who had first reached the borderlands and grabbed what they could. In this sense, the Communists followed rather than led. The party easily overlooked legal issues surrounding the transfer of ownership and the assurances given to those with priority rights and took a pragmatic approach that won them the greatest number of supporters. This solution served Communists well, as it did the first settlers, but it created lasting divisions within the borderlands.

The politics of expropriation went well beyond the competition among political parties in postwar Czechoslovakia. Disputes and conflicts arose at various government levels and among settlers. Germans too were involved in these politics. In some cases, Germans supported settlers in the acquisition of confiscated property by aiding their searches for hidden loot or by smoothing the transition for a new farmer or shop owner. In other cases, Germans uncovered the crimes of gold-diggers and helped the Czechoslovak state prosecute them. Germans also challenged the entire basis for ethnic cleansing by appealing the confiscation decrees. While most Germans lost nearly everything, their involvement in the politics of expropriation defy many of our assumptions about ethnic cleansing. Rather than hatred and violence, Czechs and Germans negotiated and bartered. Nonetheless, property expropriation served as a key component of ethnic cleansing; it fostered migration to the borderlands and forced Germans from their homes. The plan to use expropriated property as the basis for successful settlement, however, began to crumble as gold-diggers took advantage of the opportunity to take what they could while the getting was good. The confusion and conflict generated by the confiscation program hampered settlement as well. Partly as a result of these dynamics, the vision of successful settlement which sought to unite the borderlands with the rest of the country lost its importance. Instead, concerns about the economy moved to the fore. These concerns not only involved the question of who received what property, but also issues of labor and economic restructuring.

4   German Workers, Czech Settlers and Labor Politics

Expulsion or Retention?

In Česká Kamenice, where Adolf Charous, and Vilem Dovara imprisoned the first national committee chairperson, Karel Caidler, reports that old settlers protected Germans were only half true.[1] As Caidler later explained, during the first expulsions several local factory managers "emphatically protested against the transfer of their employee-specialists." In the case of the Česká Kamenice paper mill, the largest factory in town, the head of Czechoslovakia's army headquarters, General Boček, authorized the Local National Committee to exempt its workers from the transfers.[2] Throughout the borderlands, requests and demands to retain German workers poured into national committees in the summer of 1945. This chapter examines how the critical issue of replacing Sudeten German workers shaped resettlement and expulsion priorities and plans. While the focus shifts to labor and industrial policy, property, the expulsions and the future of the borderlands remain central to the dynamic relationships and policies that emerged. Local officials, factory managers and even workers did not see a contradiction in their efforts to retain German workers and re-establish industrial production while at the same time expelling the vast majority of the local population and taking over their homes. These policies and attitudes demonstrated that Czechs could compartmentalize their attitudes based on immediate needs or demands and did not see Germans solely through nationalist lenses. In the same way, Germans experienced labor policies in very different ways. Czechs treated many Germans as forced laborers, as had been typical of wartime policies throughout Central and Eastern Europe. Czechs considered other Germans as specialists and extended privileges to them in return for their productive experience or trade knowledge. Finally, the labor debates also divided central and local officials over control of the borderlands' fate. Examining the debates, experiences and policies surrounding labor issues

---

[1] See Chapter 2 for more on the situation in Česká Kamenice.
[2] Protocol of Karel Caidler, March 15, 1947. Národní archiv, Prague (NA), f. Ministerstvo vnitra-Nová registratura (MV-NR), karton (k.) 1943 inventární číslo (inv. č.) 1602 signatura (sign.) B2111.

in the postwar borderlands demonstrates how they too defined the character and extent of ethnic cleansing.

Amid the increasing tempo of expulsions during June and July 1945, military leaders cared little about the borderland economy. Central directives issued in June ordered that economic interests should be respected during the expulsions, so that enough German workers remained to continue production.[3] A directive from the Provincial National Committee in Prague, for instance, offered detailed instructions about what kinds of workers should be kept. It gave preference to Germans over the age of thirty-five without children who looked after livestock or worked in specialized agricultural production, such as hop growing and sugar-beet cultivation, and workers in public utilities and mining.[4] Such orders, however, proved less important than forces on the ground. For example, on June 18, 1945, the commander of the 28th Infantry Regiment ordered the Local National Committee (MNV) in Polevsko to prepare a transfer for the following day. In his meeting with local officials the commander referred to official policies that stated which Germans should be selected for expulsion, especially NSDAP members and those unfit for work. He also mentioned that under no circumstances should glass experts be removed because they were needed for local industry. The Local National Committee responded by drawing up a list of roughly 140 Germans for expulsion. Displeased with this low figure, the commander instructed the MNV to produce at least 50 percent of the local population for immediate transfer, and consequently expelled nearly 220 people, including many glass workers. The MNV, which had already forced a majority of Sudeten Germans from the district, complained that such acts wreaked havoc in the town.[5]

Military officials saw little reason to allow Germans to remain. Their mission was to secure the borders and cleanse the region of Germans. In the northern mining town of Most, for example, a local lieutenant warned mining officials that Sudeten German miners would not be exempt from the transfer. This was despite the fact that the Minister of Industry,

[3] Směrnice k nařízení zemského národního výboru o vystěhování Němců č.874, Zemský národní výbor (ZNV) Prague, June 12, 1945. NA, f. MV-NR, k. 7443 inv. č. 4148 sign. B300; 75 Taj.1.odděl.1945, June 19, 1945, Vojenský historický archiv (VHA) Prague, f. Velitelství první oblasti (VO1), k. 48 inv. č. 263; Zásadení směrnice pro řizení a provádění akce k vyčíštění Moravy a Slezska od Němců, Velitelství 3. oblastí (VO3), 25 June 1945. Státní okresní archiv (SOkA) Bruntál, f. Okresní národní výbor (ONV) Bruntál I, k.13 inv. č. 81; S. Biman a R. Cílek, *Poslední mrtví, první živí: České pohraničí květen až srpen 1945* (Ústí nad Labem, 1989), 44–45; Tomáš Staněk, *Odsun Němců z Československu, 1945–1948* (Prague, 1991), 155.
[4] Směrnice k nařízení zemského národního výboru o vystěhování Němců č.874, ZNV Prague, June 12, 1945. NA, f. MV-NR, k. 7443 inv. č. 4148 sign. B300.
[5] Zápis o stěhovací akcí za voj. součinnosti, Československý Národní výbor v Polevsku, June 20, 1945. VHA, f. VO1, k. 49, inv. č. 267.

Bohumil Laušman, had expressly prohibited expulsions of miners from the North Bohemian Brown Coal Mines (Severočeský hnědouhelné doly, SHD), and threatened reproach for any violations. Mining officials invoked his authority when they voiced complaints to the lieutenant that expelling Germans from the mines disregarded official policy. The lieutenant replied simply that "indeed he had received such orders, but that each district should do things according to its own will."[6] The tensions between military and civilian authorities in the borderlands reflected the military's overall control of the expulsion process as well as its power vis-à-vis local officials at a time when the state administration was still forming.[7] From the perspective of soldiers, the conflicts over German workers also raised doubts about borderland officials' national loyalty; allowing Germans to stay undermined the goals of the expulsions and the authority of military officers at a time of national reckoning.

Within the context of ongoing expulsions, borderland national committees faced difficult decisions concerning the fate of German workers. In some places, national committee members sought to protect Sudeten Germans from the expulsions because they had close personal relations with local Germans, or because they wished to take advantage of cheap labor to benefit themselves and their friends who controlled local firms. For the most part, however, national committees, urged by factory managers, farmers and others, retained Sudeten Germans in order to sustain the local economy. In many cases Germans possessed skills and experience vital to sustain production in local factories. Many textile manufacturing companies specialized in accessories or hand-made embellishments for garments. Producing these high-quality goods required years of experience. Likewise, the glass-making industry, often based on small-scale production, demanded craft skills and techniques not easily transferred to others. Accountants, office personnel and managers also remained in high demand in borderland firms. National committees' efforts to protect experienced German workers stemmed mainly from their desire to keep important local industries viable.

Prior to any central directives, individual national committees took the initiative to ensure that valuable Germans continued to work for local firms as early as May 1945.[8] In Jablonec nad Nisou (Jablonec), for

---

[6] Pamětní záznam, July 14, 1945. Státní oblastní archiv, Litoměřice, pobočka v Mostě (SOA, p. Most), f. Severočeský hnědouhelné doly-generalní ředitelství (SHD-GŘ), sign. 5–3-10 č. 279 01, 03.

[7] See report on the meeting of various district officials about problems with expulsion of miners, August 22, 1945. SOkA Teplice-Šanov, f. ONV Teplice-Šanov, k. 8 inv. č. 239.

[8] See examples in the following: Proposal for the organization of the Local National Committee, undated (likely early May 1945). SOkA Jablonec n.N., f. Městský národní vybor (MěNV) k. 123 inv. č. 58; Minutes from meeting of the Revolutionary National Committee, Děčín, May 20, 1945. SOkA Děčín, f. MěNV Děčín, k. 1 inv. č. 39; See lists

instance, national administrators and local officials issued so many exemption certificates to protect glass makers and their families from the expulsions that reportedly 80 percent of local Germans could remain.[9] In the summer of 1945, however, this situation was untenable and increased tensions between those connected with the glass industry and others who wanted the Germans gone. The rumor that the Allies would not support a total expulsion of Germans bolstered the case for the latter group and provided them the impetus to take matters into their own hands.[10] Led by the Communist security chief, Karel Šilhan, the Revolutionary National Committee decided to begin organizing their own expulsions from Jablonec in stages, beginning with members of the NSDAP who would not face trials in the People's Courts. In the middle of June, after receiving assurances from a Soviet general that he would accept a contingent of Germans across the border, they gathered 2,000 local Germans for expulsion. The transfer went poorly. The local administrative commissioners had only two days to prepare and they transported the Jablonec Germans into Polish controlled territory, where authorities refused to accept them. The Polish military, with Soviet support, forced the Germans back across the border, and many returned to Jablonec, where anxieties continued to run high about the German workers' fate.[11]

Jablonec and the glass-making industry became a focal point in discussions concerning the future of skilled German workers. This district specialized in the production of glass jewelry and other glass artifacts primarily for export, which brought in valuable foreign currency. At the time of the Nazi occupation, an estimated 120,000 workers participated in the glass industry statewide, one-third of whom lived in and around the district of Jablonec.[12] Production of these goods depended on the work of skilled laborers, the vast majority of whom were Germans. Central authorities had recognized the need to protect glass workers from indiscriminate expulsions, but, as noted earlier, such strictures meant little to those expelling Germans from the country. Following the failed expulsion from Jablonec in June 1945, officials

---

for requests of exemption from local factories. SOkA Chomutov, f. MěNV Vejprty, k. 16 inv. č. 20.

[9] Report from Josef Gottwald to the Office of the Presidium of the Government, August 11, 1945. NA, f. Ministerstvo průmyslu, 1945–1950 (MP), k. 1141 inv. č. 3631.

[10] Stěhování Němců z Jablonec n. N., June 11, 1945. SOkA Jablonec n. N., f. Jablonec ONV, k. 23 inv. č. 23.

[11] Ibid.; Vystěhování Němců z Jablonec n.N., Ministerstvo vnitra (MV), July 24, 1945. NA, f. Úřad předsednictva vlády-tajné (ÚPV-T), k. 308 inv. č. 1635 sign. 127/2. See testimony of Bruno Hofmann, May 15, 1950, accessed on November 20, 2015, winterson nenwende.com/scriptorium/english/archives/whitebook/desg10.html.

[12] Report from Josef Gottwald, August 11, 1945. NA, f. MP, k. 1141 inv. č. 3631; Vl. Mikolášek, "Jak je postupováno v odsunu německých odborníků na jablonecku," *Stráž severu*, December 8, 1946.

at the Ministry of Industry and local supporters in Jablonec finally compelled the central government to action. The Interior Ministry reissued the general order to leave enough German workers to maintain production, and the government named a special representative to the district to monitor the local authorities' actions concerning the expulsion of Germans.[13]

The difficulties that Jablonec officials faced when dealing with local German glass workers, often referred to as specialists, gave shape to more general debates about which German workers should remain. Although instructions existed to leave enough Germans behind to ensure continued production, by July 1945 central officials had accomplished little regarding the future labor needs of the borderlands and the organization of the expulsions.[14] This lack of central guidance forced factory managers and national committees to work out their own solutions. National administrators of factories sometimes refused to accept Czech workers because they argued that the factory had enough workers.[15] At times, they refused such workers in order to continue employing Germans, whom they did not have to pay as much. In other cases, factory managers sought to keep Germans because they needed their skills and know-how to run these firms. For example, one national administrator of a firm which produced mechanical weavers explained that during the revolutionary period after the war, ten of the firm's eleven technical and administrative personnel left. The remaining accountant provided a key link for maintaining production during the summer. The national administrator requested that officials allow the accountant to continue working for the firm because "in the nation's interest it is more beneficial, if in this case the German's knowledge is fully used for a definite period of time, than if the aforementioned employee became a cleaning woman in a local bar."[16] Highlighting Germans' specialized skills and know-how became a common trope in managers' efforts to justify the retention of enemy workers.

During the summer of 1945, factory managers' efforts to keep German workers forced the central government to develop more concrete solutions to the looming labor crisis. By the fall of 1945, Prague officials who

---

[13] Interior memo from Department 13, MP, September 5, 1945. NA, f. MP, k. 1140 inv. č. 3631; Oběžník B-2111–11/7–45-II/1, MV, July 10, 1945. NA, f. MV-NR, k. 1948 inv. č. 1602 sign. B2111; Reports from Úrad národní bezpečnosti, Jablonec n.N., July 4 and 20, August 1, 1945. NA, f. MV-NR, k. 7445 inv. č. 4148 sign. B300.

[14] Internal memo for minister from Department II, Ministerstvo hospodářství a práce, July 25, 1945. NA, f. Ministerstvo ochrany práce a sociální péče, 1945–1951 (MOPSP), k. 556 inv. č. 1131 sign. 2246.

[15] Odgermanisování podniků v pohraničí, Okresní úřad ochrany prace (OÚOP), Ústí n. L., July 27, 1945. Archiv města (AM) Ústí n. L., f. ONV Ústí n. L., k. 9 inv. č. 49.

[16] Žádost o přikázání a ponechání něm. stát. příslušnice. Národní správa fy. Carl Herliczka, September 1, 1945. NA, f. MP, k. 1140 inv. č. 3631.

oversaw industry in the borderlands began serious discussions about replacing German workers. Two considerations dominated these discussions. The first concerned the possible loss of highly skilled experts that would severely threaten certain domestic industries and promote the construction of competitive industries in Germany. The Interior Ministry, otherwise opposed to any talk of keeping Germans for economic reasons, appeared more committed to keep key industrial leaders and experts in the country.[17] Its officials wished to stop the possible transfer of production secrets and technical engineers. The ministry worked to keep these leading Sudeten Germans in the country and formally prevented their voluntary departure in October.[18]

The second consideration, which local officials promoted, involved safeguarding borderland industries so that productive capabilities could be returned to prewar levels. In order to make this vision a reality, the loss of the Sudeten Germans who had built these industries had to be stemmed. People who held such views might usefully be considered "productionists," a term used by Christopher Browning to describe certain German officials and industrialists' attitudes toward Jewish labor during the Holocaust.[19] Productionists were often German industrial leaders or bureaucrats who sought to make the best use of Jewish labor for the war economy, placing economic interests ahead of Nazi ideology. In the Czechoslovak case, certain departments in the Ministry of Industry and the Ministry for the Protection of Labor and Social Welfare, directors of nationalized firms, as well as business organizations such as The United Federation of Czechoslovak Industry, and The Chamber of Business and Trade, often supported the use of German labor and, thus, productionist regulations. More importantly, local borderland officials and settlers frequently adopted productionist perspectives to justify their efforts to retain Sudeten German workers. This outlook may appear counterintuitive, considering that local officials could lose their posts and national administrators their newly acquired positions and property had they appeared to be protecting Germans. Yet, somewhat ironically, both settlers and national committee members strove to maintain the unique industrial character of their towns, despite its "German" heritage. Their efforts meshed with the image of resettlement based on upward mobility and a brighter future. Such a vision neither presupposed the retention of Germans, nor precluded support for the expulsions. Nevertheless, as

---

[17] Letter from MV, August 19, 1945, ibid.; See also directive Z-1 11856/1945–9, MV, September 13, 1945. Ibid.

[18] B-300/951/45- Ref B, MV, October 18, 1945. NA, f. MP, k. 1142 inv. č. 3631.

[19] Christopher Browning, *Nazi Policy, Jewish Workers, German Killers* (Cambridge, 2000), 65–68.

local officials and managers attempted to put local economies back on track, they promoted productionist policies which meant keeping much of the enemy workforce.

The move to protect specialists in Jablonec raised the possibility that several thousand Germans would remain following the transfer. Indeed, by September 1945 the District Administrative Commission (OSK) had distributed 30,000 registration forms to protect workers in the district from expulsion. This possibility created a delicate political situation for local and District Administrative Commission members. Reports of Germans carrying out industrial sabotage, like the explosion in Krasné Březno, undermined the idea of indefinitely retaining German workers. In Jablonec, despite the efforts of the central government's representative, local expulsions continued. On September 8, 1945, the Local National Committee in Kokonín, a town that specialized in jewelry production, sent twenty families to the camp in Rychnov with permission from the District Administrative Commission in Jablonec.[20] Later that month, the OSK issued orders restricting the freedom of Germans. In response, Germans began voluntarily leaving the area. One case involved two factory owners who attempted to escape with some of their equipment through the aid of Soviet soldiers. On October 6, a sixty-four-year-old Sudeten German murdered the Czech national administrator of a glass factory and then turned the gun on himself. In retaliation, 600 Germans were expelled to a nearby camp. Despite the tensions, or possibly because of them, the OSK had registered 9,816 skilled workers and 11,229 of their family members by October 24, all of whom were slated to receive exemption from the expulsions.[21] While many opposed the idea of retaining Germans for any reason, the success of the Jablonec registration campaign reflected the growing consensus that some German workers were worth keeping.

First Settlers, Labor Shortages and German Migrant Workers

Future concern for the economy was not the only issue fueling efforts to keep German workers in Jablonec and elsewhere in the borderlands. Immediate labor shortages, both in the borderlands and in the interior,

[20] Report from Josef Gottwald, September 18, 1945. NA, f. MP, k. 1141 inv. č. 3631; Report from Josef Gottwald, September 13, 1945. NA, f. MV-NR, k. 1943 inv. č. 1602 sign. B2111.

[21] Reports from Josef Gottwald, October 10 and 24, 1945. NA, f. MV-NR, k. 1943 inv. č. 1602 sign. B2111; Report from Zemský odbor bezpečnosti odd. II., ZNV Prague, October 18, 1945, ibid.

also drove the demand for German labor. The expulsions were to blame for some of the shortages, but the resettlement campaign also left vacancies in its wake. While the immigrating Czechs should have offset most of the labor loss created through the expulsions, shortages still abounded. Meanwhile, the emigration of tens of thousands of people from the country's interior created labor shortfalls there, particularly in agriculture. In Chapter 3 we saw how resettlement, based on the confiscation and redistribution of German housing and property, created pressures that supported the expulsions. Even in the district of Jablonec this was the case. For instance, the security chief of the OSK made it clear that the need to free up housing had sparked the transfer of families from Kokonín in September.[22] Still, resettlement pressures did not produce a singular response from officials concerning German inhabitants. Some local officials lobbied for their removal, while others pursued productionist policies. Which policy they chose had much to do with the pace and nature of resettlement.

First settlers arriving in the borderlands during the summer and fall of 1945 did not gravitate toward industrial employment. Part of this phenomenon had to do with the wartime experience. The war and occupation took its toll on Czech workers and altered the structure of the labor force. Women and young adults, for instance, accounted for much of the 30 percent increase in industrial employment from 1938 to 1945. Immediately after the war, many of these new workers left their posts for a short while, until labor shortages caused by the departing Sudeten Germans made it necessary for them to return.[23] Some who worked for the Nazi war economy, often those in industry and mining, moved into administrative and managerial positions following the war and the expulsion of Germans. Others sought easier work in the borderlands. Indeed, by September 1945, Czechs working in borderland industries numbered just over 10 percent (122,000) of the total number of Czech inhabitants there, even though many were new arrivals and were without their families.[24] Local officials, from security chiefs to industrial leaders, continually commented on this problem.

---

[22] Report from Zemský odbor bezpečnosti odd. II., ZNV Prague, October 18, 1945. NA, f. MV-NR, k. 1943 inv. č. 1602 sign. B2111.

[23] Václav Průcha et al., *Hospodářské a sociální dějiny Československa, 1918–1992*, vol. 2 (Brno, 2009), 140–44; Anna Beinhauerová and Karel Sommer, "K některým aspektům průmyslové zaměstnanosti v českých zemích od osvobození do zahájení dvouletky," *Československý časopis historický* 37, no.3 (1989): 322–25.

[24] L. Ruman, "Vývoj průmyslové zaměstnanosti od března do července 1946," *Statistický zpravodaj* 9, no. 10 (1946), 315; Karel Janů, "Pohraničí, průmysl a dvouletý plan," *Osídlování*, December 10, 1946. This article gives 122,000 as the number of Czechs in industry to July 31, 1945, though this does not correspond with other labor figures.

The availability of agricultural workers was a second area of the postwar labor market negatively affected by expulsion and resettlement. The rush to occupy borderland farms eased officials' fears that crops and livestock there would go untended, but had the corollary effect of leaving many farmers in the interior without the laborers necessary to collect that year's harvest. In total, a shortage of roughly 300,000 workers existed. Officials made plans to retain German workers until the final transports and, in the long term, to look for agricultural workers from Slovakia, Italy and the Balkans. In addition, in early 1946 the government called upon eighteen- and nineteen-year-olds to work three-month stints on farms for the fall harvest and the spring planting in 1947. This measure, which was later sanctioned by Law 176/46, yielded more than 100,000 young men and women to help with agricultural work.[25] In some ways, this program presaged the worker brigades that became common during the Communist era.

Incoming settlers and labor shortages in the interior worked in tandem to turn thousands of Sudeten Germans into internal forced migrants. To compensate for the shortage of agricultural workers, the Interior Ministry issued a directive to use Germans from the borderlands for interior farm work, especially professionals, such as lawyers or office personnel, who would not be missed in local industry.[26] By September 1945, for instance, nearly 2,000 German workers were sent from the Krnov district to work in the interior. As the fall planting needs increased, district officials dispatched more Germans, so that by the end of October more than 6,500 of those able to work had been transported from the district. During the same period, the city of Krnov experienced a sharp increase in the number of Czech residents, from 480 to 8,598.[27] This rapid pace of immigration put a premium on decent housing, especially because only limited numbers of Sudeten Germans had been expelled from the district during 1945. Therefore, forcing the remaining Germans to work in the interior offered officials an alternative to expelling them abroad, which was becoming increasingly difficult by the fall, and it appeased incoming settlers' housing demands. In this case, housing and labor pressures worked together to force Germans from their towns.

---

[25] Průcha, 145; Lubomír Slezák, *Zemědělské osídlování pohraničí českých zemí po druhé světové válce* (Brno, 1978), 35; Karel Jech, ed., *The Czechoslovak Economy, 1945–1948* (Prague, 1968), 43.

[26] Z-3751/1945/II, MV, July 10, 1945. NA, f. MOPSP, k. 556 inv. č. 1131 sign. 2246.

[27] Report on population and workforce, OÚOP Krnov, November 1, 1945. SOkA Bruntál, f. OÚOP Krnov, k. 6 inv. č. 21; For Krnov's population growth compare reports: Situační zpráva – úřad Národní bezpečností (SNB) Krnov, July 11 and October 15, 1945. SOkA Bruntál, f. ONV Krnov I, dodatek, k. 11 inv. č. 92.

Like agriculture, the mining industry in the borderlands faced severe labor shortages. In July 1945, mining officials estimated that to reach production goals after the expulsions nearly 50,000 more workers would be needed – a 75 percent increase in the total number of miners.[28] Although the expulsion of Sudeten Germans from areas like Most had already hurt production, the loss of Czech miners was just as critical. Czechs, rather than Germans, had comprised the majority of miners before and during the war. In the late nineteenth century the expanding scope of mining operations in Northern Bohemia began attracting Czech migrants in search of work. From 1880 to 1910, the percentage of Czech speakers in the lignite district around Most, for instance, rose from 8 to 21 percent.[29] During the war Nazi officials forced even greater numbers of Czechs to work in the mines. Liberation in May 1945 offered Czech miners a chance to escape from the harsh working conditions. Many took the opportunity to resettle in the borderlands, while others found positions in the expanding state administration of the economy.[30] The departure of Czech workers came at a critical time, when mining output had fallen drastically and the military was expelling experienced German miners.

Prague officials, however, found few solutions to the labor problems facing the mines. In August 1945, the Ostrava-Karviná mines (OKD) needed an additional 15,000 miners to meet their production requirements and planned on using Germans to reach half of this figure. In a letter to the Ministry of Industry, the directors complained that all attempts carried out centrally from Prague had failed to produce even one worker. Thus it was clear, the letter continued, "that OKD must help itself."[31] Together with the district labor office, they organized a campaign to round up Germans from neighboring districts in Silesia. While the campaign successfully gathered more than 5,500 Sudeten Germans for work in the mines, reliance on these workers did not provide a sound basis for future labor policy.[32] Around the same time, district officials in Northern Bohemia met with the regional labor office and military

---

[28] Stav osazenstva dolů dle revírů v červenci, MOPSP. NA f. MOPSP, k. 477 inv. č. 1068 sign. 2140.

[29] Elizabeth Wiskeman, *Czechs and Germans* (London, 1967), 55.

[30] Zpráva na schůzi na Ministerstvo prumysl, October 29–30, 1945. NA, f. Osídlovací komise při ÚV KSČ (f. 23), a.j. 349/1; *Dnešek*, May 2, 1945; Beinhauerová and Sommer, "K některým aspektům," 325–26, 330–33; Staněk, *Odsun Němců*, 156.

[31] Letter from Ústředí ostravsko-karvinského kamenouhelného revíru, August 16, 1945. NA, f. MOPSP, k. 477 inv. č. 1068 sign. 2140.

[32] Německé pracovní síly v hornictví-návrh, OÚOP Mor. Ostrava, November 5, 1945. Ibid.; Zpráva o politického a hospodářského situace, SNB Krnov, October 15, 1945. SOkA Bruntál, f. ONV Krnov I, dodatek, k. 11 inv. č. 92.

authorities in an attempt to locate much-needed German labor for the mines in the area.[33] Central officials condemned such campaigns to collect Germans because they argued that many local Germans escaped abroad in fear of being sent to the mines, which in turn undermined the local industries where they had been employed.[34] However, the critical labor shortage in 1945 left mining officials with few options except to pursue Sudeten German workers. Such ad hoc measures reflected the lack of central coordination and set the stage for future problems regarding the retention of German labor during the Allied transfers in 1946 and 1947.

Despite the pressures on the housing market and the need for workers in the interior, borderland national committees kept the majority of Sudeten Germans for labor in their own districts. Figures from the Ministry of Labor and Social Welfare indicate that, of the roughly 763,000 Germans working in October 1945, 663,000 remained in their own districts.[35] They worked primarily as agricultural workers and unskilled laborers. There were several reasons why local authorities were reluctant to send German workers away. First, officials in the interior of the country wanted only able-bodied (*práce schopných*) Germans. For borderland national committees, this meant deporting useful workers for the benefit of interior districts, while increasing the already difficult burden of supporting those who could not work. In addition, Czechs did not seek low paying jobs in the borderlands, and this work was readily performed by Germans, regardless of their abilities. Finally, by October 1945, both the pace of resettlement and the need for agricultural workers following the fall planting began to dissipate. Because regulations for the official transfer required that people be transferred from their own districts, it made little sense to send them away a few months before the official expulsions were set to begin in 1946.

The migration of settlers in search of a new home or farm aggravated many of the labor problems initially caused by expelling Sudeten Germans. Yet, the opportunity to acquire property at little cost motivated people to relocate to the borderlands and became a focal point for the official resettlement program. For the Settlement Office (OÚ), the challenge of "settlement politics" became connecting settlers' desire for cheap property with the

---

[33] Minutes from a meeting of OSK and ONV, military and OÚOP officials, August 22, 1945. SOkA Teplice-Šanov, f. ONV Teplice-Šanov, k. 8 inv. c. 239.

[34] Interior memo for minister, December 22, 1945. NA, f. MOPSP, k. 477 inv. č. 1068 sign. 2142. For other measures carried out at Severočeský hnědouhelné doly (SHD), see Zdeněk Radvanovský, "The Social and Economic Effects of Resettling Czechs into Northwestern Bohemia, 1945–1947," in *Redrawing Nations: Ethnic Cleansing in East-Central Europe, 1944–1948*, eds. Philipp Ther and Ana Siljak (Lanham, 2001), 247–48.

[35] Reports from district labor offices, MOPSP, November 10, 1945. NA, f. MOPSP, k. 556 inv. č. 1131 sign. 2246.

responsibility to work. Both borderland and Prague officials felt that grave problems faced borderland industries. By the end of 1945, one settlement official estimated that settlers' occupational structure was 30 percent in agriculture, 25 percent in industry, 25 percent in business and trade and 20 percent in remaining occupations.[36] This estimate indicated the large extent to which settlers avoided industrial work during 1945. Comparable figures for employment in the Sudetenland prior to the war were 28 percent in agriculture, 48 percent in industry, 14 percent in commerce and trade and 10 percent in other professions.[37] That Germans kept working and early settlers searched for other employment, or none at all, posed a serious threat to the long-term health of the borderland economy.

Settlement officials recognized the need for a concerted effort to find replacement workers in borderland industry. In the second meeting of the Central Commission for Interior Settlement in August 1945, one official reported that they needed to encourage factory national administrators to accept Czech workers so that they would be able to gain experience and be ready to continue production after the Germans were gone.[38] Yet it was the settlers themselves, rather than national administrators, who were responsible for the lack of workers. Settlement officials sought new ways of encouraging Czechs, Slovaks, re-emigrants and others to take up industrial positions. Driven by settlement politics, which utilized confiscated property to lure settlers to the borderlands, they planned to solve the pressing labor shortages by offering attractive incentives to settlers who moved there to work. For instance, in September 1945 the Settlement Office declared as part of its mission: "we must offer hesitant colonists a better living standard than they have in the interior. For our workers this means that order must be brought to the housing market and that nervousness surrounding prices must be removed." It continued, "the Settlement Office will even try to propose the correction of wages in those categories in which there is little interest and great demand."[39] Planning continued throughout 1945. In November, Miroslav Kreysa, the OÚ chairperson, reported that the planning department had been busy studying the needs of individual economic sectors and ways to bring necessary workers to the borderlands. In addition to improving wages and living conditions, the department considered other incentives, such as offering small plots of land to workers who wished to also do some

---

[36] Settlement report, č.3421/46, Osidlováci úřad (OÚ), March 1946. NA, f. 23, a.j. 359.
[37] Table on inhabitants from May 17, 1939. NA, f. Úřad předsednictva vlády – Tajná spisovna (ÚPV-T), k. 308 inv. č. 1635.
[38] Report on current settlement activities, Central Committee for Interior Settlement (ÚKVO), August 27–28, 1945. NA, f. MV-NR, k. 12145 sign. 1651/2.
[39] Mission statement, OÚ, September 18, 1945. Ibid.

farming.[40] A few weeks later, at a meeting with regional OÚ officials, Kreysa stressed the importance of finding permanent homes for workers. He noted that while agricultural and business resettlement was largely complete, the resettlement of workers was not. He gave regional officials two months to work with national committees and create lists of homes earmarked for workers. He declared: "Then the allocation of homes for textile, glass workers and miners would begin, and which homes they can receive will be outlined for individual regions. This will build people's interest about entering certain production branches"[41] OÚ officials sought to manage the flow of settlers into industrial production with carrots; the problem was that most settlers sought the benefits of property and social mobility without the burden of factory work.

Yet settlement politics also offered a way for those pursuing productionist policies to bolster their arguments for keeping German workers. Although the number of Czech workers in industry finally exceeded the number of Germans by March 1946, the fear was that production would still suffer dramatically once the Germans were gone.[42] Beginning already in the fall of 1945, national administrators, workers and industrial officials argued that it would be necessary to retain Germans to successfully reach prewar production levels. They utilized the image of a prosperous borderlands, created in part by settlement officials, to substantiate their need to keep German workers. One group of local leaders, for instance, argued that the labor question "concerns all Czech people, who listened to the calls of government functionaries and went to build the foundations of a stable borderland. What happens with those people after the transfer of Germans?"[43] Such questions linked future productive concerns to property gains and revealed a broader conceptualization of settlement politics than one predicated on the quick and cheap transfer of property. For many borderland officials and industrial managers, keeping German workers became a means to ensuring the success of resettlement.

Labor Relations

In sharp contrast to the Czech settlers being wooed to work in the borderlands with better wages and other incentives, the bulk of Sudeten

---

[40] Zpráva o činnosti, OÚ, November 29, 1945. Ibid.
[41] Meeting with Regional representatives of the OÚ, December 7, 1945. AM Ústí n.L. f. MěNV Ústí n. L., k. 2 inv. č. 24.
[42] Minutes from the meeting of the Oversight Council for the FNO, April 25, 1946. NA, f. 23, a.j. 310.
[43] Resoluce národní správy podniků průmyslových, exportních obchodních a řemeslných, October 17, 1945. NA, f. MP, k. 1141 inv. č. 3631.

Germans faced difficult and unpleasant working conditions. Putting Germans to work served as punishment, as well as a means to fill labor shortages. A general directive concerning Germans in May 1945, for example, ordered that males from ages fourteen to sixty should be collected into work camps "in order to use them for the most strenuous work, so that they repay the war damage created by the German armies." It suggested using former concentration camps, POW camps, empty factories and other suitable venues to house Germans.[44] Early labor regulations followed a similar pattern, whether issued by local or central authorities. For example, instructions issued in June 1945 by officials in Šumperk sanctioned what amounted to the forced labor of Sudeten Germans.[45] On the day after the Allies formally endorsed the transfer of Germans from Czechoslovakia – August 2, 1945 – the Interior Minister noted the need to legalize the labor responsibilities of those who lost their citizenship. He received support for the idea from the Prime Minister (a Social Democrat) and a leading member of the National Socialists, who mentioned only that they wished to enact such provisions without the publicity of a decree.[46] Nonetheless, Decree 71, issued in September 1945, forced all males from ages fourteen to sixty and all females from ages fifteen to fifty who had lost their citizenship to work "toward the removal and repayment of damages caused by the war and bombardment and also toward the renewal of economic life disrupted by the war."[47] The idea that Sudeten Germans should pay for the war and occupation through their labor and property was a common theme in the decrees and regulations established against them, and stemmed from the notion of collective responsibility that underpinned the expulsion policy.

The system of labor camps that emerged in postwar Czechoslovakia combined solutions for labor and housing shortages with the punitive nature of the expulsions. A May 1945 general directive that suggested placing all males into work camps reflected these different goals. For instance, it stated: "In these camps Germans will be treated harshly, in order to guarantee discipline, but also humanely and justly." It noted that decent quarters will be found to house them and sufficient provisions will

[44] Prozatimní všeobečné směrnice o Němcích, SNB Brno, May 20, 1945. SOkA Bruntál, f. ONV Krnov, k. 217 inv. č. 262.
[45] Announcement, OÚOP Šumperk, June 27, 1945. NA, f. MOPSP, k. 120 inv. č. 3611. Reprinted in Theodor Schieder, ed., *The Expulsion of the German Population from Czechoslovakia*, vol. 4, *Documents on the Expulsion of the Germans from Eastern-Central Europe*, trans. G.H. de Sausmarez (Bonn, 1960), 306–7.
[46] Karel Jech and Karel Kaplan, eds. *Dekrety prezidenta republiky 1940–1945: Dokumenty* (Brno, 1995), 1: 383–84.
[47] Jech and Kaplan, 1:454.

be supplied, "since we want productivity from them."[48] Even though by the middle of June 1945 the government ruled against such a general policy, many labor camps had already been established. Some of them began as outgrowths of general internment camps or later became attached to the larger camps. At least seventy-three independent labor camps existed by September 1945, and another forty-seven served both labor and internment purposes.[49] Sudeten Germans living in other collection centers or internment camps also worked in factories or farms, though in fewer numbers. In addition, dozens of factories had their own camps, not included in these figures. The experience within such company camps varied widely. For instance, in the Chlupáček textile factory in Krnov, two young Czechs were assigned to guard 430 Germans. As one of the guards reported: "For this many Germans the number of guards is inadequate, so that, as if intentionally, this gives Germans various possibilities to move about and conduct meetings." He further commented that Germans did not work in the factory, but often sat around reading books. The other guard recalled that Germans from the factory were given permission to go collect mushrooms in the nearby forest – a seemingly dangerous policy given security officials' claims that Germans were organizing sabotage missions.[50]

In other camps, especially camps attached to mines, conditions were horrid and managers forced Germans to work from dawn until dusk. The reputation of certain camps, such as the Hanke Camp in Ostrava, preceded them and served as a further means of punishment and intimidation. Following purported attacks on two internment camps in Frývaldov, which resulted in several executions, men between the ages of fifteen and sixty were given to the district labor office for transfer to the Ostrava mines.[51] The recently organized August campaign for German miners at OKD facilitated such actions. A month later, security officials reported that the continuing campaign for the work columns attached to the mines "likely contribute[d]" to the lack of "any special optimism" on the part of the Germans.[52] In this way, work and retribution went hand in hand.

---

[48] Prozatimní všeobečné směrnice o Němcích, SNB Brno, May 20, 1945. SOkA Bruntál, f. ONV Krnov, k. 217 inv. č. 262.

[49] Tomás Staněk, *Tábory v českých zemích, 1945–1948* (Opava, 1996), 37, 45, 52.

[50] Protocols of two guards, September 1945. SOkA Bruntál, f. ONV Krnov I, k. 18 inv. č. 72.

[51] Mesíční zpráva o politické situace, OSK Frývaldov, August 20, 1945. SOkA Jeseník, f. ONV Jeseník, k. 2 inv. č. 63. The shooting was reportedly carried out by a small group on August 14 and 17. See Staněk, *Tábory*, 48–49; Jana Hradilová, "Internace německého obyvatelstva v adolfovickém táboře 1945–1946," *Jesenicko* 2 (2001): 28.

[52] Mesíční zpráva o politické situace, OSK Frývaldov, September 20, 1945. SOkA Jeseník, f. ONV Jeseník, k. 2 inv. č. 63.

The retributive aspect of camps facilitated the use of Germans for manual labor without pay. With the exception of mining districts, most Germans living in camps during the fall of 1945 performed agricultural or other non-skilled labor. In November 1945 district national committees took financial control of the camps, but their administration remained in the hands of military or police authorities and local national committees.[53] Accounting for confiscated property and German labor did not figure high in these officials' priorities. During 1945, camps calculated wage rates according to their own needs and often negotiated directly with individual firms. In one case, a sugar refinery complained that the Germans' wages together with payment for room and board made them more expensive than the wages paid to Czech women.[54] These wages rarely went to the Germans living in camps, who often received nothing more than a few crowns for their work. Instead, it appears that camp officials directly benefited from a system with little effective oversight. The report for the work camp in Krnov, for instance, noted that no accounting records had been kept until August, and that the camp used German money and property to pay for bills and wages of camp employees.[55] Camp administrators were unconcerned by Germans' productivity and thus did little to improve their living conditions. Germans showed up to work without any provisions of their own, having been stripped of their possessions by national committees or camp officials.[56] Prague authorities did not fully grasp the extent of camp officials' mismanagement until the camps were shut down at the end of 1946.[57]

Despite the problems associated with the camps, labor officials at the Ministry for the Protection of Labor and Social Welfare planned to use them to help direct labor to farms and factories. In September 1945, following a government order about quickly getting Germans to fulfill work obligations, labor officials met with Interior Ministry officials about placing work camps under their authority.[58] Yet even though it had the Ministry of Interior's support, the Ministry for the Protection of Labor and Social Welfare never established a separate administrative body for

---

[53] Staněk, *Tábory*, 111. For more on the administration and operation of the camps see Chapter 1.

[54] Letter from Česka spol. pro průmysl cukerni, Mělnik, October 27, 1945. NA, f. MPSP, k. 556 inv. č. 1131 sign. 2246.

[55] Zpráva o provedené revisi, OSK Krnov, September 5, 1945. SOkA Bruntál, f. ONV Krnov I, k. 217 inv. č. 261. See also the reports in September and October for other camps in Krnov with similar problems. Ibid., k. 7 inv. č. 63.

[56] Report from work camp Hustopeči, October 15, 1945. NA f. MOPSP, k. 556 inv. č. 1133 sign. 2303; B300/1264, MV, November 19, 1945. Ibid.

[57] See, for example, notice by MV, August 30, 1946. NA, f. MOPSP k. 398 inv. č. 835 sign. 2246; *Stráž severu*, May 22, 1947; Staněk, *Tábory*, 136, 156.

[58] Jech and Kaplan, 1: 384.

work camps.[59] Instead, district ministry officials supervised the use of camp labor and helped organize special transfers of Germans for work outside the camp, but nothing more. For instance, the Krnov District Office for the Protection of Labor in 1945 helped to organize the relocation of nearly 6,000 Germans for work. It sent some of them to the mines and steelworks in Ostrava and organized others into transports for the sugar-beet harvest.[60] Yet, they had little authority to compel camps into relinquishing Germans. In June 1946, borderland camps indicated that they had few Germans available for agriculture work outside the district. The district of Česká Lípa, for example, reported that it could not release any Germans for transport to the interior. They were either being prepared for expulsion or local farms needed them.[61] As the official transfer unfolded during 1946, central labor officials had to look elsewhere to find new workers.

The story of the Peschke family's experience offers a good example of how labor needs influenced the treatment of Sudeten Germans. The mother, Elisabeth, recounted her family's ordeal from the arrival of Soviet soldiers in May 1945 until their expulsion just over a year later.[62] Immediately after the war, as soldiers, both Czechoslovak and Soviet, looted their farm, Elisabeth resigned herself to the situation, noting that "we had to accept the fact that we lost the war, that sacrifices had to be made, and that one simply had to hope to make up for the loss by hard work during the coming years." Such reflective comments, it should be noted, are rare among the recorded testimonies of Sudeten Germans. The immediate future for the Peschkes, however, proved more difficult. They were rounded up during the expulsions from the Krnov district in mid-June 1945 and brought to the local school, which served as a makeshift camp. After spending a short time in the camp the women and children were released, but Elisabeth's husband remained in custody. Soon after their return home, a Czech father and son arrived to claim the Peschke's farm as their own. The Peschkes gathered some of their belongings and moved into the annex where her mother-in-law lived. Two days later, other Czechs arrived and expelled them from the annex. Despite their constant moves, the Peschkes continued to work the fields that they had

---

[59] Directive č. II 5310–8/9, MOPSP, September 8, 1945. NA, f. MOPSP, k. 556 inv. č. 1131 sign. 2246. See also background discussion to this directive. NA, f. MOPSP, k. 556 inv. č. 1156 sign. 5310; Staněk, *Tábory*, 65.

[60] Transporty, odeslaný ze sberného tábora ve Krnově, OÚOP, Krnov. SOkA Bruntál, f. OÚOP, Krnov, k. 6 inv. č. 21. For more on the collection of workers for the sugar-beet harvest, see NA f. MOPSP, k. 556 inv. č. 1133 sign. 2303.

[61] See this report and others from June 1946. NA, f. MOPSP, k. 398 inv. č. 835 sign. 2246.

[62] Her story and the quotations for the next two paragraphs can be found in Schieder, 4: 415–20.

planted, but which now belonged to someone else. Later, the local commissar put Elisabeth and other Sudeten Germans to work for several weeks repairing the roadways. Her husband had already been sent to Ostrava to work on construction projects, and the August campaign to recruit Germans for the OKD mines took her fourteen-year-old son.

At the end of September 1945, Elisabeth and her remaining three children were sent to the interior for agricultural work. The trip lasted several days, and they were only allowed to bring a few of their remaining possessions. They lived in an old farm building previously inhabited by rabbits, chicken and geese, and now infested with mice. Elisabeth recalled their meager rations: "In the morning we had coffee with two slices of bread, for lunch potatoes with horrible gravy, in the evening potatoes in a watery soup and no bread." The work routine reflected forced labor conditions. The farm was behind schedule and much of the fall harvest had yet to be collected. In fact, they continued to work in the fields through December picking potatoes, even in the snow. Elisabeth and her children remained on the farm until February, when they received notice to return to their district in preparation for transfer. Despite regulations that stated that families had to be transferred as a single unit, it took the Peschkes several months, a trip to Ostrava, and the help of someone who knew Czech to obtain the release of their son from the mining camp. Finally, in June, they were expelled. For most Sudeten Germans, as for the Peschkes, a combination of labor needs and repression made life arduous and uncertain.

Germans who worked in local industry had better wages and living conditions than those who worked in agriculture, though much depended on local attitudes and practices. Prior to Decree 71, local officials and factory management decided for themselves how much – or how little – to pay German employees. Some Sudeten Germans, such as office personnel, received wages above 10,000 Kčs a month, while those who lived in camps and worked on local farms received 30 Kčs a day, not including deductions for room and board.[63] Industrial officials clamored for some guidance on how much to pay Germans. National committees created their own rules to make certain that Germans did not receive exorbitant wages.[64] In September 1945, officials at the Ministry for the Protection of Labor and Social Welfare responded by saying that they were still working on the problem. The Finance Ministry had already limited Germans from receiving more than 2,000 Kčs in cash monthly; wages exceeding this sum

---

[63] Compare, for example, Letter from Hospodářská skupina oděvního průmyslu, June 22, 1945, and Letter from Pracovní tábor, Opavská ulice, Krnov, August 26, 1945. NA, f. MOPSP k. 489 inv. č. 1085 sign. 2160/25.
[64] Directive on wages from OSK Teplice-Šanov, August 15, 1945, ibid.

were to be placed in blocked accounts.[65] Financial considerations influenced such decisions as much as the desire to punish Germans.

Decree 71 provided general instructions about German wage rates, but in practice wages continued to vary. According to a directive for Decree 71 from November 1945, Germans' wages were not supposed to differ from those of Czechs, except for an additional 20 percent tax.[66] The directive also allowed other deductions for room and board, unproductive family members and poor production. Such stipulations gave space for national administrators and others who wished to use Germans as cheap labor or profit for themselves. Yet many national administrators ignored official regulations and paid highly valued and productive employees more than was technically allowed. Even factory councils approved wage hikes for German workers. For instance, the factory council of one textile firm praised the production of German workers and requested significant pay increases for them.[67] From the fall of 1945, factory managers and factory councils in the borderlands acted to improve the living conditions of their German employees. Skilled German workers were often excused from extra weekend labor, such as cleaning up the town or other public work required of other Sudeten Germans.

Not all such requests were motivated by good will. Germans with enough productive power were able to pressure borderland managers and even fellow workers into supporting such demands. A letter from one factory council indicated that the leading German workers produced only as much as was necessary to ensure that they received the 2,000 Kčs maximum wage after the 20 percent deduction. The factory council requested that officials cancel the 20 percent tax on their wages.[68] Many ministry officials felt the same way. Labor officials reported that the German wage regulations "brought about several undesired phenomena, such as a drop in worker morale and the flight of Germans from their

---

[65] Proclamation č.461/45, Ministry of Finance, June 22, 1945. Reprinted in Schieder as Annex 6, 219–22. It incorrectly lists the amount at 200 Kčs. As the transfer came to a close in late 1946, the Ministry of Finance realized that many Germans were owed money in wages that they earned while awaiting transfer. Because they earned this money after their property had been confiscated, the ministry feared that it would create a future debt against the country. Considering that many workers were held for the final transports until the end of 1946 and early 1947, this debt must have been considerable. See Záznam o poradě konané v Hospodářské radě, November 5, 1946. NA f. MV-NR, k. 1787 inv. č. 1581 sign. B-1700.

[66] II-1620–3/11–45-V/4, MV, November 2, 1945. NA f. MOPSP k. 489 inv. č. 1085 sign. 2160/25; Reprinted in Schieder, 4:268–72.

[67] Letter from factory council Optimit, Odry, November 20, 1945. NA, f. MP k. 1142 inv. č. 3631.

[68] Letter from factory council Ditmar, March 1946. SOkA Teplice-Šanov, f. ONV Teplice-Šanov, kn. 1 inv. č. 1. See also Letter from Kovoděiné zavody Rachmann, Česká Lípa, August 2, 1945. NA, f. MP, k. 1140 inv. č. 3631.

jobs."[69] They also feared the productive consequences of paying well-qualified Germans less than Czechs. Officials at the Ministry of Industry even supported national administrators' requests to allow German specialists to remain in their apartments. The Interior Ministry responded negatively to one such request by arguing that "if so the settlement of the borderlands would be severely hampered by a housing problem."[70] Despite the Interior Ministry's position against extending housing benefits to Germans, however, following their formal exemption from the transfer in early 1946, German specialists received the right to retain their property and were released from the 20 percent tax.[71] While these benefits placated those who depended on German labor for their livelihood, specialists' protected status raised apprehensions among those who did not share productionist concerns.

Organizing Labor and Expulsion

During 1945, central officials had done little to coordinate settlement, expulsions and labor needs. Instead, they had simply reacted to situations as they developed. The shortage of miners in Ostrava and Most, for example, became so acute that plans to import Reich Germans from abroad to help alleviate the shortage were considered. One official at the Ministry for the Protection of Labor and Social Welfare immediately recognized the problems with such a plan, and further noted that such ideas underscored "the illogical process, that in the period when we are expelling experienced miners from Most and Duchcov districts, we want to bring unqualified Reich Germans here."[72] This was the legacy of a policy that prioritized expulsions and rapid settlement over labor needs. This policy had given military officials in the borderlands carte blanche to expel whomever, whenever, as long as they could move them across the border. Likewise, the opportunity that settlement had offered to thousands of Czechs to become independent property owners skewed the balance of labor in many borderland communities. Another labor official complained that of the Czech settlers heading to Liberec, 12,000 had applied for national administrator positions and only 72 for positions in

---

[69] Internal memorandum, odd. 2 MOPSP, February 7, 1946. NA, f. MOPSP, k. 489 inv. č. 1085 sign. 2160/25.

[70] Letter from MV, September 29, 1945. NA, f. MP, k. 1141 inv. č. 363.

[71] B-300/3825–46, MV, Směrnice o úlevách pro některé osoby německé národnosti, May 27, 1946. Předpisy z oboru působnosti OÚ a FNO: Zákony (dekrety), vládní nařízení, vyhlášky, 2 vols. (Prague, 1947), 2:305–12.

[72] Použití německých pracovních sil v průmyslů, MOPSP, July 25, 1945. NA, f. MOPSP, k. 561 inv. č. 1152 sign. 5200.

industry.[73] Although these officials blamed poor planning, the pressures of settlers in search of property and social mobility helped to starve the labor market of new recruits.

Settlement officials continued to make plans and offered incentives to try to lure workers to the borderlands. The OÚ, along with the Ministry for the Protection of Labor and Social Welfare, issued regulations which reduced rent in the borderlands by 25 percent compared to the interior. In addition, the law of extraordinary provisions for housing welfare from July 1946 capped the rent of large working families at 15–18 percent of their incomes.[74] Kreysa argued that this provision supported the OÚ's efforts to create a "biologically healthy generation" in the borderlands.[75] In early 1946 OÚ officials also proposed that qualified settlers should receive a supplement or allowance (*příspevek*) for moving to the borderlands. Again, they used such directives to encourage industrial workers in certain branches to relocate. The Justification Report for the proposed allowance noted two interrelated goals for the allowance: to bring more workers to the borderlands, and to ensure the full financial revenue from confiscated enemy property.[76] This latter goal, rarely a priority for the OÚ, simply meant trying to make sure that the state was not left carrying the maintenance costs for property confiscated, but not claimed by settlers.

Along with the allowance for moving to the borderlands and the lowering of rents, the OÚ propagated the advantages that settlement politics provided, in order to generate more interest in the program. The Settlement Office instructed industrial officials not to speak of the general need for workers when trying to raise interest in borderland industries, but to indicate that

there are homes and apartments, provisions, and rents for such and such a cost. They receive the settlement allowance. Wages are at such and such a rate, you have the opportunity for such and such benefits, advancement, and recreation. [Tell them] what is there in the surroundings and countryside, etc. Do not only speak about fantastic "valiant work" and Stakhanovites, but also how much is earned as a good worker.[77]

[73] Summary of meeting at MOPSP, July 13, 1945, ibid. Others also commented on the overwhelming interest in national administrator positions. See, for instance, *Stráž severu*, June 8 and 26, 1945.

[74] Miroslav Kreysa, *Budujeme pohraničí* (Prague, 1946), 12.

[75] Čestmír Heller, *Volné byty, levnější nájemné* (Prague, 1946), 7.

[76] Návrh vládního usnesení o jednorázovém prlatovém příspěvku osidlovacím pro veřejné a některé jiné zaměstnance v pohraničí č.19702/46, OÚ, May 14, 1946. AM Ústí n.L., f. MěNV Ústí n. L., k. 2 inv. č. 24.

[77] Doplnění pracovníků průmyslových jako základní úkol pro dokončování osídlení našeho pohraničí, OÚ, June 17, 1946. NA, f. 23, a.j. 349/1.

Thus, Settlement Officials, many of whom were Communists, realized that tangible benefits, rather than socialist zeal, would be more effective incentives to get workers to move.

The Settlement Office's information department helped to publish materials supporting the idea that the borderlands had a lot to offer workers. One article in *Osidlování*, for example, argued that it was hard to find a reason why more Czechs had not come to get a job at the J. Kunert and Sons stockings company in Varnsdorf. Not only were workers' wages and living conditions looked after, but it also had a nursery and offered maternity leave.[78] The Kunert factory had already engaged in its own efforts to bring workers to Varnsdorf. In the late summer of 1945 it sent out hundreds of posters to promote the factory (see Figure 4.1). While this campaign helped to yield dozens of new workers, certain problems persisted. The national administrator reported that a father had come to the factory with his young daughter, but because the housing question had not been appropriately resolved he decided not to leave his daughter for training there. Nonetheless, the national administrator assumed that such problems could be overcome and that 1,700 workers would be added by early 1946.[79]

Despite such efforts and plans, the fact that by early 1946 Czechs occupied fewer than half of the jobs in borderland industries did not reassure those who depended on these firms. In addition, the deep-rooted sense that in certain industrial branches some German workers were simply indispensable gave additional weight to national administrators' and national committees' calls to protect German workers. Because of this pressure, in January 1946 the government decided to exempt a limited number of German miners from the transfer. This decision was expanded in February to include nearly 50,000 industrial specialists, and again in March to cover specialists in industry and agriculture – up to 60,000 in each sector, not including family members.[80] In addition, the government established more concrete plans to ensure that qualified workers remained until the final transports in order to maximize the labor power of remaining Germans.

The Interior Ministry official who oversaw the transfer process, Antonín Kučera, immediately challenged such productionist policies. In an April 1946 bulletin sent to provincial national committees' security officials, he raised the specter that the exemption of specialists with their family

[78] "Kunertova punčochárna ve Varnsdorfu," *Osidlování*, September 27, 1946.
[79] Report from the national administrator of the Kunert factory, September 1945. Státní oblastní archiv, Litoměřice, pobočka v Mostě (SOA Litoměřice, p. Most), f. Kunert k. 2 inv. č. 8.
[80] Usnesení, Úřad předsednictva vlády, March 19, 1946. NA, f. Úřad předsednictva vláda-běžná spisovna (ÚPV-B) k. 720 inv. č. 2908 sign. 753/1; Staněk, *Odsun Němců*, 305.

Figure 4.1 Youngsters come to Varnsdorf! Courtesy of the State
Regional Archive, Litoměřice

members, together with those in mixed marriages, would leave between
700,000 and 750,000 Germans in the country. He then warned: "it is
extremely imprudent to sidestep an acute or drastic solution to this problem,
which keeps a strong fifth column in the republic."[81] Subsequent directives

<hr />

[81] Zpráva z MV odbor pro celostátní politické zpravodajství, April 9, 1946. Zemský Archive
(ZA) Opava, f. Expozitura Moravskoslezského ZNV 1945–1949, k. 140 inv. č. 273 sign.

dealing with the certification of specialists ensured that Interior Ministry and security officials were in a powerful position to decrease the number of exempted Germans. In June 1946, as the official transfer gained momentum, the ministry sent a report to the government, in which it complained about efforts to retain German workers and reiterated the central government's commitment to the expulsions. It noted that cuts in production should be expected soon.[82] For Communist leaders, the retention of German workers threatened the expulsions, which they not only championed, but for which they held primary responsibility through their control of the Interior Ministry. While the specialist program proved an easy target for security officials, for national committee members, including Communists, the issue was much more complex. Borderland labor politics entailed more than inter-party disputes and anti-German campaigns – it revealed competing visions of the borderlands' future and produced disagreements about who had the authority to bring such visions to life.

For those controlling mining production at the North Bohemian Brown Coal Mines, the loss of German workers presented bleak options in 1946. If they transferred all of the Germans, officials estimated that output would drop to May 1945 levels, or less than half of current production. Even a partial expulsion would have reduced production by 15 percent.[83] SHD officials met with representatives of workers' councils in early June 1946 to agree on how many Germans could be transferred and recently raised production goals still be reached. While a representative from the Czechoslovak National Assembly spoke in inspiring terms about the need for fewer absences and higher individual output, workers voiced more concrete concerns. The factory council chairman for mines Quido I and III, where nearly 75 percent of the workers were Germans, asked: "What happens with our mine after the transfer? It would have to be completely shut down." The representative requested replacement workers prior to expulsions.[84] Although the majority of miners expressed the desire to rid the country of Germans, they likewise demanded compensation workers on a one-to-one basis. Their meetings concluded with the decision to keep 4,500 German miners and to find 10,000 replacements. Where those replacements would be found remained unclear.

Taj. This report was earlier sent as a letter to the Presidium with additional comments. See NA, f. ÚPV-T, k. 308 inv. č. 1635 sign. 127/2.

[82] Odsun Němců a situace ve výrobě průmyslové a zemědělské, Vládní zmocněnec pro provádění odsunu Němců, June 9, 1946, ibid.

[83] Záznam o vývoj těžby při odsunu, SHD, July 25, 1946. SOA, p. Most, f. SHD-GŘ, sign. 5–3-10 č. 279 01, 03.

[84] Jednání na dole Masaryk, June 15, 1946. Ibid.

Yet even keeping 4,500 Germans, less than a third of the number working at SHD in the spring of 1946, proved difficult. For example, Ervěnice, a town in the middle of the northern Bohemian mining strip, resisted mining officials' attempts to determine which Germans would remain. In August 1946, defying a ban on the expulsion of miners, the Local National Committee in Ervěnice transferred several miners and their families. When questioned about this violation, the MNV responded that it had only expelled those physically unfit for mining, even though records indicated that almost all of the town's remaining Germans had recently received specialist status.[85] On September 25, 1946, the MNV sent the following appeal to the Interior Ministry: "in the interest of guaranteeing the national identity, the inviolability of state sovereignty and the security of the social achievements of the memorable May 1945 revolution, we request that [the transfer of Germans] be carried out consistently and without regard to the temporary economic losses, which by our own persistence we can surmount."[86] Such requests were followed by more direct action. In early November the chairman of the MNV pressured the workers' councils at local mines to release more Germans for expulsion. After reminding them about "the great struggles in the past for a Czech school and Czech language" in the region, he asked that they cut the number of German specialists in half.[87] Heeding these calls, the workers' councils made several Sudeten Germans available for the transfer, though not the total number requested by the MNV.

The national committee's reference to past national disputes may have given more substance to calls for expulsions. Ervěnice, like dozens of other towns in the border regions of Bohemia, had large numbers of Czechs living alongside Germans prior to the war. Many of these places along the language frontier had experienced nationalist struggles over language rights and schools from the nineteenth century until World War II.[88] In 1946, national committee members in Ervěnice demonstrated through words and actions that they remained displeased with the slow pace of the transfer. Yet even with the support of several central agencies, they still had to find ways around labor regulations that allowed

---

[85] Minutes from the meeting of the Místní národní výbor (MNV) Ervěnice, September 25, 1946. SOkA Chomutov, f. MNV Ervěnice, k. 2 inv. č. 125.
[86] Letter from MNV Ervěnice, June 25, 1946. SOkA Chomutov, f. MNV Ervěnice, k. 101 inv. č. 237.
[87] Letter from MNV Ervěnice, November 1, 1946, ibid.
[88] Mark Cornwall, "The Struggle on the Czech-German Language Border, 1880–1940," *English Historical Review* 109, no. 433 (1994): 914–51; Tara Zahra, *Kidnapped Souls: National Indifference and the Battle for Children in the Bohemian Lands, 1900–1948* (Ithaca, 2008).

others to decide which Germans would remain. After learning of the MNV's efforts to expel local Germans, mining officials successfully intervened to stop the transfer in late 1946.[89] They requested an investigation into the matter, which the Interior Ministry and the District National Committee subsequently carried out. The Local National Committee in Ervěnice defended its actions by arguing that it had not violated the provisions regarding the transfer of miners, but rather had allowed the workers' council to determine the needs of the firm.[90] Considering the Interior Ministry's support for the official transfer, members of the MNV in Ervěnice had little to fear in the way of reprimands.

Elsewhere in the borderlands, national committees allowed firms to retain large numbers of Germans, especially where settlement had been weak. Large textile firms in the borderlands became particularly dependent on German labor. For instance, the textile firm Ed. Grohmann in Vrbno near Bruntál supplied a list of 138 Germans for specialist legitimacy certificates. In August 1946, the chairman of the ONV reported to textile industry officials that many of those selected were not really specialists, some having only worked one year at the factory. According to him, because of insufficient Czech workers, "the management did not see any easier way than to propose almost all the workers for specialist status." He recommended in turn that no more than fifty Germans remain, "so that there would not be a significant German work group at the factory."[91] In the nearby town of Lichtvard, the linen factory G.A. Buhl, which lost 38 percent of its employees between February and October 1946, requested that over half of its German employees be given specialist certification.[92] While the district's textile industry suffered only a 17 percent decline in overall employment during the year, this figure disguised the fact that several factories had shut down or relocated to Slovakia, and that employee fluctuation rates had remained high.[93] Under such conditions, many textile factory managers did their best to retain whomever they could, German or Czech.

[89] Letter from SHD, November 6, 1946. SOA, p. Most, f. SHD-GŘ, sign. 5-3-10 č. 279 01, 03.
[90] Letter from MNV Ervěnice, August 19, 1946. SOkA Chomutov, f. MNV Ervěnice, k. 101 inv. č. 237.
[91] Letter from ONV Bruntál, August 16, 1945. SOkA Bruntál, f. ONV Bruntál, k. 145 inv. č. 126.
[92] Potvrzené legitimace něm. specialistů o vynětí z odsunu, MV, October 1, 1946. Ibid.
[93] Compare labor reports from OÚOP, Opava, February and October 1946. NA, f. MOPSP, k. 401 inv. č. 841 sign. 2306; Otákar Kaňa, *Historické proměny pohraničí* (Ostrava, 1976), 66–67. For more on continued fluctuation during the Two-Year Plan, see Anna Beinhauerová, "Pracovní moralka a vykonnost v průmyslové výrobě v českých zemích v období dvouletky," *Slezský sborník* 88, no.2 (1990): 131–36.

Indeed, the problems posed by the lack of replacement workers continued to plague many borderland communities. The expulsions in 1946 removed nearly three-quarters of the 225,000 German workers from Czechoslovak industries. Over the course of that year, however, as countless observers pointed out, 210,000 Czechs entered – or in many cases re-entered – the industrial workforce, nearly covering the loss.[94] These figures, however, do not accurately describe the changes to the borderland workforce. Many of the new workers had little experience in these industries and many were quite young. In addition, almost equal numbers of Czechs took jobs in borderland factories as they did at companies in the interior. In 1947 nearly two-thirds of the labor force's growth occurred in the interior parts of the Bohemian lands.[95] In other words, just as the need for labor in the borderlands reached its peak after the Germans had been expelled, the arrival of workers began to slow.

In addition to the difficulty of luring new workers to the borderlands, several other problems plagued postwar production. Postwar labor productivity remained below prewar rates until 1949.[96] Worker morale was low and, especially in the borderlands, fluctuation rates remained high. Fluctuation rates reached 80 percent in some borderland textile firms. In addition, during the Two-Year Plan (1947–48), industries in the Bohemian lands lost an average of 12–14 percent of scheduled shifts due to absenteeism, illness and other reasons. Faced with these realities, government officials sought several solutions to improve worker productivity and to limit fluctuation. One effort was to find and to encourage experienced workers to return to their original professions. Another program, begun in late 1948, involved cutting thousands of public sector positions and shifting those people into productive work. In addition the government promoted factory competitions, "national" volunteer shifts, and improved pay and working conditions as far as possible.[97]

Despite the government's attempts to address problems with Czech workers, one of the main difficulties remained the lack of experienced or skilled workers. This obstacle could not be addressed by government fiat and was one reason that borderland industries sought to keep German

---

[94] L. Ruman, "Pracovní silý začetkem r.1945: Odsun Němců a vývoj celkové zaměstnanosti v r.1946," *Statistický zpravodaj* 10, no.3 (March 1947): 90–93; V.O. Nimmerfoth, "Několik pohledů do vývoje našeho průmyslu," *Československý průmysl* 2, no.11 (Nov. 1946): 410.

[95] Generální sekretariát Hospodářské rady, *Průběh plnění hospodářského plánu rok 1947* (Prague, 1948), 244.

[96] *Statistický zpravodaj* 11, no.12 (Dec. 1948): 417; Beinhauerová, "Pracovní moralka a vykonnost," 132.

[97] Beinhauerová, "Pracovní moralka a vykonnost," 131–35; Anna Beinhauerová and Karel Sommer, "Některé problémy průmyslové zaměstnanosti v českých zemích v období dvouletého plánu (1947–1948)," *Slezský sborník* 88 no.1 (1990): 11–13.

workers. In particular, German women were central to borderland industries in ways that went beyond simply being able-bodied workers. Even in
places where settlement was strong economic concerns put a brake on a
complete expulsion. In Liberec more than 750 textile specialists remained
at the end of 1946.[98] That the majority of textile specialists were female
challenges some historians' assumptions that the large numbers of
women and children among Germans represented an economic burden
on the postwar government.[99] In the Buhl plant, for instance, district
officials surprisingly supported the idea of repatriating fourteen Sudeten
German husbands of local textile workers. The chairman of the ONV
argued that the women would be restive if they were not reunited with
their husbands and supported the national administrator's extraordinary
request. Unsurprisingly, an Interior Ministry official refused to be swayed
by productionist arguments and replied simply that such an action would
be "undesirable."[100] In other cases, managers employed women already
expelled who illegally re-crossed the border to work.[101] The great
demand for labor in certain sectors of the economy forced managers
and officials to take radical steps to make the use of any and all available
labor. Mrs. Peschke and her children, after all, were assigned not to daily
work on a local farm, but transported over 200 km away and then back
again after less than two seasons of work. Sudeten German women were
not merely mouths to feed, they helped several sectors of the economy
regain their footing following the war.

National committees and others who supported the retention of
Germans for industrial production did not necessarily oppose the expulsion. The government's representative for mining, who spearheaded
many efforts to retain Germans for SHD, called the continued use of
Germans for mining production a "national disgrace" for which he did
not want to be blamed.[102] In that sector and in textile production, the

---

[98] Lists of specialists. NA, f. MV-NR, k. 1949 inv. č. 1602 sign. B2111.

[99] Václav Průcha and Karel Jech, "First Steps in Post War Economic Reconstruction
(1945–1946)," in *The Czechoslovak Economy 1945–1948*, ed. Karel Jech (Prague,
1968), 42; Beinhauerová and Sommer, "K některým aspektům," 336. The number of
certified female textile specialists was 3,966 compared to 2,977 males. See Výkazy
německých specialistů v průmyslu a hornictví, November 1947. NA, f. 23, a.j. 378.

[100] Letter to Minister of Interior, ONV Bruntál, April 29, 1947 and Minister of Interior
response, August 11, 1947. SOkA Bruntál, f. ONV Bruntál, k.145 inv.č.126; Protocol
from revision at Moravolen, Lichtvard, February 12, 1947. NA, f. MP, k. 1153 inv. č.
3631.

[101] See, for example, Odsunutí Němci-ilegální přechody státních hranic, MV, January 22,
1947. NA, f. MP, k. 1152 inv. č. 3631.

[102] Dr. Vlk, the government representative for the mines, called for the creation of an office
with dictatorial powers that would resolve problems with the lack of Czech miners. See
Zápis ze schůze ve Svazu průmyslu, November 22, 1946. NA, f. 23, a.j. 349/1.

problem remained one of numbers – not enough qualified settlers could replace the German speakers. Why, then, did some national committees, such as the MNV in Ervěnice, take such a strong stance against the remaining German miners, while others supported the idea of keeping German workers? In the former case, the particularly strong tradition of nationalist politics there certainly played a role. So, too, did the evolving roles of national committees within the state. While national committees had been promised great power to control local communities, they continually struggled against central agencies to implement their own agendas. The official provisions for protecting miners and specialists excluded the participation of local national committees from the selection process. Thus, those who most closely controlled other aspects of the transfer and settlement had little say in the matter of which Germans would remain in their communities after the expulsions ended. From the perspective of national committee members in Ervěnice, German miners were allowed to remain because mining directors and the central government's economic plans demanded it.

"Little Berlins"

Despite several shortcomings, most officials in Prague had reason to be happy with the overall results of the expulsion and resettlement. In his official report to the government about the transfer, the Communist Minister of Interior, Václav Nosek, noted that the ministry was able to press on with the transfer despite American concerns about its effects in their occupation zone in Germany and the fears of "productive circles" within Czechoslovakia.[103] While the overall success of the transfer supported a bit of Communist propaganda and self-promotion, the big picture concealed the difficulties that still beset the borderlands. In March 1947 roughly 50,000 German workers in large- and small-scale industry still remained at their posts; roughly half of them had official specialist protection.[104] The problem was that the remaining Germans were not dispersed evenly across the borderlands, but often remained concentrated in certain locations. In one textile mill, Germans maintained such a noticeable presence that the local Czechs referred to it as a "little Berlin."[105] High concentrations of Sudeten Germans evoked

---

[103] Souhrnná zpráva, MV, November 29, 1946. NA, f. ÚPV-B, k. 720 inv. č. 2908 sign. 753/4.

[104] Karel Janů, "NPF žádá o spolupráci místní národní výbory," *Osidlování*, November 10, 1946; Slezák, *Zemědelské osídlování*, 54; *Průmyslová statistika*, April 3, 1947. NA, f. 23, a.j. 360.

[105] Report from Ministry of Defense, September 30, 1947. NA, f. MP, k. 1157 inv. č. 3631.

protests and demands for their removal – if not from the country, then at least from borderland areas where settlers saw them as outsiders and officials considered them security risks. In an attempt to gain political capital the Communist Party also condemned the use of German specialists and insinuated that reactionary forces were behind their protection. Yet Communists could distance themselves from the specialist program only to a limited degree; because they led the government's Two-Year Plan, also known as the Reconstruction Program, its success depended to a large degree on coal from borderlands. Moreover, Communist leaders in the borderlands had even greater responsibilities to protect local industries, which often meant protecting German workers. Even after the Communist Party's February 1948 seizure of power, efforts to remove every last German from the borderlands remained difficult to achieve.

Demand for German labor hinged on the ability to replace them with others. In 1946 Czechs began working in borderland industries in greater numbers, but still did not produce the levels that settlement and industrial officials had set. By the end of 1946, after the official transfer ended, settlement officials still hoped that 80,000 more Czech industrial workers would move to the borderlands.[106] Despite their best efforts and plans, however, these workers failed to materialize. Attempts to encourage Czech workers from abroad to return generally fell short; the chance to acquire land was a better draw for most emigrants. Slovaks already played a productive role across all economic branches in the borderlands in 1945 and 1946, though many industrial workers had only temporary work assignments. The Bratislava Settlement Office wished to keep Slovak workers to settle its southern border regions, from where it planned to expel Magyars.[107] By 1947 the prospect of locating new labor power for borderland industry looked bleak and thus increased firms' tendency to hold onto German workers.

Other pressures worked in the opposite direction. The politics of permanently keeping Germans remained divisive at both the local and national levels. In late 1946, the Interior Minister authorized revisions (*revise*) of current specialists. Investigative commissions were established to check on the credentials of those Sudeten Germans who had received permission to remain. These investigations involved the same group of officials – District National Committee members, district security officials, and regional representatives from the relevant ministries, as well as the factory management and workers' representatives – who had, in most

---

[106] Karel Janu, "Pohraničí, průmysl a dvouletý plan," *Osidlování*, December 10, 1946.
[107] Oľga Šrajerová and Karel Sommer, "Migrace Slovaků do českých zemí v letech 1945–1948," *Slezský sborník* 98, no.1 (1998): 25.

cases, comprised the original committee to select German specialists.[108] Unsurprisingly, these investigative commissions failed to cancel many specialist certificates. The government's representative for the transfer, Antonín Kučera, reported in April 1947 that, of the 37,613 industrial specialists (not including miners) given specialist protection, central officials had already cancelled 21,728 certificates outside of the district revision process. The revisions themselves reduced the number of specialists by only 2,867. In the end, Kučera expected that 13,000 German specialists in industry and 10,000 in mining would remain.[109] Although he was largely correct, perceptions about a lingering problem continued to exist. The fear expressed by the Regional Settlement Office in Opava that the 194 German specialists in the district of Bruntál and the 130 in the Frývaldov district would hinder settlement was a complete exaggeration.[110] Elsewhere, however, real concentrations of Germans persisted, often in connection with large borderland firms. These "little Berlins" sustained the tensions created by the permanent retention of German workers. Because district authorities had been given responsibility for the revisions, the pressure was on them to resolve this question once and for all.

The revisions in the Šluknov district, in the northernmost part of Bohemia, began in early February 1947. This district had traditionally been a center of artificial flower production, which brought in over 80 million Kčs in direct export and employed 18,540 Sudeten German workers in 1938, many of whom worked from their homes.[111] The 1945 expulsions had drastically reduced the number of these workers, despite protests about the consequences for local industry. At the outset of the revision process, the chairman of the ONV, Karel Mikovec, urged the commission to reach a compromise between the political viewpoint of cleansing the borderlands and the economic position of protecting against the rise of foreign competition.[112] During the investigation, the commission found problems with certain firms' retention of unqualified workers or office personnel and cancelled 13 percent of the legitimacy certificates. In his late February report about the revisions, the district representative for the Ministry of Industry suggested that the main reason for the

[108] Odsun Němců, revise německých specialistů vynatých z odsunu, MV, December 11, 1946. NA, f. 23, a.j. 378.
[109] Letter from Vládní zmocněnec pro odsun Němců, MV, April 18, 1947. NA, f. 23, a.j. 378.
[110] Letter from OÚ, Oblastní úřadovná, Opava, April 7, 1947. NA, f. MP, k. 1153 inv. č. 3631.
[111] Letter from Ústřední kancelář továren na umělé květiny, Dolní Poustevna, October 31, 1945. NA, f. MP, k. 1141 inv. č. 3631.
[112] Zpráva o revisi německých specialistů, Oblastní referent minsterstva průmyslu, February 5, 1947. NA, f. MP, k. 1152 inv. č. 3631.

relatively high number of remaining specialists was "poor settlement," due, in part, to the isolation of many communities. About the settlers who had already arrived, he reported that "the quality of their labor was comparatively poor, so that even when firms hired a greater percentage of Czech employees, they were forced because of the insufficient and low value of production to release them."[113] In order to address this problem they divided the specialists into two groups. The first group consisted of younger German specialists who spoke Czech. These workers would be sent to the interior of the republic to teach their skills to Czechs and create a new center of artificial flower production there. The remaining Sudeten Germans, mainly older workers, would stay in the Šluknov district and gradually be replaced.

Some members of the ONV, however, saw the problem differently. Mikovec argued that the representative for the Ministry of Industry had been too lenient during the revision process, and the ONV Council agreed to appeal the results.[114] Apparently, these appeals failed. Thereafter, Mikovec, along with the security official of the ONV and a few other local officials, took it upon themselves to carry out a "super-revision" (*super-revise*) of specialists at the end of March. They focused on the artificial flower firms in Horní Poustevna, where high numbers of specialists remained. As various letters from these factories indicate, Mikovec and others used intimidation to force members of the factory council and managers to release more specialists for the transfer.[115] After getting word of these additional revisions, the Minister of Industry requested a halt to all transports of Germans from the area and sent an investigative team to the district. While this commission heaped blame on Mikovec, pressure to expel more specialists stemmed from the Regional Representative for the Transfer of Germans under the Interior Ministry, who had earlier made the point that Šluknov was the one district in the region that had failed to meet its quota for the transfer.[116]

The "super-revision" carried out in Horní Poustevna was not unique. That Czechs were able to separate their opinions about the exemption of specialists and the expulsion of Sudeten Germans only hindered a defi-nitive resolution to the issue. Mikovec described well the intractable situation:

[113] Zpráva o revisi německých specialistů, Oblastní referent minsterstva průmyslu, February 20, 1947. Ibid.

[114] Minutes from the ONV Council meeting, ONV Šluknov, February 20, 1947. SOkA Děčín, ONV Šluknov, k. 3 inv. č. 46.

[115] See various letters. NA. f. MP, k. 1152 inv. č. 3631.

[116] Zápis o pracovní poradě členů rady, ONV Šluknov, April 2, 1947. SOkA Děčín, ONV Šluknov, k. 3 inv. č. 46.

At public meetings people radically demand that officials indiscriminately transfer Germans, but immediately the next day, those in industrial firms who supported the transfer repudiate it with the reason that the transfer of German specialists threatens production, or that Czech and Slovak workers are leaving their jobs, or that without the German specialists they cannot go on.[117]

Such attitudes highlighted the protean nature of productionist and nationalist stances and the lack of simple solutions to the borderlands' labor problems.

The revision process in Jablonec had been particularly tumultuous. On October 1, 1946, the Czech workers at one factory threatened to strike in order to protest the continued presence of Germans, specialists or otherwise, who got drunk and threatened Czechs on the streets at night.[118] Following the results of a special *revise* established for the district at the end of 1946, the Minister of Interior requested that the Ministry of Industry carry out an additional inspection that would, above all else, reduce the number of Germans in the district.[119] Even after this *super-revise*, 186 small firms still had a majority of German employees. The ONV remained displeased and divided, and the issue of German specialists dominated the district's political life. In August of 1947 the District National Committee council discussed how to resolve the retention of German specialists. C. Mrazek, a Social Democrat, blamed the security department head, a Communist, for not following regulations concerning the retention of specialists. The Communist security chief had released several protected specialists without the consent of factory managers.[120] Although he was careful to mention that he did not support Germans, Mrazek argued that the legal order must be upheld. After further finger pointing, the council reissued its original directive concerning the retention of specialists. This order declared that specialists chosen by a firm's management, usually a national administrator, should not be transferred. However, it also permitted the security official to expel or retain Germans "who were originally defined for transfer out of Czechoslovakia."[121] Such an order merely prolonged the stalemate within the ONV about how to

---

[117] Ibid.

[118] Situation report on conditions in Jablonec n. N., SNB Jablonec n. N., October 24, 1946. SOkA Jablonec n. N, f. ONV Jablonec n. N., k. 29 inv. č. 52.

[119] Legitimace německých specialistů na jablonecku; revise, MV, December 16, 1946. NA. f. MP, k. 1147 inv. č. 3631.

[120] See his comments in the meetings of the District Presidium of the KSČ, Jablonec n. N., June 19 and 26, 1947. SOkA Jablonec n. N., f. Presednictvo Okresní výbor KSČ Jablonec n. N., L-I 204/3.

[121] Minutes from the ONV Council meeting, August 6, 1947. SOkA Jablonec n.N, f. ONV Jablonec n. N., k. 1 inv. č. 3.

resolve the situation. As one member of the council put it, "the Germans were breaking up the National Front."[122]

The dispute between the Communists and the other parties of the ONV came to a head at the following meeting. Although the specialist issue did not directly precipitate the walkout of the non-Communist parties from the council, it remained the major dispute dividing them.[123] After a month's impasse the Social Democrats came back to the meetings and changed their tactics regarding the specialist question. They proposed a plan to transfer Germans to the interior and simultaneously attacked the security chairperson for allowing politically unreliable Germans to remain.[124] By proposing to send Germans to the interior the Social Democrats shifted their position on the retention of German specialists. They now supported removing German specialists from Jablonec, which the Communists also favored.[125] Yet by attacking the Communist security department head, the Social Democrats indicated that they too were willing to use the German question for political ends. Communists were well aware of the political dangers that the retention of specialists brought. In Nejdek, for instance, local Communist authorities reported that local textile workers planned to go on strike if the remaining Germans were not transferred. They further reported that the district party leaders could not prevent this because their "actions regarding specialists compromised our comrades and the workforce here no longer believes in them."[126] In Jablonec the security official defended his record of expelling Germans, arguing that expulsions should not be carried out on a massive scale, but considered individually.[127] He lost his job in 1947, in part for his cautious approach to Jablonec specialists. He was replaced by a fellow Communist from outside the district, who had few qualms about expelling Germans.

While the issue of protected specialists threatened local Communist functionaries, their leaders in Prague hoped to use the impression that the borderlands were filled with "little Berlins" for political goals. In July

[122] Ibid. In several ways, the debate over German specialists mirrored the conflict within the nationality committee, which began earlier in 1946. See Chapter 2.
[123] Minutes from a meeting of ONV Jablonec n. N., August 6, 1947. Ibid.
[124] Letter from Československá socialní demokracie, Okresní sekretariat, Jablonec n. N., September 17, 1947. Ibid. See also minutes from meeting of the ONV Jablonec n. N., October 1, 1947. Ibid.
[125] Meetings between Social Democratic and Communist leaders in Prague sought to find a common approach to the question of German labor during this same period. NA, f. 23, a.j. 375.
[126] Letter from District Secretariat KSČ, Nejdek, March 24, 1947. NA, f. 23, a.j. 378.
[127] Minutes from the meeting of the District Committee KSČ, Jablonec n. N., October 25, 1946. SOkA Jablonec n. N., f. Presednictvo Okresní výbor KSČ Jablonec n. N., L-I 204/3.

1947, Dr. Bedřich Steiner, a leading party spokesperson on borderland issues, led several other parliamentary deputies in criticizing key aspects of the specialist program. They argued that the government had meant to give legitimacy "only to a narrow circle of people with entirely extraordinary qualifications, which are entirely irreplaceable, possessors of different production secrets or those having knowledge, which requires a long training period to acquire."[128] Steiner also argued that the existence of German groups in the borderlands threatened the settlement of Czech inhabitants. He noted that specialists received exemption from the confiscation of property, which served as the basis for bringing settlers to the borderlands. He also suggested that Germans had "an entirely different position towards the state and Czech inhabitants" in places where Germans lived in large numbers, compared to places where they were an insignificant minority. He argued that they already demanded cultural rights, such as schools, newspapers and cinemas.[129] Steiner hoped that attacking the specialists would win the party political support by tapping into settlers' resentment at Germans, who enjoyed the right to retain their property and their jobs. The KSČ distributed a copy of Steiner's attack on specialists to its party branches, noting that it provided "guidance, which would clarify that it was really the Communist Party that ensured cleansing the borderlands of unwanted elements."[130]

In response to the Communist attack on specialists, the Ministry of Industry, under Social Democratic control, argued that the concept of expertise could not be interpreted as narrowly as Dr. Steiner suggested. Aside from specific branches of the economy where larger contingents of Germans remained, as, for example, in Jablonec goods, the official noted that Germans were necessary to train Czechs, otherwise the number of specialists would have been considerably fewer. The letter continued: "it was necessary not only to keep real specialists in the narrow sense of the word, but also a cadre of expert employees, if these firms were to be brought into operation and provide a livelihood to Czech settlers."[131] This ministerial official echoed earlier arguments about successful settlement hinging on German labor. As scheduled 1948 elections approached, "little Berlins" were cast again into the political spotlight. The Communist Party in

---

[128] Interpelace 736, Ústavodárné Národní shromáždění republiky Československé 1947, July 7, 1947. NA, f. MP, k. 1154 inv. č. 3631. Steiner had earlier begun attacks against the idea of keeping German workers. See Slezák, *Zemědělské osidlování*, 36.

[129] Interpelace 736, Ústavodárné Národní shromáždění republiky Československé 1947, July 7, 1947. NA, f. MP, k. 1154 inv. č. 3631.

[130] Letter from Komise pro otázky osidlení při UV KSČ, July 18, 1947. NA, f. 23, a.j. 378.

[131] Partial response to the questionnaire of Dr. Steiner, MP, August 30, 1947. NA, f. MP, k. 1154 inv. č. 3631.

particular sought to benefit from nationalist politics and to distance itself from any measure that benefited Germans.[132]

Germans' Dispersal as Economic Necessity

In certain ways, the politics surrounding the remaining Sudeten Germans grew more critical as fewer of them remained. In October 1947, the MNV Ervěnice appealed to district authorities to transfer Germans to the interior and "to deliver this land from wicked elements." It blamed recent borderland fires on Germans. In early 1948, the District National Committee in Chomutov replied that, based on similar concerns and interventions, the Ministry of Interior had decided to relocate Germans to the interior and disperse them into different communities.[133] What became known as the dispersal (*rozptyl*) program had its roots in late 1946 as transports ended in the fall and several thousand Germans were stranded in collection camps for the upcoming winter.[134] Once it became clear early in 1947 that further general expulsions under Allied supervision would not continue, the government planned to move all Germans slated for the "transfer" to interior parts of the country. The need for agricultural labor in the interior, just as in 1945, reinforced demands to deport Germans from the borderlands. The central government authorized an initial relocation (*přesun*) of Germans, mainly to help alleviate the dire labor shortage facing interior farms. Antonín Kučera warned district national committees that they should realize the importance of this provision and release the greatest number of Germans. He argued that this action had various advantages. For interior districts, it was supposed to relieve serious labor strains. For the borderlands, the transfer of Germans to the interior would meet security concerns and give settlers assurances about their jobs and property.[135]

Satisfying borderland settlement and security concerns by transferring Germans to the interior, however, ran into resistance. Local

---

[132] See, for example, comments made on provisions to return citizenship to Germans in late 1947. NA, f. 23, a.j. 375.

[133] Letter from MNV Ervěnice, October 2, 1947 and response from ONV Chomutov, February 5, 1948. SOkA Chomutov, f. MNV Ervěnice, k. 101 inv. č. 237.

[134] Adrian von Arburg, "Zwischen Vertreibung und Integration: Tschechische Deutschenpolitik, 1947–1953." (Dissertation, Charles University, Prague, 2004), 175–90. See also Tomáš Staněk, *Německá menšina v českých zěmích, 1948–1989* (Prague, 1993), 57–66. The reasons for the Allies' reluctance to continue with the expulsions are aptly covered in R.M. Douglas, *Orderly and Humane: The Expulsion of Germans after the Second World War* (New Haven, 2012), chapter 7.

[135] B300/11949–47-ref. B, MV, May 21, 1947. NA, f. MP, k. 1155 inv. č. 3631.

management and factory councils attempted to retain their German workers either because of production concerns, poor settlement, or both. Vejprty, a town located in a mountainous region in northwest Bohemia directly on Germany's border, was a perfect example of how the lack of settlers affected the labor market. In October 1947, Germans comprised over a quarter of the town's 5,834 inhabitants. District totals were roughly the same.[136] In connection with the 1947 relocation to the interior one District National Committee member proposed to transfer 1,500 Germans.[137] As the action began, however, local textile firms raised a series of objections and pressured the Ministry of Industry to request a halt to further transfers. They did so because they lacked Czechs to replace these Germans. In one factory, for instance, over half of the Czech employees hired in 1945 had left less than two years later.[138] Problems with wages, housing and provisions, not to mention the presence of many Germans, made Vejprty unattractive to new settlers. In such places using German labor was often a factory's only hope for continued production. In August 1947, the Interior Ministry reported that the campaign to relocate the remaining Germans had been unsatisfactory. Of the estimated 70,000 Germans eligible for relocation – most of whom had been kept until the final transports because of their economic value – only 2,550 families were actually transferred.[139]

Despite the shortcomings of the campaign, in October 1947 the government authorized the Ministry of Interior to carry out the dispersal of the remaining Germans into the interior. As Minister Nosek noted in a speech to lower officials, the final purpose of the action was the assimilation of the Germans, so that they would no longer present a security threat to the state.[140] At the same time, labor needs continued to fuel plans to deport Germans to the interior. For instance, on February 4, 1948, at a meeting in Prague to organize the dispersal, the representative for The United Federation of Czech Farmers requested 7,830 agricultural workers for transfer to the interior.[141] Following the meeting, an internal memo to department heads at the Ministry of Industry urged its officials to quickly propose their own requests for German workers "because

---

[136] *Soupisy obyvatelstva v Československu v letech 1946–1947* (Prague, 1951), 547.
[137] Němci-odsun do vnitrozemí na zemědělské práce, ONV Vejprty, May 23, 1947. SOkA Chomutov, f. ONV Vejprty, k. 25 inv. č. 108.
[138] Odsun německých zaměstnanců z továren, Raimund Bittner, August 5, 1947. Ibid.
[139] Minutes of a meeting at MOPSP, August 11, 1947. NA, f. MP, k. 1155 inv. č. 3631.
[140] Přesun a rozptyl Němců z pohraničních krajů, MV, 1948. NA, f. Ministerstvo vnitra-Nosek (MV-N), k. 254 inv. č. 160.
[141] Záznam o poradě ve věci přesunu a rozptylu, MV, April 2, 1948. NA, f. MOPSP, k. 378 inv. č. 805 sign. 2119.

otherwise, it creates the danger that agricultural demands will be satisfied before the demands of industry will be met."[142] However, the race between ministries to collect German workers from the borderlands proved pointless. There was endless pressure to keep Germans in the borderlands, just as the need for interior labor reached its peak. The failure of the campaigns to reallocate workers forced the Communists, now in sole control of the country, to re-evaluate their entire position on German labor. The population policies of the former National Front government, though written and approved by Communists in most cases, were not working. By the end of May, the Interior Ministry reported that nearly 9,000 Germans had been dispersed throughout the interior, but most of the people were unproductive family members who could contribute little to resolving the labor shortages.[143]

Just as in previous campaigns to relocate Germans to the interior, Czechoslovak officials had to reconcile labor and settlement pressures with the needs of the borderland economy and the state's security demands. Throughout the dispersal action, the general directors of nationalized industries, district industrial officials, factory managers and workers complained of the dispersal's effects and warned that the economic objectives of the Two-Year Plan would not be met. For instance, the directors of the Czechoslovak Textile Factories national enterprise argued that the plans to transfer Germans to the interior would bring considerable losses to the firm, since most of its plants were in the borderlands. They further noted that "any attempts to obtain new Slavic workers for the borderlands have come to naught recently." As a result of such pressure, the Ministry of Industry received the right to retain German workers in the interests of borderland industrial production.[144] The overall labor shortage caused by the expulsions meant that both industry and agriculture endlessly demanded more workers and could easily justify their need, so that the scramble for German workers stalled the plans for their dispersal.

Likewise, Communist control did not translate into more orderly rule, and the practices of the past continued. Germans themselves found ways to escape deportation to the interior. For instance, in early 1948, the district of Vejprty sent roughly one hundred families and dozens of individual Sudeten Germans to the interior district of Louny for

---

[142] Letter from MP, February 9, 1948. NA, f. MP, k. 1156 inv. č. 3631. According to incomplete lists the Ministry of Industry requested 3,502 Germans.

[143] D-300/9299/1948-DN, Odsun a přesun Němců, MV, June 8, 1948. SOkA Chomutov, f. ONV Vejprty, k. 25 inv. č. 108.

[144] Letter from Československé textilní závody, April 13, 1948. NA, f. MP, k. 1156 inv. č. 3631. See also Staněk, Německá menšina, 76–77.

agricultural work.[145] The district labor office later accused the District National Committee of covering up the return of some of these workers. In response, the ONV in Vejprty claimed that some of the Germans had received permission to return from the labor office itself, while others had been exempted from the transfer; still others had not returned to Vejprty, but had left for Germany instead. Although the ONV may not have actively encouraged the Germans to return, it clearly did not want more of them to leave. In August, the ONV decided to keep all Germans without specialist legitimacy in the district for road work. In November 1948 it challenged the Interior Ministry's dispersal order on the grounds that the campaign to gather Germans for the nearby uranium mines at Jachymov in the borderlands signaled that they should no longer be liable for transfer based on security concerns.[146] Borderland national committees continued to demand their say when it came to questions about the economic future of their towns.

The labor politics concerning German workers highlight several overlapping agendas related to settlement and expulsion. The slow pace of settlers' entry into industrial jobs reflected the borderlands' draw as a place of rapid social mobility based on confiscated property, and hindered the region's economic recovery. The vacuum of farm labor in the interior and the labor shortages in the mines made borderland Germans into a migrant labor force. Such movements often did not make economic sense, but reflected the disorganized manner in which the state approached labor problems. Many national committees and local factory managers worked to retain Sudeten German labor, even in the face of pressure from military commanders and the Interior Ministry. While concerns about the local economy generally resulted in keeping German workers in place, such decisions were rife with political fallout. The MNV's stand against keeping German miners in Ervěnice raised issues of power, as did the Vejprty Local National Committee's challenge to the Ministry of Interior about retaining German workers for borderland industries. Each national committee felt entitled to decide how many Germans should stay to work, regardless of central authorities' wishes. Inter-party disputes also played a role. The debates in the Jablonec national committee demonstrated that nationalist and economic imperatives were subject to political posturing in order to gain voter support. Therefore, exploring labor politics explains much more than the relative

---

[145] Report from Oblastní zmocněnec Ministerstva vnitra pro Odsun Němců, Litoměříce, February 20, 1948. SOkA Teplice-Šanov, f. ONV Teplice-Šanov, k. 225 inv. č. 280.

[146] Inquiry by the ONV Vejprty, November 11, 1948. SOkA Chomutov, f. ONV Vejprty, k. 25 inv. č. 108. For more on the transfer of Germans to Jachymov, see Arburg, "Zwischen Vertreibung und Integration," 413–60.

importance of economic issues during the Sudeten German expulsions. The political disputes about German workers and labor shortages provide a window into the broader goals of political parties, government organs and settlers about the transformation of the borderlands. From this vantage, it becomes clear that ethnic cleansing was not an all or nothing proposition.

5 Consolidating Borderland Industries: From Confiscation to Nationalization

Factory Control

While skirmishes over retaining German workers and distributing German belongings and homes could at times be fierce, the struggles for factory control held even greater stakes. Everyone from the workers themselves to national administrators, and even former German owners, felt they had a say in how individual firms should be run. At the heart of the matter, though, was not only individual firms, but the future of the borderland economy. This chapter examines the conflicts that emerged as settlers, political leaders and government officials attempted to remake borderland industries. Because the state confiscated German-owned firms without clear plans for their future the majority of borderland factories became the source of competing interests. The postwar government had also embarked on a nationalization program of large factories and several particular industries. How confiscated factories fit into these provisions was not always clear and the relationship between confiscated factories and nationalized ones became intricately intertwined. Local officials were often at loggerheads with central officials' plans for the use of confiscated factories. Workers pleaded to keep factories local as central officials began relocating borderland factories to Slovakia and elsewhere with the hope of creating jobs. They invoked the populist rationales for nationalization in order to support their efforts to keep production in the borderlands and in their hands. The restitution of Jewish factories was also caught in the confluence of these developments. As this chapter explains, Jews faced several obstacles to reclaim their property, which became particularly contentious and complex in the borderlands. As the politics surrounding the nationalization and confiscation came to a head in early 1947, it was the fate of one Jewish owner's factory that turned the tide and led to the further nationalization of many confiscated firms. The Communist Party played a central role in this event. Nationalization became a means for it to increase the state control of the economy, and local Communists were able to mobilize enough workers to press for this agenda. The struggle over factory control in the borderlands flowed from the vacuum created by ethnic cleansing and redesigned the borderland economy on the Communists' terms.

Prior to the war the industrial composition of the borderlands had been quite varied. In the northern and western parts of the country most factories were relatively small and had a distinctive local character. They reflected all types of specialized production based on craft skills, including: luxury textile accessories, glass-beaded jewelry, pistols, artificial flowers and musical instruments. Some of these factories, such as the Kunert factory in Varnsdorf, reached world-renowned status. It became the largest European producer of women's cotton hosiery and had strong ties to the British market. In 1938, the export of Kunert leggings to England alone brought in 59 million crowns. The factory employed 4,300 workers and produced 80,000 pairs of stocking per day. The first postwar national administrator faced several immediate problems regarding available workers, raw materials and foreign contacts, but still sought to overcome these obstacles and reclaim the Kunert market abroad.[1]

Thanks in part to the various small producers situated in the borderlands, the Czechoslovak economy had already industrialized to a degree far above other countries in Eastern Europe. From 1913 to 1929, the Bohemian lands had among the highest growth rate of any economy in Europe, and, in 1930, Czechoslovakia was among its top eleven industrial producers.[2] Many of the special export industries earned substantial sums in foreign trade prior to the war. From 1927 to 1929, exports accounted for nearly one-third of Czechoslovakia's national income. Jablonec industries, for instance, had generated more than 1 billion Czechoslovak Kčs in annual sales during the prewar years.[3] Ownership of these small-scale firms was mostly in local German hands. However, during the Great Depression these industries' dependence on foreign markets meant that they experienced some of the highest levels of unemployment. In many borderland districts, unemployment exceeded 25 percent. By the early 1930s, exports had plummeted, dropping to nearly one-third of 1929 levels.[4] During the long recovery that lasted until 1937, a shift began

[1] Report from the National administrator, September 1945. Státní oblastní archiv, Litoměřice, pobočka v Moste (SOA Litoměřice, p. Most), f. Kunert, karton (k.) 2 inventární číslo (inv. č.) 8.

[2] Charles Feinstein, Peter Temin, and Gianni Toniolo, *The European Economy between the Wars* (Oxford, 1997), 55.

[3] Alice Teichova, *The Czechoslovak Economy, 1918–1988* (New York, 1988), 55; Report from Josef Gottwald, August 11, 1945. Národní archiv, Prague (NA), f. Ministerstvo průmyslu, 1945–1950 (MP), k. 1141 inv. č. 3631.

[4] Teichova, *The Czechoslovak Economy*, 61; Alice Teichova, "Industry," in *The Economic History of Eastern Europe, 1919–1975*, eds. M.C. Kaser and E.A. Radice, vol. 1, *Economic Structure and Performance between the Two Wars* (Oxford, 1985), 235; Elizabeth Wiskeman, *Czechs and Germans* (London, 1967), 191.

toward greater emphasis on producer goods for the overall Czechoslovak economy.[5] Although this trend was modest prior to the war, and related mostly to the increasing importance of armament production, it represented a change in the Czechoslovak economy that would continue into the 1950s. The Great Depression made many Czechs wary of a full-scale return to the export dominated industries of the borderlands, and for some it served as justification for the consolidation and liquidation of these industries after the war.

Mining operations, energy production, and heavy industry were also key sectors in parts of the borderlands. Two large sources of coal lay in the northern borderlands. The brown coal basin in Northern Bohemia stretched from Chomutov in the northeast to Most and a bit beyond. The other borderland deposit of coals – anthracitic, coking, and gas – swept along the outskirts of Ostrava and helped to support the growth of that industrial city, which straddles the provinces of Moravia and Silesia. Other borderland cities also contained important heavy industrial production. Aussig, for instance, was a major center of chemical manufacturing, and Komotau contained several metalworking plants. These firms were central to the Nazi war effort and became some of the first to face takeover attempts by the Nazis, many of them owned by Jewish or foreign capital.[6]

The Nazis' attempts to Aryanize these industrial properties became a testing ground for the methods of expropriation that would characterize their rule throughout Europe. Hermann Goring's attempts to acquire ownership of the Rothschilds' Witkowitz steel plant in Ostrava were ultimately stymied by the owners' ability to shift controlling interest in the firm abroad. Julius Petschek, a Jewish mine owner from Aussig, was able to sell his firms to Nazi Germany for foreign currency; a policy the Nazis quickly abandoned because of its substantial costs. These were early exceptions to the Nazis' tightening economic noose around Jews, as well as Czechs and others.[7] In Aussig, two *Treuhänder* – temporary state-empowered managers, much like the postwar national administrators – one of whom was a manager for I.G. Farben, were appointed to control the United Chemical and Metallurgical Works. The Prague owners were eventually forced to sell the company to I.G. Farben under heavy pressure by the Nazis. Another way in which the Germans took control of property in the Sudetenland was to gain access to company shares

[5] Teichova, "Industry," 240–41.
[6] Václav Kural and Zdeněk Radvanovský et al., *"Sudety" pod hákovým křížem* (Ústí nad Labem, 2002), 116–19; Vilem Brzorad, "Fuel, Power, and Producer Goods Industries," in *Czechoslovakia*, eds. Vratislav Busek and Nicolas Spurber (New York, 1957), 298–99.
[7] Raul Hilberg, *The Destruction of the European Jews*, 3 vols. (New York, 1985), 1:102–22.

through control of the banks which held their portfolios. Several purchases of property in the Sudetenland were also made with Czechoslovak currency exchanged for Reich marks, thereby foisting the costs of these property exchanges onto the citizens of Czechoslovakia.[8] Indeed, such tactics proved vital to the Nazi war effort. By the end of the war, Germany had stripped as much of the country's gold stock as possible, created inflation by purposefully deflating the currency and accrued significant debts in their clearing accounts.[9]

The Munich Agreement in 1938, which dismembered the Czechoslovak state, reshaped the economy of the borderlands in other important ways. The areas directly annexed by Nazi Germany accounted for roughly 22 percent of Czechoslovakia's prewar industrial production.[10] Although the bulk of Czech armament production was located in the interior, the Nazis improved existing mining facilities as well as some industrial enterprises in the borderlands, and even constructed new ones. For example, production at the large mines of Northern Bohemia was rationalized and mechanized in order to aid the Nazis' military needs.[11] The Germans also constructed a large synthetic fuel plant in Oberleutensdorf near Brüx to convert brown coal into motor fuel. They renovated other factories from peacetime production to wartime needs: textile factories made clothes for the Wehrmacht and glass firms produced specialized optical parts for the Luftwaffe. Some shifts were more dramatic. For instance, a textile firm near Böhmisch Kamnitz was retooled to produce parts for "Weser" aircraft, a firm headquartered in Bremen.[12] The Sudetenland's contribution to the Nazi war economy, though only a small share of its total industrial production, grew rapidly in the last two years of the war as other parts of Germany became subjected to more frequent bombing raids.[13]

---

[8] Antonin Basch, *Germany's Economic Conquest of Czechoslovakia* (Chicago, 1941), 12–13; J Hoffman, "Začlenění do ekonomiky Velkoněmecké říše," in *"Sudety" pod hákovým křížem*, eds. Václav Kural and Zdeněk Radvanovský (Ústí nad Labem, 2002); See also Götz Aly, *Hitler's Beneficiaries: Plunder, Racial War, and the Nazi Welfare State*, trans. Jefferson Chase (New York, 2006).
[9] E.A. Radice, "Changes in Property Relations and Financial Relationships," in *The Economic History of Eastern Europe, 1919–1975*, eds. M.C. Kaser and E.A. Radice, vol. 2, *Interwar Policy, the War and Reconstruction* (Oxford, 1986), 329–65; Aly.
[10] Teichova, *The Czechoslovak Economy*, 83; E.A. Radice, "The Development of Industry," in *The Economic History of Eastern Europe*, 421.
[11] See comments during June 15, 1946 meeting at the Masaryk mine. SOA Litoměřice, p. Most, f. Severočeský hnědouhelné doly-generalní ředitelství (SHD-GŘ), s. 5–3–10 č. 279 01, 03; J Hoffman, "Hospodářství sudetské župy pod tlakem prohrávané války," in *"Sudety" pod hákovým křížem*, 222, 235.
[12] Petr Joza, *Rabštejnské údolí* (Děčín, 2002).
[13] Radice, "The Development of Industry," 423–27.

Turmoil and disarray would be two apt words to describe the scene in many factories throughout the borderlands at the end of the war. The Red Army roamed throughout the borderlands claiming factories as well as personal belongings. In Ostrava, local Soviet officials took matters into their own hands and began dismantling not only machinery, but also the factory kitchen and dining room as well as 185 worker apartments and dormitories of the Vitkovice Iron Works, leaving behind a path of destruction.[14] Widespread labor shortages, caused by expulsions and Czechs leaving industrial firms, became endemic. Even Germans shunned factory work when possible. Poor working and living conditions and the onset of expulsions kept their productivity and morale low. Another immediate problem facing the borderland economy was the lack of capable and trustworthy managers to get production back on track. Some factory national administrators were simply gold-diggers. The selection and oversight of national administrators proved to be a continual complication for local and central officials who sought to restart borderland industrial production – one which, like the labor problems, proved central to the broader policies concerning the future of the border- land economy. Several structural obstacles, such as the lack of raw mate- rials and coal, transportation difficulties, as well as direct damages to factories and equipment in some places, likewise hindered the resumption of production.[15] Finally, the economic program of the National Front government did not support investment or resources in the dominant borderland industries. In fact, the Communist-led economic agenda, as presented in the Two-Year Plan (1947–1948), sought to utilize confis- cated factories to support statewide initiatives rather than strengthening the industrial basis of local borderland communities.

Despite this bleak picture, Czechoslovakia emerged from the war with much of its industrial base intact and relatively better poised to recover more quickly than most of its European neighbors. While the Nazis had profited both financially and militarily from their control of the Bohemian lands' banking and industrial enterprises, large-scale

[14] Žádost ministerstva průmyslu k ministerstvu zahraničních věcí o intervenci u sovětského velvyslanectví ke zjednání nápravy ve věci škod, působených Rudou armádou Víkovickým železárnám a obyvatelstvu moravskoostravského kraje, May 29, 1945. Karel Jech and Karel Kaplan, eds., *ČSR a SSSR 1945–1948 dokumenty mezivládních jednání* (Brno, 1997), 39.

[15] Direct war damage varied considerably across the country. In parts of Northern Bohemia Allied air raids had damaged several industrial installations. In places further east some areas avoided such war damages. For instance, the Provincial National Committee in Ostrava reported in August that two-thirds of Silesian industry survived the war unscathed. Economic report, Zemský národní výbor (ZNV) Moravská Ostrava, August 12–19, 1945. Zemský archiv (ZA) Opava, f. Expozitura Moravskoslezského ZNV (ZNVMO) 1945–1949, k. 906 inv. č. 932.

destruction and dismantling of machinery, witnessed elsewhere from 1939–1945, was kept to a minimum. While machinery had been over-worked and poorly maintained, and supplies had run low, the absence of any physical assault on buildings and equipment placed the Bohemian lands in a unique position among Central and Eastern European produ-cers. Czechoslovak authorities' first actions concerning the postwar econ-omy sought to stabilize the oversight of firms in enemy or traitors' hands as well as firms that were abandoned. Decree 2, issued on February 1, 1945, on the "extraordinary provisions for the securing of economic life in the liberated lands," sketched out the basic lines of authority over this property. It also established important precedents for Decree 5 on national administrators, which followed in May. First, Decree 2 noted that prop-erty exchanges after September 29, 1938, under the threat of national, racial or political persecution would be declared invalid. Second, it gave authority to district national committees to appoint interim management for small to medium-sized firms.[16] Decree 5 followed the same pattern. Local national committees named national administrators in industrial firms with 20 or fewer employees, district national committees named national administrators in firms with 21 to 300 workers, and provincial national committees installed management in the largest firms.[17] This system reflected the consensus among wartime politicians to decentra-lize the governing structure – a key part of their so-called democratic revolution.

Once back in Prague, central officials began to reconsider how indus-trial national administrators should be assigned. Less than a week after Decree 5 was published, officials at the Ministry of Industry began to worry that the system of assigning national administrators had gone awry. They argued that people who came to the ministry in search of positions in key firms "were proposed for interim management by the factory council or a representative of the workers, who are not able to judge their personal quality and expertise."[18] To add to the difficulties, local and district national committees simultaneously appointed national administrators to companies that Ministry of Industry or provincial national committees had the authority to select.[19] The resulting confusion

---

[16] Decree 2/45. Karel Jech and Karel Kaplan, eds., *Dekrety prezidenta republiky 1940–1945: Dokumenty* 2 vols. (Brno, 1995), 1:148–49. In May 1944, Czechoslovak planners in London spoke of "enabling the direct influence of regional national committees to correct economic life in production and distribution." See ibid., 157.

[17] Decree 5. Jech and Kaplan, 1:217.

[18] Postup při dosahování správců prozatímních. Záznam from odbor II, May 25, 1945. Národní archiv, Prague (NA), f. Ministerstvo průmysl (MP), k. 1163 inv. č. 3633.

[19] See, for example, Letter from Správa severočeského uhelného syndikatu, Ústí n. L., June 22, 1945 ibid.

is not difficult to imagine; multiple national administrators showed up to run the same firm with authority from different governmental bodies. In some cases, a collegiate national administration was created for particularly large operations, but this was the exception. When multiple people were named for a single spot, the nominees often worked to undo and oust their rivals. Officials at the Ministry of Industry later admonished one Local Administrative Commission, arguing that through "its illegal actions the MSK permitted several national administrators to be named to these properties whose authority is not and cannot be clearly delimited so that not only is there no cooperation among national administrators during the management of the firm. Instead the managers negate each other's work, because each of them controls his affairs from different perspectives."[20]

In addition, the naming of more than one national administrator led to further bureaucratic infighting. In mid-June 1945 the Ministry of Industry issued instructions concerning the assignment of national administrators, which, among other things, allowed it to reverse Provincial National Committee appointments. Such a stance contradicted the policies outlined in Decree 5, which the Provincial National Committee in Prague (ZNV) was quick to point out. Despite the Provincial National Committee's arguments, however, the Interior Ministry sided with the Ministry of Industry.[21] The Ministry of Industry also began installing national administrators in small and medium-sized firms technically outside its jurisdiction. In the middle of July 1945, the ZNV in Prague issued its own directive concerning national administrators and appealed to the ministers about overstepping their authority: national committees "are and should be the carriers of the people's just democracy and their competence cannot be disregarded by central offices, because this would destroy their activity and initiative still in its nucleus."[22] Despite such arguments, central officials continued to seek greater control over factory management. The confiscation of German factories unleashed a struggle within the state that revealed the lack of clear lines of authority and clear plans for the future of the borderland economy.

---

[20] Letter from MP, November 2, 1945. NA, f. Ministerstvo vnitra-Nová registratura (MV-NR), k. 1778 inv. č. 1577 sign. B1471.

[21] Response to ZNV Prague letter concerning the directive on national administrators, July 31, 1945. NA, f. MP, k. 1168 inv. č. 3633. See also the correspondence about this issue in NA, f. MV-NR, k. 1769 inv. č. 1576 sign. B1470.

[22] See Directive from ZNV Prague, July 16, 1945. *Předpisy z oboru působnosti OÚ a FNO: Zákony (dekrety), vládní nařízení, vyhlášky*, 2 vols. (Prague, 1947), 2:155–70; Memorandum o dosazování národních správ, ZNV Prague, August 21, 1945. NA, f. MP, k. 1274 inv. č. 3633.

National administrators often first dealt with former German owners
when they assumed control of the factory. In some cases German owners
attempted to make the most from their former firms before being forced
out. For example, in one leather goods factory in Northern Bohemia, the
national administrator was unable to assume his post because Red Army
representatives controlled the factory and had reportedly reached agreement with the former German owner to receive a large supply of black
leather hides.[23] Other German owners were able to negotiate with local
and central leaders to continue managing their factories. In Varnsdorf,
for example, the Kunert brothers initially received special protection
from the Ministry of Interior to remain in the country. In the chaos
that characterized conditions in the borderlands, the Kunert brothers
appealed for Czechoslovak citizenship in an effort to retain control of
their firm. Their justifications ranged from having resisted efforts to shift
production toward the Nazi war economy to protecting the factory for the
new Czechoslovak republic. A backlash against the Kunert brothers
quickly developed, however, supported by the factory committee and
the local youth league. They attempted to distribute a flyer entitled:
"We Won't Stand with Hyenas in a United Front," which alleged that
the Kunerts were collaborators who attempted to stash a cache of valuables out of the state's reach. The workers threatened to strike. In the end,
the Kunert brothers were forced to abandon the firm and flee the country,
though not before cashing in several of the firm's accounts.[24] While it
remains unclear whether or not the Kunerts were playing up their wartime allegiances in order to keep the firm, pressure from workers and
others demanding the removal of a German factory owner proved powerful in the postwar context of ethnic cleansing.

In other cases, German speakers smoothed the transition to state
ownership. German owners possessed key information that national
administrators needed to restart production. Everything from inventories and production methods to debts and customer contacts were
important for getting these firms back on their feet. Among the many
duties of national administrators when assuming their posts was to take
inventory of the firm's various components. Several such inventory lists

[23] Letter from národní správce fm. Ludvík Strobach, Kamenický Šanov, July 6, 1945. NA,
f. MP, k. 1171 inv. č. 3633.
[24] According to one report, they had more than 10 million crowns transferred to their
personal accounts during late April and early May 1945. Report on the firm Kunert
and Sons, undated. SOA Litoměřice, p. Most, f. J. Kunert a synové, Varnsdorf, 256, k. 2
inv. č. 8. See also the flyer and undated report on the Letáková akce. On their efforts
starting a new factory, see Report to Security referent at ZNV, May 21, 1946. ZA, f.
ZNVMO, k. 140 inv. č. 273 sign. Taj.

were counter-signed by the German owner.[25] Because of this knowledge, national administrators and others protected German owners from the earliest expulsions. Sometimes gold-digger national administrators kept Germans around to help locate and secure money or other valuables. Germans benefited from such relationships as well.[26] However, the unsettled conditions in 1945 and early 1946 were replaced by revisions and greater oversight one year after the war. In many cases, once Czechs from the interior dominated factory councils they often pressured German owners to leave larger factories. Still, in Jablonec, where small-scale production was the norm, national administrators proposed more than seventy German owners for exemption from the expulsions in late 1946.[27] Because they often needed help, it proved particularly beneficial for national administrators to keep German owners around.

By August 1945, more than 9,000 national administrators of industrial firms had been established throughout the Bohemian lands. Local national committees named nearly half of these, although these factories accounted for less than 2 percent of the total number of employees in confiscated firms. The Ministry of Industry, on the other hand, assigned national administrators to the 450 largest firms, representing 664,556 workers.[28] National administrators came from a variety of backgrounds. While some were unqualified and others were gold-diggers, for the most part these positions brought professionals and skilled workers to the borderlands. Most of these new managers had education or some relevant experience, though rarely both.[29] For instance, one national administrator of Greifenhagen and Co., a forty-three-year-old native of Pardubice, had worked at several textile firms in Prague and elsewhere after attending a two-year trade school. He then worked at his father's textile firm, helping to manage it prior to the war.[30] Others had at least technical experience in their field, though many were not up to being managers in the unsettled conditions of postwar borderland industry.

Workers enjoyed a significant degree of oversight in factory settings, which included determining the fate of national administrators. Factory councils became a formal part of the postwar order in firms with at least twenty employees. The Decree on Factory Councils (Decree 104) gave workers formal input into the working conditions as well as the operation

---

[25] See for instance, SOA Litoměřice, p. Most, f. A. Schmidl, k. 40 inv.č. 17.

[26] In one case, a German owner helped the national administrator embezzle some funds from the company and in return was kept on and given a handsome salary. See correspondence in Chlupáček, Státní okresní archiv (SOkA) Bruntál, f. ONV Krnov I, k. 142 inv. č. 155 sign. II.

[27] NA, f. MP, k. 1148 inv. č. 3631.   [28] *Československý průmysl*, no. 4 (Oct. 1945).

[29] See NA, f. MP, k. 1163–1171 inv. č. 3633.

[30] SOA Litoměřice, p. Most, f. M. Greifenhagen a spol., k. 9 inv. č. 9.

Figure 5.1 Female workers at the Kunert factory. Courtesy of the State Regional Archive, Litoměřice

of the company. From the government's perspective, clarifying the role of factory councils through legislative means offered a corrective to the practices during the First Republic, when the employer had had unlimited decision-making power.[31] In borderland firms, where Czech employees remained in the minority, factory councils developed slowly. Once they emerged, however, they proved adept at pressuring officials to consider their input when installing or removing national administrators. In one textile firm, the factory council argued that the national administrator was not an expert and made several poor decisions. In addition, it noted that he had not entered into the accounting books several stores of cloth, which it argued were being used for his personal gain. The District Administrative

---

[31] See Justification Report for Decree on Factory Councils, October 24, 1945. Jech and Kaplan, 2:815; See also comments from Jan Šrámek, minister for the People's Party: "In the new social order we must deal with the upheaval of revolutionary extent. It is necessary to look after the wishes and opinions of workers and miners and the position, which they received in this revolutionary period." Minutes from the 38th meeting of the government, July 10, 1945. Jech and Kaplan, 2:823.

Commission recalled the national administrator and allowed the factory council to nominate his successor.[32]

Factory councils initiated proposals to get rid of a national administrator for a variety of reasons. They stressed his or her lack of qualifications or antagonistic position toward workers. Other times they pointed to specific problems such as preventing the factory council from checking the accounting books or from offering input on hiring and firing decisions.[33] Often a series of problems led the factory council to request a change. The factory council of W. Krusche and Company, for instance, argued that the current national administrator did not possess the proper abilities from the perspective of "planning, organization, construction, [and] craftsmanship . . . as is necessary to run the firm." It further noted that he did not cooperate with the factory council and did not leave instructions for production in his absence. On the basis of these complaints, the ZNV removed him from the position and named another national administrator in his place.[34] Factory councils used their postwar legitimacy to voice demands concerning who should manage their firm. Together with national committees, national administrators and central ministries, they were one more force in the complex matrix of postwar industrial politics.

Confiscation and Nationalization

Nationalization measures swept throughout Central and Eastern Europe after the war. The support for nationalization in the region varied and was conditioned by the war experience and prewar influence of cartels and the Great Depression. The influence of the Soviet Union was also critical to the extension of nationalization policies in the region. In 1946, a referendum in the Soviet occupational zone of Germany registered 77.7 percent agreement for the idea of confiscating war criminals' and Nazis' factories.[35] In Poland, where there was less support for nationalization, a decree of January 1946 nationalized all factories of 50 or more workers as well as some smaller key firms. Formerly German-owned firms were expropriated without compensation, while other owners were supposed

---

[32] Letter from the Factory Council, fy. Fr. Czerný, Krnov, February 4, 1946. SOkA Bruntál, f. ONV Krnov I, k. 142 inv. č. 155.

[33] See, for example, letters in NA, f. MP, k. 1274 inv. č. 3633.

[34] Letter from ZNV Moravská Ostrava, June 16, 1946. SOkA Jeseník, f. ONV Jeseník, k. 109 inv. č. 56.

[35] Norman Naimark, *Russians in Germany: A History of the Soviet Zone of Occupation, 1945–1949* (Cambridge, 1995), 185.

to receive some compensation. By 1948, nationalized firms in Poland accounted for roughly 86 percent of the workforce.[36]

The postwar Czechoslovak leaders had decided to pursue nationalization even before the war had ended. As in other European countries, the depression of the 1930s led many people to see capitalism's failure as the catalyst for fascism's success. In response, many postwar politicians shunned the principles of capitalism. Jaromir Nečas, a minister in Czechoslovakia's London-based exile government, characterized this opinion in a speech before the State Council: "enterprise must take account of the interests of the whole and not private profits. This brings to an end the old theory that private profit through 'the free play of economic forces' is simply the best and most effective stimulus of initiative and enterprise."[37] President Beneš had likewise spoken of "a national and social revolution" and "the fulfillment of democratic principles in economic and social spheres."[38] The nationalization program, like land reform, emerged in part from the postwar government's attempts to enact socially progressive policies that would improve workers' living conditions and remove power from large landowners and capitalists. Nonetheless, disputes emerged about how far to carry these ideas. Most of the National Front parties agreed that mines, banks, and other financial institutions should come under state control. The Social Democrats and the Communist Party sought widespread nationalization in industry as well. Social Democrats had outlined various nationalization plans before and during the war, and Bohumil Laušman, one of the party's leaders, became the postwar Minister of Industry.[39] A special committee under his purview drafted the first nationalization proposal for industry, energy and mining, which it presented to the government on August 25, 1945. Although the proposed decree remained generally limited to key industries, the Democratic Party of Slovakia and the People's Party in the Bohemian lands considered the list of firms too extensive. They also complained that they had not been consulted during the preliminary drafting of the decree and were now being placed before a fait accompli. The Social Democrats and Communists pressured these and the other

[36] Zbigniew Landau and Jerzey Tomaszewski, *The Polish Economy in the Twentieth Century* (London, 1985) 199.
[37] Speech of J. Nečas, February 16, 1942. Jech and Kaplan, 1:497.
[38] Karel Kaplan, *Nekravá revoluce* (Prague, 1993), 21; Eduard Beneš, "Czechoslovakia Plans for Peace," *Foreign Affairs* no.1 (October, 1944): 37; Jan Kuklík, *takzvaných Benešových dekretů* (Prague, 2002), 329.
[39] Stanislav Šaroch, "Názory na hospodářskou politiku v Československé sociálně demokratické straně v letech 1945–1948." *Acta Oeconomica Pragensia* 4, no.3 (1996): 37–66; Nina Pavelčíková, "Znárodnění průmyslu v české a zahraniční literatuře," *Slezský sborník* 91 (1993): 73; Kuklík, 326.

parties to accept the decree by arguing that after September 20, 1945, President Beneš declared he would no longer sign decrees. This deadline preceded the convocation of the Provisional National Assembly, which Laušman and others feared would become a forum for greater, and less favorable, debate about nationalization.[40] However, the September 20 deadline passed without occasion and gave proponents of nationalization a chance to expand its scope even further.

In its final form, the decree on the nationalization of key enterprises designated twenty-seven different industrial categories – fifteen more than in the original draft. For most branches of industry the average number of employees determined if it was eligible for nationalization. For instance, metal works, electro-technical, optical and light mechanical firms that averaged more than 500 employees from 1942 to 1944 were nationalized. For wood mills, the government set the employment figure at 150 from 1938 to 1940. At the insistence of the outspoken Communist Minister of Information, Vladimír Kopecký, all record album factories were nationalized.[41] The government worked out these details through intense negotiations during September and October 1945. The most important of these meetings involved debates about extending nationalization beyond the scope of "key industries." Communists justified their demands for greater nationalization in the name of the working class. For instance, Kopecký claimed that "[o]rganized workers expect that nationalization will be carried out in the shortest time span."[42]

The Communists were not alone in their efforts to use nationalization to woo working-class support. Hubert Ripka, a National Socialist, considered nationalization a key part of refiguring Czechoslovakia's postwar economy and society, and supported Communist proposals to extend nationalization. Speaking to the other ministers, he considered the question of "how far we go in nationalization and which sectors of industry we nationalize, [to be] of the same importance as the basic question, of whether we carry out nationalization at all."[43] Support for nationalization ran deep among socialist leaders, who saw it not only in terms of social justice, but in terms of national justice as well. The first postwar Prime Minister and leader of the Social Democrats, Zdeněk Fierlinger, argued

---

[40] Karel Kaplan argues that as early as July 1945 there had been a shift away from the idea of presenting the nationalization decree to parliament. Karel Kaplan, *Znárodnění a socialismus* (Prague, 1968), 22; See Laušman and other ministers' comments concerning the need to quickly finalize the decree. Minutes from the 53rd meeting of the government, September 13, 1945. 532–47.

[41] Decree 100, part 1, sec. 1, par. 6, 18, 27. 481–83.

[42] Part of 53rd meeting of the government, September 13, 1945, ibid., Jech and Kaplan, 1:537.

[43] Ibid., 541–42.

that "the word 'nationalization' acquires a really complete meaning under the circumstances. What is happening is the return to the nation of enterprises stolen by the Germans or placed at the service of the Reich. The industrial sector, which will be nationalized, was in the hands of the enemy or of his agents. It is therefore an act of justice."[44] The Justification Report of the nationalization decree likewise emphasized its national meaning: "nationalization is prompted by the calls of the entire nation. It is the pillar, on which the national whole establishes its new state organization."[45] Such arguments meshed with the notion of the "national and democratic revolution," and were another way that leaders invoked the nation to pursue the expropriation of property.

Like confiscated property, the government sought to take over nationalized firms at no cost or risk to the state. National Front leaders decided to insulate the state from the possible debts accrued by nationalized firms as well as from the cost of compensating former owners. They employed the concept of nationalization, rather than state ownership (zestátnění), as the legal basis for this argument.[46] In order to implement this policy, the government established nationalized enterprises as financially independent organizations. At the same time, the government claimed ownership over these firms.[47] While the state's status as an owner without financial obligations appeared advantageous from the perspective of future claims against it, in practice it gave nationalized firms a tremendous amount of independence. As one Slovak minister argued: "A 'national enterprise' no longer belongs to the state, it does not turn over its profits to anyone and the enterprise is not in any way nationalized, because the nation-state does not have in any form influence over its management."[48] Indeed, nationalized firms became powerful institutions in their own right, and played a central role shaping the borderland economy.

Nationalized enterprises were organized as a conglomerate of individual factories and companies. They were grouped together by sector and controlled by regional and central directorates in Prague. Unlike national administrators of individual confiscated firms, whom national

---

[44] Jean Danes, "Z. Fierlinger on Nationalization," *The Central European Observer* 22, no. 21 (1945): 333.

[45] Důvodová zpráva k upravené osnově dekretu o znárodnění dolů a podniků energetického, zbrojního, klíčového a velkého průmyslu, September 10, 1945. Jech and Kaplan, 1:522.

[46] See comments by the Minister of Finance on the proposed nationalization decree, September 5–6, 1945. Ibid., 516; Důvodová zpráva for the proposed nationalization decree, September 10, 1945. Ibid., 522; See also Kuklík, 334–35.

[47] Decree 100, part 1, sec. 4, par. 1 and sec. 5, par. 4. Jech and Kaplan, 1:484–85; Part 3, sec. 13, par. 1 and sect. 18, par. 1. Ibid., 488–89.

[48] Excerpt of minutes from the extraordinary meeting of the government, September 13, 1945. Ibid., 536.

committees named, the directorates, which the central government appointed, controlled individual nationalized firms. While coordination among the chemical goods branch, for example, was necessary to reach the government's economic targets during the Two-Year Plan, the general directors possessed considerable authority to manage the firms under their control.[49] By the end of 1946 nearly 3,000 individual factories had been nationalized in the Bohemian lands. As the nationalized sector grew, it also increased its power to claim other firms. Because confiscated firms that had not been nationalized remained under national administrators and were state controlled, they provided easy targets for expanding nationalized enterprises. Together, nationalized enterprises and confiscated companies placed the state in firm control of the country's industrial economy. By the end of 1946, nationalized and confiscated firms together accounted for roughly 75 percent of industrial firms, based on employee numbers and overall production.[50]

The disputes and uncertainties associated with the nationalization decree delayed the passage of the confiscation decree, which had been prepared for the President's signature already on August 14, 1945. There had been several different proposed drafts for the decree confiscating non-agricultural property. The first working proposal, from May 24, 1945, for the protection (*zajištění*) of enemy property gave national committees and the state administration office authority to manage seized firms.[51] However, such an arrangement contradicted the central government's intentions, since it had requested the draft as a result of local national committees' inconsistent treatment of this property.[52] A new draft emerged as the decree for the protection and confiscation of enemy property. Officials' shift from calling solely for the "protection" of German property to its "confiscation" (*konfiskace*) reflected new opinions and conditions concerning the control of former German property by the

[49] Václav Lhota, *Znárodnění v Československu, 1945–1948* (Prague, 1987), 202–7; Václav Průcha, *Hospodářské a sociální dějiny Československa: 1918-1992*, vol. 2 (Brno, 2009), 103–4.
[50] Karel Kaplan argues that confiscated, nationalized, cooperative and public enterprises accounted for 70–73 percent of production in 1946. Kaplan, 100; 3,391 medium and larger confiscated, non-nationalized, firms represented 13 percent of industrial employees. Anna Beinhauerová and Karel Sommer, "Mocenské pozice ve znárodněném průmyslu (1945–1948)," in *Stránkami soudobých dějin: Sborník statí k pětašedesátinám historika Karla Kaplana*, ed. Karel Jech (Prague, 1993), 61; Růžena Hlušičková, *Boj o průmyslové konfiskáty v letech 1945–1948* (Prague, 1983), 38–41.
[51] Earlier drafts of this decree had been proposed while still in exile. See London proposal from May 24, 1944. Jech and Kaplan, 2:862.
[52] A282–0/5–1945, Ministerstvo vnitra, May 30, 1945. NA, f. MV-NR, k. 477 inv. č. 1028 sign. A2826. See also the correspondence and other proposed drafts of the confiscation decree in NA, f. Úřad předsednictva vláda-běžná spisovna (ÚPV-B), k. 708 inv. č. 2866 sign. 741/4.

summer of 1945. Initially, when exiled leaders planned for the expulsions, they had to take into account the attitudes of international leaders, especially the British; therefore, they had promised not to confiscate Sudeten German property without indemnity.[53] By the summer of 1945, with the expulsions successfully underway and Allied leaders' attention elsewhere, Czechoslovak officials pursued more thoroughgoing policies against Germans.[54]

Just as the confiscation decree was set for publication in August 1945, Minister of Industry Laušman requested that it not be issued because it conflicted with the nationalization decree, which the government continued to debate. He worried that many confiscated firms would also be liable to the nationalization provisions, which would complicate matters of compensation, especially concerning non-German capital in German-owned firms.[55] In particular, Laušman sought to coordinate the date in the two decrees that determined whether such capital would be eligible for compensation. Unlike the draft of the confiscation decree, which confiscated only wartime investment in German firms, the nationalization decree backed by Laušman sought to withhold compensation for any capital investment in German firms dating back to 1918, the founding of the Czechoslovak Republic.[56] Such a policy would have considerably increased the amount of property exempted from compensation. However, as an Interior Ministry official noted, this provision would concern foreign investors, including current allies, who should not face the "police character" of the confiscation decree. The official argued instead that if the Ministry of Industry wanted to take over foreign capital it should do so through the nationalization decree which it could "justify by the new economic and social character of the state."[57]

The nationalization and confiscation decrees differed in form, but not in substance. While political parties and ministerial officials held different conceptions of how far these provisions should go, they agreed with the general need to restructure property relations and the economy. The impetus for this transformation involved not only socialist ideology and

---

[53] US Department of State, Historical Office, *Foreign Relations of the United States* (FRUS), *Europe 1945*, vol. 2, *General Economic and Political Matters* (Washington, DC, 1960), 1234.

[54] Jan Kuklík argues that Czechoslovak legal measures against German property were in line with other states' policies and laws concerning enemy property. See Kuklík, 291–96. What is different, however, was that in the other countries enemies did not comprise a substantial portion of the prewar citizenry of the country.

[55] Letter from Minister Laušman, August 23, 1945. NA, f. MV-NR, k. 477 inv. č. 1028 sign. A2826.

[56] See Proposal for the decree on the nationalization of mines, energy firms, defense and key industries, part 2, sec. 7, par. 1c, August 25, 1945. Jech and Kaplan, 1:503.

[57] Interior memo of MV, August 23, 1945. NA, f. MV-NR, k. 477 inv. č. 1028 sign. A2826.

prewar experience, but also the structural changes brought by the war. World War II had created a unique opportunity for states in Central and Eastern Europe to redefine their economic priorities. Nazi Aryanization policies along with state control over other industries left the issue of property rights open to debate at the end of the war. Because the state de facto controlled these properties as well as the decisions about their fate, it was easy for central leaders to pursue an ever-expanding nationalization program. The expulsions provided even more justification for increased state intervention in the borderland economy, where former owners were not simply powerless to prevent the takeovers, but were declared enemies. Together, the confiscation and nationalization decrees dramatically changed the borderland economy and property rights for the next fifty years.

Central Planning

Prague officials began concrete planning for the borderland economy in the fall of 1945 as drastic changes were still unfolding and as problems brought by the initial expulsions and settlement emerged. At the first meeting of the Central Commission for Interior Settlement, the Ministry of Industry representative noted that they had begun "to make up lists of firms where production should be continued, and lists of firms that would be temporarily closed or liquidated."[58] By the end of August 1945, officials at the Ministry of Industry began to distinguish between confiscated industrial concerns that did not fall under nationalization provisions, but which were nonetheless of key importance in the borderlands.[59] This process evolved into the classification of confiscated firms, according to three categories: those of statewide importance where production would continue (category A), those which would be temporarily closed (category B) and those set for liquidation (category C). Such a policy allowed for short-term plans to direct labor, both Czech and German, as well as energy and material supplies to the most important firms. For the long term, this policy provided a basis to begin the consolidation of borderland industries. However, these categories became points of contention, rather than final decisions. The number of confiscated firms under state control continually fluctuated in the immediate postwar years. By the summer of 1945, some firms existed only on paper; they

[58] Minutes from the first meeting of Central Commission for Interior Settlement (Ústřední komise vnitřího osídlování ÚKVO), July 30, 1945. NA. f. MV-NR, k. 12145 sign. 1651/1.

[59] See čj. I/2 179.682/1945 outlining the early part of this procedure. MP, Department 1, August 28, 1945. NA, f. MP, k. 1140 inv. č. 3631.

had closed before or during the war, but were still counted in industrial statistics. Confiscated firms also changed classifications as they were liquidated, temporarily closed or resumed operations. Figures concerning the number of firms in these categories changed accordingly. For instance at the end of 1946, 1,790 borderland enterprises existed in category A. By April 1947 the number of seized A-level firms jumped to 4,569 in the borderlands as national committees, national administrators and others continued to request that local factories remain open.[60] The Settlement Office, which considered the reduction of industrial firms as part of its mandate, support the quick categorization of borderland firms in order to permit a more organized approach to settlement.[61]

In addition, the confiscation program involved using borderland firms to bolster the industrial base of Slovakia and underdeveloped regions in the Bohemian lands. Increased industrialization was a basic tenet of Czechoslovakia's postwar economic plans and the shortage of workers in the borderlands meant excess machine capacity could be used to meet needs elsewhere. Relocating confiscated borderland firms to Slovakia also served as a way to bridge the prewar and wartime divisions between Prague and Bratislava. Indeed, Communist leaders promoted the program as a way to satisfy Slovak demands for immediate industrialization.[62] President Beneš likewise supported the idea. In an August 1945 speech to the Slovak National Council, the ruling body for Slovakia, he connected the removal of German workers to the possibility of bringing borderland factories to Slovakia. He argued that the transfer of factories "will be by itself a certain kind of political and economic revolution."[63] While central leaders clearly understood that borderland national committees would resist such a policy, leading Communist officials believed they could get borderland comrades on national committees to accept their decision.[64] During the Two-Year

---

[60] Hlušičková, 47–48; Tomáš Staněk, *Odsun Němců z Československu, 1945–1948* (Prague, 1991), 349. There were 670 confiscated category A firms in the interior of the country as well. Zapis o poradě at Osidlováci úřad (OÚ), April 11, 1947. NA, f. MV-NR, k. 2487 inv. č. 2053 sign. B2653/1.

[61] See the Settlement Office's Program Statement and minutes from the 3rd meeting of ÚKVO, September 18, 1945. NA. f. MV-NR, k. 12145 sign. 1651/1; See also letter from MP about the categorization provisions, October 16, 1945. NA, f. MP, k. 1140 inv. č. 3631.

[62] See Klement Gottwald's remarks cited in Anna Beinhauerová, "Problémy likvidace a přemisťování průmyslu z pohraničí v letech 1945–1948." *Slezký sborník* 83, no.1 (1985), 27–28; E. Kafka, "Industrialisace Slovenska a přemisťování průmyslových podniků z pohraničí." *Osidlování*, July 10, 1946.

[63] Edvard Beneš to Slovak National Council, August 1945. Edvard Beneš, *Edvard Beneš: Odsun němců z Československa*, ed. Karel Novotný (Prague, 1996), 152.

[64] Minutes from the Narodohospodářská komise (NHK) KSČ meeting, October 9, 1945. NA, f. Narodohospodářská komise (NHK) KSČ, a.j. 4 sv. 1.

Plan, the government pledged to create 26,000 jobs by moving confiscated factories to Slovakia.[65]

The government attempted a trial run for the relocation program by targeting textile firms in the Silesian district of Krnov in the autumn of 1945. Slovak Communists had hoped to use the relocation of the Krnov firms as a publicity campaign for the general relocation program. The other members of the KSČ's National Economic Committee agreed to support it.[66] During initial discussions to designate which factories would be moved to Slovakia, however, the District National Committee's industrial representative remained adamant about protecting the district's leading firms. After protracted negotiations the Slovak delegation had to settle for some of the district's weaker factories. The Krnov ONV chairperson congratulated the industrial department head upon his return from Prague for the "tireless and efficient work in the protection of Krnov's textile industry, and through it also the possibility for the livelihood and employment for relocated Czech workers."[67] Such a reaction to the initial steps toward factory relocation did not bode well for the central government's plans for the consolidation of borderland firms. Rather than a publicity campaign for the relocation of borderland firms to Slovakia, the program was quietly pursued, with many voices raised against it. National committees' responses to such pressures revealed a deep commitment to local industry as a key component of successful resettlement.

In the face of local resistance, the central government struggled to get beyond the planning stages and to begin actual consolidation and distribution of machine equipment and entire factories. Ministry of Industry officials first compiled preliminary lists of A-level firms during September and October 1945.[68] At a three day meeting in late October, various government officials began to separate the most important firms and those easily slated for liquidation. However, the lists prepared by the Ministry of Industry proved incomplete and prevented a comprehensive approach to liquidation. Even after these lists were finalized in late November, they continued to change and remained, in many cases, incomplete.[69] In addition, different

[65] Law for the Two-Year Economic Plan, part 4 sec.7 par.3, October 25, 1946. *První československý plán* (Prague, 1946), 117. According to projections from the Ministry of Industry the figure was 24,000. See I/2–230498/46, MP, August 15, 1946. NA, f. MP, k. 1788 inv. č. 1581 sign. B1700.

[66] Minutes from the NHK KSČ meeting, October 9, 1945. NA, f. NHK KSČ, a.j. 4 sv. 1.

[67] Report on meetings with representatives from Slovakia and Brno, MP, September 23–24, 1945. SOkA Bruntál, f. ONV Krnov I, k. 7 inv. č. 63.

[68] NA, f. MP, k. 1140, 1141 inv. č. 3631.

[69] Dr. Piskač from the Ministry of Industry stated that the ABC lists were prepared at the 5th meeting of ÚKVO, November 29, 1945. NA, f. MV-NR, k. 12145 sign. 1651/1. For different complaints about the lists from central government officials see Letter from MV, December 14, 1945. NA, f. MP, k. 1142 inv. č. 3631; Letter from Okresní úřad ochraný

government organs had their own conception about which firms should be designated as A, B or C. In a sign of further problems to come, a Ministry of Industry official rebuked representatives of the Provincial National Committee in Brno for requesting that printing firms in their region remain open by arguing that "people's organs, or no people's organs, all that matters to us is industry."[70] Technical problems and governmental infighting hindered the process of reorganizing the borderland economy at every turn.

By early 1946, the Settlement Office, along with the Ministry of Industry and other officials, had decided which borderland firms to liquidate and which would continue production. Miroslav Kreysa, the OÚ's chairman, reported that in the first group (A-level) were 2,260 firms with 286,000 employees, of which 142,000 were Germans. In the remaining categories there were 1,528 (B) and 1,910 (C) enterprises.[71] While the plans to redirect resources to A-level factories and to liquidate many others made practical sense and allowed officials to finally begin consolidating borderland firms, this process also proved lengthy and painstaking. First, central plans developed slowly, which allowed firms slated for liquidation to continue hiring settlers and planning for future production. In addition, authority between ministries and other central offices continued to collide and slowed the process of liquidation and the relocation of equipment. Most importantly, national committees and settlers fought to protect local firms. At times they did so by making claims to these industries in the name of nationalization or settlement. In other cases, they simply ignored central orders to stop operating. As central authorities increasingly sought to control confiscated firms, settlers reacted to do the same.

At the beginning of 1946, the Czechoslovak government created twelve Regional Industrial Reconstruction Commissions to streamline the liquidation of borderland firms. They had the task of organizing the closure of factories so that raw materials, machinery and labor could be best utilized for the remaining companies.[72] Despite hopes that the liquidation process would begin in early 1946, the reconstruction commissions faced numerous obstacles. One official complained that the commission spent much of its time collecting information by personally visiting each firm. In many instances the trips were pointless because the firm was in shambles or no

práce (OÚOP) Karlový Vary, October 8, 1946. NA. f. Ministerstvo ochrany práce a sociální péče, 1945–1951 (MOPSP), k. 406 inv. č. 842 sign. 2307.
[70] Minutes from the meeting at the MP, October 29–31, 1945. NA, f. Osídlovací komise při ÚV KSČ (f. 23), a.j. 349/1.
[71] Stráž severu, April 5, 1946.
[72] Směrnice pro obnovovací komise, OÚ, February 11, 1946. Předpisy, 2:449; Martin Rais, "Naše osidlovací politika," Osidlování, June 25, 1946.

longer existed. He reported that he "did not receive the impression of timely and directed planning from the Ministry of Industry, at least not from the perspective of economy."[73] Indeed, the Ministry of Industry decided to scrap B-level factories already in April 1946. This created further delays because commissions had to revisit firms and create new inventories before the entire process could move forward.[74]

Party disputes over the fate of confiscated firms slowed the process even further. During the final debates about the nationalization decree the Communist Party agreed that no further nationalizations would occur. The other parties believed this pledge applied to former German firms as well.[75] However, the Communist Party saw confiscated factories as an excellent way to strengthen the nationalized sector's size and power. The attachment of confiscated firms to nationalized enterprises, or affiliation (*afiliace*), as the Communists called it, theoretically provided an easy, low-cost way to build up the nationalized sector's capacity. In April 1946 the KSČ's National Economic Committee discussed ways that nationalized enterprises' "general directors could have influence over chosen confiscated firms until the time that their closure and attachment will be decided."[76] National Socialists, on the other hand, sought to use confiscated firms to develop an independent business class, and wished to prevent confiscated industries from being subsumed by the nationalized sector.[77] The fate of many confiscated factories, which had either been listed at the B-level, or which were actively operating C-level firms, therefore remained in contested limbo into 1947.

Although party leaders differed on the final provisions for confiscated firms, they agreed that these assets should remain under centralized control. This policy developed in response to various demands for confiscated property made by ministries, state offices and other officials. At one meeting in late 1945, an auction-like atmosphere emerged as different ministries demanded control of this or that property. The Ministry of Education recommended that church and school property be excluded from allocation

---

[73] Report on activities of industrial reconstruction commission in Opava, August 7, 1946. NA, f. MOPSP, k. 401 inv. č. 841 sign. 2306.

[74] Minutes from the sixth meeting of Industrial Renewal Commission in Liberec, April 29, 1946, ibid. See other commissions' complaints about further changes in the ministry's decisions. NA, f. MOPSP, k. 406 inv. č. 842 sign. 2307.

[75] Lhota, 245.

[76] Agenda for upcoming NHK KSČ meeting, April 13, 1946. NA, f. NHK KSČ, a.j. 19 sv. 2.

[77] For support of entrepreneurs, see "Nerozdávejte velké konfiskaty," *Svobodné slovo*, November 23, 1946 (found in NA, f. 23, a.j. 349/1.); see Kreysa's comments that national socialists did not want to attach medium and large confiscated firms to nationalized ones. Minutes of the Osidlovácí komise při Ústřední výbor KSČ, September 13, 1946. NA, f. 23, a.j. 14.

provisions. The Minister of Foreign Trade argued that things of cultural value should be retained by the Cultural Fund under its jurisdiction. The representative from the Ministry for the Protection of Labor and Social Welfare requested control over all housing, or at least housing under rental contracts.[78] The extent of such demands forced Prague officials to search for alternative ways to distribute this property without going through the allocation provisions outlined in the confiscation decree. Decree 108 provided for allocation commissions, established at the local, district and provincial levels, to decide on a case-by-case basis the fate of permanent confiscated property. Central government officials, however, considered such a process too slow and unwieldy, not to mention that it gave local authorities extraordinary power over confiscated property. In July 1946 the OÚ published two key directives concerning the fate of borderland firms. The first, number 1586, outlined more precisely the process for liquidating C-level firms, while the second, number 1587, involved plans to use confiscated property "in the interest of public work or for the economic construction of the state."[79] Directive 1587 allowed various state bodies, like education and cultural organizations, to request the allocation of confiscated buildings and equipment for their use. It provided buildings and supplies for schools, nurseries and recreation centers in local communities throughout the country. The Settlement Office touted this aspect of Directive 1587 as fulfilling the cultural and social demands of the people.[80]

While various ministries and national committees acquired confiscated homes and other buildings for their use, Directive 1587 also offered a way for nationalized enterprises to expand their scope. The Communist Party, in particular, sought to utilize this aspect of the directive to attach confiscated industrial firms to nationalized enterprises, and had begun discussing such plans by April 1946. Immediately after Directive 1587 came into effect, national enterprises began requesting confiscated firms in large numbers.[81] The National Socialist paper *Free Word* (*Svobodné slovo*) reacted with surprise that nationalized enterprises had requested 686 confiscated firms by September 1946, some with as few as 6 employees.[82] The Settlement Office, under Kreysa's authority, often expressed socialist themes in its efforts to allocate confiscated firms to the nationalized sector.

---

[78] Minutes from a meeting at OÚ, November 8, 1945. Archiv Města (AM) Ústí n. L., f. MNV Ústí n. L., k. 2 inv. č. 24.

[79] *Předpisy*, 1:86–89.

[80] Eduard Tomáš, "Konfiskáty do služeb lidu," *Osidlování*, April 25, 1947. See also more detailed lists of property and their purposes, October 25, 1948–March 31,1950. AM Ústí n. L., f. ONV Ústí n. L., k. 38 inv. č. 202.

[81] Agenda for upcoming NHK KSČ meeting, April 13, 1946. NA, f. NHK KSČ, a.j. 19 sv. 2; Staněk, *Odsun Němců*, 349; Hlušičková, 48–49.

[82] "Co se stane s prumyslovými konfiskáty," *Svobodné slovo*, September 21, 1946.

For example, at a meeting of regional settlement officials in late 1946, a Prague official from the OÚ argued: "The state's economic construction closely connects with nationalized industry, with the undisputed need to productively and organically expand it, so that it really uses these confiscated factories for the complete improvement of our economy." He added that nationalized enterprises will receive priority during the allocation of firms that complement their production.[83] In early 1947, the Communist Party compelled the directors of nationalized enterprises to increase their demands for the allocation of expropriated German companies.[84] With the support of the Communist Party and such prodding by settlement officials, the momentum behind affiliating confiscated firms with nationalized enterprises continued to grow. However, it was an unrelated case in a remote place that finally tipped the scales in the Communists' favor.

Restitution

Companies and property under national administration, which were neither confiscated nor nationalized, still became entangled in the politics surrounding property rights after the war. Some cases involved Czechs who were forced to leave their homes to make space for Nazi military training grounds.[85] Jewish owners, or their heirs, who survived the war and returned for their property had important claims as well. In theory, Jewish property should not have been involved in the confiscation process at all. Decrees 2 and 5 declared all forced property transactions after September 29, 1938, invalid, which would have included property Aryanized once the Nazis annexed the Sudetenland. However, by the war's end, with Jewish property in Germans' hands, it was unclear to incoming Czechs how such property would be handled, particularly because Jewish survivors had not yet returned. When Jews did return to their old jobs and homes they encountered hostility from settlers and received little official support. Pressure against Jews reclaiming their property surfaced elsewhere in East Central Europe after the war.[86] In

---

[83] Referát o výhlášce 1587 pro schůzí přednostů obl. úřad, November 21, 1946. Zemský Archiv (ZA) Opava, f. Oblastní osidlovací úřad, Opava, k. 12 inv. č. 20.

[84] Meeting of the NHK KSČ, January 19, 1947. NA, f. NHK KSČ, a.j. 4 sv. 1; Internal report of the Settlement Committee of the KSČ, March 17, 1947. NA, f. 23, a.j. 349/1. Communists held the most directorships within nationalized industry. See Beinhauerová and Sommer, "Mocenské pozice," 71–72.

[85] Some 46,000 inhabitants moved to make space for military training grounds. Problémy osídlení a hospodářské výsledky FNO v Praze a v Bratislavě, MV, late 1950. NA, f. Ministerstvo vnitra – tajná (MV-T), k. 196 inv. č. 3582 sign. 280.

[86] Jan Gross, *Fear: Anti-Semitism in Poland after Auschwitz* (New York, 2006), 39–51.

part, the resistance to returning Jewish property was due to discrimination and opportunism, but it also fit with the government's objectives – both local and central – to control property. With property rights in flux and widespread hostility toward Jews, the possibilities for unencumbered restitutions were slim. Indeed, of the 16,000 individual requests for restitution made by Jews in Czechoslovakia after the war, only 3,000 were granted by the end of 1947.[87]

The Jewish community of prewar Czechoslovakia had distinctive characteristics that often broke down along regional lines. In the eastern parts of the country, particularly Sub-Carpathian Ruthenia, most Jews were Orthodox, whereas in the western portions more Jews were secularized. In the Bohemian lands, for instance, Bohemian Jews had a higher incidence of intermarriage with the gentile population compared to those in Moravia.[88] During the interwar years three broad categories of Jewish identity had emerged in Bohemia: German Jewish, Czech–Jewish and Zionist. However, even these categories must be approached with caution given that people changed categories or may not have considered themselves as belonging to any one of these three.[89] Nonetheless, Jews were forced to choose sides, either in elections or in censuses, and their choice in the 1930 census, though again not necessarily a true measure of their self-identity, held significant consequences for those who survived the Holocaust and returned to Czechoslovakia following the war. In 1930, based on the census of that year, so-called German Jews numbered roughly 35,000 out of 117,000 Jews in the Bohemian lands.[90] As Kateřina Čapková argues, German Jews living in the Sudetenland tended to speak German for socio-economic reasons, but were more likely to choose Jewish nationality when given the chance during the interwar censuses. In Bohemia, this switch came at the expense of Germans more so than it did for Czechs. Those who continued to declare themselves as German Jews may have done so for reasons of cultural affinity or simply as a reflection of their spoken language.[91] Jews comprised a small percentage of the borderland population before its annexation in 1938. They lived primarily in the larger cities of the region: Reichenberg,

---

[87] Helena Krejčová, "Židovská očekávání a zklamání po roce 1945," in *Češi a Němci: ztracené dějiny?* (Prague, 1995), 247.

[88] Kateřina Čapková, *Czechs, Germans, Jews? National Identity and the Jews of Bohemia*, trans. Derek and Marzia Paton (New York, 2012), 22.

[89] Čapková; Wilma Abeles Iggers, ed., *The Jews of Bohemia and Moravia: A Historical Reader* (Detroit, 1992), 321–22.

[90] Tomás Staněk, "Němečtí židé v Československu v letech 1945–1948," *Dějiny a současnost* 5 (1991): 42.

[91] She points out that this was in sharp contrast to the situation in Prague, where Jews and Germans intermingled more easily: Čapková, 62–73.

Karlsbad, Aussig and Teplitz-Schönau. Only in Teplitz-Schönau did they comprise more than 10 percent of the population; in other cities they represented less than 5 percent.[92] In general, they participated in a broad cross-section of the economy as shop owners, officials and workers. Their economic role also depended on location. In spa towns they ran hotels and guesthouses, and in places like Gablonz they were heavily involved in the glass-making industry.[93] Several Jews were also factory owners in the typical industries that comprised the Sudetenland's industrial economy.

By early 1938, the situation for Jews in the borderlands had become increasingly desperate. Sudeten German Nazi supporters had begun to isolate Jews during the summer of 1938 through the spread of anti-Semitic propaganda, a boycott of Jewish businesses and sporadic episodes of robbery.[94] When the Nazis took over, further abuses ensued. The Gestapo began arresting perceived enemies of the regime, including Jews. The Nazi government extended anti-Jewish provisions in place elsewhere in German territory so that Jews could not practice certain professions, and their property was confiscated. These developments culminated in Kristallnacht in November 1938, when pogroms swept through the borderlands and Sudeten German Nazis burned synagogues and ransacked Jewish businesses. By November 1938, between 15,000 and 17,000 Sudetenland Jews fled to the interior parts of the country, in particular to Prague. Those who remained lost their property and ultimately their lives. During the war several hundred were sent to Theresienstadt and later to the gas chambers in Auschwitz. Others who had fled first to the interior, but not abroad, met a similar fate.[95]

For many Jews, the postwar experience in Czechoslovakia was anything but liberating. Anti-Semitism widely propagated during the war continued to shape people's views afterward.[96] Popular hostility was also supported by official discrimination. For instance, a September 1945 general directive from the District Administrative Commission in Ústí nad Labem to local national committees outlined provisions for determining who should lose citizenship. It noted that anyone who had registered

[92] Jörg Osterloh, *Nationalsozialistische Judenverfolgung im Reichsgau Sudetenland, 1938–1945* (Munich: Oldenbourg, 2006), 53.
[93] Ibid., 62–65; Livia Rothkirchen, *The Jews of Bohemia and Moravia* (Jerusalem, 2005), 37–38.
[94] Osterloh, 152–54; Rothkirchen, 60; Kural and Radvanovský, 52–54.
[95] Rothkirchen, 79–80. Kural and Radvanovský, 81–82.
[96] For the wartime period, see Benjamin Frommer, *National Cleansing: Retribution Against Nazi Collaborators in Postwar Czechoslovakia* (Cambridge, 2005), 165–79. For the postwar period, see David Gerlach, "Beyond Expulsion: The Emergence of 'Unwanted Elements' in the Czech Borderlands, 1945–50," *East European Politics and Society*, 24 no. 2 (May, 2010): 269–93; Kevin McDermott, "A 'Polyphony of Voices'? Czech Popular Opinion and the Slánský Affair," *Slavic Review* 67, no. 4 (Winter, 2008): 863.

themselves as German in the 1930 census, including Jews who had been persecuted during the war, should be considered as German.[97] The Council of Jewish Religious Communities for Teplice-Šanov challenged the OSK chairperson's interpretation of the citizenship decree. In response the chairperson, Maria Vobecká, wrote: "Racial persecution is not solely the legal condition, since the law requires that such a person 'remained true to the democratic republican state idea of the Czechoslovak Republic.' For many Jews this second condition is not fulfilled."[98] Vobecká later justified her views by arguing that "the majority [of Jews] do not know the state language and go around Ústí speaking German, which upsets the Czech inhabitants who desire the 'de-Germanization (*odgermanizace*) of the borderlands." She noted that it would be best if such people were not sent there.[99] Such interpretations and renegade actions of local authorities forced central officials to define more clearly which Jews should be considered German and what constituted "Germanization activities."

In September 1946, the Interior Ministry issued an order that attempted to clarify the position of "people of Jewish origin" regarding their citizenship. The order first presented a sympathetic tone toward the suffering of Jews. It noted that

barbaric Nazism ... directed itself primarily and in the greatest extent against people of so-called "Jewish origin" and so-called "mixed Jews". It is also well known that from those people, as far as they were in regions subjected to the Nazi reign of terror, only about ten percent survived, while close to half of these, however, returned from concentration camps with greater or lesser injured bodies and health.[100]

The order stated that the Czech and Slovak nation refused to recognize such racial distinctions and discrimination. With regard to Decree 33, on citizenship, and Decree 108, on the confiscation of non-agricultural property, it argued that because of their suffering under Nazi terror they fulfilled the conditions for exemption from these decrees. At the same time, the order outlined other conditions by which Jews could face loss of property and citizenship for their support of "Germanization" or "Magyarization." Here too the Interior Ministry stressed the fact that

---

[97] Čis. 476/Dr.H/M-1945 from Okresní správní komise Usti n.L., September 18, 1945. NA, f. MV-NR, k. 1769 inv. č. 1576.

[98] Věra Hladíková and Vladimír Kaiser, "Resituce majetku ústecké židovské rodiny Pisků, 1945–1961," *Ústecký sborník historický* no. 27 (2000): 197.

[99] Letter from Chairperson of ONV Ústí, November 2, 1945. NA, f. MV-NR, k. 1807 inv. č. 1602 sign. B2111.

[100] Z/S-3559/89–17/9–46, Instructions on determining the establishment of Czechoslovak state citizenship for people who were listed as "people of Jewish origin" by the occupiers and permission for expatriation, if it relates to people of German or Magyar nationality, MV, September 13, 1946. *Předpisy*, 2:315.

Jews, for the most part, would not be liable to the retributive nature of the decrees, even if they had listed German as their nationality in the 1930 census. The instructions noted that Germanization or Magyarization could not be determined simply by "the use of German or Magyar language (often from the lack of knowledge of a Slavonic language) and participation in German or Magyar organizations or cultural life, as long as it did not support the attempt at Germanization or Magyarization."[101] Germanization was described in broad terms as extraordinary support for German schools or organizations, pressuring Slavic employees to send their children to German schools and hiring Germans rather than Czechs. But even in these instances the order noted that such actions were deemed traitorous only if they occurred "in Slavonic regions."[102] Thus, for German Jews in the borderlands the allegation that they supported Germanization should have required substantial proof of exceptional support for German political parties or nationalist organizations intent on subverting the republic.

One of the most prominent restitution cases involved a textile mill in the northern borderland town of Varnsdorf. Emil Beer, the pre-1939 owner of the firm, came from a Jewish family that had owned the company for many years. Beer and his family had fled Czechoslovakia after selling the company to a Reich German named Eichler for a nominal sum.[103] Following the war, Beer returned to Varnsdorf and was reportedly welcomed with music and a celebration; his former chauffeur, and the firm's current national administrator, greeted him warmly.[104] In November 1945, Beer requested the cancellation of the national administrator and the return of his property. The District Administrative Commission, after checking with the employees, approved the idea of returning the firm to him.[105] From this point forward, however, the situation deteriorated.

During 1946, the factory council pressured the then District National Committee to sustain its original confiscation ruling after a series of disagreements and misunderstandings between Beer and some of the employees. It likewise demanded that the factory be nationalized through affiliation to a local nationalized enterprise.[106] The ONV in Varnsdorf

[101] Ibid., 316; Šárka Nepalová, "Die jüdische Minderheit in Böhmen und Mähren in den Jahren 1945–1948," *Theresienstädter Studien und Dokumente 1999*, 337–38.
[102] *Předpisy*, 317.   [103] Hlušičková, 54.
[104] "Dozvuky k varnsdorfské stavce," *Stráž severu*, March 8 1947; for many other facts regarding Beer's background, see Petr Sedlák, "Jmenuji se Emil Beer aneb pokus o životopisné porozumění," in *Německy mluvící obyvatelstvo v Československu po roce 1945*, eds. Adrian von Arburg, Tomáš Dvořák, David Kovařík a kol. (Brno, 2010), 352–59.
[105] Minutes from the meeting of the ONV, September 6, 1946. SOkA Děčín, f. ONV Varnsdorf, k. 1 inv. č. 47; Hlušičková, 55; Sedlák, 359, n.14.
[106] Hlušičková, 56.

began debating the case in earnest again in the fall. In a meeting on September 6, 1946, after hearing arguments from both sides it voted 10 to 9 against restitution. Much of the argument against Beer involved claims that he did not choose Jewish nationality and that he was truly German.[107] In early 1947, however, the ZNV in Prague decided to cancel the confiscation proceedings against Beer, because he had declared Jewish nationality in the 1930 census and was thus exempted from the confiscation provisions. In response, the factory council, with the support of the district trade union, which local Communists controlled, protested the ruling. They threatened to organize a strike if the confiscation process was not restarted. The Prague government sent an official committee to help prevent unrest and resolve the case. It met with the ONV in Varnsdorf on February 27, 1947. The representative from the Interior Ministry reported that new evidence about Emil Beer's past behavior emerged at the meeting concerning his "Germanization activities." Therefore, he recommended "that the district national committee debate the entire case again and consider whether or not the activities of Emil Beer are based on realities, for which it is possible to order confiscation without regard to nationality."[108]

The ONV had already been taking a hardline approach to the issue of restitution. In a meeting in January 1947 it denied the requests of two Czech women to have their share of property owned with their German husbands restituted. The cases were complicated, but as one of the members added to the record in regard to the second case: "This ruling contradicts the clear tenor of the directive."[109] The Communist Party in Varnsdorf had an eleven-member majority on a twenty-person plenum of the District National Committee; they also controlled the council and chairperson post. This meant that they could, and did, dictate policy. In the Beer case, the meeting called on February 27 was much more of a show than the previous debate on his case had been. It was held in the dining hall of a local factory and was open to the public. It was over in the first act. The first witness against Beer declared: "National conditions during the First Republic were very difficult and complicated and all the factory owners propagated and supported German thinking and supported Germanization. Mr. Beer belonged among them." From there,

---

[107] Minutes from the meeting of the ONV, September 6, 1946. SOkA Děčín, f. ONV Varnsdorf, k. 1 inv.č. 47.

[108] Zpráva o jednání ve Varnsdorfu. Konfiskace firmy Beer, MV, February 28, 1947. NA, f. Ministerstvo vnitra – Nosek (MV-N), k. 227 inv. č. 146.

[109] Minutes from the meeting of the ONV, January 31, 1947. SOkA Děčín, f. ONV Varnsdorf, k. 1 inv. č. 47.

others came out and attacked every aspect of his national character.[110] The Communist members of the ONV all voted in favor of confiscation, which, thanks to their majority, was enough to carry the motion despite the other parties' opposition. As the Interior Ministry representative reported, a Social Democrat on the ONV stated that they abstained from voting because "the entire meeting was forced by terror and that even though they otherwise agreed with the proposed confiscation, they did not participate in the voting." The National Socialists, in a sign of their protest against the manner of the proceedings, did not even show up to the meeting.[111]

The accusation that Emil Beer had been a Germanizer prior to the war appeared highly dubious. In fact, he appears to have been one of the Jews in Czechoslovakia whom Helena Krejčová might consider "a sort of connector between Czechs and Germans. Their bilingualism became a natural and significant intermediary between us."[112] Beer spoke Czech and German and apparently moved in social milieus that were, at times, distinctly Czech or distinctly German. He attended Czech schools, though, as his detractors noted, he sent his children to German schools.[113] He went to Czech football matches before the war as well as other Czech and German cultural events.[114] Beer also served as the secretary for the Jewish Community of Rumburk. As Petr Sedlák suggests, his faith likely supported his decision to choose Jewish nationality in the 1930 census – a decision which played a major role in his restitution case.[115]

While the appeals to the district and provincial national committees were being processed, Beer had turned to the courts for support in his quest for restitution. A formal restitution law (Law 128/46) provided a second way for people to claim property taken by the Nazis, but which had not been returned within three months of submitting an appeal against the national committee's ruling.[116] Indeed, just after the District National Committee voted against restitution in early March 1947, the district court restored ownership of the factory to Beer. This event finally ignited strikes in Varnsdorf, which quickly got out of hand. Reportedly, 10,000 people turned out for the strikes, though it seems that Communist

---

[110] Minutes from the meeting of the ONV, February 27, 1947, ibid.
[111] Ibid.; Zpráva o jednání ve Varnsdorfu. Konfiskace firmy Beer, MV, February 28, 1947. NA, f. MV-N, k. 227 inv. č. 146.
[112] Krejčová, 245. See also Herman Kopecek, "Zusammenarbeit and Spoluprace: Sudeten German-Czech Cooperation in Interwar Czechoslovakia," *Nationalities Papers* 24, no.1 (1996), 68.
[113] Letter from RŽNO, March 7, 1947. NA, f. 23, a.j. 344; Hlušičková, 54.
[114] "Na okraj případu ve Varnsdorfu," *Stráž severu*, March 5, 1947.   [115] Sedlák, 354.
[116] Eduard Kubů and Jan Kuklík jr., "Reluctant Restitution: The Restitution of Jewish Property in Bohemia after the Second World War," in *Robbery and Restitution: The Conflict over Jewish Property in Europe*, eds. Martin Dean, Constantin Goschler and Philipp Ther (New York, 2006), 228.

union officials forced some people into participating. Beer and his lawyer were physically threatened, though recollections vary on the exact course of events.[117] Various reports point to a Communist-led event. Representatives of the three other Czech parties requested that an independent central committee come to Varnsdorf to investigate the events "considering the destructive activities by members of the KSČ."[118] While lower Communist functionaries may have been acting alone, Prague Communists had also recently made plans to challenge the restitution provisions in an effort to strengthen the nationalized sector.[119] In addition, *Stráž severu* reported that the police often exacerbated problems of public disorder during the strikes. Amid such scenes, a Communist member of the ONV allegedly proclaimed: "they give laws in Prague and we change them here according to our needs. Nothing will help; our party will not stand for any private firm."[120] Whether the initiative against Beer came from local Communists or the Central Committee was less important than the indication that the Communist Party was willing to work around the law to achieve their goals.

The strikers had their demands met, and the very next day the Communist Party felt emboldened enough to demand that all confiscated factories be affiliated to nationalized firms.[121] The actions against Beer not only undermined Jewish demands for restitution, but also served the Communists' goal of strengthening nationalized firms by attaching confiscated factories to them. Rudolf Slánský, at a meeting of Communist Party leaders, declared shortly afterward: "In the question of confiscated firms we achieved great success ... what is already in the state's hands (confiscated firms under national administration) must not be returned back to private hands."[122] In the wake of the Varnsdorf strike, the government established official commissions to resolve disputes about restitution and national administrators. In order to prevent further strikes and unrest, the government underscored the importance of obtaining the workers' input for these meetings.[123] Effectively, this decision meant

[117] Official Transcript, Ministry of Interior, March 6, 1947. NA, f. MV-NR, k. 2625 inv. č. 2051 sign. B2624; *Svobodné Varnsdorf*, March 14, 1947; Sedlák, 366.

[118] Letter from Representatives of the Czechoslovak National Socialists, Czechoslovak Social Democrats and People's Party, March 6, 1947. NA, f. MV-NR, k. 2625 inv. č. 2051 sign. B2624; *Stráž severu*, March 8 and 15, 1947.

[119] See minutes from the meeting of the NHK KSČ, January 16, 1947. NA, f. NHK KSČ, a. j. 11; Certain reports noted that similar events had occurred elsewhere, suggesting some coordinated initiative, see *Stráž severu*, March 14, 1947.

[120] *Svobodné slovo*, March 22, 1947.   [121] Hlušičková, 61.

[122] Minutes from the meeting of the NHK KSČ, March 27, 1947. NA, f. NHK KSČ, a.j. 11.

[123] See 12218-II-3681/47 from ÚPV, 25.3.47, which became B-2610/1–26/3–47-R-II/1, MV, April 1, 1947. Also see follow-up instructions from the ÚPV on May 13, 1947. NA, f. MV-NR, k.2348 inv.č.2004 s.B2610/1.

that confiscated firms would not return to the private sector. The Communists had won in their efforts to strengthen the nationalized sector with confiscated firms. It also bears mentioning here that the combination of official and unofficial pressure prevented Jews from restarting their lives in many places. Although this policy was less direct than the expulsion of Germans, it effectively forced many Jews to emigrate.[124]

Affiliation, Liquidation and Relocation

While the Communist Party's efforts to control confiscated factories were strengthened by the events in Varnsdorf, the struggle to determine these companies' future and the economic fate of the borderlands was far from over. Conflicts continued between local and central officials, often regardless of party membership, over the different plans to combine borderland factories through affiliation, liquidation and relocation. The district of Frývaldov, renamed Jeseník in 1947, faced both external and internal pressures concerning the future of its two strongest sectors: quarry-stone mining and a thriving tourist trade connected with local spas. The stone industry had been progressively growing since the mid-nineteenth century thanks in part to the natural surroundings with significant supplies of high-quality granite. Likewise, the world-famous Gräfenberg spa, established in the foothills of the Rychlebský/ Reichensteiner Mountains just outside of Freiwaldau, attracted thousands of visitors to relax in its tranquil setting, and spurred the growth of other tourist institutions in area.[125]

Following the war, these industries faced uncertain futures. The District Administrative Commission in Frývaldov decided that it would be in the best interests of the district to combine all of the confiscated stone works into a single unit. Only gradually did this plan become voiced in terms of nationalization.[126] The Ministry of Industry had slightly different designs for the stone companies in and around Frývaldov. In early 1946 it named Jaroslav Michl, who was the national administrator of the Albert Förster stone works and one other firm, as the Ministry's representative for the region's quarries. In conjunction with this appointment the ministry began to consolidate all of the confiscated quarry works

---

[124] Staněk writes that of roughly 50,000 Jews in Czechoslovakia, more than 17,000 left, many for Israel. Staněk, "Němečtí žide," 45–46; Krejčová, 247.

[125] Report of the Confiscation, National Administrator and Settlement Chairman given at the First Bi-Annual Meeting of the ONV Frývaldov, April 22, 1947. SOkA Jeseník, f. ONV Jeseník, k. 2 inv. č. 63a.

[126] Proposal of the ONV Frývaldov Council, November 28, 1946. NA, f. MV-NR, k. 2532 inv. č. 2021 sign. B2612/7.

into a single enterprise under the leadership of the firm Förster and Michl. Michl proved to be a bad choice. While a thorough revision did not clearly answer the question of whether Michl was a gold-digger or simply a bad manager, by the middle of 1946 Förster was in such a poor financial state that the employees demanded Michl's recall and the firm's nationalization.[127] After initially agreeing to nationalize the district's stone works, a commission representing the Ministry of Industry and Konstructiva, a nationalized enterprise in Prague, visited the district in late August 1946 to choose which firms Konstructiva would take over. Rather than trying to rebuild the district's leading industry, these officials intended to liquidate many of its quarries and leave the remaining ones under Konstructiva's control. Only after heated debate with local officials did they agree, instead, to establish a regional directorship and to keep most of the district's quarries working under Konstructiva's leadership. The ministry also promised to recall Michl and install a government commissar for the Silesian stone industry. However, the situation dragged on until the workers finally ran out of patience and threatened to strike because Michl remained in the firm and the ministry failed to follow through on its promise to nationalize it.[128] On December 3, 1946, the Frývaldov District National Committee's plenum overwhelmingly voted to support nationalization.[129]

The District National Committee faced similar threats to its second leading industry as well. At a December 1946 meeting the ONV decided to merge spas from three different communities into a single enterprise. These spas, which provided accommodation and various health treatments, had been taken over for the most part by individual national administrators during the first months after the war. The ONV used their poor performance, in part, to argue for the creation of a single management for the neighboring communities' spas. It argued: "The current results of their leadership from the revolutionary period, which led to scandals and irreparable economic losses, supports the proposal that a single united leadership, as suggested by the law on nationalized firms, guarantees the prosperity of the entire spa and tourist trade in

---

[127] Ibid.; Letter from the factory council A. Förster, August 9, 1946. NA, f. MV-NR, k. 1791 inv. č. 1587 sign. B1720. See also the 86-page audit of Förster under Michl's authority. It found him responsible for 4,258,892 Kčs in losses. NA, f. MP, k. 1298 inv. č. 3645.

[128] Proposal of the ONV Frývaldov Council, November 28, 1946. NA, f. MV-NR, k. 2532 inv. č. 2021 sign. B2612/7; Letter from enterprise council A. Förster, Cukmantl, November 19, 1946. Ibid.; Report of the Confiscation, National Administrator and Settlement Chairman given at the First Bi-Annual Meeting of the ONV Frývaldov, April 22, 1947. SOkA Jeseník, f. ONV Jeseník, k. 2 inv. č. 63a.

[129] Minutes from the plenum ONV Frývaldov, December 3, 1946. SOkA Jeseník, f. ONV Jeseník, k. 136 inv. č. 120.

Frývaldov."[130] Thus, national administrators' shoddy performance and the suspicions surrounding their 1945 activities reinforced local plans to consolidate seized firms.

Central ministries also considered spas of special interest. Prior to the war they had been an attraction for foreign tourists and generated significant foreign currency. Following the war the government planned to use spas for workers' recreation and rehabilitation. In the case of the Frývaldov district spas, the Ministry of Health, which along with the Ministry of Domestic Trade had some jurisdiction over the fate of these firms, continued to change its stance over their future. In late January 1947, officials from these organs met in Frývaldov to discuss the proposed union. At that time they agreed to unite only the firms in the hamlet of Dolní Lipov and to attach the remaining hotels and spas in other towns later. However, the Ministry of Health soon changed its position and refused to recall the national administrators in Dolní Lipov, reportedly because the ONV had stirred up unease in its campaign to unite these firms.[131] The Local National Committee and settlers in Dolní Lipov also protested the decision to consolidate all the firms under a unified management. The national administrators in the town argued that "realizing their national responsibility, they gave up their safe existence in the interior and assumed the management of property left by Germans with the hope that they would find a new existence in the borderlands."[132] Although the Local National Committee supported these national administrators, the ONV, which sought to take spas under its control, believed that these national administrators were only out to protect their own interests. The head of the District National Committee's confiscation department likewise condemned central officials for becoming overly involved in the management of local spas.[133] The efforts to control these properties divided the state administration at every level.

District officials in Frývaldov pushed to nationalize confiscated spas and quarries as a means to protect them from the liquidation plans of Prague, but the ONV misunderstood the meaning of nationalization. In early 1947, just after the deal with Konstruktiva had been reached, the Minister of Industry began to siphon off machine equipment from the

---

[130] Letter from ONV Frývaldov, December 3, 1946. NA, f. MV-NR, k. 2486 inv. č. 2053 sign. B2653/1.

[131] Report on spa firms, ONV Frývaldov, April 18, 1947. NA, f. MV-NR, k. 2350 inv. č. 2004 sign. B2612/1.

[132] Resolution from twenty-two national administrators in Dolní Lipov, August 1, 1947. Ibid.

[133] Report of the Confiscation, National Administrator and Settlement Chairman given at the First Bi-Annual Meeting of the ONV Frývaldov, April 22, 1947. SOkA Jeseník, f. ONV Jeseník, k. 2 inv. č. 63a.

confiscated stone works in the district, setting off another round of protests and negotiations. The Ministry of Industry accused the ONV of "local patriotism," while the ONV argued that the ministry was undermining resettlement.[134] The District National Committee chairman, Zdeněk Slezák, and the head of the confiscation department, both Communists, led the appeals for nationalization without liquidation. At a public meeting in April 1947, the ONV's representative for confiscation reported that the final decision regarding Konstruktiva's control of the district's quarry firms remained in doubt, though significant progress had been made. He stated: "The final solution still requires very much work and pressure, since the private capitalist opponents of nationalizing the stone industry have not capitulated. This will be one of our department's most important aims in cooperation with the industrial department for the near future."[135] Local Communists framed their struggle to control local confiscated companies as an anti-capitalist, pro-worker policy. Such a position not only indicated their support of local quarry workers, but also meshed with Communist leaders' efforts to extend the reach of nationalized firms.

Nevertheless, vast differences remained between local and central Communists' visions of what nationalization meant and who should control it. Party leaders, who sought to quickly resolve the liquidation of borderland firms in order to transfer machine equipment, supplies, and, in some cases, even workers, to nationalized firms became frustrated at the slow pace of liquidation. An October 1947 report about the liquidation process indicated that of 8,667 craft and industrial operations chosen for liquidation, 90 percent had received their closing order and 61 percent had sent in inventory lists.[136] However, progress beyond this point stalled. The Fund for National Renewal (FNO) had provided cost estimates for only about a quarter of the equipment, and only 20 percent had actually begun dismantling their machines. An internal report noted that there had been little interest in the equipment or in the FNO's work. The report also blamed national administrators and national committees for "local patriotism," which they argued slowed the implementation of central plans.[137]

In Frývaldov, the ONV disputed plans to move confiscated machine equipment out of the district on several grounds. It argued that much

[134] See folder on Kamenoprůmysl v Fryvaldově, Konstruktiva, ibid.; Minutes from the meeting of the ONV Council, March 26, 1947. SOkA Jeseník, f. ONV Jeseník, k. 135 inv. č. 119.
[135] Report of the Confiscation, National Administrator and Settlement Chairman given at the First Bi-Annual Meeting of the ONV Frývaldov, April 22, 1947. SOkA Jeseník, f. ONV Jeseník, k. 2 inv. č. 63a.
[136] Report on the State of the Closing of Confiscate C Action, Ústřední výbor KSČ, likely September 9, 1947. NA, f. 23, a.j. 349/1.
[137] Report on Liquidation of Confiscated C factories, October 9, 1947, ibid.

of the machinery was needed to replace equipment that had fallen into disrepair during the war. In a 1947 letter, Slezák noted that Konstruktiva, which had recently taken over the quarries, did not have a proper overview of such equipment. He argued that because borderland firms faced several obstacles not present in the interior, they should be compensated by other means. He also countered ministerial officials' claims that the district was only looking out for itself, arguing that "[t]he satisfactory economic development of the borderlands is surely in agreement with statewide interests."[138] Slezák, who remained the ONV's chairperson throughout this period, continually promoted borderland interests in the framework of the National Front's economic and settlement policies.

Moving factories to Slovakia created even bigger headaches and raised further protests. As local resistance to relocating borderland factories grew in 1946, officials at the Ministry of Industry decided to use individual machines, in addition to entire factories, to supplement the creation of job opportunities in Slovakia. For instance, in the department of metallurgy and metal works, the government ordered 12,605 jobs to be created from borderland firms. Of these positions, 7,200 would come from 68 complete firms and the rest from individual machines.[139] Slovaks expressed concern over the effectiveness of this and other changes to the relocation program. They claimed that they had initiated all of the efforts to implement the policy and complained about the slow progress of relocating factories. As part of their pressure on the central government to speed the relocations, Slovak representatives connected their requests for factories with the impending expulsion of German industrial workers from the borderlands. They noted that as of March 1, 1946, all that was needed to meet the factory relocation goals was a 15 percent reduction of the nearly 200,000 positions currently occupied by Germans. From their vantage, the retention of German workers to staff borderland industries countered the efforts to boost Slovakia's industrial capacity and benefited Germans more than Slovaks. By that time only 1,345 jobs had been created by moving borderland factories to Slovakia.[140]

---

[138] Letter from ONV Frývaldov, May 7, 1947. NA, f. MV-NR, k. 2486 inv. č. 2053 sign. B2653/1.

[139] The same letter stated that it was unknown how the number of textile jobs would be filled. I/2–239.287/46, MP, August 30, 1946. NA, f. MV-NR, k. 1778 sign. B1700. According to the Ministry of Industry's metal works department, 2,500 of these jobs would become piecework, thus lowering the total number of jobs to be created. See VIII/2–213.906/D/46, August 11, 1946, ibid.

[140] Comments of slov. oddělení MP k akci přemíšťování strojního zařízení z pohraničí na Slovensko, MP, May 2, 1946. NA, f. MP, k. 1266 inv. č. 3642.

In 1947, as Communist officials at the OÚ and elsewhere focused on accelerating the liquidation, affiliation and relocation programs, protests against the movement of confiscated factories reached a new pitch. *Stráž severu*, by this time a Social Democratic publication, published a protest from six factory councils in Liberec under the title "They Defend the Borderlands." These workers complained that Prague officials decided to move the factories without the input of the factory councils. While they sympathized with the need to industrialize Slovakia, they did not see the reason to close profitable factories and move them to places where reportedly few skilled workers lived. Workers also saw the relocation program in terms of a larger threat to the borderlands:

We believe that we are fighting for a just cause, for the continuation of industry in this region is not only in the interest of employees, but of all inhabitants ... We request nothing other than the right to work in factories which we entered immediately following the liberation of the borderlands and which by our own work we built up, so that today they represent well run operations and a prosperous whole.[141]

Such protests revealed how Czech workers adopted the rhetoric of settlement officials and their promise of a successful future with workers' rights to influence industrial policies. This was a powerful mix and one that could not be easily ignored in Prague.

Continued resistance to the liquidation and relocation of confiscated firms slowed the government's plans for the consolidation of the borderland economy. The government originally planned to finish physically moving factories to Slovakia by March 1947.[142] However, in a report from April 24, 1947, the Ministry of Industry reported that fewer than half of the pledged job openings had been established. In addition, it noted that they overestimated by 25 percent the number of jobs created through individual machine transfers.[143] The dates for completing the liquidation of C-level firms also continued to be pushed back. For Communist leaders, delays in liquidating and relocating factories posed political dangers because the industrialization of Slovakia was a key component of their Two-Year Plan. Even though the relocation of confiscated borderland firms played a minor role in the overall industrialization policy, the resistance it generated threatened the Communists' strong political position in the borderlands. In the political summary of a report on liquidated factories, the Communist author argued that "[t]he

[141] "Pohraničí se brání." *Stráž severu*, February 12, 1947. See other examples of protests in Beinhauerová, "Problémy likvidace a přemisťování průmyslu," 33–36.
[142] Internal correspondence, MP, July 17, 1946. NA, f. MP, k. 1266 inv. č. 3642.
[143] I/8–135.327/47, MP, April 24, 1947. NA, MV-NR, k. 2472 inv. č. 2074 sign. B2633/5.

industrialization of Slovakia means many severe cuts to local regional interests in Bohemia and Moravia. In many districts the relations between Czechs and Slovaks are worsening, [because] they are taking machines from active firms ... It is in the interests of borderland politics that liquidated C firms were liquidated and forgotten as soon as possible."[144] Despite resistance from their borderland constituents, Communist leaders continued to press forward with the liquidation and relocation policies. However, even after February 1948, Communists continued to struggle with these programs. By October 1948, just over half of the originally proposed number of positions in Slovakia had been created by moving firms and equipment from the borderlands.[145] Only after the Communists controlled the state and had nationalized virtually the entire industrial economy could they begin to pursue the complete restructuring of the borderland economy.

Brothers K

Though it may seem counterintuitive, examining the fate of one particular company provides perhaps the best way to understand the transformation of the industrial economy after ethnic cleansing. From the first nationalization proposal in 1945, nationalized enterprises became the focal point for the reorganization of the industrial sector. By the end of 1947 more than 300 national enterprises existed, which encompassed over 3,000 firms and 60 percent of the workforce.[146] The Communist Party leaders supported the increased scope of nationalized enterprises as part of their overall effort to reshape the economy. Workers and national committees in the borderlands considered nationalization as the best method to prevent confiscated factories from being sold, restituted, closed or relocated. They did not equate nationalization with centralized control; quite the opposite: they believed that by nationalizing a company they would retain control over it. They took central leaders' proclamations about nationalization at face value and believed that the specialized local industries, which Sudeten Germans had built, provided the best basis for rebuilding the borderlands. The fate of Kanneberger Brothers' Company reveals the varied ways that competing interests to control factories played out in the postwar borderlands.

Kanneberger Brothers' textile company produced textile embellishments for women's clothing and hats. It was the largest firm in Vejprty, a small town located directly across the Polava/Pöhlbach River from

---

[144] Report on Liquidation C, October 9, 1947. NA, f. 23, a.j. 349/1.
[145] *Statiskický zpravodaj*, 11 no.10 (1948), 21.   [146] Lhota, 210–15.

Germany. During the late nineteenth century it became a leading producer of its type of goods and helped to support the growth of further textile
operations in the town. After the brothers who founded the company
passed away, ownership of the firm went to six shareholders, who held a
total of 100 shares. Following the war, two national administrators were
named by the Provincial National Committee in Prague; the first,
Franitšek Kříž, was unpleasantly surprised when a second national
administrator, Josef Poslední, arrived just days later. Kříž assumed there
had been some mistake and ultimately left the firm.[147] Poslední sought to
put the firm on a profitable track and to rebuild its connections to
customers in the West. In an early report he noted that in order to secure
the company's export market they needed to find representatives who
could speak foreign languages and who had personal contacts with expor-
ters. The factory itself appeared to be in good condition. He noted that,
"The majority of the equipment was older, but basically in good working
order, so that no requests for investments were currently necessary." In an
effort to ensure enough supplies Poslední also suggested that smaller
firms in the area should be closed and their raw materials handed over
to Kanneberger Brothers.[148] The impulse of larger confiscated firms to
take over smaller ones partly emerged from the need to address shortages
in workers, machinery and raw materials, but it also reflected the logic of
massive confiscations, when multiple justifications could serve as logical
claims for property.

Kanneberger Brothers performed well, though not outstandingly. The
final balances for 1945 showed a profit of one million crowns (Kčs) after
gross sales of nearly five million Kčs.[149] By the middle of 1946, total sales
had jumped to over 18 million Kčs, though profits remained low.[150] In
the first quarter of 1947, the company showed signs of larger profits and
sales. Even export figures crept higher, though they still remained well
below their prewar levels.[151] Part of the reason for the overall decline in
exports was due to the loss of business connections that had been created

---

[147] Letter from Kříž, June 17, 1945. NA, f. MP, k. 1166 inv. č. 3633; in 1947 there were
continued disagreements between the two. See letter about a German representing Kříž
at another firm, from Brothers Kanneberger, January 6, 1947. SOkA Chomutov, f.
ONV Vejprty, k. 21 inv. č. 106.
[148] Report from Josef Poslední, late June/early July 1945. SOA Litoměřice, p. Most, f. Bratří
Kannebergerové, k. 12 inv. č. 19.
[149] Financial report for 1946. SOA Litoměřice, p. Most, f. Bratří Kannebergerové, k. 19 inv.
č. 95.
[150] Financial report for the first half of 1946, ibid. Part of the reason for the flat earnings
during this period was an adjustment for previous accounting errors and the need to
create financial reserves.
[151] Financial report for the first quarter 1947, ibid. Compare these with the monthly reports
in ibid., k. 13 inv. č. 30–31.

prior to the war. In addition, the loss of many skilled workers hampered the quality of production. The factory council and national administrator tried their best to overcome these losses, but to no avail. By 1947, one of the remaining German managers remarked that because of their poor quality many of the goods were not fit for export.[152] Returning Kanneberger Brothers to its prewar pre-eminence was unlikely under the best of circumstances.

What success the company did enjoy resulted primarily from the Sudeten Germans it managed to retain. During the 1946 efforts to protect specialists, the firm nominated 40 of its employees for exemption from the expulsions. Its request, however, failed to halt the removal of specialists, and they ended up with less than two dozen. During the later *revise* of specialists the district revision commission took note of the difficult labor situation facing the firm, but still forced them to release an additional four Germans for the "transfer."[153] Even without specialist protection, the firm managed to keep most of its German employees after the final transports: the firm still had 86 full-time German employees in September 1947.[154] Many of these had familial connections to other specialists and were thus protected from expulsion by extension. Just as important to the firm's future was the company's German management: one was the company's director and two others were top managers. A textile official sent from Prague noted in a May 1947 report that "although Czechs do occupy the leading positions, they are not completely trained and as a result the German experts really hold the leadership of the firm in their hands."[155]

Attracting suitable replacements for the departed German employees proved problematic because settlers did not flock to Vejprty as they did to other towns. Not only did Vejprty sit directly on the border, it also sat on the German side of the Krušné Hory mountain range, isolated from the Bohemian interior. Even so, Vejprty's location did not completely hinder the influx of replacement textile workers. As of January 1, 1946, more

---

[152] Zpráva o revisi fy. Kannebergerové, May 12–22, 1947, ibid., k. 13 inv. č. 28.
[153] Protocols from the revision of specialists, January 20, 1947. NA, f. MP, k. 1152 inv. č. 3631.
[154] List of employees, September 1, 1947. SOA Litoměřice p. Most, f. Bratří Kannebergerové, k. 14 inv. č. 48.
[155] One of them even earned more than the average Czech employee in a similar position. The German head of production made 5,500 Kčs and two other Germans made just under the average for office personnel. This does not include Poslední's salary of over 9,000 Kčs and other Czechs who earned more in the firm. See Zpráva o revisi fy. Kannebergerové, May 12–22, 1947, SOA Litoměřice p. Most, f. Bratří Kannebergerové, k. 13 inv. č. 28. The average earning in 1947 for salaried employees in textile firms was 4,515 Kčs a month. *Průmyslové zprávy*, no.7–8 (1948), 47.

than 2,500 settlers worked for the textile industries in the district.[156] Keeping settlers, however, proved to be the problem. As a result of its location, procuring provisions remained difficult, and during the winter months the situation worsened, which was why some settlers left. Not only that, but because textile wages remained low, living expenses for these workers were relatively higher than for other workers. Likewise, the uncertainty surrounding the future of the textile firms in the town did not encourage people to stay. Lastly, for Kanneberger Brothers, some of Poslední's hiring practices were questionable; he actively sought to retain Germans and he hired his brother and his uncle, both of whom he overpaid. Such nepotism fueled the sense of corruption surrounding his management.[157] Together, these factors account for the high turnover at Kanneberger Brothers. In 1946, just when the firm was getting back on its feet, ninety-one new Czechs came to work there, though forty-four left. During 1947, the same number of settlers was hired at the factory, but sixty-five departed.[158] Like many borderland firms facing high employee turnover, Kanneberger Brothers could not get back on its feet.

Nevertheless, Kanneberger Brothers, classified as an A-level confiscated factory, remained a valuable asset. The national enterprise, Ribbon and Braid Mills (Továrny stuh a prýmků) took an interest in Kanneberger Brothers and moved to acquire it in 1946. Ribbon and Braid Mills, an enterprise based on confiscated firms in the borderland district of Krnov, worked through the central organization of nationalized textile enterprises in Prague to pursue its claim to Kanneberger Brothers. In July 1946, one of the Ribbon and Braid Mills' directors became the second national administrator of the firm. Although the nationalized firm promised the factory council and Josef Poslední a measured amount of independence to continue its specialized production, problems quickly beset relations between it and Kanneberger Brothers. First, Kanneberger Brothers had to go through Ribbon and Braid Mills in order to gain access to raw materials and to confirm its production plans. In addition, they became embroiled in misunderstandings about the future of other confiscated companies in Vejprty. The national administrator and factory council continued their efforts to acquire local firms, both to amass raw materials and machinery and to increase the company's leverage as a possible independent nationalized enterprise. Ribbon and Braid Mills

---

[156] *Průmyslové zprávy*, no. 8–11 (1946), 75.
[157] It was against regulations to hire relatives who did not possess proper qualifications. See letter from MP, November 21, 1947. NA, f. MV-NR, k. 2348 inv. č. 2004 sign. B2610/1.
[158] Report on the fluctuation of employees at Brothers Kanneberger, September 1, 1948. NA, f. 23 a.j. 349/2.

likewise sought to expand its holdings in the district, and raised the hostility of many locals as it acquired additional firms.[159] For instance, Poslední was irked by the nationalized firm's requests to resubmit inventories not only of his firm, but at other nearby companies not under Ribbon and Braid Mills' control. By September 1946, local control of the factory appeared jeopardized to the extent that Poslední wrote to the director and demanded, in what had become a common refrain, that as "the most important company in the production of special modern goods," Kanneberger Brothers should remain independent even after its affiliation with the nationalized enterprise. He even claimed that the other factories within the Ribbon and Braid Mills' enterprise undercut Kanneberger Brothers' deals abroad by selling cheaper wares.[160]

The District National Committee in Vejprty backed Poslední as part of a general campaign to halt the industrial exodus from the town. In a protest to central authorities, the ONV Council wrote that it did not believe the promises of government officials that companies would remain in place after they were attached to national enterprises. In order to substantiate its claims for independent operation, it wrote: "Since long ago the district of Vejprty has been known in this land and abroad by its specific industry and the production of textiles." The ONV Council also noted that 90 percent of the Germans had been expelled and that the number of Czechs had increased from 280 to more than 4,000 by late 1946. In a final appeal, it argued that settlers "who obeyed the government's pleas [to move to the borderlands] a year ago ... will be embittered and will not believe that all that has happened was done for the nation; rather, like us, they will suspect that it's all about the interests of the few, of individuals' [interests], which damage the republic."[161] National committees and settlers saw the expulsion and resettlement as sanctioning their control of local firms. From their vantage, just as German apartments, dishes and beds now belonged to settlers, so too did the factories. Moreover, local officials argued that they knew better than officials from Prague what was best for the industrial economy. Ethnic cleansing had, in this sense, empowered people to claim ownership in ways that went beyond where any Marxist or socialist justification could have gone.

---

[159] Kateřina Mertová, "Vejprtská průmyslová oblast 1945–1948," in *6. vědecká archivní conference Revoluční národní výbory, osídlování pohraničí a význam národních výborů při zajišťování národně-demokratického procesu v ČSR v letech 1944–1948* (Ústí nad Labem, 1990), 70–72.

[160] Letter from National Administrator and Factory Council, Brothers Kanneberger, September 27, 1945. SOA Litoměřice p. Most, f. Bratří Kannebergerové, k. 27 inv. č. 143.

[161] Proposals by ONV Vejprty, September 27, 1946. SOkA Chomutov, f. ONV Vejprty, k. 2 inv. č. 53.

The nearly silent death knell for Kanneberger Brothers came in a letter from the general director of the Ribbon and Braid Mills to the central director of all nationalized textile firms. He wrote, "From the beginning of our interaction with them it is clear that they do not judge things from a statewide perspective, but solely from the view of Vejprty." By the end of 1946, the reference to "local interests" already had a well-established meaning for Prague officials. In addition, the director drew attention to Kanneberger Brothers' labor problems, noting that "in Krnov we work exclusively with Czech employees and we already have enough of them, whereas Brothers Kanneberger continuously struggles with insufficient Czech employees."[162] Such "little Berlins" remained targets for those who sought to extend their power and became liabilities for places and industries that relied on German workers. Because Ribbon and Braid Mills had become recognized as the nationalized firm for specialized textile embellishments, its directors could make a strong case to overcome localized interests and put the firm to its best use.

On February 5, 1947, after further protests by workers, Poslední and the national committee, they received word from Prague that their firm would be nationalized. However, in early May the tide shifted once again against Kanneberger Brothers and the firm was officially allocated to Ribbon and Braid Mills. In the accompanying notice to the factory council a representative from the Central Trade Union Council wrote: "It is the attempt of our officials, who organize nationalized firms, to see that all of our firms are profitable and that more factories join together always to form individual national enterprises, which should mutually support each other and which should work to the benefit of the entire nation."[163] Such sentiments doubtlessly irked many at Kanneberger Brothers. Settlers who had made the trek to Vejprty to work fulfilled resettlement goals and made confiscated factories potentially profitable. Yet central planners and nationalized enterprises saw opportunities in confiscated companies like Kanneberger Brothers to concentrate what had been a disparate and diverse industry. The prewar status of a firm meant little to them. Instead, they pursued new goals to bring industrial production firmly under centralized control.

Following the Communist takeover, the transfer of Kanneberger Brothers to Ribbon and Braid Mills' control slowly proceeded. In September 1948 the highly paid German office personnel were fired,

[162] Letter from General Director of STAP, December 2, 1946. SOA Litoměřice p. Most, f. Bratří Kannebergerové, k. 27 inv. č. 143.
[163] Letter from Ústřední rada odborů, May 9, 1947. SOA Litoměřice p. Most, f. Bratří Kannebergerové, k. 14 inv. č. 57.

and Posledni's brother was next in line for removal.[164] The factory
council, which remained under the same leadership throughout these
years, now backed plans to move the firm to Jindřichův Hradec in the
interior. Only the District National Committee withheld its support,
because they realized what losing Kanneberger Brothers meant.[165]
Kateřina Mertová estimates that less than 30 percent of Vejprty's original
industrial capacity remained in the district at the end of 1948.[166] This loss
had nothing to do with wartime destruction, but stemmed directly from
the expulsion of the Germans and the conflicts between the central
government and local authorities. Its effects were clear. In the first four
months of 1950, just as Kanneberger Brothers was being moved, 264
Czechs left Vejprty in search of better prospects elsewhere.[167]

The saga of Kanneberger Brothers embodies many of the changes that
occurred within postwar borderland industries. The national administrator needed Germans – managers, skilled workers and ordinary seams-
tresses – to work because Czech workers were unwilling and unable to
fulfill the firm's production needs. Retaining Germans, however, raised
questions about the company's ability to continue without them. Ribbon
and Braid Mills, the nationalized enterprise, used this reason, among
others, to substantiate its claim to Kanneberger Brothers. Although
Germans represented the core of Kanneberger Brothers' labor force, the
national administrator and the Czech employees, as well as other settlers
in Vejprty, all hoped to keep the company in the town. Without it,
Vejprty's economic importance and attractiveness to settlers would sub-
stantially decrease. This perspective explains, in part, why settlers, workers and the national committee supported nationalization, independent
from Ribbon and Braid Mills. They believed that Kanneberger Brothers
would serve as a hub to reorganize and strengthen the town's textile-based
economy. Indeed, many settlers believed that their factory deserved to
remain open and used all possible avenues to promote their interests.
That Ribbon and Braid Mills overcame their resistance, however, pointed
to the growing strength of state-run enterprises and the weakening of
national committees' power.

Taken together, the plans and policies to consolidate borderland industry represented a powerful attack on local interests. The process ignited

[164] Protokol from meeting at Brothers Kanneberger, September 24, 1948. SOA Litoměřice
p. Most, f. Bratří Kannebergerové. k. 13 inv. č. 43.
[165] Letter from national administrator and factory council Brothers Kanneberger, August 5,
1948, ibid.
[166] Mertová, 72.
[167] Report from MNV Vejprty, April 21, 1950. SOkA Chomutov, f. MNV Vejprty, k. 15
inv. č. 20.

numerous conflicts and unrest, and left factories and settlers in limbo. Protests against factory closures and relocation to Slovakia became widespread throughout the borderlands, with national committees and settlers alike working to protect their town's firms. Restitution of factories, rather than becoming a means to restore the prewar Jewish communities, became a form of repression, which supported Communist plans for expanding the nationalized sector. While it was unlikely that the workers in Varnsdorf had any idea of the influence their actions would have, Communists took advantage of the political opening that the strikes created to press their demands forward. In some ways, it foreshadowed their tactics of eleven months later, during the political crisis in February 1948. The rationale and operation of the confiscation and nationalization programs reinforced one another at several key junctures. In 1945, the confiscation of German property supported the premise of extensive nationalizations. By 1947, nationalization seemingly offered a solution to settlers and national committees who sought to stabilize their town's economy for the future. However, as the case of the industries in Frývaldov and Vejprty demonstrate, nationalization had little to do with putting factories in the workers' hands and, instead, led to greater centralization of the economy. In this way, the path to state socialism ran through the borderlands.

6   Borderlands Transformed

Local Power and High Stalinism

Although ethnic cleansing had been successful, in the sense of removing the vast majority of Sudeten Germans, it did not result in an ethnically pure borderland region. Pockets of German speakers remained, and were sometimes concentrated in significant numbers. In addition, many non-Czechs lived scattered throughout the borderlands. That several re-emigrant groups, though nominally Czech speakers, had also moved there gave the borderlands a multiethnic dimension that it had previously not had, and which ran contrary to settlement planners' intentions for an integrated national region. The Communist Party takeover in 1948 opened the opportunity to revisit the failed promises of expulsion and resettlement by targeting Germans, old settlers and others. By the early 1950s, though, this door had closed. Communist priorities began to shift with Cold War demands, and the need for greater productivity outweighed any lingering efforts to reorder the borderlands' ethnic composition. The First Five-Year Plan placed Czechoslovak industry under centralized planning and emphasized heavy industrial development based on the Soviet model. This left little room for the specialized industries of the former Sudetenland to thrive. Collectivization began and undermined the notion of using property ownership as an incentive for settler-farmers. Lastly, the government attempted to integrate the remaining Germans by making them citizens and by offering them cultural autonomy. Local officials grappled with a host of difficulties related to these new policies, but increasing Communist Party control in Prague restricted their room for independent initiative and maneuver. This chapter demonstrates how the Communist Party struggled with the legacies of ethnic cleansing in its efforts to consolidate the party, state and economy during the period from 1948 to 1953.

During the Communist seizure of power in February 1948, district and local "action committees" became the first agents of political change. Action committees appeared in virtually every organization in the country, such as youth groups, factory councils and even national committees.

District-level action committees also formed and were comprised of Communist and often Social Democratic national committee members as well as others from various local organizations, like trade unions and veterans' organizations. In Varnsdorf, the District Action Committee took quick steps to transfer power into Communist hands. On February 24, 1948, the committee removed all National Socialists and People's Party representatives from the district and local national committees as well as several administrators from local offices. In its call to the people the leadership wrote of "the cleansing of public life in the interests of maintaining calm and order." It ended with the ominous warning: "Those who are not with us, are against us. Those who are with us, will be victorious in the end."[1] In Žatec, among other things, leaders of the takeover there reorganized the District National Committee's office, the school inspectorate, the labor office and the police force, mostly by suspending unreliable workers.[2] Leading members of the Czech National Socialist Party were often the first to go, but other parties' members also faced dismissal. In Jeseník (formerly Frývaldov), the entire District National Committee was reorganized and National Socialist and People's Party members were removed. The Communist chairperson, Zdeněk Slezák, proclaimed that "agreement and better work will now be possible in all sectors of people's self-government and it will be possible to focus on the real construction of our state and district."[3] Much of the history of the Communist Party takeover has focused on the actions in Prague and within the party's leadership. While the call to create action committees came from central Communist leaders, the rapid actions of the Communist forces in the borderlands demonstrate that the takeover was also executed from below.

The transition to Communist power in the borderlands also assumed a character of its own. While much has been written about specific groups that suffered Communist suppression in Czechoslovakia, such as religious figures and opposition politicians, the repression in the borderlands targeted those who had hindered widespread cleansing. In Varnsdorf, the Action Committee of the Elite National Enterprise – formerly the Kunert factory – took action against several individuals. It compiled a list of twenty-three people that it wanted removed from positions in the post

---

[1] Minutes from the first meeting of the Action Committee of the District National Front in Varnsdorf, February 24, 1948. Státní okresní archiv (SOkA) Děčín, f. Okresní národní výbor (ONV) Varnsdorf, karton (k.) 1 inventární číslo (inv. č.) 51.

[2] Report on the Creation of Okresní akční výbory from February 25, 1948. Národní archiv, Prague (NA), f. Ministerstvo vnitra-Nová registratura (MV-NR), k. 1943 inv. č. 1602.

[3] Minutes from District National Committee Council, Jeseník, February 27, 1948. SOkA Jeseník, f. ONV Jeseník, k. 135 inv. č. 119.

office to the tax office. It specifically targeted a judge who had taken a stand against the workers during the Varnsdorf strikes in 1947. The District Action Committee of the National Front followed up on this denunciation and punished the judge who had upheld the legal claim of Emil Beer for the return of his factory that had been Aryanized under the Nazis. The action committee of another factory in nearby Nový Chřibský likewise denounced its national administrator for not supporting those strikes.[4] Solutions for new enemies also echoed the policies of the past. In Varnsdorf, the Communist leadership of the District Action Committee of the National Front gave seven days for seven people to leave the town, lest they face more serious reprisals. The Jeseník District National Committee formed its own action committee comprised of several employees, whose first act was to request the removal of a leading politician from the Provincial National Committee in Ostrava and his expulsion from Jeseník.[5] The Communist takeover had a local flair in the borderlands, supported by local demands and resolved by local methods.

Germans too became immediate targets. The failure to remove all the Germans during the expulsions had left the question of their fate unresolved. Many settlers resented their continued presence in the borderlands, especially because Germans often occupied key positions in local industries. Not surprisingly, calls emerged to expel them once and for all, if not from the country, then at least from the borderlands. For instance, the Action Committee of Clockmakers in Liberec fired all of its German workers immediately after its founding in early March 1948. Several other committees and firms did the same, requiring the Interior Ministry to intervene in order to prevent serious economic damage.[6] In Vejprty, the District National Committee reverted to policies against Germans that resembled those from 1945. It limited the hours that Germans could go shopping, imposed a curfew on them, prevented them from leaving their town of residence and forced them to help clear trees in the forest.[7] While the ONV rescinded these policies a few months later, they suggest that many settlers still harbored resentment toward Germans.

---

[4] Minutes from the second and third meeting of the Action Committee of the District National Front in Varnsdorf, February 26 or 27 and 28, 1948. SOkA Děčín, f. ONV Varnsdorf, k. 1 inv. č. 51.

[5] Minutes from District National Committee Council, Jeseník, February 27, 1948. SOkA Jeseník, f. ONV Jeseník, k. 135 inv.č. 119.

[6] See the Circular from the Society of Clockmakers in Liberec, March 3, 1948 and Vyhláška č.j. 30 předs./48, ONV Šluknov, March 10, 1948. SOkA Děčín, f. ONV Šluknov, k. 1 inv. č. 34.

[7] Vyhláška č. 3588, March 1, 1948, and Vyhlášky 3763 and 3764, ONV Vejprty, March 2, 1948. SOkA Chomutov, f. ONV Vejprty, k. 25 inv. č. 108.

Communist targets often included those who controlled confiscated property. Local officials specifically targeted national administrators, whose "national and state reliability" was now measured by their loyalty to the Communist Party. Those who opposed Communism or the party were liable to lose their positions. The Interior Ministry wrote to national committees in March 1948 that given "national administrators' importance and meaning there is no doubt that such people can no longer be national administrators."[8] Again, National Socialists were the first to go. In one case the former chairman of the local National Socialist Party branch in Domašov lost his position as the caretaker of a local pub. He was accused of cursing the Soviet Union and poor living conditions in 1948 while drunk on a bus. He also ejected members of the Local Action Committee when they came to his home to offer him the opportunity to switch his political allegiances and join in the committee's work.[9] Across the borderlands, action committees quickly voted to remove national administrators who had been active members of opposition parties. What had been a privilege and a benefit of ethnic cleansing became a means of repression. National committees made clear in late 1948 that those who challenged Communist power would not enjoy the advantages of being a national administrator or have the right to acquire a confiscated home or business.[10]

While ostensibly directed against "enemies of the people's democracy," the post-February cleansing widened to include national administrators who had intimate relations with Germans. For example, the Czech husband from the mixed-marriage couple who ran a hairdresser's salon in Jeseník suddenly faced opposition to his request for ownership of the business. One of his employees had denounced him for being politically unreliable and for speaking German with customers in the store.[11] Such denunciations not only improved the employee's own chance to obtain the firm, which he had simultaneously requested, they revealed how questions of national reliability remained potent in the borderlands even as the regime focused its attention on class and political enemies. In Jablonec nad Nisou, where the politics surrounding the nationality commission had been so divisive before 1948, the Communist takeover presented an opportunity to remove those close to Germans or with German

---

[8] B2610/1–15/3–1948-II/6, Odvolání národních správců, MV, March 16, 1948. SOkA Bruntál, f. ONV Krnov, k. 113 inv. č. 138.
[9] Case of J.Č. SOkA Jeseník, f. ONV Jeseník, k. 71 inv. č. 109.
[10] Working program of the Action Committee in Jablonec nad Nisou, September 25, 1948. SOkA Jablonec nad Nisou (Jablonec n. N.), f. Okresní výbor Komunistiská strana Československa (OV KSČ) Jablonec n. N., Kniha (kn.) 1.
[11] See the case of J. V. SOkA Jeseník, f. ONV Jeseník, k. 55 inv. č. 109.

pasts. Of the fifty-two national administrators who lost their positions in the city, twenty-four had close relations with Germans or had claimed German nationality before the war. In the nearby town of Mšeno nad Nisou, the ratio was basically the same. Communists removed others for political reasons or because they were accused of being gold-diggers.[12] The Communist takeover opened another round of cleansing that affected those who had survived the postwar expulsions, and in some cases those who had benefited from it. These revisions were a sign that many settlers resented Czechs who received German property and yet maintained cordial relations with them. It also proved an easy way to provide property to other settlers, namely those loyal to the Communist regime.

Like the expulsions, however, the breadth of the Communist cleansing was mitigated by several factors. Most importantly, Communist leaders sought to appear responsible in the wake of their takeover. This may sound counterintuitive, given the methods they used to go after their perceived enemies, but inasmuch as Communists sought to solidify their power through repression, they also sought legitimacy. This meant that the cleansing of national administrators and others should be kept under control. Directives from higher organs stressed the need to retain specialists and to refrain from using this opportunity to settle personal scores. In addition, properties that were again vacated were supposed to be reserved for those with priority credentials. Even demands for the continued expulsion of Germans met with resistance from some local leaders. Just as with previous upheavals, a revision of the cleansing program occurred in some places to ensure that none of these measures had been superseded.[13] So, while the Communist takeover was a revolutionary process, it was also a managed one. Indeed, getting rid of political enemies allowed Communists to satisfy some demands for property that had remained unfulfilled prior to 1948.

In addition to targeting national committees and national administrators, the Communists began to police their own. The ability of local Communists to call their own shots and push against central policies

---

[12] Lists of people condemned by the action committees, 1948. SOkA Jablonec n. N. f. OV KSČ Jablonec n. N., k. 37.

[13] See Plán práce pro okresní komise lidové správy, KSČ Liberec, April 12, 1948. SOkA Děčín, f. ONV Šluknov, k. 1 inv. č. 34: Working program of the Action Committee in Jablonec, September 25, 1948. SOkA Jablonec n. N. f. OV KSČ Jablonec n. N. kn. 1; Minutes from the Plenum of the OV KSČ Jeseník, March 5, 1948. SOkA Jeseník, f. OV KSČ Plenum, k. 3 inv. č. 15; Zapisy plena rada ONV Dubá, March 18, 1948. SOkA Česká Lípa, f. ONV Dubá, k. 1 inv. č. 3; Report on Settlement and Business, ONV Teplice-Šanov. June 2, to August 24, 1948. SOkA Teplice-Šanov, f. ONV Teplice-Šanov, k. 4 inv. č. 212/4.

that conflicted with local interests was sharply curtailed as renegade leaders were removed from their posts. One case involved Zdeněk Slezák, the national committee chairperson in Jeseník who helped to usher in Communist power there. From 1945, he had been a vocal proponent of local control over the quarry industry and spas that marked the district's economy. He fell into disfavor, though, in 1948 as the Communist Party sought to remove members who did not share in the vision of a unified and disciplined movement. Slezák's comrades charged him with a series of shortcomings and misdeeds that ultimately led to his removal from the District National Committee and the party. He had mishandled the dedication ceremony for the new hospital's cornerstone, he criticized fellow party members in an uncomradely fashion, and had also been gambling, drinking and abusing the privilege of his official automobile. More importantly, as the condemnation of Slezák was building momentum, he failed to take the necessary steps to diffuse his colleagues' ire. In his response to the charge that he drank too much, for instance, the record shows that Slezák admitted "he drinks more than is good for his health, but that he was never drunk because he had a high tolerance." Such excuses, however, just made matters worse. Another member of the Presidium, Harabiš, noted that Slezák's "self-criticism" was insufficient, but that at least he accepted his faults. Others went further, noting that the criticism of his fellow members was weak and that Slezák "deviated from the masses" and "lacked Bolshevik forthrightness."[14]

The Communist Party of Czechoslovakia was in this case working in reverse. It was after the revolution that it began to create an organization that worked from the top down. Party discipline was not a priority in the immediate postwar years when filling posts with anyone who would adopt the Communist label was more important than their willingness to follow the party line. The party swelled its ranks in the postwar years, increasing membership from roughly 500,000 in mid-1945 to more than 2 million in 1950.[15] In the late '40s and early '50s, party discipline became a central component of the Czechoslovak turn toward a Soviet system. Through the *provĕrka* – the checking of members' credentials – party members in Jeseník were learning "to speak Bolshevik."[16] They also began acting like

[14] Minutes from the Presidium of the OV KSČ Jeseník, September 20, 1948. SOkA Jeseník, f. OV KSČ Jeseník, Předsednictvo, k. 7 inv. č. 30.
[15] Ben Fowkes, *Eastern Europe 1945–1969: From Stalinism to Stagnation* (Essex, 2000), 126.
[16] Stephen Kotkin, *Magnetic Mountain: Stalinism as a Civilization* (Berkeley, 1995), chapter 5. Although Kotkin uses the term to refer to workers' self-identification with the Soviet regime's goals, it seems useful to consider it here in relation to Communist Party members learning the new methods of party politics.

Bolsheviks. It was clear that most of the Presidium's members sought to protect Slezák and believed that he had done his best for the district, but that this was no longer enough. After the Communist Party had taken over the government, party unity and discipline became its guiding principles. In this new atmosphere, Slezák and several of his comrades were removed from their posts for their "fractious activities."[17] What seems more likely is that his independent initiative and his defense of local industry, which conflicted with central Communist priorities, were no longer compatible with the new party line.

The upheavals in the district continued following Slezák and company's dismissal. A *provĕrka* of the rest of the Presidium occurred in which each member had to provide a self-criticism and be evaluated by his comrades. A member of the regional party leadership oversaw the process and ensured that they carried it out correctly. Harabiš, the district party political secretary, recounted how he had worked for the party going back to the 1920s – one of the few district members who had joined the party prior to the war. He had gone to Spain in 1937 and France in 1941 to fight. He returned to the country during the war as a partisan, and the party sent him to Frývaldov (later Jeseník) in 1945 to lead the party there. In his self-criticism he noted that his mistake was that he "sometimes procrastinated when it came to less meaningful tasks." Other members of the Presidium then criticized him for other shortcomings, though the consensus was that he had done a good job and was, if anything, too hard on himself.[18] The party reconfirmed Harabiš in his position as the party's political secretary, but his *provĕrka* had not gone smoothly and his position remained tenuous. In 1950, the attacks against him and several other party members renewed. There had been a scandal involving the misappropriation of fuel and a failure to properly manage personnel issues, and many of the members were accused of living beyond their means. While Harabiš avoided punishment at that time too, twelve other members of the District Plenum were removed. In some cases they simply lost their administrative jobs and their party membership. Some, however, were sentenced to hard labor and were named enemies of the working class.[19] The Jeseník district party members' actions and past was not new or unknown to the regional party leadership before 1950. What changed was the increasing effort of the central party leaders to take control and remake the party along Stalinist lines.

---

[17] Minutes from the Presidium OV KSČ in Jeseník, November 22, 1948. SOkA Jeseník, f. OV KSČ Předsednictvo, k. 7 inv. č. 30.
[18] Minutes from the Presidium of the OV KSČ Jeseník, October 11, 1948, ibid.
[19] Minutes from the Plenum of the OV KSČ, March 9, 1950. SOkA Jeseník, f. OV KSČ Jeseník, Plenum, k. 3 inv. č. 16.

The party repression continued in the early 1950s, culminating in the well-known trial of Rudolf Slánský and several other leading party members, mostly Jewish, in 1951–52. Slánský had been the KSČ's General Secretary and played a leading role in party affairs going back to the 1930s. His trial was initiated by Stalin in 1951 and culminated in a show trial where he and fourteen other defendants proclaimed their guilt in the hope of some leniency. Eleven were hung; three others received life in prison. While many historians and Czech émigrés have seen the trials and purges as imposed from without as part of an anti-Zionist Stalinist campaign, newer research suggests that internal forces drove the purges as well.[20] In 1951, there were strikes in different parts of the country that brought workers into the streets and undermined the claims of the party to represent their interests. Rather than considering the Slánský affair solely as a policy enforced from abroad or as a sign of ongoing anti-Semitism, like the Slezák affair, it was a reflection of the socio-economic tensions that sprang from the war and early Cold War and the party's attempts at greater control.

Local and district national committees also came under the increasing control of regional and central organs. In 1949, a statewide reorganization of administrative boundaries based at a new regional level brought with it the diminution of local power. In July 1950, local national committees were put under the additional control of district authorities who were supposed to more closely monitor their actions. As the authority of national committees dissipated they became more administrative than political organs. At the same time, district-level authorities complained that local national committees were no longer fulfilling their functions. In Bruntál, for instance, a report noted that local department heads distanced themselves from criticism for not fulfilling their duties and asked to be relieved of their posts rather than accept extra responsibilities. Many members did not have the qualifications to carry out the necessary work and resented the "paper pushing" demanded by central organs. In addition, members of other organizations – like the action committees, the Communist Party and the United Federation of Czech Farmers, among others – also sat in on meetings of local national committees and sometimes led the meetings themselves. As the chairman of the District National Committee in Bruntál reported to his superiors, "This method of meeting caused definite stagnation in the activity of MNVs and many functionaries of the people's administration report that the MNV means almost nothing."[21]

---

[20] Kevin McDermott, "A 'Polyphony of Voices'? Czech Popular Opinion and the Slánský Affair," *Slavic Review* 67 n. 4 (Winter 2008): 840–65.
[21] Situační zprává za měsíc leden 1951, February 9, 1951. ONV Bruntál. SOkA Bruntál, f. ONV Bruntál II, k. 20 inv. č. 88.

By the early 1950s, the function of national committees had dramatically changed. No longer were they organs that debated with central officials and defined the shape of borderland communities. While they continued to serve as conduits of local problems, they no longer sought to solve those problems with their own solutions. Yet, the tensions remained, among settlers, local Germans, Jews and others. Property remained at the center of such disputes, and thus pitted Czech against Czech in most cases. Still, it was connections with Germans that tipped the balance against national administrators and old settlers in most cases. Local authorities easily labeled such support as dishonorable, and many settlers recognized it that way. Party leaders were moving in a different direction, however. Given the priorities of the early Cold War and the political and economic reorganizations underway, Communist leaders sought control and moved to prevent locals from doing as they pleased. Soon, the struggle against the West and the need to fulfill the Five-Year Plan subsumed efforts to ease the tensions or problems that still plagued the borderlands.

The Making of an "Industrial Graveyard": The First Five-Year Plan (1949–1953)

In the spring of 1947, following the Varnsdorf strikes that gave the Communist Party a victory in its efforts to prevent the restitution of Jewish property and to expand the scope of nationalization, the Social Democratic newspaper *Free Word* (*Svobodné Slovo*) ran a short piece that underscored the continuing problems in the borderlands. Among other things, it noted that elected officials no longer controlled the removal of competent national administrators or the movement of factories to Slovakia. In near despair, it asked "Who has interest in transforming the region from Aš to Vejprty into an industrial graveyard?"[22] This was a dig at the increasing administrative control that Communist Party bureaucrats in Prague exercised on confiscated factories. While socialists, in general, favored greater governmental oversight of industrial firms, the Social Democrats perhaps realized the direction things were heading. With central officials rather than local leaders in charge of the borderland economy, it departed from its prewar structure of small-scale export-oriented production. The making of an industrial graveyard had perhaps started before World War II, but through ethnic cleansing and Communist economic policies the unique industrial character of the borderlands was put to rest. Over the next several years the borderland economy, like its politics, felt the effects of Sovietization: Five-Year Plans, shock work, a focus on heavy

---

[22] "Zkazky z pohraničí," *Svobodné slovo*, April 18, 1947.

industry and increasing centralized control came to characterize economic life. These changes also brought to an end to the debates about what to do with confiscated factories and the efforts to protect local industries. As Communist power and policies became increasing linked to Cold War priorities the industrial capabilities shifted to meet the military, energy and metal needs of the new state. This was the final stage in the destruction of local economies that left a host of empty factory buildings to dot the borderlands like gravestones.

Communist Party leaders in Czechoslovakia imposed Soviet-style economic planning on the country soon after coming to power. The first signs of this change came in April 1948, when the party extended the nationalization laws to include nearly the entire industrial economy to firms with as few as fifty employees. National administrators were installed in roughly 1,300 firms taken over by the state. In addition, the shift to heavy industrial development in terms of investment and production goals above all other sectors indicated further change. The Communists also changed the organizational structures of industrial management. The State Planning Office became the main body for developing and measuring the plan. The government created new ministries to oversee individual branches of the economy divided between light and heavy industry. The Communists eliminated the General Directorates, which had directed national firms through 1949, and installed ninety-four Chief Administrations that more directly managed the implementation of the plans at the enterprise level. These moves mirrored Soviet economic organizations. National firms were also broken into smaller units and the Domestic and Foreign Trade Offices took over their commercial activity. Planning targets were tightened as well, so that the First Five-Year Plan was much more detailed than the Two-Year Plan had been, particularly after 1951 when the Communists increased targets for all sectors of the economy. Together, these changes gave greater influence to central authorities and eliminated the autonomy that the national enterprises had hitherto enjoyed.[23]

Because the textile industry had been a distinguishing feature of the borderland economy, it serves as a good measure of the changes brought by Communist economic policies there. Plans for the textile industry reveal both the inability of Communist planners to work out the immediate technical and logistical problems facing the industry as well as the

---

[23] Václav Průcha et al., *Hospodářské a sociální dějiny Československa, 1918–1992*, vol. 2 (Brno, 2009), 253–56, 264–69, 372–76; Alice Teichova, *The Czechoslovak Economy, 1918–1980* (London, 1988), 135–36; Otakar Mrázek, "Course and Results of the Nationalisation of Industry," in Karel Jech, ed., *The Czechoslovak Economy, 1945–1948* (Prague, 1968), 116–21.

shortcomings of working within the centrally planned economy. The textile industry had demonstrated signs of growth after the war. Its production value was the highest of all branches in 1948 and planners expected it to be second only to metal production for the entire First Five-Year Plan.[24] Yet, much of the industry's machinery was outdated. In a planning report from July 1948, officials noted that textile industries were among the "most backward" and "most dispersed" sectors of the economy. The machinery, they argued, was fifty years old, and after the war "they had to put into operation machines, which are museum pieces and need relatively more workers than modern machines."[25] This assessment represented an economic planner's harshest critique and most coveted opportunity. Only through the modernization of production equipment and the reconfiguration of the industry into an organized whole, they argued, could production become the "most rationalized" and "most economical." They therefore sought to obtain much-needed investment to rejuvenate textile factories in the country. They pointed out that textiles were integral to the Five-Year Plan's goal of raising people's living standards and should be given more investment and, even, respect.[26]

Despite the pleas from officials and managers in the textile industry, however, economic planners allocated less investment to the textiles industry than was necessary to meet even modest increases in production. Textile officials had initially called for heavy investment in updated machinery in order to make existing factories more efficient. However, the requests for new machines – central to modernizing the industry – required planners in the machine-building sector to produce such equipment, which they were not able to provide.[27] This meant that the outdated machinery remained in place with little hope for replacement. There were also shortages in raw materials necessary to meet export orders because central planners sought to avoid spending hard currency on imported supplies. Furthermore, the ongoing process of closing and relocating borderland textile factories did little to increase efficiency, sapped investment opportunities and equipment and encouraged workers to look for opportunities elsewhere. Officials in Liberec, for instance, noted that the consolidation of industry had done nothing more than to decrease the number of workers in light industry in their region, thus putting greater pressure on

---

[24] Report on the Fulfillment of the First Year of the Five-Year Plan, 1949. NA, f. MP, k. 1345 inv. č. 3652.
[25] Report on the Textile Industry in the First Five-Year Plan, July 2, 1948. Presidium of the Working Group on Textile and Clothing Production. NA, f. MP, k. 1362 inv. č. 3652.
[26] Ibid.
[27] Report on the Textile Industry in the First Five-Year Plan, July 2, 1948. Presidium of the Working Group on Textile and Clothing Production. NA, f. MP, k. 1362 inv. č. 3652.

the productive capabilities of remaining workers to reach the planned targets.[28]

The biggest difficulty facing the textile industry, as indeed with all sectors of the economy, was the lack of workers. From the factory level to the State Planning Office, reports always indicated labor shortages as the primary reason for failing to meet quotas or to expand production. Textile planners argued that because of the expulsion of experienced German workers it would take some time for new Czech workers to gain efficiency in this kind of work. In 1949, textile planners noted that the general shortage of workers was compounded by the fact that the average age of workers in the industry was forty-seven, which meant that in addition to the roughly 25,000 new workers needed to increase basic production in the Bohemian lands, about 50,000 more workers were necessary to replace those who would be retiring over the course of the First Five-Year Plan. Nonetheless, they predicted that by 1953 they would nearly reach 1930 levels of production (the highest prewar year) even with 100,000 fewer workers.[29] Of course, such projections depended on a greater investment into equipment upgrades and worker training. Yet, in early 1950, Communist leaders reached a decision to reallocate male workers from light to heavy industry and gave each branch of light industry a quota to reach. For textiles the number was over 4,500 out of a total workforce of roughly 230,000. Although the number of workers siphoned from the industry by this policy was relatively low, these decisions from above undermined the industry's stability.[30]

The decision to move men into heavy industry did not come at the expense of textiles alone. All sectors provided some manpower for the campaign. Yet this policy reinforced the gendered division of labor in textiles that existed before the war and continued thereafter. The expulsions created greater demand to bring women into the socialist economy as a key source of new labor power. For the Bohemian lands, the planned number of all workers for the end of 1948 in textiles and footwear production was just over 200,000. By the end of 1953, the figure was to increase to over 230,000 with the addition of over 37,000 women, while reducing the number of men by nearly 9,000. The number of women planned for metal work was to increase by 38,000 during the same

---

[28] Report on the State and Development of the Economy in 1953, Regional Planning Commission in Liberec, February 25, 1954. NA, f. Úrad předsednictvo vlády - Tajné (ÚPV-T), k. 480 inv. č. 1750.

[29] Report on the Textile Industry in the First Five-Year Plan, July 2, 1948. Presidium of the Working Group on Textile and Clothing Production. NA, f. MP, k. 1362 inv. č. 3652.

[30] Comments on the fulfillment of the plan for the III and IV quarters in 1950, June 12, 1950. NA, f. MP, k. 1345 inv.č. 3652. See also the Situation Report from the Referent of Work and Social Welfare in Bruntál, May 1951. SOkA Bruntál, f. ONV Bruntál, k. 20 inv. č. 88.

period.[31] In some ways the labor drives succeeded. In the first three-quarters of 1951, for example, more than 65,000 new workers were added to heavy industry, roughly half of whom were men transferred from other occupations. The rise in the number of female workers was likewise impressive. In a 1954 report that outlined regional aspects of fulfilling the plan, Liberec leaders noted that there had been a 14 percent increase in the number of women joining the workforce in 1953 compared with 1949. While textile officials had some success reducing labor shortfalls by adding women who had been outside the labor market, their contribution was still not enough to cover the overall shortage. Furthermore, women frequently left work as well. In a typical month for Bruntál, May 1951, 148 new housewives entered the labor force, but 224 other women departed.[32] What planners referred to as "fluctuation," of course, was not just a problem associated with female workers or the textile industry, but just one of the many obstacles that economic officials faced attempting to manage a centralized economy.

In addition to mobilizing female labor, Communists also adopted the practice of shock work and worker competitions to help make up for labor shortages. Czechoslovak factories imported this system of labor campaigns from the Soviet Union prior to 1948.[33] Production campaigns involved workers signing agreements to fulfill monthly and yearly quotas, even if that meant working overtime. Shock work was a similar effort to meet production quotas through extra shifts and fast-paced production. A third campaign was named after a Soviet labor hero, Alexei Stakhanov, and emphasized individual workers' attempts to set production records in a single shift.[34] These campaigns melded socialist zeal for labor with the concrete productive needs of the postwar Czechoslovak economy. Communist leaders also had to find a way to reverse the negative attitudes toward work that had emerged during and after the war. During the expulsions the economy required the greatest input of Czech workers, but some of them wished to escape manual and factory labor, while others wished to stop working altogether. The expulsions offered much greater social mobility to Czechs than a simple factory job – at least, that had been the implication of settlement policies and promotions. Following the years

---

[31] Report on the Fulfillment of the First Year of the Five-Year Plan, 1949. NA, f. MP, k. 1345 inv.č. 3652.

[32] Situation Report from the Referent of Work and Social Welfare in Bruntál, May 1951. SOkA Bruntál, f. ONV Bruntál, k. 20 inv. č. 88.

[33] Peter Heumos, "State Socialism, Egalitarianism and Collectivism: On the Social Context of Socialist Worker Movements in Czechoslovakia Industrial and Mining Enterprises, 1945–1965," *International Labor and Working-Class History*, 68 (Fall, 2005): 47–74.

[34] For the origins of this campaign in the Soviet Union, see Lewis Siegelbaum, *Stakhanovism and the Politics of Productivity in the USSR, 1935–1941* (Cambridge, 1990).

of working for Nazi bosses, ethnic cleansing had opened the opportunity for something much better than factory labor. These postwar attitudes toward work had negative effects for the productivity and profitability of the Czechoslovak economy. For example, mining production struggled to reach planned targets, even though the number of workers in mining continued to rise. Throughout 1947, productivity rates remained at three-quarters of prewar rates. Labor problems, concerning absenteeism, poor qualifications and labor turnover, plagued both the Ostrava-Karviná mines and the North Bohemian Brown Coal Mines during these years. One historian found that despite a 40 percent increase in the number of workers between 1937 and 1948, mining productivity remained at 81 percent of 1937 levels at the end of this period.[35] Socialist competitions and shock work were ways for planners to try to reverse such trends by attempting to instill pride in worker achievements and the socialist economy as a whole.

Increasing worker productivity held both economic and political importance. Economically, increasing productivity was another way that planners could minimize the impact of labor shortages and meet planned targets. Politically, planners and other Communist leaders considered worker morale as a key measure of the system's vitality. They monitored the workers' willingness to participate in socialist competitions and touted it as another sign of the system's success.

The continually growing organization of shock work, which moves from individual production to shock work of the whole shop and entire factory or firm, and socialist competitions, which also successfully spread and encompass continually greater number of workers and finally raises the consciousness of working people, are a guarantee that the future course of the Five-Year Plan will meet with continually better results, that we will continually draw nearer to the excellent Soviet model, and that the construction of our socialist economy will continue smoothly and permanently improve.[36]

While not all workers participated in or appreciated labor campaigns, many did support them during the initial years of the First Five-Year Plan (see Figure 6.1). For example, at the Elite National Enterprise in Varnsdorf, 75 percent of the workers joined in socialist competitions in order to fulfill the plan in 1950.[37] Such enthusiasm appeared promising to

---

[35] Anna Beinhauerová, "Pracovní moralka a vykonnost v průmyslové výrobe v českých zemích v obdobi dvouletky," *Slezský sborník* 88, no.2 (1990): 132; Generální sekretariát Hospodářské rady, *Průběh plnění hospodářského plánu rok 1947* (Prague, 1948), 86–87; Generální sekretariát Hospodářské rady, *Průběh plnění hospodářského plánu III čtvrtletí 1948* (Prague, 1949), 33–34.

[36] Report on the Fulfillment of the First Year of the Five-Year Plan, 1949. NA, f. MP, k. 1345 inv. č. 3652.

[37] Letter from Elite National Firm, January 15, 1951. SOkA Děčín, f. ONV Rumburk, k. 128 inv. č. 366.

Figure 6.1 Beating the plan! Courtesy of the State District Archive, Bruntál

planning officials as they increased the planned quotas in 1951. Yet, as Peter Heumos points out, underlying the official statistics on labor competitions was a growing distrust and rejection of them by some segments of the working class.[38]

The relative success of labor campaigns during the First Five-Year Plan became a key way of making up shortfalls, but was not a solution to preventing them. Even Communist leaders admitted that relying on labor campaigns to meet quotas was unsustainable. In Liberec, for instance, one official noted that even though two-thirds of the workers had signed on to socialist competitions, the plans were still not met: "This proves that socialist competition still isn't completely aimed at deciding productive work and that it is too formally organized."[39] Moreover, because of the monthly quotas, working on weekends and overtime shifts at the end of the month to meet targets became common features of the system and began to wear on workers.[40] Some Communists recognized this trend and warned of the dangers it posed to the economy. In a report

[38] Heumos, 57–61.
[39] Report on the State and Development of the Economy in 1953, Regional Planning Commission in Liberec, 25 February 1954. NA, f. ÚPV-T, k. 480 inv. č. 1750.
[40] Heumos, 51.

on mining production, one planner noted that even though shock work helped to achieve the monthly target, they needed to find a better way to increase production "so that fulfillment of the plan must not be, again and again, catch up at the end of the month with extraordinary Saturday and Sunday shifts."[41] While some Communist planners worried about the future bases of the economy, these voices were generally drowned out by supporters of the planned economy and enthusiasts of shock work and socialist competition. In a 1952 meeting about a Jablonec export firm's inability to meet its quota, one local leader was chastised for suggesting that the plan was unrealistic and needed to be decreased.[42] As Communist leaders and Czechoslovak workers made their way through the First Five-Year Plan the political meaning associated with economic goals grew increasingly important. To question those goals, or the methods of achieving them, had become politically dangerous.

After the first year of the First Five-Year Plan, authorities congratulated themselves that the targets had been surpassed – 102.8 percent for industry overall. In textiles, in particular, total output goals reached 106.4 percent of the target. In a report on the results of the first year, officials proclaimed that "these significant results clearly prove the success of our planned economy and that particularly the direction of our First Five-Year Plan is correct."[43] This became a common refrain throughout the early 1950s. For instance, the State Statistical Office's final report on the plan only voiced praise for the planned economy: production increased, heavy industry grew as part of the overall economy and Slovakia became industrialized. Even in light industry, one report noted, production increased and expanded. With regard to the textile industry, it spoke about new factories that were put into production, the greater use of automated machinery and the increased number of new products – from nylon stockings to printed tricot dresses – that were now available.[44]

But few of these changes were in evidence in Liberec, where textile firms still comprised the bulk of the factories. Officials from the region noted that they were still waiting for new technology to increase productive capacity. The Communists' shift to focus on heavy industry had siphoned workers from textile factories and other borderland firms. Regional officials argued that a more balanced approach to the

---

[41] Report from State Planning Office, February 1950. NA, f. ÚPV-T, k. 320 inv. č. 1715.
[42] Report on Jablonex, May 2, 1952. SOkA Jablonec nad Nisou. f. OV KSČ Jablonec n. N. kn.1.
[43] Report on the Fulfillment of the First Year of the Five-Year Plan, 1949. NA, f. MP, k. 1345 inv. č. 3652.
[44] Report on the results of the First Five-Year Plan, State Statistical Office. NA, f. ÚPV-T, k. 480 inv. č. 1750.

development of both light and heavy industries should be pursued.[45] However, central planners made a choice to dedicate investment and labor resources to heavy industry, despite the price that it cost the borderland economy. Planners noted that while producer goods industries were performing well, consumer goods industries were failing to keep pace. At the end of 1949 textile production remained at 81 percent of the 1937 level, with employment at 83 percent and worker productivity at 98 percent. The quality and quantity of textiles and other borderland export industries also began to suffer. For instance, in an October 1950 report, officials noted that there was a serious problem with quality and the production program, which called for "the fewest number of old standard types of cloth in a limited number of assortments."[46] Similar problems plagued the glass industry in Jablonec. In both cases, foreign orders were either not being met or foreign consumers returned goods because of their poor quality.[47] These shortcomings continued into the 1950s. In 1953, textile officials noted that in specialized industries, such as glass jewelry and women's stocking production, new workers lacked experience to return production output and quality to previous levels.[48] Communist Party policies and the consequences of ethnic cleansing left borderland industries vulnerable in the face of competing priorities after the war.

The transformation of the borderland economy also reflected the sharpening divisions of the Cold War and the country's new responsibilities as part of the Soviet bloc. In 1951, Czechoslovakia reached an agreement with the Soviet Union to increase armament production. Between 1950 and 1952, Czechoslovak armament production rose four times. By 1956, brown coal production had doubled.[49] Textile and glass production, on the other hand, were sharply reduced and repurposed from their traditional export sales. Czechoslovakia also faced greater pressure to reorient its trade toward fellow East European members of the Council for Mutual Economic Assistance. Between 1948 and 1953, exports to socialist countries rose from 39 percent to 78 percent of Czechoslovakia's total exports. As trade with western European countries declined, so too did the need to

[45] Report on the State and Development of the Economy in 1953, Regional Planning Commission in Liberec, February 25, 1954. NA, f. ÚPV-T, k. 480 inv. č. 1750.

[46] Report from State Planning Office, October 1949. NA, f. f. Úřad předsednictva vlády – Tajná spisovna (ÚPV-T), k. 320 inv. č. 1715. See also Results of the Fulfillment of the First Five-Year Economic Plan, State Office of Statistics, 1953. NA, f. ÚPV-T, k. 480 inv. č. 1750.

[47] Reports from State Planning Office, October 1949 and January 1950. NA, f. ÚPV-T, k. 320 inv. č. 1715.

[48] Report on the State and Development of the Economy in 1953, Regional Planning Commission in Liberec, February 25, 1954. NA, f. ÚPV-T, k. 480 inv. č. 1750.

[49] Průcha et al., 273–74; Teichova, 136–37; B.R. Mitchell, *International Historical Statistics: Europe 1750–1988*, 3rd edn. (New York, 1992), 416.

rebuild the export sectors, like glass and textiles. That these special exports survived at all was thanks in large part to the Sudeten Germans who remained behind and to those Czechs in the borderlands who supported them. Much to the chagrin of Czechoslovak officials, Sudeten Germans expellees in the Federal Republic of Germany began successfully rebuilding those industries in the 1950s. This was one small indicator, among many, of the widening gap in Cold War Europe.

By 1953 there was no returning to the prewar borderland economy. Ethnic cleansing gutted the workforce and management of borderland factories, upon which much of its success depended. Communists had alternative priorities that left little possibility for the return to the kind of small-scale production that had previously defined economic life there. Nonetheless, Communist officials were speaking Bolshevik when they glossed the production figures and exaggerated the scope and depth of economic development in sectors of the economy that were actually contracting. This was part of the new Communist system and reflected the way in which labor and industrial production had become politicized. The reality was that borderland factories were failing to provide market-worthy goods. This likewise became a feature of the Communist economy. While the increased targets of the First Five-Year Plan were nominally met, ongoing problems with labor shortages and fluctuation, lower-quality goods and shock work necessary to meet quotas signaled future problems. The enthusiasm for celebrating production campaigns also began to wane as the promised benefits of socialist production failed to materialize for the average worker. As Communist officials reorganized the borderland economy and focused on its mining and heavy industrial sectors, the smaller and medium-sized towns that depended on other types of enterprises failed to attract new setters and set the trend for their long-term economic decline.

Germans at Home in the Borderlands

As the Cold War assumed sharper divisions and the Czechoslovak Communist Party continued its economic and political consolidation, party officials sought to ameliorate the condition of the remaining Germans. This volte face came during the height of the dispersal action, which had been planned in 1947 as a way to remove Sudeten Germans from the borderlands when the option to ship them to Germany ended. The government first rescinded the 20 percent deduction from Germans' wages in the middle of 1948. Other policies followed. By the early 1950s the Communists embarked on a much broader integration policy for Germans and other minorities in the wake of ethnic cleansing. They

promoted this program under the principle of "proletarian internationalism," which prioritized socialist unity over ethnic divisions. Communists
did not apologize for the "transfer," and, in fact, they argued that it had
resolved the problems of the past.[50] For them, however, it was time to
move on. The increasing tensions of the Cold War in the early 1950s
demanded unity from Soviet bloc countries and forced officials to deal
directly with national minorities. While small-scale transfers to western
parts of Germany and relocations to other parts of the country continued
into the 1950s, most Germans who remained after 1948 still resided in
the borderlands. Only two years after the end of the expulsions,
Czechoslovak officials began considering ways of making Germans feel
at home.

Giving Germans citizenship, considered politically inexpedient several
months earlier, began with German miners in early 1948 and was permitted for all Germans by 1950. Politically, the turnaround in thinking
involved members of the Interior Ministry who began to re-evaluate the
dispersal actions as they considered the future of minorities in the state
more generally.[51] While this did not stop the deportations already in
progress, by early 1948 Communist thinking began to shift. In April
1948, the government issued a new ordinance that allowed Germans
to apply for state citizenship. Germans who were over fifteen years of
age and had a working knowledge of Czech or Slovak could apply.
Applications went through the national committees, though factory
councils and local law enforcement also had to review them. Progress
was slow and administrative delays were not the only problem; unsurprisingly, not all Germans wanted to apply. The initial deadline, set for the
end of 1949, was later extended to the end of 1950 and the language
provision was dropped. By early 1950, the central government began to
focus more intently on improving Germans' living and working situation.
In a March 1950 circular, the Interior Ministry urged national committees to eliminate any remaining discriminatory local policies toward
Germans and to expedite their requests for citizenship.[52] Later that
year, district national committees set up coordinating commissions
comprised of representatives from additional organs, such as action

---

[50] Zacházení mit osobami německé národností, MV, March 21, 1950. NA, f. Ministerstvo
vnitra – Tajné (MV-T) k. 73 inv. č. 2601, sign. 24; Tomáš Staněk, *Německá menšina
v českých zemích, 1948–1989* (Prague, 1993), 80.
[51] Adrian von Arburg, "Zwischen Vertreibung und Integration: Tschechische
Deutschenpolitik, 1947–1953" (Dissertation, Charles University, Prague, 2004), 462–
68. For the start of the dispersal program see Chapter 4.
[52] Zacházení mit osobami německé národností, MV, March 21, 1950. NA, f. MV-T, k. 73
inv. č. 2601, sign. 24.

committees, local police and the trade unions, to carry out these tasks. These commissions, in turn, met with local communities to try to convince all Germans to submit their requests for citizenship. While many Germans requested the return of citizenship, some also held out, and the process continued into 1951.

One reason that officials were so intent on extending citizenship was to secure their labor for the future. In June 1948, a directive from the Interior Ministry gave Germans the same rights and obligations at work by removing the 20 percent wage reduction and providing sick and vacation pay to them.[53] However, central authorities did not yet relent on deporting Germans to the interior for work duty, and the dispersal campaign continued into 1949. In August 1948, the Interior Ministry issued a directive to district national committees that prevented the return of Germans to the borderlands under any circumstances.[54] In December 1949, regional borderland officials reiterated these instructions. They reasoned that if resettled (přesídlení) Germans were allowed to return, the 1950 agricultural plan would be threatened and remaining resettled Germans' morale would be crushed.[55] German labor was needed to fill gaps, particularly on interior farms where few people wanted to work as day laborers. As part of the dispersal program the Czechoslovak government deported somewhere between 15,000 and 20,000 German speakers into the interior from the end of 1946 to the beginning of 1949.[56]

Under Communist rule, work became a means for Germans to prove their loyalty to the state and the regime. In their efforts to step up the progress of the citizenship drive, regional party officials instructed district officials to give the applicants who were committed to the socialist economy priority consideration. Model German workers, in turn, were seen as valuable tools for the promotion of the citizenship campaign. Officials in Teplice solicited activist members of the Revolutionary Trade Union to spread the word about the opportunity for citizenship and to encourage other Germans to apply. Many German workers took the opportunity to become active functionaries in Communist Czechoslovakia. Some were wartime antifascists, others had newly joined the party and helped in its efforts to reach German speakers. Sudeten Germans also participated in the production feats of the socialist economy in the early 1950s. The state,

---

[53] Staněk, Německá menšina, 77–78.
[54] D-300/11978–1948-DN, Ministerstvo vnitra, August 13, 1948. SOkA Teplice-Šanov, f. ONV Teplice-Šanov, k. 225 inv. č. 199. Staněk, Německá menšina, 76.
[55] 5151/1949-V, Krajský národní výbor v Ústí nad Labem, December 4, 1949. SOkA Teplice-Šanov, f. ONV Teplice-Šanov, k. 225 inv. č. 199.
[56] Arburg, "Zwischen Vertreibung und Integration," 482.

eager to promote Germans when it could, officially recognized them for these accomplishments.[57]

Less easy for local officials was the question of German property. In their discussions with Germans about the return of citizenship, local Germans frequently raised the issue of getting their property back. During the so-called "get togethers" (*aktiv*) in the Ústí nad Labem district during late 1951, property and confiscation questions dominated the discussions.[58] Sensing such concerns, the Interior Ministry specifically mentioned in its March 1950 circular the need to allow Germans to remain in their homes and within their rental contracts. By the middle of 1951 it was willing to go further, and the ministry put a halt to further confiscation of German homes and rescinded the allocation proceedings where they had not yet been finalized.[59] However, the regulations only covered homes where the former German owners still lived; in cases where the home was already allocated to a settler, there was no chance of redress. Even when a settler had been promised a German's house one party had to agree to an alternative property through negotiations. Unsurprisingly, as the process of "deconfiscation" unfolded there were conflicts. In Jablonec, where many Germans were able to hold onto their original homes, the district coordinating commission ran into trouble. Although they successfully resolved many of the 100 or so cases where a German owner requested the return of his or her property, the dearth of appropriate empty homes to offer as compensation ensured that future disputes would arise.[60] Even so, officials there went to great lengths to try to appease German speakers' demands for the return of their homes.

By the early 1950s, the Communist Party even promoted German cultural events in their efforts to integrate Germans into socialist Czechoslovakia. By the end of 1951, national committees were promising to show German-language films and were organizing cultural nights with German speakers and singers. In some cases, German musical groups were organized locally, in other cases officials brought in entertainment

---

[57] Zn: 216–25.4.1950-I/4-Kč, Krajský národni výbor (KNV) Ústí nad Labem, April 27, 1950. AM Ústí n. L., f. ONV Ústí n. L., k. 635; Minutes from the meeting of the Coordinating Commission for national questions ONV Teplice-Šanov, November 22, 1951. SOkA Teplice-Šanov, f. ONV Teplice-Šanov, k. 236 inv. č. 918; Staněk, *Německá menšina*, 111; Elisabeth Wiskemann, *Germany's Eastern Neighbours: Problems Relatng to the Oder-Neisse Line and the Czech Frontier Regions* (London, 1956), 282–85.

[58] Minutes from the get-together in the Cultural Home of the Chemical Factories in Ústí nad Labem, October 4 and 6, 1951. AM Ústí n. L., f. ONV Ústí n. L., k. 635 inv. č. 2381.

[59] Zn. 215–30/4–1951-IV/2, Zacházení s osobami německé národnosti – konfiskace a příděl rodinných domků, MV, June 12, 1951. SOkA Bruntál, f. ONV Krnov II, k. 326 inv. č. 478. Staněk, *Německá menšina*, 104–5.

[60] Proposal by the Coordinating Commission concerning the Allocation of Houses, September 16, 1951. SOkA Jablonec nad Nisou, f. ONV Jablonec n. N., kn. 2 inv. č. 7.

from elsewhere, including the German Democratic Republic (GDR). Beginning in September 1951, a German-language weekly, *Aufbau und Frieden* (*Reconstruction and Peace*), was published, which both reflected the broader changes in nationality politics and propagated them. Magazines and local factory newsletters in German or with German articles appeared later. In local borderland libraries and bookstores, German-language book collections were rebuilt and filled with ideologically proper authors. In terms of school policies, local efforts to integrate German-speaking children resulted in some unusual experiments. In parts of Northern Bohemia, for example, mixed groups of Czech and German children shared German-language classes.[61] While the government did not go so far as to create separate German schools, the efforts to appease German cultural demands stood in stark contrast not only with the ethnic cleansing that had just occurred, but also with the nationality battles in the realm of culture, education and language rights in Bohemia and Moravia that characterized the previous century.

Yet central policies to pursue integration only went so far. The efforts to end discrimination were a top-down affair that contradicted everything that had happened since the end of the war. The Communists themselves had enabled the targeting of Germans after they took power. In the early 1950s, local officials and settlers were apprehensive about what it meant to end the discrimination against Germans. In order to allay one of their fears, district and regional officials stressed that the return of citizenship did not entail the return of property.[62] Even so, a continued German presence rattled some settlers and discrimination toward Germans continued in many places. In Velké Březno, for instance, conflicts over property return and other misunderstandings among locals led to ongoing tensions between Czechs and Germans.[63] National committees, as one 1950 circular noted, did not always treat Germans "politically correct," even though, "they actively participate in constructive work."[64] The

---

[61] Report of Referent III for the Council of the KNV on nationality politics, May 19, 1952. SOkA Teplice-Šanov, f. ONV Teplice-Šanov, k. 236 inv. č. 918; Report on state citizenship, ONV Chomutov, November 10, 1951. SOkA Chomutov, f. ONV Chomutov, k. 347 inv. č. 525; Report on the nationality question, Jednotný národní výbor Ústí n.L., October 15, 1951. AM Ústí n. L., f. ONV Ústí n.L., k. 737 inv. č. 1155; Staněk, *Německá menšina*, 126–34.

[62] See, for example, Zn: III-216–1951-S from ONV Teplice-Šanov, March 15, 1951. SOkA Teplice-Šanov, f. ONV Teplice-Šanov, k. 236 inv. č. 918.

[63] See reports on the situation in Velké Březno in March 1952. AM Ústí n. L., f. ONV Ústí n. L., k. 653 inv. č. 2381. See also Matěj Spurný, "Nejsou jako my: Sociální marginalizace a integrace v období budování nového řádu na příkladu menšin v českém pohraničí, 1945–1960" (Dissertation, Charles University, Prague, 2010), 220–23.

[64] Zacházení mit osobami německé národností, MV, March 21, 1950. NA, f. MV-T k. 73 inv. č. 2601 sign. 24.

coordinating commission in Teplice criticized party members in late 1951 for not understanding that "our enemies were not Germans, but German fascism." At the same time, though, it reassured settlers that "We will not open German schools and there will not be any revision of the confiscation [provisions]."[65] While Communists were willing to make some adjustments to the treatment of Germans, they were unwilling to entirely reverse course. Communists continued to validate "the transfer" as inviolable – a good and necessary thing – and defended the resettlement program and the confiscation of German property that came with it.

Given these factors, that the citizenship campaign failed to get all Germans to apply should have been expected. In late 1951, roughly 40,000 of the more than 160,000 officially registered Germans remained without citizenship and were technically "stateless."[66] In Jablonec officials lamented that throughout 1951 the number of applicants for citizenship declined, with only 368 requests submitted through November. They blamed foreign radio for broadcasting reports that "all the Germans will return," as well as their own insufficient efforts to convince Germans of the benefits of citizenship. At that point roughly 4,000 German speakers in the district had applied for citizenship and 3,000 others held out.[67] Communist officials refused almost no one who applied, so the application process was more or less a formality. Even so, local officials seemed pessimistic that all of the remaining German hold-outs would opt to become citizens. Indeed, some Germans remained hostile to Czechoslovakia. Nazi activists and sympathizers still lived in the borderlands, though only in pockets. Some had been Nazi Party members or even former members of the SA or SS. In 1951, when local officials near Chomutov went to discuss with certain holdouts why they would not apply for citizenship, some said they wanted to leave, others wanted their property back first, and yet others said they were waiting for the Nazis to return.[68] Turn out for such "get togethers" was generally poor. In Ústí nad Labem, for instance, of 350 invited Germans who had not yet requested citizenship only 70 attended.[69] Such attitudes signaled

[65] Minutes from the meeting of the Coordinating Commission for national questions ONV Teplice-Šanov, November 22, 1951. SOkA Teplice-Šanov, f. ONV Teplice-Šanov, k. 236 inv. č. 918.
[66] Arburg, "Zwischen Vertreibung und Integration," 500; Spurný, 200–2.
[67] Report for the ONV Council on state citizenship, matrimony and nationality, November 22, 1951, and Council Meeting September 1951. SOkA Jablonec nad Nisou, f. ONV Jablonec n. N., kn. 2 inv. č. 7.
[68] III/1–21–951–Kč, Krajský národní výbor Ústí nad Labem, August 24, 1951. SOkA Chomutov, f. ONV Chomutov, k. 3 inv. č. 177.
[69] Report on the nationality question, Jednotný národní výbor Ústí n. L., October 15, 1951. AM Ústí n. L., f. ONV Ústí n. L., k. 737 inv. č. 1155. See also, Report on the care of

to the Communist Party that it had to devise other plans to make all Germans citizens. Finally, in March 1954 the state enacted a law that automatically gave Germans and others citizenship as long as they met certain residency requirements. For Sudeten Germans remaining in Czechoslovakia, Law 34/54 simply overrode Decree 33 that had stripped Germans of their citizenship and paved the way for the mass expulsions in 1945–46. The remaining holdouts mostly accepted the new law, though there were some reports of refusal and protest. In the district of Jablonec, thirty-eight Germans still refused citizenship in 1959. Although this was a very small number of Germans in the district, seventy more requested to leave every month, and some who were able to travel to the GDR simply did not return.[70]

German migration continued throughout the early 1950s. Migrants left or wanted to leave for a number of reasons: worsening economic prospects, wanting to live with their relatives, resentment at Communist leaders or locals, for example. In an operation that the International Red Cross organized, several thousand Germans who had been separated from their immediate families were reunited with family members in both Germanys during 1950.[71] Most Germans who sought a way out, however, had little success. For example, an instrument maker's wife requested permission to move to Germany in order to care for her sick mother and brother in 1950. The woman and her husband remained without Czechoslovak citizenship. The representative from Czechoslovak Woodworking Factories argued that it would be unwise to approve her request because a similar factory was being built in Germany and required skilled workers. The official feared that it would have to release eighty other Germans who also wanted to leave because they faced continuing discrimination.[72] Even though local authorities supported their departure, the Ministry of Interior had already issued instructions forbidding the loss of skilled workers, even for the purpose of reuniting families. The logic of the Czechoslovak government in preventing Germans from leaving was similar to the motivations that drove East German Communists' efforts to curtail *Republikflucht* – the emigration of Germans to West Germany. Politically, it was untenable to see millions to flock to the West as a repudiation of their system. The economic consequences would likewise have been disastrous.

Germans in Jablonec, June 3, 1953. OV KSČ Jablonec nad Nisou. SOkA Jablonec n. N., f. Okresní výbor národní front, k. 6.
[70] Report on the work with German inhabitants, May 18, 1959. OV KSČ Jablonec nad Nisou. SOkA Jablonec nad Nisou, f. Okresní výbor národní front, k. 6.
[71] Arburg, "Zwischen Vertreibung und Integration," 513–530; 712–15.
[72] See the case of P.R. from Kraslice. NA, f. MV-NR, k. 10311 inv. č. 6013 s. 573.

The vast majority of Sudeten Germans accepted their situation and Czechoslovak citizenship by 1954. Of course, many wanted to leave, but active holdouts remained on the margins. In the Teplice-Šanov district, by 1953 over 5,400 requests for citizenship had been received and only 398 holdouts remained.[73] German demands for cultural events, political representation and better living standards continued into 1954 as they began to voice more ordinary concerns to local officials. Sudeten Germans also tried to regain their property, even when they did not meet the necessary legal conditions. Their efforts depended upon the willingness of settlers to move and the availability of other homes, neither of which was guaranteed. Still, national committees worked hard to try to appease Germans' demands and assuage settlers' fears about the return of confiscated homes. Some Germans even returned to the borderlands. German speakers who had been deported to the interior migrated back to the borderlands as policies against them began to ease. Some wanted to reclaim their properties, others wanted to move back to familiar surroundings and people. The return migration of Germans who had been dispersed further underscored the extent to which Communist policy had changed since 1948.

The Czechoslovak government's efforts to integrate Germans was part of a broader strategy to deal with national minorities and make them equal participants in the efforts to construct a socialist society. Communist policies toward Germans shifted with Cold War politics, and fit into a broader spectrum of postwar migration and minority politics in Czechoslovakia.[74] Indeed, the program went beyond simply trying to remove legal discrimination that targeted Germans or Magyars because of the war. It meant trying to change attitudes, both Czech and German, as well as resolving bread and butter issues. As we will see in the next section, a similar process evolved regarding Roma. In some ways the integration policy of the early 1950s was a kind of affirmative action program that gave Germans legal rights and promoted German culture, assuming that this would convince them to help create a successful socialist society. The Soviet Union experimented with similar policies in the 1930s regarding national minorities. In the USSR the institutionalization of national categories worked toward ethnic cleansing in the 1930s and 1940s as the international and internal political dynamics became

---

[73] Report on the nationality politics in 1952, ONV Teplice-Šanov, January 13, 1953. SOkA Teplice-Šanov, f. ONV Teplice-Šanov, k. 236 inv. č. 918.

[74] On the Cold War politics, see Staněk, *Německá menšina*, 66–136. For the connection to minority politics, see Arburg, "Zwischen Vertreibung und Integration," 486–507.

increasingly divisive.[75] In the Czech borderlands, the promotion of German cultural and political rights in the 1950s grew from ethnic cleansing. Here too Communist ideology played a large role, as did the early Cold War context. The notion that "if you are not with us, you are against us," which permeated Communist policies and thinking, required giving Germans a chance to prove themselves as loyal citizens. Many German speakers did prove their loyalty through work in the mines and in textile factories. Most others resigned themselves to at least remaining in the country, if not in their homes.

"It looks like the Balkans here"

By the early 1950s, Sudeten Germans comprised only one minority group in the borderlands and the settlement process remained unfinished. In fact, people from a variety of cultural backgrounds and places populated the region, and migration to and from the borderlands continued. In 1950, according to official statistics, 87 percent of the borderlands inhabitants were Czech.[76] Adrian von Arburg estimates that this figure should be more like 83 percent since most Germans did not register themselves as such. While the 160,000 officially registered Germans comprised less than 2 percent of the overall population, in borderland districts they sometimes comprised between 6 and 11 percent of the population.[77] Moreover, many German speakers "became Czech" through marriage or by other means. Other minorities abounded. There were Slovaks, who were officially welcomed, but often wished to leave. Re-emigrants from a variety of countries lived there. Magyars, some of whom had been deported to the borderlands in 1948 from southern Slovakia, also remained. While Czech speakers predominated in most towns, different dialects and customs meant that a diversity of people became common. In some places settlers noted that the variety of languages and dialects spoken and different ways of life made the place feel foreign. In one case, a settler remarked "It looks like the Balkans here."[78] Well after the

[75] Terry Martin, *Affirmative Action Empire: Nations and Nationalism in the Soviet Union, 1923–1939* (Ithaca, 2001); Rogers Brubaker, *Nationalism Reframed: Nationhood and the National Question in the New Europe* (Cambridge, 1996), 23–54; Pavel Polian, *Against Their Will: The History and Geography of Forced Migrations in the USSR*, trans. Anna Yastrzhembska (Budapest, 2004).

[76] Vladimir Srb, *Populační, ekonomický a národnostní vývoj pohraničích okresů ČSR od roku 1930 do roku 2010* (Prague, 1989), 18; Adrian von Arburg, "Tak či onak," *Soudobé dějiny* 10, no.3 (2003): 281.

[77] Staněk, *Německá menšina*, 86–87.

[78] SOkA Jeseník, *Historický a sociologistický průzkum, 1949–50.* Dodatek D/7, *Vidnavska,* Mobilita, 2. It is difficult to tell for sure if this quote was meant as negative reflection on the ethnic makeup of the town or if it was meant literally.

expulsions ended, far from becoming a unified part of the country the borderlands appeared as a place apart, marked by exceptional diversity, pockets of economic malaise and continued migration.

By the early 1950s, Communist leaders sought to make Roma productive members of socialist Czechoslovakia under the guise of proletarian internationalism. Like their position on the Germans, this effort stood in sharp contrast to the attitudes of many settlers and national committee members who had actively sought to remove Roma from their towns in the immediate postwar years. The policies followed the same logic for Germans, and often local Communists listed both groups under the heading of "nationality politics" in their reports. The policies were similar in that they provided special cultural and educational opportunities for them, but differed from policies toward Germans with regard to things like health and hygiene. While officials focused on Germans' cultural needs and citizenship status, they inspected Romani living quarters and reported on their illiteracy rates. When pressed to solve the nationality problems, local officials reacted to Germans' actions and demands, but treated Roma as inferior people in need of assistance. If anything, the state's approach to Germans and Roma, as well as to Magyars and others, reinforced the biases against them by emphasizing their particular cultural needs or by focusing on their supposed shortcomings. Rather than being a progressive response to the diversity of the borderlands, the shift to proletarian internationalism demonstrated the embedded nationalist attitudes and stereotypes toward minority groups, particularly among the Communist officials who were supposed to combat them.

The tension between promoting Roma integration and overcoming old stereotypes was evident throughout the early 1950s. In early 1952, central officials initiated a program to improve Romani living and working conditions by directing local officials to coordinate their care. By encouraging Roma to permanently settle and to engage in steady employment, officials hoped that they would become integrated citizens. The goal of the program was "to reeducate gypsies so that they become orderly citizens of our land." The Local National Committee in Krnov put it in slightly more lofty terms: "The care of people of gypsy origin with a view toward their reeducation as a new man."[79] Local officials varied in their dedication to the integration of Roma. Some experimented with new policies regarding schooling; others worked with local factories to get Roma more stable jobs. Teplice-Šanov officials in 1951 noted that "several factories had

[79] II/3–215.13/2–1952, Úprava poměrů osob cikánského původu, Ministerstvo vnitra, March 5, 1952. SOkA Děčín, f. ONV Rumburk, k. 35 inv. č. 230; The care of people of gypsy origin with a view toward their reeducation as a new man, ONV Krnov, November 2, 1953. SOkA Bruntál, f. ONV Krnov, k. 326 inv. č. 478.

positive experiences with gypsy workers and that the majority assumption that they could only be used in agriculture or construction was already disappearing."[80] Even so, old attitudes proved difficult to dislodge. In 1953, factory managers in the district were still unwilling to hire Roma because they believed they were lazy. Local officials sought to use local success stories to change such attitudes. They lauded the work of model Roma workers, noting that several Roma employed at the Teplice machine works "overfilled the norms and never refused work, even on Sundays."[81] For some local Communists, work proved to be a means by which Roma demonstrated that they could be worthwhile citizens, just as it had with the remaining Germans.

Suspicions and doubts, however, underlay the premise of the project to integrate Roma. The March 1952 instructions to national committees for the care of Roma included the need for constant surveillance of homes and health. For instance, it instructed national committees to carry out hygiene examinations in order to "gradually obtain the evidence of gypsy health and the basis for the protection against disease, particularly contagious ones, and the removal of potential epidemic danger."[82] Officials considered Roma from the beginning as unkempt and as a threat to public health. Local officials and settlers also responded to Roma integration in ways that reflected earlier animosity and continued prejudice. In 1952 some communities in the Ústí nad Labem region still banned Roma from going to the pool or visiting the spas. Such discrimination reveals the ways in which old fears that Roma were unclean manifest themselves. Officials tried to downplay the meaning of such policies as "a lack of understanding on both sides," but such reports should be read as evidence of ongoing prejudice toward Roma.[83]

Of course, one of the main problems was that Roma did not necessarily want to be integrated according to Communist intentions. One response was that Roma left in search of other opportunities. While Czech and other settlers frequently moved around, for local officials this was an indication that Roma were unruly nomads. In Šluknov, for instance, local officials criticized Roma for moving from house to house even though this was still common practice in many borderland towns into

[80] Minutes from the meeting of the Coordinating Commission for national questions, ONV Teplice-Šanov, November 22, 1951. SOkA Teplice-Šanov, f. ONV Teplice-Šanov, k. 236 inv. č. 918.
[81] Report on the nationality politics in 1952, ONV Teplice-Šanov, January 13, 1953. Ibid.
[82] II/3–215.13/2–1952, Úprava poměrů osob cikánského původu, Ministerstvo vnitra, March 5, 1952. SOkA Děčín, f. ONV Rumburk, k. 35 inv. č. 230.
[83] Report of the referent for internal matters of the JNV about nationality politics, Jednotný národní výbor Ústí n. L., December 1952. AM Ústí n. L., f. ONV Ústí n. L., k. 653.

the 1950s.[84] Roma had plenty of reasons for wanting to leave. They often lived in substandard housing, even when they were employed. Many worked on state farms, which did not have the money for new housing. As part of the integration program, local national committees carried out home inspections to see how Roma lived as a first step toward improving their situation. Some Roma lived as their neighbors did and sent their kids to school. Others shared decrepit buildings and used the furniture to build fires. Just as there was no single Roma response, there was no simple solution regarding Roma re-education. Officials focused on dozens of issues, but resolved few.

The effort to integrate Roma was short-lived and unsuccessful. By 1956, the situation had changed again. Matěj Spurný argues that local officials and settlers' negative response to the Roma integration program and discrimination toward Roma helped to undermine and ultimately to end it. The constant reports of theft and a lack of progress toward transforming Roma eventually changed central officials' goals. Instead of a paternalistic approach based on proletarian internationalism, they began to use tougher tactics against Roma. In 1957, the Communist Party moved toward banning nomadism altogether.[85] The prejudices and biases against Roma were never completely removed and surfaced in officials' discourse about how best to integrate them. Roma also responded to the integration initiatives in ways that forced the government to alter its course. Just as central officials were frustrated by German holdouts, negative Roma reactions to integration policies also tested officials' patience. One local official lamented that he lacked "the power" to change Roma behavior.[86] The notion that Roma were at fault for not behaving differently gave officials a clear target to blame for the failure of the integration policies. Even for more benevolent officials, the presuppositions about Roma and the goals of the integration program reinforced what they already believed.

Other migrants from Slovakia, both Magyar and Slovak speaking, were technically internal migrants, though their reasons for moving to the borderlands differed. As "co-nationals", the government encouraged Slovak

[84] Report about the national question of gypsies, MNV Šluknov, August 3, 1954. SOkA Děčín, f. ONV Rumburk, k. 35 inv. č. 230.
[85] Spurný, 272–76. They would reverse course again in the 1960s and attempted some of the same policies that had previously failed. See Eagle Glassheim, "Most the Town That Moved: Coal, Communists and the 'Gypsy Question' in Post-War Czechoslovakia," *Environment and History* 13 (2007): 463–69.
[86] Report on the conditions of people of gypsy origin, MNV Jiříkov, January 15, 1953. SOkA Děčín, f. ONV Varnsdorf, k. 35 inv. č. 230.

migration to the borderlands, though not many came and few felt welcome. Magyars generally occupied low-paid positions in agriculture. They were necessary laborers in an economy that was shifting to heavy industrialization and drawing off all available labor. As early as mid-1948, officials began working to find ways to keep them on the job. In the fall, the Ministry of Interior issued instructions to begin giving Magyars citizenship and equalizing wage regulations.[87] Their integration supported the German policies that followed. Slovaks and Magyars had fewer cultural opportunities than Germans – the 130 Magyar books in Teplice district libraries was hardly something noteworthy.[88] The effort to successfully integrate Slovaks was seemingly an afterthought. In a 1952 report on the status of borderland education policy, the Ministry of Education not only mentioned looking after the delicate needs of German and non-Czech students, but specifically noted that Slovaks also did not have the necessary educational support. The official recommended that the same kind of attention being given to Roma and Germans should also be extended to Slovaks.[89] While Germans and Roma stood out as problems to be solved, officials had not paid Slovaks any attention.

The presupposition that as "co-nationals" Slovak speakers would feel at home in the borderlands was belied by their exodus. Slovaks were among the most mobile and most willing to leave.[90] Many were agricultural laborers or forest workers who earned little and had few reasons to stay. Reports in one district claimed that Slovaks went from hut to hut, collecting what they wanted before they returned to Slovakia. Officials noted that it had been a region of gold-diggers and that some were still being cleared out. So Slovaks, or for that matter Roma, who were blamed for stealing were simply following established practice. Yet, for local officials it meant more than that. Slovaks became another suspect group, whose dedication to the settlement program was doubted. Slovaks had an established history of return migration, and the distances to cover in this case were not so large.[91] Unlike other non-Czech migrants, Slovaks could more easily return to their homes. So, when wage discrepancies emerged or seasons ended, Slovaks packed up and left.

---

[87] Situation report, ONV Teplice-Šanov, July 1948. SOkA Teplice-Šanov, f. ONV Teplice-Šanov, k. 4; MV B-2111–8/9–1948-N-II/1, MV, September 8, 1948. SOkA Chomutov, f. ONV Vejprty, k. 25 inv. č. 108.

[88] Report for October 1952, state citizenship and nationality politics, ONV Teplice-Šanov. SOkA Teplice-Šanov, f. ONV Teplice-Šanov, k. 236 inv. č. 918.

[89] S/4/134/52 Tajné, Reply to the report on problems in the borderlands, Ministerstvo školství, věd a umění, February 7, 1952. NA, f. MV-T k. 116 inv. č. 3284.

[90] Report on the situation in the borderlands, MV, February 13, 1952. Ibid.

[91] Mark Wyman, *Round-trip to America: The Immigrants Return to Europe, 1880–1930* (Ithaca, 1993).

Figure 6.2 Re-emigrant family. Iljič Holoubek, CTK

Re-emigrants also remained on the fringe of many settler communities. The larger groups of re-emigrants, like Czechs from Volhynia and Slovaks from Romania, came from distinct backgrounds and were conspicuous because of it. In one corner of the borderlands, researchers conducted a study of three districts that had been resettled, which investigated almost every aspect of life there in 1949. Among other things, their reports highlighted the diverse nature of these communities by examining the different background of settlers. They did not just consider Germans and Roma as distinctive, but also considered the varied backgrounds of re-emigrants and Czech speakers.[92] Reports noted that re-emigrants lived as

---

[92] These are located in the State District Archive in Jeseník. My thanks to Jana Hradilová for making these reports available to me.

a community within a community, mostly keeping to themselves and with those from their place of origin. They were seen as backward, lazy and uncultured. One report noted: "Re-emigrants drink a lot of alcohol and live a very primitive life. When they came they didn't know how to prepare meat as a meal, they didn't cook or even eat it."[93] Officials singled out re-emigrants as poor farmers who were unable to manage independent holdings and did not understand proper farming methods. They saw them as a drag on their communities and a drag on the success of settlement. Officials apparently did not consider that they may have been the "most disorganized" farmers because their farms were the poorest quality and the least equipped. Still, officials refused to see them leave. In 1948, as Slovak re-emigrants from Hungary and Romania sought to relocate from the Czech borderlands to Slovakia, agricultural officials warned them that they would not be allowed to settle there, or return back to the borderlands, if they left.[94]

Volhynian Czechs managed to maintain a distinct identity after their resettlement, despite being widely dispersed. They established their own organizations and newspaper, and in some places they established their own church.[95] Even though the 1949 program for the Union of Volhynian Czechs in Žatec gave priority to assimilating the Volhynian Czechs, its very existence worked against such ends.[96] In addition, religious differences in some cases brought them closer to Germans. For instance, Catholic Volhynian Czechs attended church with Germans, which made them seem suspect in the eyes of some settlers. Because they kept mostly to themselves, but comprised only a small minority in most towns, this only further distanced them from new settlers from the interior. For instance, in Bernartice, a town of 1,373 in late 1949, there were 26 Volhynian Czech inhabitants. In this region, researchers claimed that they occupied the highest rung on the social ladder, even compared with Czechs from the interior.[97] This was not typical. Even though Volhynian Czechs had priority status for confiscated farms, the late arrival of many after 1946 put them at a disadvantage for settlement options. Bernartice was not located in a desirable region in terms of its agricultural potential and sat directly on the Polish border. Settlement officials may have been able to hold some land there for priority applicants, or perhaps it was land freed up during one of the revisions. Regardless, most

---

[93] SOkA Jeseník, *Historický a sociologistický průzkum, 1949–50*. Dodatek D/7, *Jeseníka*, Horní Lipová.

[94] Circular 54/48 Národní pozemkový fond, May 26, 1948. NA, f. NPF, k. 3 inv. č. 4.

[95] Spurný, 311.

[96] H. Nosková, *Návrat Čechů z Volyně: Naděje a skutečnost let 1945–1954* (Prague, 1999), 150–53.

[97] *Historický a sociologistický průzkum, 1949–50*. SOkA Jeseník. Dodatek D/7, *Javornika*, sociální charakteristika, 3.

Volhynian Czechs did not sit atop the social ladder elsewhere in the borderlands. It was one reason that they were willing to emigrate when things did not go well for them.

In 1948, a general exodus from the borderlands began, particularly from confiscated farms. The reasons had less to do with where a settler came from, and reflect in many ways the failure of the resettlement program. A report from late 1949, which discussed a host of problems plaguing borderland agriculture, cited settlers' lack of experience first.[98] Officials should have expected this. Land reform, under Communist aegis, generally allotted land to agricultural laborers, many of whom had scant savings and young children, rather than to experienced farmers. A report from one borderland district touted this result. It argued that large families would help bring population levels closer to prewar levels, which signaled the "national" success of land reform. It also noted that "80 percent of the people are former farm hands and agricultural laborers, the poorest of the poor. Land reform made these people farmers and improved their existence . . . This is the social success of our land reform."[99] That these settlers were, for the most part, unqualified to manage independent farms was beside the point. Land reform did not simply seek to improve agricultural production, but served as a popular program that both punished Sudeten Germans and rewarded landless laborers. However, agricultural production suffered, and many farmer-settlers failed to make a successful living in the borderlands. This, in turn, caused people to move at another time. From 1946 to October 1949, at least 34,000 out of roughly 120,000 holders of ownership decrees to confiscated farms had left the borderlands. In smaller communities the effects of ongoing migration were drastic. For instance, in Javorník, a town of roughly 1,700 people after the war, nearly 400 emigrated in 1948 alone. High rates of fluctuation remained common into 1949, with 265 coming into the town and 195 people departing. Only the National Land Fund's refusal to take back the ownership decrees prevented more agricultural settlers from leaving.[100]

[98] The Problems of Agriculture in the Borderlands, Ministerstvo zemedělská (MZ), December 1949. NA, Ministerstvo zemědělská – Sekretariat (MZ-S), k. 371 inv. č. 191.
[99] Výsledky osidlení zeměděské půdy na Českolipsku, Osídlovací komise ministerstva zemědělství, Česká Lípa, January 19, 1946. NA, f. Národní pozemkový fond (NPF), k. 10 inv. č. 16.
[100] The Problems of Agriculture in the Borderlands, MZ, December 1949. NA, MZ-S, k. 371 inv. č. 191. See also Lubomír Slezák, "Pohraničí českých zemí na pokračování (Dosídlování v padesátých letech 20. století)," *Acta Oeconomica Pragensia* 15 no. 7 (2007): 385; Slezák, *Zemědělské osidlování*, 119–126. For Javorník, see *Historický a sociologistický průzkum, 1949–50.* SOkA Jeseník. Dodatek D/7, *Javornícka*, Javorník, sociální charakteristika, 2.

Communist policies made things worse. Collectivization came in waves in Czechoslovakia. Farmers in some places had formed a Joint Farming Cooperative (*Jednotné zemedělské družstvo*; JZD) soon after the war. These slowly became the basis for collectivization following the Communist takeover. In addition, the government created state-run farms from holdings that it confiscated either from national enemies or former estate owners whose holdings were deemed too large for individuals to take over as national administrators. In 1949, the Communist Party began more earnestly to encourage farmers to band together and form JZDs. They were organized into four different categories based on their ownership and work policies. Type 1 JZDs were considered the lowest kind according to Communist standards, because property remained in privately owned hands. Type 4 JZDs, by contrast, were run with collective labor and common ownership of machinery, animals and harvests. In 1951, the government abandoned the voluntary nature of the early policies and they gave farmers little choice but to join. By the second half of 1953 there were more than 7,000 type 3 and 4 JZDs in the country, representing 80 percent of all collective enterprises.[101] The collectivization campaign was accompanied by positive propaganda encouraging peasants to join, as well as an attack on wealthy farmers called *kulaks*, an often misleading term directly appropriated from the Soviet experience of collectivization. Even with onerous delivery quotas and high taxes facing private farmers, many resisted collectivization. Local officials from one district struggling to meet its deliveries noted that many people wanted to leave the collective farms because of high quotas and a lack of assistance.[102]

Volhynian Czechs had already been expecting as much. The most unique characteristic of the Volhynian Czechs was their previous experience under Soviet Communism. This experience had encouraged their migration from the USSR after the war, and many of them were apprehensive about the future after the Communists took power in Czechoslovakia.[103] In particular, they feared a return to collectivization.

[101] Jan Rychlík, "Collectivization in Czechoslovakia in Comparative Perspective, 1949–1960," in *The Collectivization of Agriculture in Communist Eastern Europe: Comparison and Entanglements*, eds. Constantin Iordachi and Arnd Bauerkämper (Budapest, 2010): 189–96; "Collectivization of Agriculture in Czechoslovakia," Radio Free Europe News and Information Service, September 11, 1957. Open Society Archives (OSA), Central European University, Budapest, Hungary, accessed on September 15, 2014, http://osaarchivum.org/greenfield/repostitory/osa:b457fb52-1cc3-44a5-945f-09d5fae3fade.
[102] Minutes from the working meeting of MNV chairpersons, October 10, 1953. SOkA Chomutov, f. ONV Chomutov, k. 118 inv. č. 292.
[103] H. Nosková, Osídlovací komise ÚV KSČ"; "H. Nosková, "Osídlovací komise ÚV KSČ a reemigrace v letech 1945–1948, *Historické studie* (1998): 116–29; Lubomír Slezák, *Zemědělské osídlování pohraničí českých zemí po druhé světové válce* (Brno, 1978), 139; Karel Bertelman, *Vývoj národních výborů do ústavy 9. května.* (Prague, 1964), 149.

One Volhynian Czech recalled his response to another Czech settler who
blamed the Volhynians for the imposition of collectivization: "Yeah,
right, we brought it here to you! We just fled from it there!"[104] Under
the postwar settlement policies that incentivized immigration to the borderlands with sweet deals on property transfers, it had seemed that their
newly won property would remain in their hands. However, with the
onset of collectivization in the early 1950s, many Volhynian Czechs
became migrants again. A representative from the Ústí nad Labem region
where they settled in large numbers reported that 700 families left following the collectivization campaign.[105] They did not necessarily leave the
borderlands, but relocated to cities and became factory workers instead.
Others did their best to hold out as long as possible, but this may have
only made things worse. In a 1954 meeting of Volhynian Czechs, those
who had joined late or had left the collective farms complained of receiving poor land from which they could not meet their quotas.[106] Trapped in
a poor situation, many were willing to get on the road once again.

Central officials began meeting with borderland representatives to try
to end "the flight from the borderlands" in the early 1950s. Central
officials blamed settlers and local officials. As one official put it: "a lot of
people came [in 1945 and 1946] led by their own personal interests in
order to take property into their personal possession. When the change to
a higher social form happened, people began to leave the borderlands."
They demanded that more attention be given to mass organizing, that
settlers just saw their time there as temporary, and that quotas went
unfulfilled.[107] Collectivization was an aggravating factor, rather than the
root cause. In some areas, it may have been that collectivization helped to
organize farmers and supply them with the tools, tractors and livestock
that they were lacking. In addition, when settlers entered JZDs their debts
for confiscated farmland were relieved. While farmers did eventually leave
collective farms in large numbers, this was not the case in the early
1950s.[108] Instead, it appears that poor housing, a lack of livestock and a
lack of money to invest drove many farmer-settlers to depart. For
instance, in the district of Bruntál a review of the cases of people leaving
demonstrated that most left because the houses were dilapidated and

[104] Jana Nosková, *Reemigrace a usídlování volyňských Čechů v interpretacích aktérů a odborné literatury* (Brno, 2007), 87, 119, 121.
[105] Minutes from the meeting about flight from the borderlands at the Ministry of Agriculture, March 16, 1951. NA, f. MV-T k. 116 inv. č. 3284.
[106] Report on the district gathering of Volhynian Czechs in Krnov, December 2, 1954. SOkA Bruntál, f. ONV Krnov, k. 90 inv. č. 144.
[107] Minutes from a meeting at the Ministry of Interior, February 2, 1952. NA, f. MV-T k. 116 inv. č. 3284.
[108] Slezák, "Pohraničí českých zemí na pokračování," 390–92.

settlers had not received any help to improve them. Many other settlers switched properties within the district as others departed for good. In 1951, a similar review in the Chomutov district gave three main reasons for the departures: sickness, lack of qualification and speculation.[109] In an effort to forestall total collapse, the Communist Party even began forcing *kulaks* from interior parts of the country into unsettled border regions. Between 1951 and 1953 more than 1,400 families faced these relocations, most ending up as laborers on state farms.[110] The use of forced migration as punishment and as a means to meet economic needs was, by that time, considered reasonable practice in Czechoslovakia.

Settlers who had occupied a confiscated German home had fewer reasons to leave. The allocation of homes to settlers finally began in 1948. The procedures for selling homes to settlers had been organized prior to the Communists taking power, and from an organizational standpoint things went mostly according to plan. The Communists did make it clear that political considerations would play a role in the selection of those finally getting home ownership. In Jablonec the ONV chairperson told the allocation commission that people with morally suspect backgrounds or those who held antagonistic attitudes toward the socialist state should not be approved. Mixed-marriage couples, too, should only be approved according to the strict letter of the law. Finally, he told the commission workers that a settler who had occupied the homes prior to April 1947 "has priority rights even before a so-called priority applicant under another title."[111] Such policies continued the promotion of early settlers at the expense of re-emigrants and undermined the efforts to integrate Germans. By early 1950 the allocation of homes was mostly complete. Even so, in several of the towns and small cities the closure of factories encouraged ongoing emigration. A typical report from the Rumburk district from 1954 noted that "as a result of the closure of factories (i.e. the firm Rössler, factory for the prod. of metal goods, which was attached to the firm SOPOS in Šluknov; Drátovna, the firm Fründ, producer of aluminum goods) many families moved away."[112] In fact, the entire Liberec region witnessed massive migration in the early 1950s. Between 1951 and 1953 more than 52,000 people

[109] See minutes of the meetings of the District Commission for the Solution of Departed (Resettled) Settler-Farmers from the Krnov District, 1949–1950. SOkA Bruntál, f. ONV Krnov, k. 96 inv. č. 164. For Chomutov, see Úmyslné opuštění zemědělských usedlostí, Okresní velitelství Národní bezpečnosti Chomutov, May 12, 1951. SOkA Chomutov, f. ONV Tajné Chomutov, k. 3.
[110] Rychlík, 196.
[111] Minutes from the 33 Allocation Commission meeting, Jablonec nad Nisou, November 11, 1948. SOkA Jablonec n. N., f. MNV Jablonec n. N., k. 2 inv. č. 29.
[112] Report from Dolní Poustevna, May 1954. SOkA Děčín, f. ONV Rumburk, k. 35 inv. č. 229.

left the region, and over 45,000 people arrived. While most districts ultimately grew during the 1950s, the overall growth hides the great fluctuation that characterized life in the borderlands.[113] Ongoing migration
demonstrated that the borderlands remained quite unsettled years after
ethnic cleansing.

In 1954, the government's efforts to resolve the problems of flight and
poor agricultural performance coalesced into a program known as the
"final settlement" (*dosidlování*) of the borderlands. It focused on particular borderland regions in the west, south and east, where population levels
remained low and agricultural production was weak. The government
plans involved everything from bringing in more teachers to building new
housing. Yet even with massive state intervention and investment, the
situation did not reverse. During the first year of the program, housing
construction lagged behind intended targets. Central officials blamed
local authorities for not going far enough with their own work or helping
themselves.[114] Regional officials who had long experience in the borderlands felt their own frustrations mounting at the neglect of settlers'
concerns. They argued that central officials had not given serious consideration to those problems, and argued that the "ministries should give
material help, not just advice."[115] Their complaints, however, could do
little to improve the basic lack of people's interest or desire to live in
certain parts of the borderlands. Nor did central efforts to promote the
"final settlement" campaign amount to much. By the middle of 1954, the
government had managed to resettle just over 2,000 workers, which
reached almost 17 percent of the overall goal for the year. Despite the
investment and the efforts, settlers continued to move into, out of, and
around the borderlands into the late 1950s.[116]

Communist rule cut against the promises of resettlement and ethnic
cleansing. The initial burst of repression in the wake of the Communist
takeover signaled that many considered the remaining Germans and old
settlers as obstacles still to be overcome. The Communists had other
priorities, such as reigning in party officials and gaining greater control
of the levers of government power. The extension of nationalization was
one of the crowning achievements of the Communist takeover, but it

[113] Report on the State and Development of the Economy in 1953, Regional Planning
Commission in Liberec, February 25 1954. NA, f. ÚPV-T, k. 480 inv. č. 1750.
[114] Report on the Fulfillment of Work Related to the Economic Development Plans for
Borderland Districts in 1954, Ministry of Agriculture, September 2, 1954. NA, f. ÚPV
Vládní komise pro otázky osídlení pohraničí, k. 2 inv. č. 6.
[115] Minutes from the Working Meeting on Concerning the Inclusion in the Settlement
Zone, Ostrava Regional National Committee, June 9, 1954. NA, f. ÚPV Vládní komise
pro otázky osídlení pohraničí, k. 1 inv. č. 6.
[116] Slezák, "Pohraničí českých zemí na pokračování," 388–89.

encouraged emigration in the wake of factory relocations or closures. The decision to close and move borderland factories dovetailed with postwar labor realities and with postwar priorities to industrialize other regions of the country. Collectivization also encouraged emigration, in part because it ran counter to the entire premise of the settlement program, based on the transfer of confiscated property into settlers' hands. New settlers did arrive when others departed, though this only added to the mixture, as after 1949 when the government settled Greek refugees in some outlying regions of the borderlands. The ongoing migration left areas of the borderlands short of workers and sparsely populated, and demonstrated that the resettlement program had failed to meet settlement officials' visions of a uniform and unified country. Rather than promoting ethnic homogeneity, which is its ultimate goal, ethnic cleansing created a diverse and rootless society.

Conclusion

This book has explored the actions and attitudes of locals to make better sense of the Sudeten German expulsions and ethnic cleansing more generally. It does not propose that a simple 'rational actor' explanation, where economic calculations determined people's decision making, accurately reflects the historical dynamics at play. For the historian, determining motives is a slippery slope. There are few records explaining clearly why someone did something; something that he may not even be able to explain himself. The effort here has been to investigate people's actions and attitudes from a variety of sources, and, based on these, to explain why the expulsions happened the way they did. From the perspective of people in the borderlands economic matters were often at the forefront of public discussion and private correspondence. Even so, economic concerns were not an either/or proposition; in other words, what drove the expulsion process and shaped Germans' experiences was not the domination of one attitude, but rather an ongoing dialogue. As this book has shown, this dialogue involved many different actors and reached from borderland towns and villages to Prague and back. Individual views and motives shifted depending on the locality, the year and the circumstances. Recall that even productionists could support calls for a total expulsion of Germans, but still attempted to keep their German workers around. Czech bartenders served beer to German patrons in pubs, which had been German owned. Communist leaders went to great lengths to meet the desires of Germans for movies and theater in German in the 1950s. These apparent contradictions demonstrate that ethnic cleansing did not center on nationalist divisions, but that a multitude of actors – Czechs, Germans, settlers, workers, national administrators, Prague officials, and others – drove the economy of ethnic cleansing in the Czech borderlands. Their relations reveal a much more complex picture of experience and motive than an analysis based strictly on national actors.

This approach differs from previous accounts of ethnic cleansing that focus on violence. Most of the major studies of ethnic cleansing are largely dismissive of economic factors and material interests. For some it is not even examined, for others it is merely a by-product. Instead, nationalist violence drives their narratives of ethnic cleansing. Violence was indeed widespread in the borderlands, but it was no more than one in a host of factors that characterized the postwar expulsions. As Chapter 1 argued, the violence associated with ethnic cleansing needs to be examined in its specific context. What appears as nationalist mob violence from the perspective of Sudeten German memories looks different from other sources that point to the military's leading role. One of the arguments here has been that the movement of the Czech military into the borderlands resembled an occupation more than a liberation. That one unit, in this case the 28th Infantry Regiment, took a hard line on expulsions and was involved in some brutal attacks indicates the need to examine such actors in detail. Given a free hand, they were particularly devastating. Moreover, nationalist hatred cannot solely account for the violence that did occur. In fact, the war experience itself is a key factor that many scholars overlook. It may seem a self-serving way for officials of the time to exonerate their men from any culpability, but unlike most Czech speakers who went to the borderlands, the soldiers deployed there had experienced the fighting first hand. Of course, not everyone who carried out a sadistic deed was part of the military, and ethnic cleansing created space for little dictators, like Adolf Charous and Vilem Dovara, to emerge and terrorize German speakers, old settlers, Jews or whomever. Even so, specific perpetrators carried out the violence of ethnic cleansing, not a nation.

Nationalist attitudes certainly played a role – in fact, they were quite widespread. There was clearly general support for the expulsions throughout 1945 and 1946. These attitudes resurfaced during the revisions of specialists and again after the Communists usurped government authority. But what they meant regarding people's actions and experiences in the borderlands is difficult to unravel. Czech–German attitudes were enmeshed in long-term struggles over education and language rights, though these too had often been localized. Yet, these political disputes were hardly reason for killing. Similarly, while the occupation had clearly done the most to enflame national passions, it remains unclear how this connected to specific episodes of violence after the war. In the spring and summer of 1945, Czechoslovak leaders did their best to establish an atmosphere where revenge was not only accepted, but encouraged. Yet a storm of popular violence did not manifest, and instead nationalist unity among Czechs was challenged by other formidable factors, particularly property and political power. Thus, while nationalist politics – including symbols, speeches and commentary – were pervasive, they alone could do little to move Germans. The expulsion of the Sudeten

Germans presented a nationalist goal of removing Germans and offered substantial material incentives to implement it. This was a powerful combination, to which state and society wholeheartedly responded.

The state, led by the National Front government, intervened first and foremost by sending in the military to carry out ethnic cleansing. It also sought to control resettlement. The Settlement Office attempted to coordinate the arrival of settlers and to evenly disperse the population according to housing availability and labor needs. The central government took advantage of the spoils to promote the nationalization of industry and land reform. The Ministry of Industry sought to manage the movement of whole factories to Slovakia, the consolidation of confiscated firms and the concentration of labor in certain industries. These were rational plans for the remaking of the borderlands that dovetailed with the government's broader agenda for social and economic change. Yet, state power remained fleeting and unstable in the immediate postwar years. While the central government was generally effective at expelling Germans, it struggled to assert its authority over the borderlands. Constant inspections and countless directives from officials in Prague suggested not effective oversight, but its absence. The revision of specialists and farm and housing allotments were marred by inconsistencies and corruption. For central officials the borderlands appeared to be an unruly and disorganized place.

The state was hardly a monolith, however, and things looked very different to local officials in the borderlands. State power developed from the ground up within the context of resettlement and expulsion in the borderlands. Old settlers established national committees in Česká Kamenice, Jablonec nad Nisou and elsewhere before the arrival of other outside officials. These were often disbanded as new settlers arrived and began to make their presence and demands felt. National committees which had been granted broad powers were thrust into the melee of migratory forces brought by expulsion and resettlement, which they were ill-equipped to handle. In many places national committee members themselves were the source of corruption. Even so, local officials often had a vision of the borderlands from the past: a local economy based on a specific industry that had been successful for many years before the war. National committees pursued this vision, quixotic as it might have been, with vigor and consistency. Only as plans for factory relocation and liquidation moved forward and as nationalized enterprises' appetite for confiscated firms continued to grow did centralized authority over the economy increase beyond national committees' power. In the early 1950s national committees lost even more control as the Communists weakened their authority to the point that they became mere administrators with little input into central policies. By that time the central government had dramatically shifted the political and economic landscape and sealed the borderlands' fate.

Hundreds of thousands of Czechs responded enthusiastically when given the opportunity to migrate to the borderlands, but they did not go there for revenge. Instead, Czech speakers participated in ethnic cleansing by moving into Germans' homes and stripping them of their livelihoods and possessions. Partisan and military units had already expelled many, interned some and brutalized others, leaving easy pickings for gold-diggers and early settlers. Germans experienced expropriation as a traumatic event and felt its effects long after their arrival in Germany. That property became a source of conflict among Czechs also reveals how national divisions were sometimes less important than local ones. Volhynian Czechs who went to the borderlands as soldiers had trouble laying claim to the land they had cleansed. The Volhynian Czechs who arrived later were treated less like welcomed brethren and more like people who should be kept under surveillance. Other re-emigrants faced discrimination because they appeared poor and uncivilized – a vision that became self-fulfilling as many were left with the worst that resettlement had to offer. Old settlers were certainly wary of their Czech counterparts from the interior. New settlers, in turn, considered old settlers as possible obstacles in their own efforts to speed the cleansing of the borderlands and to seize German property. Far from acting as a nation, Czech speakers pursued individual material and political interests in the borderlands.

The drive for property shaped the migration of Czech settlers to the borderlands, which, in turn, played a key role in creating demand for German laborers. As Czech farmhands from the interior moved to the borderlands to take over confiscated farms, labor authorities moved Sudeten Germans into the Czech interior to work as agricultural laborers. The story of the Peschke family, in Chapter 4, who was sent to work on an interior Czech farm, demonstrated how such policies added to their tribulations in postwar Czechoslovakia. It also reveals the economic logic of ethnic cleansing: work could be seen as punitive – a form of reparation for war damages – so moving Germans where they were needed was deemed a deserved punishment. Likewise, because Czechs did not assume positions in borderland factories and mines, local authorities and managers needed to keep German workers for those production lines running and refused to release them for labor in the interior. In this case, the failure of Czech migrants to fill industrial jobs drove retention policies. Relying on German labor became problematic after 1946 and added extra impetus to the drive for specialists as factories and mines began facing severe labor shortages. For thousands of Germans, their profession saved them from expulsion. That many German specialists sought a way out of Czechoslovakia in the 1950s suggests that "saved" is not the right word.

Ethnic cleansing transformed the economy of the borderlands. Gone were the specialized industries that gave the borderlands their unique character. This is not a nostalgic observation; given the direction of the modern world economy, the majority of these firms likely would not have survived in their prewar form anyway. Likewise, the larger economic consequences of ethnic cleansing cannot be untangled from the Communist policies of nationalization and collectivization, or, for that matter, from the Nazi policies that preceded them. As Chapter 5 demonstrated, nationalization and confiscation dovetailed with Communist policies and created a broader state role in the economy than would have necessarily been the case. Settlers and national committees, however, believed that nationalization would mean greater local control. In the end, nationalization became a means toward increased centralization, as the story of the textile industry and Brothers Kanneberger reveals. Collectivization likewise meant a dramatic state intervention in land ownership and reconfigured agricultural production. The effects these policies had in the borderlands were particularly thoroughgoing, much more so than in other areas of the country. What had been prominent industries either disappeared or relocated to West Germany, where some thrived. Farming also gave way to heavy industrial production, which siphoned off labor and investment. Just as migratory forces and material incentives help explain how the expulsions operated, Communist economic priorities and ethnic cleansing together transformed the borderland economy.

The general dynamics of this story are hardly unique. As this book argues, the expulsions were intertwined with wider World War II horrors and developments and cannot be divorced from them. That Czechs mimicked Nazi policies with concentration camps, armband IDs and minimal rations shows not genocidal policies, but reflected general attitudes pervasive at that time. Nazi and Soviet priorities as well as the war had shaped Central and Eastern Europe in many critical ways that made ethnic cleansing a seemingly reasonable solution in 1945. This was not something new: by 1936, the Soviet Union had already carried out deportation actions against borderland residents based on ethnic criteria.[1] Nazi population policies, labor needs and shifts in the battle

---

[1] Kate Brown, *A Biography of No Place: From Ethnic Hinterland to Soviet Heartland* (Cambridge, 2004), 173–191; Terry Martin, *Affirmative Action Empire: Nations and Nationalism in the Soviet Union, 1923–1939* (Ithaca, 2001), 328–41; Pavel Polian, *Against Their Will: The History and Geography of Forced Migrations in the USSR*, trans. Anna Yastrzhembska (Budapest, 2004), 95–96, 126–39, 243–49, 277–303.

front forced more than 50,000,000 people into the status of migrants, forced laborers and displaced persons. During the war, ethnic cleansing emerged elsewhere – between Poles and Ukrainians and between Serbs and Croats, for example – as secondary conflicts in the shadows of the war. With the disappearance of interwar states and the uncertainty about the political outcomes following the war, nationalist and underground groups sought to create homogeneous ethnic space as a precondition to demands for independent statehood. These projects continued during the postwar period. German speakers across the region left homes that their ancestors had occupied, sometimes centuries earlier. In Poland, the movement of displaced persons, expellees, repatriates, settlers and Jews reached 15,000,000 between 1945 and 1947 alone.[2] While not all were forced migrants of the same kind, Central and Eastern Europe was a sea of movement through the late 1940s. For many who experienced it, these migrations brought trauma and misery. War, the Holocaust and ethnic cleansing ended the rich mixture of cultures, languages and peoples that had hitherto distinguished many Central and Eastern European countries.

While moving populations was the goal, economic factors shaped the ideologies, the organization and planning, and the everyday interactions of ethnic cleansing. As Timothy Snyder points out, "Nazi colonization and Soviet self-colonization could function only when economic interests and ideological presuppositions seemed to confirm each other."[3] Nazi plans for German expansion into the East combined the creation of a Greater German Reich with plans for agricultural development and ethnic domination in Poland and Ukraine.[4] As these plans were put into practice they faltered in many ways because economic goals and migratory currents collided, leaving people stranded and factories and fields untended. Additional plans were improvised, but did little to alleviate the problems that had already emerged. Soviet cleansing of the western borderlands likewise contained an economic rationale. Deportees served as an available source of mobile labor for development projects in remote parts of the country.[5] Ethnic cleansing connected states' efforts to control

[2] United Nations, *Economic Survey of Europe* 1, no.1 (1949): 16; See also the chapters on Poland in the following: Steven B. Várdy and T. Hunt Tooley, eds., *Ethnic Cleansing in Twentieth Century Europe* (Boulder, 2003); Philipp Ther and Ana Siljak, eds., *Redrawing Nations: Ethnic Cleansing in East-Central Europe, 1944–1948* (Lanham, 2001).
[3] Timothy Snyder, *Bloodlands: Europe Between Stalin and Hitler* (New York, 2010), 394.
[4] Götz Aly and Susan Heim, *Architects of Annihilation: Auschwitz and the Logic of Destruction*, trans. A.G. Blunden (Princeton, 2002).
[5] J. Otto Pohl, *Ethnic Cleansing in the USSR, 1937–1949* (Westport, 1999), 46; Brown, 173–191; Polian, 243–49, 277–303.

labor, land and industrial production with personal interest in social mobility and material gain.

The expulsion of Germans from postwar Poland most closely resembled that of Czechoslovakia. The rapid reshuffling of populations there brought similar opportunities for enrichment, raised key labor issues and connected with Cold War priorities and Stalinist politics. Gold-diggers (in Polish *szabrownicy*), swarmed the western borderlands searching for available loot and adding to the chaos of the region. As David Curp argues, this posed a dangerous situation for Germans who had fled the front and then returned, only to find that their property had been taken.[6] Officials encouraged settlers to move there by offering them material incentives and sought to bring large numbers of emigrants back, though the number of re-emigrants failed to meet expectations. Even so, the settlers who stayed struggled to overcome the sense of foreignness that came with living in other people's homes and sleeping in their beds – what Gregor Thum aptly terms "the impermanence syndrome."[7] Similarities also occurred in the area of labor. Settler-farmers there demanded that German workers remain during the harvest and planting seasons in order to mitigate productivity declines. Skilled workers were retained, though not to the extent that they were in the Bohemian lands. Settler diversity hindered the coalescence of communities even around the notion of national identity.[8] All of these trends characterized the ethnic cleansing of Germans at war's end.

In postwar Germany the arrival of millions of expellees put different pressures on society and the government than in Poland and Czechoslovakia. In many ways the situation worked in reverse. Rather than being indebted to their governments, many expellees felt betrayed and sought redress. This was particularly the case in the Federal Republic, where expellees pressured the government to keep open the question of border revisions and of possible return. That West German leaders at times supported such calls only further deepened the Cold War divide.[9] In the GDR, the expellee issue was quickly buried in socialist rhetoric and in many ways resembled the party's approach to the remaining Germans in Czechoslovakia. The economic effects of absorbing

[6] T. David Curp, *A Clean Sweep? The Politics of Ethnic Cleansing in Western Poland, 1945–1960* (Rochester, 2006), 43. See also Gregor Thum, *Uprooted: How Breslau Became Wrocław During the Century of Expulsions*, trans. Tom Lampert and Allison Brown (Princeton, 2011), 118–26.
[7] Thum, chapter 5.   [8] Ibid., chapter 2.
[9] Pertti Ahonen, *After the Expulsion: West Germany and Eastern Europe* (Oxford, 1993); Andrew Demshuk, *The Lost German East: Forced Migration and the Politics of Memory, 1945–1960* (Cambridge, 2012), 67.

millions of expellees also produced different outcomes. Rather than labor shortages, expellees proved to be important contributors in both Germanys, providing a mobile labor force to rebuild the country. That expellees, once across the border, faced very similar circumstances in terms of housing, food, wages and even suspicion likewise speaks to the interconnected history of these migrations. It also suggests that ethnic cleansing is a lengthier process for its victims than simply leaving their homeland. Their experiences improved somewhat once they crossed the border, but ongoing difficulties as well as painful memories followed them to their new homes.

Just as the expulsions and resettlements emerged from World War II, they also fit into the calculus of the early Cold War. The emptied lands became spaces for regimes to pursue new political, economic and cultural programs. As Padraic Kenney argues in the case of Poland, "[t]he social revolution, so evident and probable an outcome of the war, had by 1948 become something quite different; and the components of a state socialist – or stalinist – revolution began to fall into place."[10] These components included five-year plans and tighter political control. By 1953 this revolution had run its course and state and society had achieved a significant measure of stability. The 1953 upheavals in the GDR did not spread to the borderlands. There were some protests and signs of resistance, quickly blamed on Germans, but authorities labeled it capitalist and imperialist.[11] That the new "imperial fascist state," the Federal Republic of Germany, was also the former imperial fascist state, and harbored more than a million Sudeten Germans, probably helped Czechs to accept the early Cold War propaganda directed against West Germany. The notion of being surrounded by the enemy was a leftover from the war as much as it was a part of Soviet-inspired propaganda. The shift in Czechoslovak policies toward remaining Germans in the early 1950s, which coincided with the purge of party members and widespread anti-Semitism, meant that the targets had changed, but not yet the atmosphere created by the war and ethnic cleansing. The Czech border with the Federal Republic and that between the two Germanys became new borderlands within Europe. A period of intense migration and political and economic upheavals would only be seen again when the Communist edifice crumbled in 1989.

There were no winners in this story. The idea that the Communist Party somehow "won" in its contest for political control or that Czechs

---

[10] Padraic Kenney, *Rebuilding Poland: Workers and Communists, 1945–1950* (Ithaca, NY, 1997), 190.

[11] Czechoslovak Communist Party Information Bulletin, July 1, 1953. Wilson Center Digital Archive, accessed on January 19, 2015, digitalarchive.wilsoncenter.org/docu ment/112625.

triumphed in their conflict with Germans seems misplaced given the history of the past seventy years. The Communists established rule through tough tactics and various forms of patronage. Having control over the key levers of power in the borderlands surely helped in this regard. Land reform and nationalization programs grew from the expulsions and the confiscation of German property. Yet Communist rule proved unstable and unpopular. Barely twenty years after Communists had seized power a serious challenge to their tactics and policies materialized, and the reform-minded Alexander Dubček opened the door to new voices. This door was quickly shut thanks to the Soviet-led intervention and a general crackdown in August 1968. The Communist Party in Czechoslovakia then held out for another twenty years. Within that forty-one year period few voices debated the reasons for and meaning of the expulsions, while officially sponsored media and literature sought to justify them. For people living in the borderlands physical reminders of the prewar past surrounded them, but for the rest of Czech society the legitimacy of the expulsions was never questioned.

While in many ways the Communist past has been put to rest, if not entirely overcome, the legacies of the expulsions still linger. Politicians in the early post-Communist years, most notably Václav Havel, made symbolic gestures of reconciliation, but few politicians have said that the expulsions were wrong, and even fewer have suggested that some form of compensation should be paid. A few schemes have emerged to pay a symbolic sum to some Germans, but they have been limited to small specifically defined groups of Germans who remained in the Czech Republic. Questions about the legality of the postwar Presidential Decrees, the victimhood of Germans, and property confiscation and restitution continue to surface as matters for contemporary political debate. These debates fluctuate depending both on domestic and international politics. In the initial years following the collapse of Communism, Czechoslovakia and Germany worked to smooth relations and signed a friendship treaty in 1992 signaling Czech recognition of expulsion violence and Germany's unwillingness to support expellees' property claims. In 1997 the two governments signed a Declaration on Mutual Relations that reiterated these points.[12] Germany also pledged to work for the Czech Republic's accession into the European Union. The Czech Republic's application for European Union membership opened the door for the Sudeten German *Landsmannschaft* to intensify its

---

[12] Czech-German Declaration on Mutual Relations and the Future Development, January 1997, accessed on January 5, 2016, eudocs.lib.byu.edu/index.php/Czech-German_Declaration.

pressure against the so-called Beneš Decrees' legality.[13] Debates about postwar reckoning flared up and forced German and Czech societies to re-examine the past. The responses varied. Czech historians published a treatise "Against the Rape of History," which awkwardly attempted to justify the expulsion policy; the Czech Prime Minister labeled the Sudeten Germans "a fifth column"; and Günter Grass published *Crabwalk* (*Im Krebsgang*), which put the plight of German expellees squarely at the heart of popular political and cultural discussions in Germany. These were signs of both increasing dialogue and tensions within Germany and the Czech Republic over the fate of the expellees. Public opinion in the Czech Republic reflected these tensions; 60 percent of the respondents for one poll in 2002 supported the notion that the expulsions were justified. Only 25 percent suggested they were unjust. When the Czech Republic finally did accede to the EU in 2004 the focus on the expulsions began to wane and opinions began to shift, so that by 2011 the same poll was evenly split among Czechs on the question of the expulsions' justness.[14] Although planning for The Centre against Expulsions in Berlin has sparked new debates, they have been more muted and less important for relations between the Czech Republic and Germany.

The legal issue of property restitution has been another reason for ongoing debates about the expulsions. In fact, property disputes, more than any other issue, stand at the center of Sudeten Germans' demands. As Edvard Beneš had feared in 1945, the confiscation of Sudeten German property without indemnification has created a multitude of legal challenges to the validity of the decrees that popularly share his name. From the outset of Czechoslovakia's "return to Europe" some Sudeten Germans, their heirs and others have been challenging the confiscation laws and practices in various legal forums. There is no formal legal method of restitution as the Beneš Decrees still remain valid. The only restitution measures instituted by the Czechoslovak government involved property taken over by the Communists after 1948, which, in order for someone to make a claim, also required that they held Czechoslovak citizenship. This means that the legal challenges to the confiscation decrees have varied widely in their details and outcomes. Some challenge the specifics of their case and the way it was handled. For instance, in one case the plaintiff argued that his father had successfully appealed for his

---

[13] For more on the conflict surrounding the Beneš Decrees see, Emil Nagengast, "The Beneš Decrees and EU Enlargement," *European Integration* 4 no. 25 (December 2003): 335–50.

[14] Lukáš Novotný, "Dekrety, odsun sudetských Němců v historických paměti Čechů: Vysledky z representaetivního dotazníkového šetření," *Naše společnost* 2 (2012): 32–33.

Czechoslovak citizenship in 1946 at the local level, but then passed away before the Ministry of Interior could approve it. His family was then expelled in 1946. The court ruled that because the plaintiff lacked citizenship, he could not bring a restitution case to trial.[15] Others have challenged the very validity of the decrees themselves.[16] More noteworthy have been the cases involving former nobility who have the means to bring these cases to court and whose former properties often hold great value. The Schwarzenburgs, the Lichtenstein family, the Czernins and others have pursued both domestic and international remedies, though with little success.[17]

One of the more famous cases involves František Oldřich Kinský from an aristocratic family. He submitted 157 claims for property restitution in the Czech courts, many of which are still pending despite his death in 2009. Kinský's story began in 1940 when his mother took him to Argentina following his father's death, and he later obtained Argentinian citizenship. At that point, the property, which belonged in a trust, passed to František, who was six years old at the time. After the war the family's property was confiscated, including the baroque Kinský Palace in Prague's Old Town Square, which currently houses the National Gallery. The emergence of his case in 2001, rather late compared with other restitution claims, raised concerns across the Czech political spectrum. Particularly upsetting for some is the fact that Kinský's father actively supported the Nazis and sought German citizenship after the takeover of the Sudetenland in 1938. The legal issue has been mired in years of court cases and foot-dragging on the part of Czech authorities. In one case, defense lawyers slowed the case by challenging the legitimacy of Kinský's Argentinian citizenship. Politicians became involved with his case in the summer of 2003. Over the next several years they denounced judges who ruled in Kinský's favor, and the police even began an investigation against Kinský and his lawyer. As a result, the European Court of Human Rights fined the Czech government for interfering with the legal process associated with Kinský's claims.[18] Overall,

[15] Nagengast, 345.
[16] See, for example, the case before the United Nations Human Rights Committee, Josef Bergauer et al. v. The Czech Republic, accessed on January 5, 2016, www1.umn.edu/humanrts/undocs/1748-2008.html.
[17] Marcia Christoff Kurapovna, "Revenge of Old Europe," *New York Times*, December 9, 2003; R.M. Douglas, *Orderly and Humane: The Expulsion of the Germans after the Second World War* (New Haven, 2012), 337–41; Elazar Barkan, *The Guilt of Nations: Restitution and Negotiating Historical Injustices* (Baltimore, 2001), 137.
[18] Case of Kinský v. The Czech Republic, Strasbourg, February 9, 2012, accessed on September 16, 2016, hudoc.echr.coe.int/app/conversion/pdf/?library=ECHR&id=001-109044. For more on the Kinský legal case see Josef Benda, "Restituce majetku bývalých

only a few of his cases have been resolved, and only because those municipalities which owned his property did not want to deal with legal proceedings. That the courts have neatly sidestepped the gray areas surrounding the confiscation decrees and questions of restitution reflects the broader attitudes of the Czech public. From 1995 to 2011 less than 5 percent of Czech citizens polled about the expulsions supported any kind of payment for damages or property restitution.[19] It seems unlikely that the Czech government or courts will relent on this issue in the future.

The long-term legacy of ethnic cleansing in the borderlands has been mixed. The northern borderlands of the Czech Republic continue to struggle with higher unemployment and crime rates compared to other parts of the country. By 2000, several of the borderland districts discussed earlier here were declared to be economically weak regions or in need of structural repair. Many of them had unemployment rates in excess of 12 percent.[20] Crime rates in these regions have been higher compared to elsewhere in the country, with the exception of the bigger cities.[21] The borderlands have witnessed increased violence and discrimination, particularly against Roma, who comprise a visible minority in many places. In 1997, the Ústí nad Labem city council approved a plan to wall off a section of town where Roma lived. Violence against Roma continually punctuates the news about borderland towns. In 2011, a wave of anti-Roma demonstrations swept from Varnsdorf to Šluknov.[22] The European Union recently found the Czech government responsible for discrimination in its education of Roma children. In 2013, a survey by the Czech Schools Inspectorate found that Roma comprised 28 percent of pupils in schools for students with special learning needs, even though Roma count for roughly 3 percent of the population.[23] The Czech Republic is not unique in terms of such incidents, however, and

šlechtických rodů po roce 1989" (Disseration, Charles University, Prague, 2010), 348–78.

[19] Novotný, 32–33.

[20] See the various reports from 2006 and 2009 developed in conjunction with the Czech Republic Ministry for Regional Development, accessed on June 21, 2017, www.regional nirozvoj.cz/index.php/home.html.

[21] Report on Crime by region 2013, Czech Statistical Office, accessed on January 5, 2015, www.czso.cz/csu/2014edicniplan.nsf/engkapitola/330085-14-eng_r_2014-24.

[22] See the television documentary by David Vondráček, "Na divokém severu (Šluknovsko 2011–2012)," accessed on September 16, 2016, www.ceskatelevize.cz/ivysilani/103271 92109-na-divokem-severu-sluknovsko-2011-2012/.

[23] Amnesty International, "EU Action against Czech Republic to End Discrimination in Schools is a Victory for Rights, Justice and Roma," September 25, 2014, accessed on January 5, 2015, www.amnesty.org/en/articles/news/2014/09/eu-action-against-czech-r epublic-discrimination-schools-victory-rights-justice-and-roma/.

discrimination against Roma remains common throughout Central and Eastern Europe.

Some encouraging signs that past and current problems might be overcome have also appeared in recent years and offer a more nuanced picture of the borderlands and attitudes toward the expulsions. Antikomplex, an organization devoted to public education about the Sudetenland and discrimination, has published books and articles and held exhibitions to promote reconciliation between the past and present. A Czech–German Fund for the Future, established in 1998, supports a range of projects meant to build better relations between Czechs and Germans. Academic research also continues to foster cross-border understanding. A Czech/German Historical Commission supports ongoing research into the expulsions and Czech–German relations. Czech literature and films have also begun to grapple more openly and with more resonance about this past.[24] Local initiatives have also grown in number. Žatec celebrated its millennial festivities in the spirit of Czech/German friendship in 2004. In Ústí nad Labem a ceremony to mark and acknowledge the massacre sixty years earlier took place on July 31, 2005. Schools have developed ties across the border with German schools and offer dual language classes. Areas that had been abandoned and left to decay are now being rejuvenated. Cross-border economic initiatives, including trade and tourism, have also encouraged cross-border contacts.[25] These local efforts signify the way forward. While outside attention tends to focus on the *Sudetendeutsche Landsmannschaft* and legal claims for compensation, neither the organization nor the claims garner overwhelming support from the remaining Sudeten Germans or their heirs. One hopes that local initiatives and the passage of time will mute the more strident voices of those who want to deny or undo the past.

---

[24] Rajendra Chitnis, "'Moral Limits': The Expression and Suppression of Guilt in Czech Post-War Writing about the Borderlands," *Central Europe* 10 no. 1 (May 2012): 52–54.

[25] Caitlin Murdock, *Changing Places: Society, Culture, and Territory in the Saxon-Bohemian Borderlands, 1870–1946* (Ann Arbor, 2010), 210–11; Peter Becher, "Deutsche und Tschechen: Vertreibung und Versöhnung," *German Studies Review* 30 no. 2 (May, 2007): 259–66.

Selected Bibliography

Archival Sources

Czech Republic

Archiv města (Municipal Archive), Ústí nad Labem
Národní archiv (National Archive), Prague
Státní oblastní archiv (SOA, State Regional Archive), Litoměřice, pobočka v Most
Státní okresní archiv (SOkA, State District Archive), Bruntál
SOkA Česka Lípa
SOkA Chomutov
SOkA Děčín
SOkA Jablonec nad Nisou
SOkA Jeseník
SOkA Liberec
Vojenský historický archiv (Military History Archive), Prague
Zemský archiv (Provincial Archive), Opava

Germany

Lastenausgleicharchiv (Equalization of Burdens Archive), Bayreuth

Contemporary Periodicals

Central European Observer
Československý průmysl
Dnešek
Hraničař, Protifašistický list okresu Frývaldova
Osidlování
Rudé pravo
Statistický zprávodaj
Stráž severu
Svobodné slovo
Svobodný Varnsdorf

288   Selected Bibliography

Published Primary Sources

Arburg, Adrian von and Tomáš Staněk. *Vysídlení Němců a proměny českého pohraničí 1945–1951: dokumenty z českých archivů.* Středokluky: Susa, 2010.

Beneš, Edward. *Edvard Beneš: Odsun němců.* Edited by Věra Olivová. Prague: Knižnice společnosti Edvarda Beneše, 1995.

Edvard Beneš: Odsun němců z Československa. Edited by Karel Novotný. Prague: Dita, 1996.

Československá statistika. Pohyb obyvatelstva v roce 1945. Vol. 14, book 13. Prague: Státní úřad statistický, 1949.

Soupisy obyvatelstva v Československu v letech 1946–1947. Vol. 6, book 15. Prague: Statní úřad statistický, 1951.

Chomutovsko 1945–1948: Sborník dokumentů. Chomutov: Okresní výbor KSČ Chomutov, 1989.

Intolerance: Češi, Němci a Židé na ústecku 1938–1948. Ústí nad Labem: Albis, 1998.

Jech, Karel and Karel Kaplan, eds. *Dekrety prezidenta republiky 1940–1945: Dokumenty.* 2 vols. Brno: Ústav pro soudobé dějiny, 1995.

Jurová, Anna, ed. *Rómska problematika 1945–1967. Dokumenty.* Part 1. Prague: Ústav pro soudobé dějiny, 1996.

Kaplan, Karel, ed. *ČSR a SSSR: dokumenty mezivládních jednání, 1945–1948.* Brno: Doplněk, 1997.

Schieder, Theodor, ed. *Documents on the Expulsion of the Germans from Eastern-Central Europe.* 4 vols. Translated by G.H. de Sausmarez. Bonn: Federal Ministry for Expellees, Refugees and War Victims, 1960.

Statistický lexikon obcí v Republice československé. 4 vols. Prague: Orbis, 1934–1937.

US Deptartment of State. Historical Office. *Foreign Relations of the United States. The Conference of Berlin; The Potsdam Conference, 1945.* Washington, DC: US Government Printing Office, 1960.

Volokitina, T.V. et al., eds. *Vostochnaia Evropa: V Dokumentakh Rossiiskikh Arxikhov.* Vol. 1. Moscow: Sibirskii Khronograf, 1997.

Vondrová, Jitka, ed. *Češi a sudetoněmeká otázka 1939–1945: Dokumenty.* Prague: Ústav mezinárodních vztahů, 1994.

Zelený, Karel, ed. *Vyhnání Čechů z pohraničí 1938.* Prague: Ústav mezinárodních vztahů, 1996.

Vynání a život Čechů v pohraničí 1938–1945. Prague: Ústav mezinárodních vztahů, 1999.

Secondary Literature

6. *vědecká archivní conference Revoluční národní vybory, osídlování pohraničí a význam národních vyborů při zajišťování národně-demokratického procesu v ČSR v letech 1944–1948.* Ústí nad Labem: n.p, 1990.

Abrams, Bradley F. *The Struggle for the Soul of the Nation: Czech Culture and the Rise of Communism.* Lanham: Rowman and Littlefield, 2004.

Ahonen, Pertti, Gustavo Corni and Jerzy Kochanowski. *People on the Move Forced Population Movements in Europe in the Second World War and Its Aftermath.* Oxford: Berg, 2008.

Aldcroft, Derek and Steven Morewood. *Economic Change in Eastern Europe since 1918*. Brookfield: Edward Elgar, 1995.

Arburg, Adrian von. "Tak či onak." *Soudobé Dějiny* 10, no. 3 (2003): 253–92.

Als die Deutschen weg waren was nach der Vertreibung geschah: Ostpreussen, Schlesien, Sudetenland; das Buch zur WDR-Fernsehserie. Berlin: Rowohlt Berlin, 2005.

Auerbach, Hellmuth and Wolfgang Benz. *Die Vertreibung der Deutschen aus dem Osten: Ursachen, Ereignisse, Folgen*. Frankfurt am Main: Fischer, 1996.

Bartoš, Josef. *Okupované pohraničí a české obyvatelstvo, 1938–1945*. Prague: Český svaz protifašistických bojovníků, 1986.

Bell-Fialkoff, Andrei. *Ethnic Cleansing*. New York: St. Martin's Press, 1996.

Bertelmann, Karel. *Vývoj národních výborů do ústavy 9. května*. Prague: Československé academie věd, 1964.

Biman, S., and R. Cílek. *Poslední mrtví, první živí: České pohraničí květen až srpen 1945*. Ústí nad Labem: Severočeské, 1989.

Brandes, Detlef. *Der Weg zur Vertreibung, 1938–1945: Pläne und Entscheidungen zum "Transfer"der Deutschen aus der Tschechislowakei und aus Polen*. Munich: Oldenbourg Verlag, 2001.

Brubaker, Rogers. *Nationalism Reframed: Nationhood and the National Question in the New Europe*. Cambridge: Cambridge University Press, 1996.

Bryant, Chad. "Either German or Czech: Fixing Nationality in Bohemia and Moravia, 1939–1946." *Slavic Review* 61, no. 4 (2002): 683–706.

Prague in Black: Nazi Rule and Czech Nationalism. Cambridge, Mass.: Harvard University Press, 2009.

Čapka, František, Lubomír Slezák and Jaroslav Vaculík. *Nové osídlení pohraničí českých zemí po druhé světové válce*. Brno: Akademické nakladatelství CERM, 2005.

Cornwall, Mark. "The Struggle on the Czech-German Language Border, 1880–1940." *English Historical Review* 109, no. 433 (1994): 914–51.

Curp, T. David. *A Clean Sweep? The Politics of Ethnic Cleansing in Western Poland, 1945–1960*. Rochester: Rochester University Press, 2006.

Deak, Istvan, Jan T. Gross and Tony Judt, eds. *The Politics of Retribution in Europe: World War II and Its Aftermath*. Princeton: Princeton University Press, 2000.

Demshuk, Andrew. *The Lost German East Forced Migration and the Politics of Memory, 1945–1970*. Cambridge: Cambridge University Press, 2014.

Dostál Raška, Francis. *The Czechoslovak Exile Government in London and the Sudeten German Issue*. Prague: Karolinum, 2002.

Etnické procesy v novoosídleneckém pohraničí- dělnictvo v etnických procesech. Vol. 1. Prague: Ústav pro etnografii a folkloristku ČAV, 1986.

Douglas, R.M. *Orderly and Humane: The Expulsion of the Germans after the Second World War*. New Haven: Yale University Press, 2014.

Franzen, K. Erik. *Die Vertriebenen: Hitlers letzte Opfer*. München: Ullstein-Taschenbuchverl, 2002.

Frommer, Benjamin. "Expulsion or Integration: Unmixing Interethnic Marriage in Postwar Czechoslovakia." *East European Politics and Societies* 14, no. 2 (2000): 381–410.

National Cleansing: Retribution Against Nazi Collaborators in Postwar Czechoslovakia. Cambridge: Cambridge University Press, 2005.

Glassheim, Eagle. *Cleansing the Czechoslovak Borderlands: Migration, Environment, and Health in the Former Sudetenland.* Pittsburgh: University of Pittsburgh Press, 2016.

Hahnová, Eva. *Sudetoněmecký problem: obtížné loučení s minulostí.* Ústí nad Labem: Albis, 1999.

Hahnová, Eva and Hans Henning Hahn. *Sudetoněmecká vzpomínání a zapomínání.* Prague: Votobia, 2002.

Hayden, Robert M. "Schindler's Fate: Genocide, Ethnic Cleansing, and Population Transfers." *Slavic Review* 55, no. 4 (1996): 727–48.

Hertl, Hanns, et al. *Němci ven! Brněnský pochod smrti 1945.* Translated by Jana Šlajchrtová. Prague: Dauphin, 2001.

Hlušičková, Růžena. *Boj o průmyslové konfiskáty v letech 1945–1948.* Prague: Záře, 1983.

Hoffmann, Dierk, Marita Krauss and Michael Schwartz. *Vertriebene in Deutschland: interdisziplinare Ergebnisse und Forschungsperspektiven.* Munchen: R. Oldenbourg Verlag, 2000.

Hrabovec, Emilia. *Vertreibung und Abschub: Deutsche in Mähren 1945–1947.* Frankfurt am Main: P. Lang, 1996.

"Politisches Dogma kontra wirtschaftliches Kalkül," In *Heimat und Exil.* Edited by Peter Heumos, 163–85. Munich: Collegium Carolinum, 2001.

Hradilová, Jana. "Internace německého obyvatelstva v adolfovickém táboře 1945–1946," *Jesenicko* 2 (2001).

Jech, Karel, ed. *Stránkami soudobých dějin: Sborník statí k pětašedesátinám historika Karla Kaplana.* Prague: Ústav pro soudobé dějiny, 1993.

Němci a Maďaři v dekretech prezidenta republiky: Studie a dokumenty 1940–1945. Prague-Brno: Ústav pro soudobé dějiny, 2003.

Joza, Petr. *Rabštejnské údolí.* Děčín: Okresní museum Děčín, 2002.

Kálmán, Janics. *Czechoslovak Policy and the Hungarian Minority, 1945–1948.* Boulder, Colorado: Social Science Monographs, 1982.

Kaplan, Karel. *Znárodnění a socialismus.* Prague: Práce, 1968.

Pravda o Československu, 1945–1948. Prague: Panorama, 1990.

Aparát ÚV KSČ v letech 1948–1968. Studie a dokumenty. Prague: Ústav pro soudobé dějiny, 1993.

Kastner, Quido. *Osídlování českého pohraničí od května 1945 (na příkladu vybraných obcí Litoměřicka).* Prague: Sociologický ústav, 1999.

King, Jeremy. *Budweisers into Czechs and Germans: A Local History of Bohemian Politics.* Princeton: Princeton University Press, 2002.

Kocích, Miroslav. *Boj KSČ za prosazení národních výborů jako lidových orgánů státní moci a správy.* Ostrava: Krajské kulturní středisko, 1981.

Kovály, Heda Margolius. *Under a Cruel Star: A Life in Prague.* Translated by Franci and Helen Epstein. New York: Holmes and Meier, 1989.

Krejčová, Helena. "Židovská očekávání a zklamání po roce 1945." In *Češi a Němci: ztracené dějiny?* Prague: Bernard Bolzan, 1995.

Křen, Jan. *Konfliktní společenství.* Toronto: Sixty-Eight Publishers, 1989.

Křen, Jan and Eva Broklová, eds. *Obraz Němců, Rakouska a Německa v české společnosti 19 a 20 století.* Prague: Karolinum, 1998.

Kučera, Jaroslav. *Odsun nebo vyhnání?* Prague: Panorama, 1992.

Odsunové ztraty sudetoněmeckého obyvatelstva: Problémy jejich přesného vyčislení. Prague: n.p, 1992.

Česká historiografie a odsun Němců." *Soudobé dějiny* 1, no. 2–3 (1994): 365–373.

Kuklík, Jan. *Mýty a realita takzvaných Benešových dekretů.* Prague: Linde, 2002.

Kural, Václav. *Místo společenství – konflikt! Češi a Němci ve Velkoněmecké říši a cesta k odsunu.* Prague: Ústav mezinárodních vztahů, 1994.

ed. *Studie o sudetoněmecké otazce.* Prague: Ústav mezinárodních vztahů, 1996.

Kural, Václav and Zdeněk Radvanovský, eds. *"Sudety" pod hákovým křížem.* Ústí nad Labem: Albis, 2002.

Lacina, Vlatislav and Jaroslav Pátek. *Dějiny hospodářství českých zemí od počatku industiralizace do současnosti, 1918–1945.* Prague: Charles University, 1995.

Leff, Carolyn Skalnik. *National Conflict in Czechoslovakia.* Princeton: Princeton University Press, 1998.

Lhota, Václav. *Znárodnění v Československu, 1945–1948.* Prague: Svoboda, 1987.

Luža, Radomir. *Transfer of the Sudeten Germans: A Study of Czech-German Relations, 1933–1962.* New York: New York University Press, 1964.

Mann, Michael. *The Dark Side of Democracy: Explaining Ethnic Cleansing.* Cambridge: Cambridge University Press, 2004.

Moeller, Robert. *War Stories: The Search for a Useable Past in the Federal Republic of Germany.* Berkley: University of California Press, 2001.

Murdock, Caitlin. *Changing Places: Society, Culture, and Territory in the Saxon-Bohemian Borderlands, 1870–1946.* Ann Arbor: University of Michigan Press, 2010.

Myant, Martin. *Socialism and Democracy in Czechoslovakia.* Cambridge: Cambridge University Press, 1981.

Naimark, Norman. *Fires of Hatred: Ethnic Cleansing in the Twentieth Century Europe.* Cambridge, Mass.: Harvard University Press, 2001.

Naimark, Norman and Leonid Gibianskii, eds. *The Establishment of Communist Regimes in East Europe, 1945–1948.* Boulder: Westview Press, 1997.

Němeček, Jan. et al. *Cesta k dekretům a odsunu Němců.* Prague: Littera Bohemica, 2002.

Nosková, Helena. "Osídlovací komise ÚV KSČ a reemigrace v letech 1945–1948." *Historické studie* (1998): 116–29.

Návrat Čechů z Volyně: Naděje a skutečnost let 1945–1954. Prague: Studijní materially Ústav pro soudobé dějiny, 1999.

Nosková, Helena and Jana Váchová. *Reemigrace Čechů a Slováků z Jugoslávie, Rumunska a Bulharska (1945–1954).* Prague: Ústav pro soudobé dějiny, 2000.

Průcha, Václav. *Hospodářské a sociální dějiny Československa: 1918–1992.* Vol. 2. Brno: Nakl. Doplněk, 2009.

Radvanovský, Zdeněk. *Konec Česko.Německého soužití v ústecké oblastii.* Ústí nad Labem: University of Jan Evangelist Purkyn, 1997.

Historie okupovaného pohraničí. Ústí nad Labem: University of Jan Evangelist Purkyn, 1998.

Rieber, Alfred J., ed. *Forced Migration in Central and Eastern Europe, 1939–1950.* London: Cass, 2000.

Rohlíková, Slavěna. "Vysídlení Němců z Československa: Výběrová bibliografie literatury z let 1945–2001." *Soudobé dějiny* 9, no.1 (2002): 168–86.

Sayer, Derick. *The Coasts of Bohemia: A Czech History.* Princeton: Princeton University Press, 1998.

Schechtman, Joseph B. *Postwar Population Transfers in Europe, 1945–1955.* Philadelphia: University of Pennsylvania Press, 1962.

European Population Transfers, 1939–1945. New York: Russell and Russell, 1971.

Schwartz, Michael. *Vertriebene und "Umsiedlerpolitik": Integrationskonflikte in den deutschen Nachkriegs-Gesellschaften und die Assimilationsstrategien in der SBZ/ DDR 1945–1961.* München: Oldenbourg, 2004.

Service, Hugo. *Germans to Poles: Communism, Nationalism and Ethnic Cleansing after the Second World War.* Cambridge: Cambridge University Press, 2015.

Slezák, Lubomír. *Zemědělské osídlování pohraničí českých zemí po druhé světové válce.* Brno: Nakladatelství blok, 1978.

Snyder, Timothy. *The Reconstruction of Nations: Poland, Ukraine, Lithuania and Belarus, 1569–1999.* New Haven: Yale University Press, 2003.

Bloodlands: Europe between Hitler and Stalin. New York: Basic Books, 2012.

Spurný, Matěj. *Nejsou jako my: česká společnost a menšiny v pohraničí (1945–1960).* Prague: Antikomplex, 2011.

Srb, Vladimír. "Osídlení českého pohraničí v letech 1945–1959." In *Materialy k problematice novoosidleneckého pohraničí.* Prague: Ústav pro etnografii a folkloristiku ČAV, 1984.

Populační, ekonomický a národnostní vývoj pohraničích okresů ČSR od roku 1930 do roku 2010. Prague: Ministerstvo výstavby a stavebnictví ČSR, 1989.

Staněk, Tomáš. "Co se stalo v Ústí nad Labem 31.července 1945?" *Dějiny a součastnost* 2 (1990): 48–51.

Odsun Němců z Československu, 1945–1948. Prague: Academia Naše Vojska, 1991.

Německá měnšina v českých zemích, 1948–1989. Prague: Institut pro středoevropskou kulturu a politiku, 1993.

Perzekuce, 1945. Prague: Institut pro středoevropskou kulturu a politiku, 1996.

"Stanovisko Společné česko-německé komise historiků k odsunovým ztrátám." *Soudobé dějiny* 3, no. 4 (1996): 1–13.

Tábory v českých zemích, 1945–1948. Opava: Slezský ústav, 1996.

Tampke, Jürgen. *Czech-German Relations and the Politics of Central Europe: From Bohemia to the EU.* New York: Palgrave MacMillan, 2003.

Teichova, Alice. *The Czechoslovak Economy, 1918–1980.* London: Routledge, 1988.

Ther, Philipp. *Deutsche und polnische Vertriebene: Gesellschaft und Vertriebenenpolitik in der SBZ/DDR und in Polen 1945–1956.* Göttingen: Vandenhoeck & Ruprecht, 1998.

The Dark Side of Nation-States: Ethnic Cleansing in Modern Europe. Translated by Charlotte Hughes-Kreutzmuller. New York: Berghahn Books, 2016.

Ther, Philipp and Ana Siljak, eds. *Redrawing Nations: Ethnic Cleansing in East-Central Europe, 1944–1948.* Lanham: Rowman and Littlefield, 2001.

Thum, Gregor. *Uprooted – How Breslau Became Wroclaw During the Century*. Translated by Tom Lampert and Allison Brown. Princeton: Princeton University Press, 2011.

Várdy, Steven B. and T. Hunt Tooley, eds. *Ethnic Cleansing in 20th Century Europe*. Boulder: Social Science Monographs, 2003.

Wiedemann, Andreas. *"Komm mit uns das Grenzland aufbauen!": Ansiedlung und neue Strukturen in den ehemaligen Sudetengebieten 1945–1952*. Essen: Klartext, 2007.

Wingfield, Nancy M., ed. *Creating the Other: Ethnic Conflict and Nationalism in Habsburg Central Europe*. New York: Berghahn, 2003.

"The Politics of Memory: Constructing National Identity in the Czech Lands, 1945–1948." *East European Politics and Societies* 14, no. 2 (2000): 246–67.

Flag Wars and Stone Saints: How the Bohemian Lands Became Czech. Cambridge, Mass.: Harvard University Press, 2007.

Zarecor, Kimberly. *Manufacturing a Socialist Modernity: Housing in Czechoslovakia, 1945–1960*. Pittsburgh: University of Pittsburgh Press, 2011.

Zayas, Alfred de. *Nemesis at Potsdam: The Expulsion of the Germans from the East*, 2nd edn. Lincoln: University of Nebraska Press, 1989.

A Terrible Revenge: The Ethnic Cleansing of the East European Germans 1944–1950. New York: St. Martin's Press, 1994.

Index

Moravská Ostrava, 5, 73, 138, 166–69, 171, 194, 196
Most, 34, 35, 55, 153, 161, 171, 194
Munich Agreement, 2, 6, 34, 60, 65, 195

National Front, 2, 11, 25, 69, 71, 96, 98, 109, 110, 146, 149, 150, 185, 189, 196, 203, 205, 226, 276
National Land Fund (NPF), 118, 137, 147, 268
National Socialists, 80, 92, 165, 204, 212, 220, 237–39
North Bohemian Brown Coal Mines (SHD), 154, 175, 176, 179
Nosek, Václav, 48, 52, 63, 89, 109, 180, 188

Opava, 4, 5, 58, 182
Ostrava-Karviná mines (OKD), 161, 166, 169

People's Party, 203, 237
Poland, 15, 20, 21–25, 38, 42, 45, 84, 106, 107, 202, 203, 279–81
Postoloprty, 39–47, 48, 52, 63
Prague, 5, 8, 30–33, 35, 50, 51, 67, 70, 73, 80, 81, 104, 115, 117, 188, 194, 200, 205, 210, 216, 223, 231, 237, 284
Presidential Decrees, 10, 282, 283
    Decree 108 on the confiscation of non-agricultural property, 109, 120, 135, 149, 213, 217
    Decree 12 on agriculture property, 108, 110, 122, 127
    Decree 33 on loss of citizenship, 60, 91, 94, 108, 109, 217, 259
    Decree 5 on national administrators, 108, 121–23, 184–86
    Decree 71 on forced labor, 165, 169, 170

Red Army, 22, 30, 31, 34, 38, 42, 44, 46, 50, 51, 76, 107, 131, 148, 196, 199
Roma, 9, 11, 95, 100–2, 260, 261–67, 285, 286
Rumburk, 84, 116, 220, 271

Settlement Office (OÚ), 17, 79, 81–82, 84, 85, 96, 99, 120, 127, 141, 149–50, 162–64, 172, 173, 209, 211–14, 227, 276
Slánský, Rudolf, 221, 243
Slezák, Zdenk, 225, 226, 237, 241–43
Slovaks, 11, 80, 82, 95–103, 110, 163, 181, 226–28, 265–66
Šluknov, 5, 182, 183, 263, 271, 285
Social Democrats, 7, 91, 92, 102, 148–50, 165, 184–86, 203–5, 220, 237, 244
Soviet Union, 13, 18, 21–24, 42, 46, 96, 97, 106, 202, 239, 248, 252, 260, 269, 278
Stank, Tomáš, 15, 32, 47, 55, 75
Sudetendeutsche Partei (SdP), 6, 8, 109

Teplice-Šanov, 34, 65, 71, 72, 129, 217, 255, 258, 260, 262, 263, 265

Ústí nad Labem See Aussig, 4, 30, 40, 47–53, 59, 63, 97, 104, 123, 125, 134, 216, 217, 256, 258, 263, 270, 285, 286

Varnsdorf, 38, 173, 193, 199, 218–22, 235, 236–38, 244, 249, 285
Vejprty, 101, 104, 116, 119, 135, 187–91, 228–35, 244
Volhynian Czechs, 17, 44–46, 53, 96–97, 101, 128–30, 139, 266–70, 277
Volksdeutsche, 9, 13, 22

Žatec, 4, 41–47, 97, 124, 128, 129, 139, 237, 267, 286

Made in the USA
Columbia, SC
24 August 2023

22061020R00170